THE
GLOBAL
VILLAGE
MYTH

THE GLOBAL VILLAGE MYTH

Distance, War, and the Limits of Power

PATRICK PORTER

HURST & COMPANY, LONDON

First published in the United States of America
by Georgetown University Press, 2015

Published in the United Kingdom in 2015 by
C. Hurst & Co. (Publishers) Ltd.,
41 Great Russell Street, London, WC1B 3PL
© Patrick Porter, 2015
All rights reserved.

Printed in England

The right of Patrick Porter to be identified as the author of this publication is
asserted by him in accordance with the Copyright, Designs and Patents Act, 1988.
A Cataloguing-in-Publication data record for this book is available from the
British Library.

ISBN: 978-1-84904-545-2 *hardback*
     978-1-84904-544-5 *paperback*

www.hurstpublishers.com

This book is printed on paper from registered sustainable
and managed sources.

"In the global village, maybe I am the bobby on the beat."
—Lord George Robertson, former secretary general of NATO, in
Liverpool Echo, September 7, 2011

"Go massive. Sweep it all up, things related and not."
—Secretary of Defense Donald Rumsfeld, aide's notes, Military
Command Center, 2:40 pm, September 11, 2001

"[T]hey would march out to war against the south wind. . . . Arriving amid
the dunes, they were engulfed by sand."
—Herodotus, *The Histories*

CONTENTS

ACKNOWLEDGMENTS

Thanks are owed to many people for making this book possible. I am hugely grateful to Don Jacobs and Georgetown University Press for their professional oversight. Great thanks also go to the Leverhulme Trust for awarding me a Research Fellowship to write the book, and to colleagues Alan Cromartie, Catriona McKinnon, and Katie Powell for strengthening the bid. I am in the debt of archivists at the Library of Congress, the National Defense University, the National Archives, and the archives of the Yale and Princeton university libraries. Earlier versions of the argument took a healthy battering at conferences, including panels at the International Studies Association in San Francisco and Toronto, and gatherings at the University of Reading, the Royal Military Academy at Sandhurst, and the University of Hull. I am grateful to the Americans I met for their generosity, especially those who disagreed, and for debating the ideas that drive their foreign and defense policies.

Many individuals shaped the thinking behind the book, in conversation or writing. Warm thanks also go to Jonathan Golub, Burak Kadercan, Huw Bennett, Jonathan Boyd, Daniel Deudney, Colin Gray, David Blagden, Michael Horowitz, Justin Hastings, Andrew Hurrell, John Mearsheimer, Daryl Press, Joseph Parent, Daniel Drezner, Keir Lieber, Christopher Coker, Theo Farrell, Hew Strachan, Stephen Walt, Taylor Owen, Robert Saunders, Andreas Behnke, Tarak Barkawi, Christopher Layne, Marc Mulholland, David Adesnik, Justin Logan, Micah Zenko, Michael Cohen, Hugh White, Lawrence Freedman, Ryan Grauer, Robert Dover, Oisin Tansey, Daniel Nexon, Stephen Biddle, Campbell Craig, Daphne Halikiopoulou, Christopher Fettweis, Chris Tripodi, Tim Vlandas, Geoff Sloan, Angus Trumble, Christina Hellmich, Josh Shifrinson, and Edward Hampshire.

Continents of love go to Jane Rogers, Emily Porter, Patrick Doyle, Gus, and Molly. This book is dedicated to my parents, Brian and Muriel, who need no advice on the power of distance.

INTRODUCTION

Strife in the Village

Ours is an age of anxiety. Many of America's foreign policy experts believe the world is getting more dangerous. They see the world as equally or more insecure than it was during the Cold War against the Soviet Union of 1947–1991, when a clash between nuclear superpowers could have devastated human life.[1] Though there has been a striking decline in the overall rate of armed conflict and war-related deaths in the past two decades, security elites in the American-led West see a grim present and a bleak future.[2] The world is "more dangerous than it has ever been," insists Gen. Martin Dempsey, chairman of the Joint Chiefs of Staff, the "most uncertain, chaotic and confused international environment" since World War II, according to Lt. Gen. Michael Flynn, chief of the Defense Intelligence Agency.[3] For soldiers who once trained to fight the Warsaw Pact, those are striking claims. The conceit that our era is deadlier and more complex than the simpler, more stable Cold War is widespread, even though problems we associate with our time were then worse, from nuclear proliferation to refugees.[4] Many believe the United States lives in an age of terror, though successful terrorist attacks against America are scarce compared to the 1970s.[5] Given the successes of the United States and its allies, these fears seem odd. The Soviet Union is gone. Menaces to the countries of the Atlantic basin play out more through banks than tanks. Continental Europe is pacified and under the shield of a large military alliance. The North American landmass has unthreatening neighbors, and a powerful military shield that guards its ocean flanks. The world is no longer split into two, ideologically hostile camps. Despite brutal clashes in the Middle East and Eastern Europe, conditions do not pose armed existential threats to the West. If that does not warrant triumphal declarations of the end of history, neither does it deserve inflated fears. Nevertheless, makers of strategy voice an ancient, visceral fear identified by Thomas Hobbes as the starting point of politics, the fear of violent death. This alarm has many roots. One of them is the belief that the world is getting smaller.

We have been here before. The deadly cliché of the "shrinking world" stretches back at least to World War II. George Orwell noticed similar rhetoric in 1944, even after the Axis powers with their dreams of global conquest and their rapid, mobile war machines were blunted by determined resistance across the frozen wastes of the Soviet Union, the English Channel, and the Pacific. Orwell mocked "the automatic way in which people go on repeating certain phrases . . . two great favorites are 'the abolition of distance' and the 'disappearance of frontiers'" at a time when states re-erected frontiers, dominated radio to broadcast propaganda, and controlled travel and migration as never before.[6] But he was pushing against a Western strategic tradition that would prove resilient. The belief that the world is dangerously small and must be policed has never gone away. It gets more pronounced in the wake of violent shocks from Imperial Japan's attack on Pearl Harbor in 1941 to Al Qaeda's strike on New York and Washington, DC, in 2001. Due to this fear, what ought to be one of the most secure states in history feels perpetually insecure, haunted by rumors of chain reactions and falling dominoes.

Does technology kill distance? Many policymakers and scholars think so. The "globalized" nature of our world is a mantra of the modern corporation, the university, government, and military. Those who embrace it not only call for more open markets, more "international" citizenship, or greater attention to the world beyond. They also assume the passing of an old territorial, state-based order.[7] Fear is never far away from the rhetoric of globalism, about new vulnerabilities and the ease with which aggressors can apply violence over large spaces. Notions of a fragile small world are pervasive in debate about security, from the preservation of biological life to the defense of a way of life.

Globalists claim that a revolution in information, communications, transport, and weapons technology has reduced the transaction costs of interaction over space and linked the world to the point where it has shrunk or even collapsed distance. This creates an unprecedented condition of vulnerability, sensitivity, and connectedness, making the United States and its allies increasingly open to violent threats. Globalists rarely specify exactly the extent to which this has happened. Regardless, they claim that the net effect is to transform international relations and make the world an intrinsically dangerous place.

This book takes aim at globalism, challenging its empirical claims and what it tends toward, the waste of blood and treasure in a utopian impulse to pursue security by remaking the world. My focus is not geography, or the description of the earth. Instead, the focus is geopolitics, or how people interact with nature in pursuit of security and the relationship between politics, location, and material things.[8] Above all, it is a study of "distance," or that which separates us, and how it is generated. And it is a caution against liberal wars, or the pursuit of security through the creation of liberal subjects abroad. The cause of armed liberalism, especially of the kind that puts troops on the ground, is now in low water. But the ideas that power it endure. As after Korea and Vietnam, those ideas may make a comeback.

Globalism is several things. A theory about security, it is also an ideology about Western power, and as a powerful set of images and memories, a myth that shapes debate about what the United States and its allies should bleed and kill for. I argue that globalism is a misleading half-truth at best. It is empirically unfounded. Its logic points to endless war. Rather than being a self-evident truth about the security environment, it reflects a dangerous ideology inherited from the past, a "myth of empire" that tempts states into self-defeating behavior. I use the term "global village," first coined by the media theorist Marshall McLuhan, as shorthand for this brew of theory, ideology, and myth.[9]

Globalism derives from a broader theory of change, known as "globalization," the "dynamic shrinking of distance on a large scale" that proponents argue is the dominant pattern of international politics.[10] All versions of the theory refer to four linked processes: *extensity* (the stretching of activities), *intensity* (the intensification of activities), *velocity* (the acceleration of interactions), and *impact* (the growing significance of events and decisions in distant places).[11] By circulating capital, goods, people, and information, the process creates endless transnational "flows" and networks of activity. This enables not only accelerated material interactions but the production of virtual identities that leap over soil. It obliterates old boundaries and, in the interpenetration of the international and the domestic, gives worldwide dimensions to national security. It is a theory of political time as well as space. In particular, its proponents date it around two moments in recent history, the "fall of the wall" that signaled the end of the Cold War and the terrorist attacks on 9/11, both of which allegedly signaled a new more integrated, and more insecure, condition. On both sides of the Atlantic, the mytho-history of a shrinking world getting more dangerous after the Cold War view is entrenched among the security establishment. For Britain's former chief of defense staff, "the world today is not a safer place and the distinction between home and abroad is strategically obsolete."[12] Ultimately, globalization theory reflects ambitions and fears about change, creating "a horizon of political imagination structured around expectations of transcendence."[13] Most versions regard the process not as something consciously willed by human agents, but made by the invisible hand of stateless forces. In the fatalistic words of Anthony Lake, former national security adviser to President Bill Clinton, "globalization is like the weather: It simply is."[14]

If globalization theory looks to a technology-driven process of physical compression, globalists argue that this leads to strategic compression, so that violence can be exported more easily. In particular, globalists claim that distance, or that which separates, has been significantly downgraded as a shaping and protective force. In the world of armed conflict, this process makes the "offense" easier and defense harder to the point where geography offers little protection. The process of globalization breeds a new kind of enemy, unconstrained by geography, and a new kind of vulnerability, where inventions create a deadly material context for the struggle for power.

People who see the world this way do not agree on what should be done about it, exactly. Some believe that the new environment calls for a more aggressive pursuit of self-interest, that states must take radical offensive action and stand in a constant state of emergency in order to secure themselves. Others lean toward a more cosmopolitan vision of global governance in the world village. But in common they assume that the closeness and interdependence of peoples makes them increasingly vulnerable. In common they are predisposed to regard almost any issue as a security issue. In common, they believe a small world of fragile states, transnational threats, and general volatility demands active internationalism rather than restraint. Generally globalists converge on a vision of "empire lite," or of a world so fragile that it must be superintended by a benevolent liberal hegemon.

The 9/11 terrorist attacks became a potent symbol for all these fears, marking the world's dangerous proximities and the inability of communities to wall themselves off. Contemplating the devastation, the 9/11 Commission concluded that it proved there was no longer an "over here" distinct from an "over there," that "the American homeland is the planet."[15] In a similar vein, President George W. Bush saw that day as a lesson in the irrelevance of traditional security barriers: "It used to be that oceans would protect us, that we saw a threat, we didn't have to worry about it because there were two vast oceans. And we could pick and choose as to how we deal with the threat. That changed on September 11th."[16] Because technology compressed physical space, it also shrank strategic space, denying America discretion. This left the superpower with little option but to strike back on a grand scale.

Visions of a "global village" can inspire optimism. Hope that a smaller world is a better world ran through early Western perceptions of the Arab Spring, the wave of revolts beginning in 2010 against dictators across North Africa and the Middle East. Some argue that the internet, digital commerce, and social media hold out new possibilities of emancipation and internationalism. New "ethnoscapes," "technoscapes," or "mediascapes" transcend borders and state censorship. Tweets overcome the bullets of the old order.[17] For cosmopolitans looking on the bright side, where once oceans, deserts, and mountains divided humans, new inventions transcend the old topography and flatten the world.[18] But anxious versions of the myth endure. Because the United States is the prime superpower shaping world order, it seems to be globalization's main target as well as its beneficiary.

Globalism matters because wars are waged in its name. It drives ambitious military campaigns in the Gulf and Central Asia, leads to increased drone killings from the Horn of Africa to Pakistan, and underpins calls for the expansion of the NATO alliance and its missions. In our time, the United States waged the War on Terror, with wars in Afghanistan and Iraq, on the premise that the world has become one battlespace and that America could only secure itself against the borderless Islamist terrorist network of Al Qaeda by waging a global war of ideas that know few limitations, politically transforming nations in its image. As well as militarizing statecraft, the sense of heightened insecurity in a small world has other weighty policy implications. It calls forth doctrines of preemptive war. It prompts calls for new defenses such as missile defense shields and extraordinary new presidential powers such as an internet "kill switch" that would empower the president unilaterally to shut down "critical" parts of the Web without judicial review, creating a kind of cyber monarch.[19] The stakes are high. And the policy agendas urged on by globalists expose the contradiction at the heart of their doctrine. Proclaiming the coming of a global political-economic order that eclipses state power, territory, and nationalism, they advocate measures to strengthen the state, fortify territory, and claim extraordinary privileges for select nations.[20]

Doctrines of globalism lie at the heart of America's activism abroad and its grand strategy of exerting worldwide hegemony to ensure a liberal peace on its terms. In Washington, DC, the capital of a consciously global superpower with earth-spanning military might, a guiding assumption is that American security is now implicated everywhere. A state failure, a dangerous ideology, or disorder anywhere on the periphery threatens American interests at the core. Now that the politics of the Middle East can erupt violently in Manhattan, it is feared, the very distinction between core and periphery is outmoded. Fear of the dangerous interconnectedness of things rings loudly in Western security debate, from Tony Blair's Chicago speech in April 1999 making the case for idealistic armed internationalism in an interdependent world, to the "Bush Doctrine" of 2002 that adopts first strikes and "regime change" in the name of anticipatory defense, to President Barack Obama's claim in 2013 that America should bomb the Assad regime in Syria to protect American children in the long run.[21] Against the threat of "dark" globalization, America would oversee the creation of an enlightened one under its hegemony.[22] If "globalism" is the shorthand for the shrinkage of the world into a borderless and closed system, it is also a "post-national" doctrine by which Washington and its allies permit themselves to override state sovereignty and intervene at will.[23] To be sure, globalism is not all-powerful. There are multiple strategic traditions, and America does not always follow its logic. But the notion of insecurity in a shrunken world is enduring and influential.

Because the stakes are high, the myth deserves further scrutiny. Of course, technologies of globalization can have an effect, whether the invention of bridges to cross water, the invention of railways to cross land, the invention of TVs or phones or cyberspace to accelerate communication or exchange. An intercontinental missile strike, a plane hijacking, or a cyber assault were obviously impossible a century ago. But beyond the literal, technical level, in the world of human politics has technology really conquered space to the point where we inhabit a village? Has it generated a world so interconnected that it is increasingly threatening, demanding that the West reimpose order? Globalization has already drawn debate in other fields, especially in political economy, the study of the economics of polities. But the literature has not properly addressed central questions about how it applies to armed conflict. If globalism is both a hypothesis about the nature of modern conflict and an ideology about Western power and vulnerability, where does it come from? How accurate is it as an account of today's security environment?

Distance was once regarded as a "tyranny" to be suffered or exploited. Historian Geoffrey Blainey coined it to describe Australian history, shaped by the unforgiving force of the vast interior and the stretches between expatriates and their motherlands.[24] So too in armed conflict, distance exerted a decaying effect that sapped strength.[25] The further a state extended its reach from home, the less force it could apply and sustain. Napoleon's wars made the point. The civil engineer Charles Joseph Minard captured the depleting effect of space in his diagrammatic data map of Bonaparte's "March to Moscow and Retreat in 1812." Captured as a data flow, the thinning line of the invading and withdrawing *Grande Armée* reflected the brutal attrition of space, time, and climate. Prussian soldier and theorist Carl von Clausewitz wrote that distance worked its ironic force through the cycle of military offensives over land. The farther the invader lunged into hostile territory, the more its power was sapped by casualties, by desertion, by the need to guard ground taken, by the strains on supply and lengthening lines of communication. And there was a psychological dimension. The more the defender retreated toward its vital center, the greater its political will to survive, while the aggressor's efforts slackened. That was his warning to any invader.[26]

The relationship between humans and their environment has never finally stood still. Historically, as innovations or markets changed, so too have the benefits and costs of location. Mountains or seas could be obstacles or sources of security. Peoples once sought safety in the vastness of the Eurasian steppe, only to be fallen upon by mounted conquerors. In turn, the horsemen met their limits. Geography, as historian Ian Morris argues, unleashed possibilities of development, but development then changed what the geography meant.[27]

Oblivious to this historical dynamism, globalists today fear that the process of change is fixed at a dangerous point, that nomadic predators have closed the gap. Today, the tyranny of closeness is a greater source of anxiety. Dangerous proximities allegedly pose maximum threat to once-secure Western heartlands. In starker versions of the argument, this spells the "end of geography," as we cannot hold off the rising tides that bring uncertainty and terror to our doorsteps.[28] According to Robert Keohane, "geographical space, which has been seen as a natural *barrier* and a locus for human barriers, now must be seen as a *carrier* as well." If "threats of violence to our homeland can occur from anywhere," then "the barrier conception of geographical space, already anachronistic with respect to thermonuclear war and called into question by earlier acts of globalized informal violence, was finally shown to be thoroughly obsolete on September 11."[29]

The most sophisticated articulation of the argument comes from Daniel Deudney, who argues that science and technology altered nature irresistibly, leaving states to adapt or suffer. Deudney argues that given humanity's condition of "violence-interdependence," and its capacity to destroy itself, world government is the species' only viable political response and the only way to bound power and its destructive capacity. The image of the global village,

> imperfect in its connotations of stability, provides a good first-cut mapping of where we most fundamentally are. It is a simple summation of the single most important fact about the actual situation of the human species: intense interdependence and particularly intense violence interdependence is occurring on a global scale. Humanity is in something roughly resembling a global village situation, not because it wants to be and not because domesticated neighborly relations have been established among the members of this village. Rather . . . nature as it presents itself for human activity has changed profoundly. To acknowledge this as the primary political fact is simply to recognize that the natural-material context of all practical human security activity has been altered radically and irreversibly (barring some very deep and universal civilizational collapse) by modern science and technology . . . global technological interdependence has altered the scope of interaction and hence number of humans and human groups among whom restraint of violence is necessary for security. While it is possible to choose and alter how we and our neighbors interact, we cannot alter the fact that the neighborhood of all humans now encompasses the entire planet.[30]

Deudney's argument reclaims geopolitics for republican security theory, a theory that looks to achieve security with and from the state, as well as between states. He develops a critique made by thinkers from Reinhold Niebuhr and Hans Morgenthau to Campbell Craig, that deliverable nuclear bombs compress time and space to the point where they can destroy cities instantly, and their proliferation means that the species finds itself in a thermonuclear "village" defined by the possibility of apocalypse. The strategic order of the world can never be the same and humanity must find new ways to govern itself.[31] In the hands of nonstate actors without a return address, many fear, the problem gets worse. The shrinking world links up weak states in a vortex of illicit economies, proliferation of weapons of mass destruction (WMDs), and safe havens whence guerrillas can "strike out at adversaries in very distant lands."[32]

On the level of technical capability and the capacity of some actors to inflict destruction, it is indisputably true that nuclear weapons with long-range delivery systems represent shrinkage. But on a political level, nuclear weapons and conventional military and nonmilitary capabilities lower down the chain also create distance, empowering defenders and in the case of the well-armed weak against the strong, make territorial expansion politically unfeasible. As Henry Kissinger warns, any clash between developed nuclear powers would inflict casualties and upheaval "impossible to relate to calculable objectives."[33] If, between well-armed states, the link between war and rational instrumentality is thus broken, the net result is a paradox. While new systems place polities in striking distance of one another, in terms of the costs of aggression, geopolitically they are now far apart. The main nightmare of twentieth-century geopolitical thought, that one power could harness the resources of Eurasia to dominate the world, is now more remote than ever.

The resurgent power of distance does not mean we should assume peace is assured, nor that we should bid farewell to geopolitics.[34] Like any process, the power of strategic distance does not make territorial war (or the calculations that breed it) impossible. But most of the time, as Norman Angell predicted, it makes it futile. As the Iraq War brutally demonstrated, the danger is to believe that mastery of globalizing technologies by the strong makes war cheap, swift, and easy, or to believe that the shrinkage of the world existentially threatens the strong, obliging them to wage continuous wars of pacification. In contrast to Deudney and other cosmopolitans, I argue we are seeing not the obsolescence but the reassertion and resilience of the nation-state, and that sharing power prudently is the best course, to negotiate for an equilibrium in the widening spaces between us. The alternatives are implausible and dangerous. Attempts to institute a "world government" Leviathan would not bound power, including destructive power, but concentrate it dangerously and breed the violent clashes it seeks to eliminate. Similar problems befall the attempt to create an American Leviathan, to lock in and extend American hegemony. The global village mindset, which underpins both, is less the solution than the problem.

The Question and the Argument

Has technology compressed space as a dimension of strategy, armed conflict, and the pursuit of security, to the point where distance is significantly downgraded? I argue that it has not, and that the world is not small. Technology may accelerate movement, enable instant communication, and compress physical space. But it does not necessarily shrink strategic space, the ability to project power across the earth affordably against resistance. By "affordably," I mean not just dollars and material sacrifices, but the wider diplomatic price, and the political will to incur those costs. Mechanically speaking, the United States can apply force across space to invade countries, topple regimes, and install friendly client rulers, and did so in Iraq. But politically speaking, the material and diplomatic price was so unacceptably high that most Americans are reluctant to repeat the adventure.

The notion that technology kills distance in all its variants does badly when it is put through some revealing qualitative tests. These suggest two overarching problems with globalist theory. First, while technology can compress, the same instruments and other tools can be used to enlarge strategic space. And space seems not to be a one-dimensional physical site onto which inevitable forces such as globalization impose themselves, but as a contested and dynamic field that widens and shrinks through political struggle.

Second, human agency intervenes against what is assumed to be the structural fact of globalization. As well as the defensive potentialities of technology, agents especially through the state can resist and at times reverse the shrinking effect of globalizing forces. State sovereignty is a jealous force that refuses to go quietly into the night and continues to play a strong mediating role.

Overall, the offensive and shrinking power of technology-driven globalization is grossly overstated. To be clear: Technology and material culture, the circulation of ideas, capital, technology, people, can have nontrivial compressing and accelerating effects. But views of the world as a miniaturized, interconnected battlespace, driven inexorably by forces beyond our control, both overstate the threats represented by human agents and overstate the capacity of the United States to project power. At best, globalism is a mischievous half-truth that is a poor guide to the complex, uneven, and double-edged relationships between space, agents, tools, and security. As in economics, where globalization is a "choice" more than an objective "fact" of life, so too in the world of armed conflict. Globalization can happen alongside other phenomena, but it is not a fixed, independent, and irresistible force. It is something that states actively shape and resist, make and unmake. This is appreciated less in the study of modern war than in other disciplines.[35]

Crucial to the argument is the distinction between physical space, measured by miles, and strategic space, by which I mean the ability to project power over space against resistance at affordable cost. We owe a debt to Derek Gregory for this distinction, which is the starting point for my argument.[36] Distance entails the spatial dynamics of power, where space is shaped by the clash of wills, the interactions of competing agents and tools, and the problem of incurring cost over space. How far or near a community is from a source of threat cannot be measured in pure cartography, or miles on a map, but with regard to all of the intervening forces that stretch or shrink. As I will argue, 9/11 did not set the pattern and was more an anomaly than signpost for the times. Events since then suggest that states

[handwritten annotation: WMD stop global domicide if actual increase size of world]

can impose new barriers. Nukes and the means of instant devastation do more to enlarge than shrink the world strategically, checking the expansion of the strong. A world without them would more greatly empower military giants. Bodies of water can be converted into formidable barriers.

Even on its own, physical space can impose its strains on power projection. In the fields of commerce and military logistics, the actual demands of movement of large-scale military forces are easy to underestimate. The limited capacity of rapid air transport means that most goods today are still seaborne. Faster airlift can only carry a small fraction of the cargoes that seapower can deliver. But the alternative, of faster sealift, also has its limitations because accelerating it requires increasing the thrust of propulsion at sea. Thanks to physics, beyond speeds of 25 knots disproportionately more shaft horsepower is needed for small additions of pace, becoming expensive. This mode of transport is not much faster than it was a century ago, making it difficult to transport large quantities of material promptly to the battlespace.[37] Overstating the compression of time and space across trans-oceanic distances, Margaret Thatcher presumed it would take three days to get Britain's taskforce to the Falkland Islands. It took three weeks.[38]

Strategic space is more difficult to master still. Even today, it reimposes its material and psychological costs upon those who fight over it. Projecting power affordably over space is now more difficult, not less. This constrains the super-power and its adversaries. It makes the United States less powerful, but more secure, than we think.

Research Design

My aim is to lay out the theory of globalism, to provide a biography of the idea, or a historical interpretation of how and why it has been embraced by US policymakers since World War II, and then to see how well it measures up in explaining the dynamics and course of armed conflict today.

To assess the claim that globalization shrinks space to the point where the world becomes a village, I select three important cases. I use "process tracing," or the in-depth examination of evidence within a case, selected, carefully described, and analyzed in light of research questions, to test globalist theories.[39] Process tracing enables us "to evaluate the separate causal links that connect explanatory variables with the predicted outcomes" and to ask whether the makers of strategy "speak, write and otherwise behave in a manner consistent with the theory's predictions."[40] In this case, it enables us to take a closer look at the interplay of tools, space, and human agency and the chains of causation within the making of war.

This study examines territoriality and space in cases that are often assumed to be symptomatic of globalization. It builds on recent literature that focuses on territoriality in international relations, or "the attempt by an individual or group to affect, influence, or control people, phenomena, and relationships by delimiting and asserting control over a geographic area."[41] "Large n" studies of the patterns of interstate conflict demonstrate that states interact predominantly with neighbors; most armed conflicts are local in the object and location of conflict; most are fought between contiguous states; territorial disputes have the highest propensity to militarized escalation; "globalized" pairs of states are less likely to fight than more proximately located states; projecting force to distant locations is still relatively costly; and most states are not able to reach noncontiguous states by military means.[42] My work reinforces these findings by turning attention to ways in which globalism also has an impoverished view of space in ways that are not so easily quantifiable. Struggle for "space" concerns a contested political process within and over territory, the ability to project power and achieve desired outcomes at affordable price over air, sea, land, or the astral or cyber domains. Distance and distancing still takes place even between "globalized" pairs of enemies, across oceans, or in electronic battlefronts.

Taking a closer look at a few illustrative cases supports these critiques of globalism but also enables us to unpack the dynamics of distance and the ways in which technology and space interact. In this study, I select three "easy test" or "most likely" cases where the theory of globalism should perform well, and which should be difficult for my argument. These are "netwar" theory and the case of the Al Qaeda network; amphibious war and the military balance between a strong state (China) applying superior firepower against a weaker state relying on geographical defenses (Taiwan); and the case of cutting-edge technologies that are commonly regarded as transcending the limits of distance: remotely piloted vehicles (drones) and cyberwar. This approach is based on the assumption that a theory that performs badly in the most favorable conditions is unlikely to be very powerful generally. We can assess the applicability of a theory in a few in-depth cases. The theory should do a better job in "more likely" cases than typical cases. If it does badly, that bounds the theory's applicability to other cases.[43]

My method is to derive from the existing literature some specific claims about how the dynamics of armed conflict should change if globalist theorists are correct. I then compare the claims of globalism with the findings of these qualitative case studies. I will use open-source materials and archival sources, including government documents and the papers of American strategists in mid-century, and the recently declassified and translated papers from the Al Qaeda network. For issues that presently lack available archival sources, such as China-Taiwan and new technologies, I draw on official publications and statements of policymakers, as well as military estimates and formal reports that offer enough information about current capabilities to attempt a provisional estimate. Throughout, I also draw on and synthesize literature already on offer in the specific cases.

What criteria inform how we choose which cases are most likely to be reveal-ing tests? The case selection criteria are those instances where technological capa-bility seems to be most mobile, long-range, and international in its reach. They also happen to be cases often identified by globalists as demonstrations of their argument. I have deliberately steered away from focusing on cases of intensive conventional wars between states fought over large distances. These pose proba-bly the hardest test to globalization theories about the weakening of distance and its effects, because they are so logistically intensive. It would be relatively easy in those cases to demonstrate the enduring importance of transport and logis-tics capabilities over long range. It would not be as rewarding an exercise, and has already been done.[44] It wouldn't tell us very much about whether and to what extent globalism is applicable to cases where war seems more "instant" and "inti-mate," and where technology and geography square off in a fight where technol-ogy *prima facie* holds the upper hand. It is more productive to see how the theory fares on its own chosen turf.

This work is influenced by both classical and "neoclassical" realist traditions, strands of pessimistic thinking that focus on the systemic causes of insecurity but also the interaction between external pressures and the internal dynamics of states.[45] The study of geopolitics is closely tied to traditions of political realism. Both share a pessimistic view of an anarchic, conflict-prone world, and an inter-est in the material dimensions of power. This approach sacrifices the ambition and systematic rigor of "scientific" realism but gains the richness of detailed historical analysis and the particularities of a given context, to show how a range of variables are linked causally. Rather than grand theory, neoclassical realists focus on more specific problems, in this case, why the strongest superpower in history senses that it is in constant peril.[46]

There is a tension in this kind of realism. It assumes that anarchy creates inse-curity but regards the perception of American insecurity as disproportionate and a puzzle. It is prudent to assume some degree of insecurity, but not too much, which is where ideology intervenes. For powerful states like the United States, insecurity is more often a product of tragic interactions rather than the work of one enemy's evil will, and the prospects for states are strongly affected by how they perceive and misperceive their environment. Thanks to misperception, states from time to time inflate their insecurity and make mistakes, such as launching wars recklessly, and the anarchic system has a way of penalizing such behavior. The tragedy of successful states is not that they are assassinated, but that they more often perish by their own hand. In the tradition of Machiavelli, Morgenthau, and Thucydides, the realism that informs this book assigns weight to domestic ideologies, "cogni-tive variables," and power struggles that intervene to shape how people interact with their world.[47] Rather than viewing the world as a place that compels rational behavior and cold cost-benefit calculation, classical realists stress that states can suffer self-inflicted wounds when gripped by myths of empire. One such myth is the belief that the world is dangerously shrinking and needs constant policing by a benevolent hegemon, or "a bobby on the beat," that brings order into chaos without unintended consequences.

As a vision of the transformation of the world, globalization is a slippery target that has been linked to everything from hamburgers to the internet. To be clear about what I challenge in this book, globalists argue not merely for cumulative evolution, but for revolution. They do not argue that developments in technology have merely accelerated or accentuated patterns of interaction, but that they have brought about a fundamental change. Globalists in the field of armed conflict tend toward hyperbole, making absolute claims. Consider the phrases they use: The barrier conception of space is "thoroughly obsolete"; Al Qaeda is "borderless"; the world is "globalized" as an obvious, irreversible "fact"; the ability of far-off threats like terrorists to transport their cargoes and make threats appear in one's own backyard "exemplifies the death of distance"; cyberwar is "little constrained by space and obliterates traditional distinctions between local and distant conflict"; "globalization . . . renders commonly accepted modes of strategic thinking and rational deterrence increasingly irrelevant"; weapons proliferation into the hands of terrorists means "the rules must change, if the West is to survive."[48] Unmeasured claims of this kind abound, in both academic and policymaking circles, and in the dialogue between them.[49] Testifying before the 9/11 Commission, terrorism expert Magnus Reinstorp articulated the myth at its most intense:

> The world is truly a global village today and it has been made even more real than ever with September 11th. Among the first lesson is that the global community cannot allow conflict in one part of the world to fester—principally because, sooner or later, it has the propensity to reach around the globe and produce violence in any corner of the global village. The prospects of an attack against one of our nuclear facilities, rendering vast geographical or economic centers uninhabitable for hundreds of years, are no longer fiction but a possible future apocalyptic reality. Above all, September 11th showed that when globalization meets extremist violence anything is possible for the future with threats of violence that can occur anywhere and anytime within our homelands with incalculable and unimaginable consequences.[50]

In these categorical and melodramatic terms, globalists prophecy a new era, arguing for a change so profound as to alter the very scope and nature of security. That globalism lends itself to melodrama is not an accident, but a reflection of its "totalizing" nature and its vision of international life as a stark morality play.

For globalism to hold up, it must mean at a minimum that technology has shrunk the world, and done so decisively, to the point where distance is significantly weakened as a barrier. But this is where it runs into a central problem. When challenged by evidence that stateless forces have not globalized the world as fundamentally as assumed, globalists must choose whether to defend their problematic claims or modify and scale them back, with the result that they are diluted and lose their force. As Justin Rosenberg observes,

> either the accelerated rise of transnational relations was indeed of such a nature as ultimately to transgress and undermine the existing order of things—in which case it should have been possible to specify and project their transformative impact without excessive, retractive qualification; or, alternatively, it was all more complicated for some reason, in which case the original claim that "globalization" embodied a "fundamental" change would have had to be given up, and the "mantle of a new paradigm" for social science would have had to have similarly to be discarded.[51]

If globalists let distance back in, concede that territoriality, geography, and state power retain some force, their claims dissolve "in a sea of qualifications" and fall short of the decisive transformation in world affairs that they assert to begin with.[52] If distance and territoriality still count after all, the world of armed conflict is not so globalized.

In challenging globalism, this book has no "hidden agenda." It disputes both the myth's empirical claims and its policy agenda. Globalism ascended as a dominant paradigm in America, but I draw on another American paradigm to challenge it, a tradition of classical realism that was recast and articulated from mid-century. The chief proponents of this realism, such as Walter Lippmann, George Kennan, and Hans Morgenthau, argued for the limits of power, cautioned against attempts at global domination, and sought to temper universalist ambition with consciousness of the constraints of distance. This argument cannot be value-free. The conclusions this book draws are inescapably ideological in their counter-claims about what America's role in the world should be, in its assumptions about how to define the national interest as the referent object of strategy, in its conception of how security is made and unmade, and in its judgments about whether the pursuit of primacy is good for America and the world. Both "shapers" and "restrainers" offer strategic visions that are political at their core. But both rely on empirical claims—of how the world "is," from which policy consequences flow, what "ought" to be done. What matters is which one holds up better to the tests imposed by the unforgiving world of international politics, and which one offers the better guide to the superpower as it attempts to pick its way through the chaos.

Notes

1. In a 2009 survey, 69 percent of members of the Council on Foreign Relations feared that for the United States the world was as dangerous or more dangerous than during the Cold War. In another survey, 70 percent of experts feared that the world was getting more dangerous. See Micah Zenko and Michael Cohen, "Clear and Present Safety: The United States Is More Secure Than Washington Thinks," *Foreign Affairs* 91:2 (2012): 79–93, 80.

2. Bethany Lacina and Nils Petter Gleditsch, "Monitoring Trends in Global Combat: A New Dataset of Battle Deaths," *European Journal of Population* 21 (2005): 145–66; *Human Security Report 2012* (Vancouver: Human Security Press, 2012), 149.

3. Chairman of the Joint Chiefs Gen. Martin Dempsey, testimony to the Senate Armed Service Committee, *Hearing to Receive Testimony on the Impacts of Sequestration and/or a Full Year Continuing Resolution on the Department of Defense*, February 12, 2013, 22; James Kitfield, "Flynn's Last Interview: Iconoclast Departs DIA with a Warning," *Breaking Defense*, August 7, 2014.

4. Robert Golan-Villela, "The Cold War World Wasn't Simple," *The National Interest*, February 4, 2013.

5. According to the University of Maryland's Global Terrorism Database, there were 1,350 attacks in the United States in the 1970s, a figure that has declined significantly since. See Scott Shane, "Bombings End Decade of Strikingly Few Successful Terrorism Attacks in U.S.," *New York Times*, April 16, 2013.

6. George Orwell, "As I Please," *Tribune*, May 12, 1944.

7. As Rajan Menon observes, "Enough with the Globalization Hype," *Huffington Post*, April 11, 2012.

8. Definition derived from Jeremy Black, *Geopolitics* (London: Social Affairs Unit, 2009), 1.

9. Marshall McLuhan, *Understanding Media: The Extensions of Man* (London: Gingko Press, 1964, 2003), 6.

10. Joseph Nye, "Globalism versus Globalization," *The Globalist*, April 15, 2012.

11. As formulated by David Goldblatt and Jonathan Perraton, "Rethinking Globalization," in *The Global Transformations Reader*, ed. David Held and Anthony McGrew (Cambridge, UK: Polity, 2003), 67–68.

12. Lord Richards of Herstmonceux, chief of the defense staff, 2010–13, in Adrian Johnson, ed., *Wars in Peace: British Military Operations since 1991* (London: Royal United Services Institute, 2014), xii.

13. Jens Bartelson, "Three Concepts of Globalization," *International Sociology* 15 (2000): 180–96, 192.

14. Anthony Lake, *6 Nightmares: Real Threats in a Dangerous World and How America Can Meet Them* (Boston, MA: Little, Brown, 2000), xii.

15. *The 9/11 Commission Report: Final Report of the National Commission on Terrorist Attacks Upon the United States* (New York: W. W. Norton & Co., 2004), 362.

16. Remarks at Hershey, Pennsylvania, April 19, 2004, in *Public Papers of the President of the United States* (Washington, DC: Office of the Federal Register, 2004), 606.

17. Nicholas D. Kristof, "Tear Down This Cyberwall," *New York Times*, June 17, 2009.

18. Thomas Friedman, *The World Is Flat: A Brief History of the Twenty-First Century* (New York: Farrar, Straus, and Giroux, 2005); Frances Cairncross, *The Death of Distance 2.0: How the Communications Revolution Will Change Our Lives* (New York: Texere, 2001); Erik Gartzke, "The Capitalist Peace," *American Journal of Political Science*, 51 (2007): 166–91.

19. "Renewed Push to Give Obama an Internet Kill Switch," CBS News, January 24, 2011.

20. As Tarak Barkawi notes, *Globalization and War* (New York: Rowman & Littlefield, 2006), 3.

21. For the Chicago speech, see "Prime Minister's Speech to Economic Club of Chicago, 23 April 1999" (Prime Minister's Office, London, 1999); for the Bush Doctrine, see President of the United States, *National Security Strategy of the United States of America* (Washington, DC: US Government Printing Office, 2002); for Barack Obama's speech, see "Remarks by the President to the Nation on Syria," September 10, 2013, at www.whitehouse.gov/the-press-office/2013/09/10/remarks-president-address-nation-syria.

22. President of the United States, *National Security Strategy of the United States of America* (Washington, DC: US Government Printing Office, 2010), 1. References to the "dark side" of globalization were echoed by former NATO Secretary General Lord George Robertson in a speech to Chatham House, "Transatlantic Relations: A Case for Optimism," July 6, 2011; the theme was also anticipated by Anthony Giddens, *Modernity and Self-Identity: Self and Society in the Late Modern Age* (Cambridge, UK: Polity, 1991), 12.

23. As Michael Lind shows, "The Case for American Nationalism," *The National Interest* 131 (2014): 9–20.

24. Geoffrey Blainey, *The Tyranny of Distance: How Distance Shaped Australia's History* (Melbourne: Sun Books, 1966).

25. The most prominent theorist of the distance decay effect, or the "loss of strength gradient," was Kenneth E. Boulding, *Conflict and Defense: A General Theory* (New York: Harper and Brothers, 1962), 79, 230–31.

26. Carl von Clausewitz, *On War* (trans. Michael Howard and Peter Paret, 1976), Chapter 22, 572.

27. Ian Morris, *Why the West Rules—for Now: The Patterns of History, and What They Reveal about the Future* (London: Profile Books, 2010), 35.

28. Or so writes former UK secretary of defense Liam Fox, who brands those who think we can as naive isolationists. Liam Fox, *Rising Tides: Dealing with the New Global Reality* (London: Heron, 2013), 7, 10.

29. Robert Keohane, "The Globalization of Informal Violence, Theories of World Politics and the Liberalism of Fear," *Dialogue IO* 1:1 (2002): 29–43, 32, 33. Keohane has long argued that globalization creates linkages between local and far-off politics, to the extent of transforming the world: Robert O. Keohane and Joseph Nye Jr., "Power and Interdependence in the Information Age," *Foreign Affairs* 77 (1998): 81–94; *Transnational Relations and World Politics* (Cambridge, MA: Harvard University Press, 1971).

30. Daniel H. Deudney, *Bounding Power: Republican Security Theory from the Polis to the Global Village* (Princeton, NJ: Princeton University Press, 2007), 273–74.

31. Campbell Craig, *Glimmer of a New Leviathan: Total War in the Realism of Niebuhr, Morgenthau, and Waltz* (New York: Columbia University Press, 2003).

32. Jonathan Kirshner, "Globalization, American Power, and International Security," *Political Science Quarterly* 123:3 (2008): 363–89, 387, 389.

33. Henry A. Kissinger, "The Future of U.S.-Chinese Relations: Conflict Is a Choice, Not a Necessity," *Foreign Affairs* 91 (2012): 44–55.

34. Steven Van Evera, by contrast, argues that the difficulty of conquest means great powers should cease practicing geopolitics: Steven Van Evera, "A Farewell to Geopolitics," in *To Lead the World: American Strategy after the Bush Doctrine*, ed. Melvyn Leffer and Jeffrey W. Legro (Oxford: Oxford University Press, 2008), 11–30.

35. Honorable exceptions include Stephen Biddle and Michael Evans, who critically refute theories that precision technology or air power eclipse traditional land dimensions of warfighting: Stephen Biddle, *Afghanistan and the Future of Warfare: Implications for Army and Defense Policy* (Carlisle, PA: U.S. Army War College Strategic Studies Institute 2002); Stephen Biddle "Allies, Air Power, and Modern Warfare," *International Security*, 30:3 (Winter 2005–6): 161–76; Michael Evans, *The Continental School of Strategy: The Past, Present and Future of Land Power* (Australia: Land Warfare Studies Center, 2004).

36. Derek Gregory, "The Deadly Embrace: War, Distance and Intimacy," Lecture, British Academy, March 14, 2012.

37. As Kieren Webb observes, "The Continued Importance of Geographic Distance and Boulding's Loss of Strength Gradient," *Comparative Strategy* 26:4 (2007): 295–310, 302.

38. Adam Leach, " Crisis Management and the Assembly of the Task Force," in *The Falklands Conflict Twenty Years On: Lessons for the Future*, ed. Stephen Badsey, Rob Havers, and Mark Grove (London: Frank Cass, 2005), 70. I am grateful to Edward Hampshire for bringing this to my attention.

39. On the method of process tracing, see David Collier, "Understanding Process Tracing," *Political Science and Politics* 44:4 (2011): 823–30.

40. Stephen Van Evera, "What Are Case Studies? How Can They Be Performed?," in *Guide to Methods for Students of Political Science* (Ithaca, NY: Cornell University Press, 1997), 49–76.

41. Robert David Sack, *Human Territoriality: Its Theory and History* (New York: Cambridge University Press, 1986), 19; Stuart Elden, *Terror and Territory: The Spatial Extent of Sovereignty* (Minneapolis: University of Minnesota Press, 2009); David A. Carter and H. Goemans, "The Making of the Territorial Order: New Borders and the Emergence of Interstate Conflict," *International Organization* 65:2 (2011): 275–309.

42. Miles Kahler and Barbara F. Walter, eds., *Territoriality and Conflict in an Era of Globalization* (Cambridge: Cambridge University Press, 2006), especially Halvard Buhaug and Nils Petter Gleditsch, "The Death of Distance? The Globalization of Armed Conflict," 187–219; Paul Senese, "Territory, Contiguity, and International Conflict," *American Journal of Political Science* 49:4 (2005): 769–79.

43. On the principles of case study methodology and "easy tests," see Harry Eckstein, "Case Studies and Theory in Political Science," in *Handbook of Political Science*, Vol. VII, *Strategies of Inquiry*, ed. Fred Greenstein and Nelson W. Polsby (Reading, PA: Addison-Wesley, 1975), 79–137; Arthur L. Stinchcombe, *Constructing Social Theories* (New York: Harcourt, Brace, and World, 1968), 24–28.

44. Daisaku Sakaguchi, "Distance and Military Operations: Theoretical Background toward Strengthening the Defense of Offshore Islands," *Journal of Defense and Security* 12 (2011): 83–105.

45. Gideon Rose, "Neoclassical Realism and Theories of Foreign Policy," *World Politics* 51 (1998): 144–72, 146–47; Jack Snyder, *Myths of Empire: Domestic Politics and International Ambition* (Ithaca, NY: Cornell University Press, 1991), 19–20; Christopher Layne, *The Peace of Illusions: American Grand Strategy from 1940 to the Present* (Ithaca, NY: Cornell University Press, 2006), 7–11.

46. Randall L. Schweller, *Deadly Imbalances: Tripolarity and Hitler's Strategy for World Conquest* (New York: Columbia University Press, 1998).

47. Steven E. Lobell, Norrin M. Ripsman, and Jeffrey W. Taliaferro, *Neoclassical Realism, The State and Foreign Policy* (Cambridge: Cambridge University Press, 2009), 4.

48. Geoffrey Till, *Seapower: A Guide for the Twenty-First Century* (London: Routledge, 2013), 296; Lukas Kello, "The Meaning of the Cyber Revolution: Perils to Theory and Statecraft," *International Security* 38:2 (2013): 7–40, 22–23; Victor Cha, "Globalization and the Study of International Security," *Journal of Peace Research* 37:3 (2000): 391–403, 391; James Gow, *Defending the West* (London: Polity Press, 2005), 6.

49. According to an official from US Central Command, "The global nature of US interests mean that, even in a physical sense, the United States no longer is defensively advantaged. In today's globalized world . . . the notion of insularity—which, by delivering defensible borders, traditionally allowed states to privilege long-term economic growth—has virtually lost all meaning." Emily Goldman, *Power in Uncertain Times: Strategy in the Fog of Peace* (Stanford, CA: Stanford University Press, 2010), 129–30.

50. "First public hearing of the National Commission on Terrorist Attacks upon the United States: Statement of Magnus Ranstorp to the National Commission on Terrorist Attacks upon the United States," March 31, 2003, at http://govinfo.library.unt.edu/911/hearings/hearing1/witness_ranstorp.htm.

51. Justin Rosenberg, "Globalization Theory: A Postmortem," *International Politics* 42:1 (2006): 2–74, 42.

52. For instance, in an attempt at a more nuanced version of the argument, Jonathan Kirshner claims that globalization has "profoundly transformed" the "contest" with regard to the balance of power and prospects for war. But he then concedes that globalization is not all-powerful, that states can limit their exposure to it, that globalization "reshapes" the consequences of policy choices, and that globalization recasts and redistributes state power but does not diminish it. Accepting all these caveats, in the end globalization seems more to have altered than "profoundly transformed" the security environment. But to show increased connectedness to this limited degree is to fall short of proving a "profound" transformation. Jonathan Kirshner, "Globalization, American Power, and International Security," *Political Science Quarterly* 123:3 (2008): 363–89.

CHAPTER 1

So Near, So Far

Physical and Strategic Distance

What is distance? How is it generated? How does it function in relation to armed conflict? And how are globalists getting it wrong?

In this chapter, I argue that to understand how it shapes and constrains the exercise of power, we should appreciate the distinction between physical and strategic distance. The word "distance" comes from the Latin verb *distare*, to separate oneself. If we consider "distancing" as a verb, an act that separates strategically, not just "distance" as a noun, then human agency can turn spaces into what Alan Henrikson calls "distancing units."[1] A stretch of terrain easily crossed in times of peace can become a lethal barrier in times of war. Globalists tend to conflate or confuse this important difference, mistaking the ability to move in permissive spaces with the shrinkage of the world.

To argue for the distinction between physical and strategic distance, this chapter proceeds in four parts. First, I argue that geopolitical theory at times loses sight of the differences between types of space. I then place the question of the relationship between human agency and the structure of the material world in a wider historical context, with particular reference to America. Third, I demonstrate that globalist conceptions of security are more deeply rooted than just an overestimation of technology and its compressing power. They are rooted in a liberal tradition of security thinking, a tradition that is hostile to the notion of geographical limitation. This is why globalism tends toward a view of security that is indivisible and borderless. Finally, I identify five "grounds for suspicion" that should make us think again.

Understanding Distance

Distance is generated by the interplay of terrain and technology. Space can work as a barrier, especially to the "offense" that must cross it successfully to close with its defending opponent. But other than the most imposing extremes of climate and landscape, there is no such thing as a fixed, intrinsic barrier or permanent corridor. As human agency intervenes to alter the spaces that divide polities, barriers can be expanded or contracted. Diplomats were obsessed with railways in the buffer →

late nineteenth century precisely for that reason. The new locomotive transport threatened to turn buffer terrain into carrier space. Arthur Balfour believed that Afghanistan was a "non-conducting" space, an impediment to Russian adventurism that stood between it and India, but feared roads and railroads could change it. On similar grounds, Russia sought British assurances that they would not build threatening railroads in their sphere of Persia.[2] Demilitarized outer lands that separate the core of one country from another, and that are not actively defended, can play a "buffer" role in a more limited sense by providing warning time. But that too takes political agreement, conscious restraint, and the compliance of those caught in the middle.

An important context through which to unpack the concept of distance is the issue of water and "moats." Water is generally more of a potential barrier than land. When applying ground forces from water onto land, it is harder and slower to cross. But its barrier power relies upon a level of resistance. The defense will benefit where it can focus its forces on land while the attacker's forces cross only gradually and under fire. But just as humans must "man" and exploit walls for them to work, water draws its barrier power from a level of active exploitation. Undefended water and empty beaches present few obstacles to power projection, weather permitting.

Water's properties are a central issue within debate about American security. America is flanked by oceans, and it is tempting to regard them as a natural barrier. In his seminal account of great-power politics, political scientist John Mearsheimer claims that the "stopping power of water" is a permanent obstructive force in international relations.[3] The oceans, he argues, are buffers that act as a built-in check on the expansionism of would-be hegemons. Mearsheimer does not fully explain what makes water "stop." He rightly notes that transoceanic lunges are harder to pull off than snap invasions across contiguous territories. This echoes earlier American traditions that the country's geographical bounty afforded it "free security." His argument implies that physical distance naturally generates the strategic payoff of a protective "moat." But he also observes that water did not stop modern Japan's expansion against weaker Russian and Chinese defenders, implicitly conceding that it takes more than water to do the stopping.[4]

Globalists turn this picture on its head, stressing the "enabling" power of technology, the ability to overcome maritime barriers and remake oceans into corridors of travel. But this also looks past the role of human agency in the picture and jumbles the distinct concepts of physical and strategic space. When former secretary of state Madeleine Albright said that "the idea of an ocean as protection is as obsolete as a castle moat," or secretary of defense William Cohen that "the vast oceans have been reduced to ponds . . . lands across the sea are now almost as close as neighboring countries today," they relied on a mechanical view of maritime space as mere terrain to be moved through. Similarly, one security analyst stresses that whereas Christopher Columbus's return journeys from Spain to the Caribbean took months, today "the same journey can be made in a matter of hours for the price of an airplane ticket."[5] The ease of travel, he argues, physically compresses space and time in threatening ways. But this confuses the geography of a tourist or explorer with that of a military contest for the control over space. We are not dealing with space as though it were a politically uncontested thoroughfare of climate and terrain. We are considering space as the medium into which other humans intrude, space through which (and for which) violent political struggle takes place. A glance at the strategic history of the Atlantic Ocean suggests that ever since humans learned to sail and navigate, water has not derived "stopping power" or "carrying power" naturally from its physical properties. Maritime space can function as a barrier or a highway depending on the capabilities of those who would cross it, the strength of resistance, the balance between offense and defense, and the intensity of clashing wills. The Atlantic Ocean is not in itself a wide "moat." Its expanse did not prevent the expansion of the Spanish conquistadors, whose transoceanic crossings in the sixteenth century went unresisted by their victims in Central and South America who lacked a navy to shield them. For Viking amphibious raiders, unopposed at sea, water afforded the luxury to choose where and when to strike. The monasteries that they preyed on did not draw stopping power from the seas. Bodies of water *in themselves* do not obstruct as moats if there is an insufficient defense able to thwart attackers with sufficient capability to cross them. To mistake particular trends in a certain period for a geopolitical law is to overlook the impact of agency and resistance on bodies of water.

For the United States, water has functioned as both barrier and carrier. Entering World War I in 1917–18, America transported vast quantities of men and materiel across the Atlantic to deploy on the Western Front, unmolested except for a faltering U-boat campaign, thanks to Britain's Royal Navy bottling up Germany's High Seas Fleet. But against the Axis of 1941–45, crossing and securing the Atlantic shipping lanes against effective armed resistance took a colossal maritime struggle in the Battle of the Atlantic, from Washington's undeclared war in 1941 to the crescendo of the campaign in mid-1943. The United States had to fight its way in through an Atlantic stalked by U-boat wolf packs that threatened to cut Britain's maritime throat and starve it into submission. Transporting armies to Britain as a base for continental war in Europe, and supplying that base, was a high-risk proposition until the Allies had secured the sea lanes. America and Britain secured a bridgehead to northwest Africa for Operation Torch in 1943. But this was only after the Allies had tilted the Atlantic balance in their favor. Even then, to avoid Axis interception it took elaborate deception, and the penalties of error or bad luck for the invasion fleet could have been heavy.[6]

One step in America's rise to the position of global hegemon was its ability to overturn the naval "stopping power" of its rivals. As a semi-insular power with no major rivals at home, it had regional dominance that meant that it could focus its might on applying its power beyond its neighborhood, unlike continental European and Asian powers who were occupied dealing with their neighbors.[7] This achievement gave Washington what Barry Posen calls "command of the commons," the sea, air, and space domains that it can defend and threaten to deny to others.[8] As the naval supremo, it turned the oceans into a global protectorate under its sway. Geopolitically, distance yielded advantages and disadvantages. If America operated from a remove, it had the ability to withdraw. During the Cold War, the fact that America was asserting itself from a different hemisphere and could "go home" threatened the credibility of its alliance commitments and its extended nuclear deterrence toward other states. At the same time, by operating from a remove, America's insularity made it seem less dangerous and less permanent, and therefore more attractive as a balancing ally, compared to local threats that had nowhere to retreat to.[9]

As this arrangement requires a considerable level of relative power in America's favor, there is no guarantee that it will last forever. America's ability to project power at will is subject to change, and changing balances of power could revive one of its oldest fears, the fear of eviction. If the world becomes more multipolar in the distribution of power as other states rise, those states could flex their maritime muscles and we enter a new era of sea denial. Parts of the "commons" could become "contested zones" where others could find and sink American ships and threaten its bases, to the point where even the United States would find it hard to dominate affordably.[10] The strategic "size" of the maritime East Asia, for example, will continue to vary, as a product of interaction between space, material capability, and political will.

So distance in human conflict is not intrinsic to space but a product of human exploitation of it. The ever-shifting relationship between technology, terrain, and agency means that spatial barriers rarely correspond exactly to their physical size. Some relatively short physical spaces represent more of a barrier than some larger ones. Defending states can construct defenses over relatively narrow bodies of water that are more formidable than larger land barriers. It proved easier for Hitler's Germany to overrun continental Europe than prevail across the Channel in the Battle of Britain. The small state of modern Israel is traditionally anxious about a lack of strategic depth and the scarcity of time and space, fears accentuated by memory of the shock of the 1973 surprise attack and successive wars of survival. Its strategists feared that modern technology made geography an irrelevance to Israel's survival, putting Israel's airfields and any target within its narrow coastal strip within range of the aircraft and missiles of its

Arab neighbors.[11] Israel now restretches that space with its defense missile system, Iron Dome, a relatively cheap and accurate fortification that effectively pushes its adversaries farther back.

It could be objected that the ultimate destructive technologies and their delivery systems place us in a precarious "village." The physical act of applying force from afar and putting a bomb on target has in many ways obviously accelerated, through drones, aircraft, or long-range missiles. A nuclear missile fired across the world can almost instantly destroy a city and its population regardless of geographic barriers. With enough nukes, states can penetrate missile shields sufficiently to inflict catastrophic damage. It only takes a few minutes for a long-range strategic weapon to reach its target, though most states lack the capability to fire an intercontinental missile and lack the deliverable bombs.

But a narrowly technical view of war as a matter of the range and velocity of weapons or the delivery of projectiles over space fails to consider the central political problem. This is the ability of those wielding force to translate it into political opportunity at affordable cost, which is the essence of strategy. War as a political act is rarely a matter of merely applying brute force on a target with the objective of annihilation, regardless of consequences. Warring parties mostly do not opt for a pure brute force objective (annihilating an adversary) as opposed to a more limited objective of coercion (changing the adversary's behavior, extracting political concessions, or overthrowing a regime). A war aim of pure annihilation pursued with maximum intensity and with a high tolerance for costs is an unlikely ideal type.[12]

This is partly because most states perceive a limited stake in a conflict. Even states with nuclear weapons turn to the means of destruction as a means to an end, not an end in itself. The most brutal conqueror out for profit would probably not wish to destroy valuable spoils they covet by leaving the smoking ruins of irradiated cities. And even a conqueror out simply to destroy would be subject to powerful domestic and international constraints. Resorting to a war of sheer brute force can be generally counterproductive to the state's long-term security goals. Warring to wipe out an opponent can incite other parties to intervene on the target's behalf. In its war in Vietnam, the United States had the ability to apply escalating levels of violence on land and from the air but shied away from maximizing violence on Hanoi in order to avoid overescalation spilling into war with the major communist powers, to prevent a propaganda defeat in the struggle for world opinion, and for fear of growing opposition at home. Unlimited brute force can invite blowback as the means of long-range violence that in theory enable annihilation from a distance also enable retaliation in kind. And with the kinds of weapons on the market today, even an overmatched and defeated opponent can inflict a devastating dying sting. So long as the defending state with a nuclear arsenal has a

Can't try and anihilate State w/ UMD, as their final act will be taring them

secure second-strike ability to retaliate, it can devastate an aggressor even with only a few punitive strikes.[13] This makes the conquest of any nuclear state prohibitively expensive. Nuclear weapons may not be certain to deter limited wars or prevent all-out nuclear exchange, and accident or misperception can take states to the brink. But the means of destruction constrain the ability of aggressors to expand. Technical capabilities do not bypass or suspend the dynamics of distance precisely because humans are still subject to the logic of costs and consequences as well as capabilities. Now that military power is more instantaneously lethal than ever, resort to maximum violence across international borders rarely makes sense.

Appreciating distance as a dynamic human creation, it is to the modern traditions of geopolitical thought that we now turn. Distance — what you make of it.

Geography, Geopolitics, and Globalism

Geography is distinct from geopolitics. "Geography" refers to the description of the earth, and the pursuit of knowledge about it. According to some geopolitical minds, like Nicholas Spykman, geography signals permanent physical facts: "Geography does not argue, it simply is."[14] This is not entirely correct. The earth, though usually more glacial in its pace of alteration than our species, also can change, with momentous political consequences. In our time, the melting Arctic calls forth a growing competition to exploit its energy holdings, mineral wealth, and opening shipping lanes.[15] By "geography," I refer here not to permanence, but to the physical, natural environment. Geography - natural, physical

"Geopolitics," by contrast, refers to something more interactive. Geopolitics is a tradition of "historical security materialism."[16] It concerns the spatial dynamics of power, the relationship of humans seeking security from violence and their surroundings, and the practices this leads to. It asks how in each era the material environment made up by geography and technology shapes security politics. It finds significance in the combinations of forces such as location, resources, climate, offense, defense, and above all, change. It also allows for human agency. Wisely or unwisely, humans exploit their natural environment in the pursuit of security. As Hans Weigert put it, "Where the forces of the earth, where the spaces of state systems have become part of an ideology for which men are dying, we are no longer confronted with 'facts' alone: Geopolitics does argue. It argues against us."[17] In this tradition, geography generates opportunities and constraints and conditions how the "security community" thinks and behaves.

There is a renewed debate about the relationship between globalization and geography. To what extent is geography now taking its "revenge," as Robert Kaplan now argues?[18] Kaplan argues for geography's primordial power. A chastened supporter of the United States–led Iraq War, Kaplan warns that the earth's barriers constrain American military strength. By turning back to maps, this can alert us to the tragic realism of the ancients as a caution against "excessive zeal in foreign policy."

But how, precisely, does geography reimpose itself? There is an ambivalence in Kaplan's use of the term "geography," a master concept that he loads with different meanings at different times. At one level, Kaplan's work is a powerful manifesto for renewed attention to maps, showing for example how nature's unequal dispensation gives China with its 19,000-mile Pacific coastline an ability to radiate power through the open sea in ways denied to Russia, denied warm-water access and whose only ocean frontage was historically blocked by Arctic ice. But Kaplan's ambivalence over what "geography" really means and under what conditions it prevails leads him into self-contradiction. At turns he is fatalistic about geography's power, framing it as a structural fact that acts on its subjects almost irresistibly. If the earth's terrain is the base structure and "first order of reality" and "ideas, however uplifting and fortifying, only the second," the mountains and waters that divide peoples play havoc with their projects. Kaplan points to the earth's natural barriers, such as the Hindu Kush, as the most impressive force. But at other times he turns this on its head, finding that transformative human inventions count more than nature, that "individual acts of men—the building of a canal—prove more historically crucial than the simple fact of geography." But canals surely involve ideas as well as materials, so here the second order of reality overturns the first. This sounds more like the revenge of technology and human agency, not geography as Kaplan conceives it. At other times he identifies technology taking its revenge over geography and its dividing power, noting that "globalization—the information age, the collapsing of distance"—erases spatial barriers in America's Caribbean backyard.[19] Because Kaplan conflates geography—that is, the description of the earth—with geopolitics—that is, the study of human interaction with it—these contradictions do not get resolved.

Lined up against Kaplan are those who lean toward visions of humans being integrated by globalization and also liberating themselves from geographic fate by introducing revolutionary technologies or creating institutions. Believers in globalized transcendence are a broad church. They include the likes of liberal internationalist Anne-Marie Slaughter, scholar and former State Department official, who stresses the universality of American security interests, and Niall Ferguson, Daron Acemoglu, and James Robinson, who argue for agency over structure, insisting that political choices matter more than geography, and that polities can succeed through good political choices wherever they are.[20]

If Kaplan's account is ambivalent, his liberal opponents' embrace of globalization is unequivocal. Slaughter accuses Kaplan and his regard for the relief map and Thucydides of being "old-fashioned" and "very male."[21] Against backward old geography, she prefers the cosmopolitan, the new manufactured landscapes of digital communication and Google Earth, and the connecting power of new globalizing technologies. Averse to the suggestion that territory should help guide American strategy, she writes that America must define its "vital strategic interests" not in terms of "oil and geography," but "universal values."[22] This is a false antithesis. How the pursuit of universal values can succeed without attention to earthly sources of power, such as affordable transport, is not clear. But Slaughter writes as an admirer of President Woodrow Wilson and looks to the progressive application of American power in order to steer globalization in the right direction. Slaughter's world view, which she believes is less macho, is also more bellicose. In the name of advancing universal values, and addressing the insecurities of globalization, she has advocated military interventions in Rwanda, Kosovo, Afghanistan, Iraq, Libya, and Syria.[23] Few of these have been triumphs. But globalism, at least in her case, means war. To prevent genocide and advance liberalism, she regularly advocates war, a brutally illiberal and degenerate force that historically creates conditions for genocide. As Karl Marx noted when Britons debated war on China in the name of extending free trade, it is liberals who now preach "red hot steel" in the cause of ultimate peace.[24]

To debate the balance between connection and division, borders, and the borderless is to debate a deeper issue, the never-ending struggle between structure and human agency, how far "security communities" can alter their environment or are prisoners of it, and the very relationship between ideas and the material world. The word "limits" originates in geopolitics. *Limes* was the Roman term for a marked frontier, marking both the scope of power and the violent periphery where the empire's domination was contested and its vulnerability was played out. Distance was critical to the empire's success, as the imperial center tried to hold off "disorder" far away on the outer periphery.

Do the same limits apply to America? American hegemony regards itself as uniquely nonterritorial, as a liberal order of values and institutions that are emancipating and that, with enough support, can succeed anywhere, anytime. Unlike in prior empires, its proponents claim, America's creed of market democracy undergirded by alliances and institutions is universally applicable and transcends geographical limits. According to John Ikenberry, Washington's long-term "deep global engagement" and its global liberal order represents the triumph of the liberal order over geopolitics, because the strength and appeal of the Atlantic "way" makes futile any territorial struggles for spheres of influence, or any effort to counterbalance the liberal superpower.[25] At stake here is the issue of change, whether globalization has altered the rules and whether the United States can transcend the limitations that bound great powers before it. To speak of geography's "revenge," therefore, is to resist the claims of American exceptionalism.

The question of whether geography is a hard fact of life, or a political state of mind that can be altered, not only splits "realists" and liberals. It also splits classical and critical geopolitics. Classical geopolitics stresses material forces, approaching nature as the dominant structure of politics. At the extremes, there are hard "structuralists" such as Ellsworth Huntington and Jared Diamond, for whom nature's brute forces are the main engines of history.[26] This school points to the power of material context, but by minimizing the importance of intervening ideas, doesn't tell us much about variations in human behavior when placed in similar environments. Critical geopolitics, by contrast, privileges the role of ideas and discourse. It views geopolitics as a system of knowledge produced in order to achieve and sustain power. This countertradition accuses traditional geopolitics of being the handmaiden of Western imperialism, as a self-serving ideology that naturalizes imperial power politics.[27] But by treating geopolitics as little more than a cultural construct, it risks trivializing material context, losing sight of how the physical environment bites back. And it is so preoccupied by discourse that it is not very "geo" at all.

To be geopolitically minded, one does not have to believe that physical environment is destiny. At a minimum, geopolitical analysis assumes that material conditions influence whether particular modes of security-seeking can generate the results their makers desire. Geography conditions political choices though does not determine them. Location shapes how the state defines its interests, allocates its resources, and organizes its military capabilities. In moments of interstate struggles for survival, it informs "bread and butter" decisions. As Paul Kennedy suggests, a state's location posed important questions: "Was a particular nation able to concentrate its energies on one front, or did it have to fight on several? Did it share common borders with weak states, or powerful ones? Was it chiefly a land power, or a sea power, or a hybrid—and what advantages and disadvantages did that bring? Could it easily pull out of a great war in central Europe if it wished to?"[28]

But states still have choices. Agents can "misread" their environment. Resource-rich states that enjoy favorable geography can blunder. Resource-poor ones can succeed despite their location. All things being equal, states that share the same geographical conditions can make choices that give them very different futures. The diverging paths of states on the Korean Peninsula or in Cold War Germany bear this out. But things are mostly not equal, and location often weighs heavily in the balance. In our time, democratic Vietnam with its access to deepwater ports and the booming Asian market surged ahead of more democratic Bolivia, locked in mountains at high altitude.[29] People make their own history, just not in conditions of their choosing.

Since classical antiquity, "naturalistic" traditions privileged geography as the "maker," acting on human politics. Political thinkers speculated about the divide between more authoritarian land states and more democratic maritime states, and about the imprint of the natural world on politics. This was pithily expressed by Herodotus through the mouth of the Persian king Cyrus, that "soft lands are prone to breed soft men."[30] In the classical tradition, commentators on the Greek wars linked "hubris" to the question of boundaries. If hubris is self-destructive presumption in the face of the gods, the transgression of limits flouted an order laid down by heaven. Launching his unsuccessful invasion of Greece, King Xerxes yolked together the continents of Europe and Asia with pontoon bridges across the kilometer-wide water of the Dardanelles, displaying his mastery over nature, "to hold / The raging Bosphorus, like a slave, in chains."[31] In Greek portrayals, when a storm swept away the first attempt, Xerxes had the sea lashed for its disobedience. Presuming to enslave nature, he invited punishment that was meted out in military defeats at Salamis and Plataea. In the language of social science, this tradition framed the power of geography as the independent or causal variable, and politics as the dependent variable or the thing effected. This tradition persisted. Philosopher Charles de Montesquieu (1689–1755) argued that the western Roman Empire doomed itself when its territory exceeded the power of its forces to guard it. European states lacked the natural buffers that large Asian states had, like deserts, oceans, and mountain chains. Nature set frontiers that in the long run no state can dare to cross without being punished.[32]

All of this changed with modern geopolitical thought, which centred on the great disruption of the industrial revolution and the consequences of sudden, dramatic, and accelerating change. New tools and the sheer scale of activity held out the possibility that humans could master their environments and transform their worlds. The essential move of modern geopolitics is to switch geography from independent to dependent variable, becoming the thing acted upon, making technology the independent or causal variable that changes the world around it.

Debate shifted to how the changing material forces of each period functioned and what they mean for power struggles, focusing on the relative balance of land versus sea power, offense versus defense, and given the new possibilities for conquerors, continent versus continent. The father of modern geopolitics in the Anglosphere, Halford Mackinder (1861–1947), argued that the coming of the railways for the first time would enable a conqueror to seize command of Eurasia, the world's pivotal power center, and harness the resources of this vast continental landmass to gain access to the oceans and make a bid for world mastery.[33] The fear of a Eurasian continental superpower became very real and reached a crescendo in World War II. If Nazi Germany could conquer the Soviet Union, it could unite "Germany's science with Russia's manpower and pivotal geopolitical position," enabling it to prepare for a hegemonic clash of continents against America. Mackinder privileged railways and land power.[34] By contrast, the American naval historian and imperial visionary

Alfred Thayer Mahan (1840–1914) saw navies and seapower rather than the land battles as the key to history, and the steamship as the revolutionary device. Neither foresaw that air power too would add a third domain to the struggle. But both looked to human inventions exploiting and shrinking geography as the central issue in the conflict between landlocked and oceanic states.

Modern geopolitics grew out of an anxiety about the relationship between tools, space, and struggle that was recast with every new tide of technology, from the telegraph to the television, from the steamship to the airplane. Maps have a long association with military activity, imperialism, and power struggles abroad. Modern cartography evolved as a discipline closely tied to professional militaries and became a device to aid military operations. Its roots lie most strongly in nineteenth-century Prussia-Germany, which studied it more intensely than in the Anglosphere. The general staff of the *Kaiserreich* employed over five hundred officers in a land survey section to study cartography, trigonometry, and topography.[35] Geopolitics found especially fertile ground in Germany. The growth of geopolitics as an intellectual pursuit was stimulated by German power struggles and anxieties about its vulnerable Central European location, its recurring antagonisms with Russia and France, the spawning of nationalism and the quest for *Lebensraum*, and the capacity of new means of transport to deliver threats to the doorstep.

For Karl Marx, the industrial revolution and the coming of new machines that accelerated movement and reduced its transaction costs pointed to "the annihilation of space by time."[36] What Marx saw coming from new means of production of modern industrial technology, others now see coming from new means of destruction. Where once it was transport technologies applied to war such as the railway and air power, it is now primarily the information revolution (including the internet, instant communications, the flow of digitized capital, and the shift from industrial to information-based economies) that globalists identify as a powerful world-integrating forces. By closing the gap between people, these forces render security indivisible as technology heightens violent interdependence.

From different directions, the premise of a radically altered security environment underpins thinking about "new" versus "old" wars, the applicability in a new age of classical strategy theory, the rise of "new" terrorism, the emergence of a cyber domain of conflict, and the future of nuclear deterrence, and in contestation about the meaning of security itself.[37] The proposition that modern inventions shrink space with profound consequences is strongly contested in other fields, but in the study of security has become a "recurrent cliché."[38] The "Copenhagen School" of new security theory, led by Barry Buzan and Wolfgang Reinecke, stresses the changes wrought by new kinds of actors and a broadening of the security in ways that render distance less relevant. The "London School" of risk theory, inspired by Ulrich Beck and Mikkel Rasmussen, sees security problems embedded in an emerging political economy, a world in which chaotic flows and the empowerment of new actors make nonsense of classical geopolitics where security communities could protect themselves through the control of space and the accumulation of material power. Writes Beck, "We have already seen the *death of distance* in the cultural sphere—now we are experiencing it in the military sphere; indeed, we are witnessing the end of the state's monopoly on violence in a highly technologized world where anything can ultimately become a missile in the hands of determined fanatics."[39] Forecasting a grave new world, Rasmussen argues that "the study of strategy is still deeply rooted in the analysis of structural conditions like geography and enduring national interests," at a time when globalization is creating "a new breed of strategic agents . . . able to operate because globalization makes the world easily accessible to terrorists as well as traders."[40]

Literature on international security on a "macro" scale also takes the concept of a new globalized security environment as a premise. Studies of the relationship between law and security, such as those of James Gow and Philip Bobbitt, argue that the world has changed so much since the advent of transnational threats, weapons of mass destruction, global communications, and trade networks that international law must now accommodate anticipatory or "preclusive" defense.[41] They have in mind nightmare scenarios like urban nuclear terror and pandemics. Robert Cooper, former adviser to Tony Blair, in the lead-up to war in Iraq in 2003 reasoned that the danger of premodern failed states called for a new liberal imperialism.[42] It is not hard to see the contentious ideology in these visions, where the West is the agent of order with the foreknowledge, power, and authority to act without becoming the unwitting bearer of chaos.

The main focal point of globalist speculation is the United States. If globalization is real, America is both its main engine and its main target. America is an unusual superpower in the scale of its reach and the global breadth of its ambitions. Its military horizons are vast. The yardstick of military clout for successive presidencies has been the ability to deter adversaries in multiple theaters, counterattack in others, and take an enemy's capital all at once. Its Unified Command Plan, created in 1946, divides the planet into military commands. Its defense budget exceeds most of the other major military powers combined.[43] It has munitions, equipment, and personnel prepositioned around the world, both onshore and afloat. Its diplomacy is worldwide, and with its spying casts a long gaze across the world's surface. The range of its weapons enables it to penetrate from the seas to deep inside countries, and from high altitude. No hegemon before has so strongly dominated the two traditional domains, primacy on land and dominance at sea. It seems to have transcended the seapower-based limits of nineteenth-century Britain and the land limits that constrained twentieth-century Germany.[44] It designed the world's financial and trade architecture with its "Bretton Woods"

[handwritten: Globalisation leading from Cold War — need for ... National security states]

institutions. This places it in the eye of the storms attributed to globalization, such as the spread of dangerous ideologies, state breakdown, spiralling ethno-religious wars, and the proliferation of weapons of mass destruction.

The United States entered what some supposed was its "unipolar moment" after the Cold War, when for the first time, it had a preponderance of power with no peer or plausible rival.[45] Washington cast around for a new organizing idea to inform its diplomacy and defense. Globalism became the ascendant world view in government and the received "common sense" of the political class. Consecutive US administrations and the American foreign policy establishment embraced it. It forms the premise of successive post-9/11 strategy documents such as the National Security Strategies of 2002, 2006, and 2010, which offer "generalized discourses on global threats."[46] President Barack Obama also propagates the myth, even though his record of strategic words and actions is more conflicted. At times, Obama warns against falling into a state of "continual war" and has tried to limit America's liability by ending wars he inherited, avoiding ones that look too hard, and extricating the United States from the wildly difficult jobs it set itself in the Middle East and Central Asia. Yet he too has perpetuated the mentality that underpins "continual war." According to him, "the security of the American people is inextricably linked to the security of all people," and his National Security Strategy of 2010 rededicates the United States to the task of underwriting global security in a dangerous globalizing era.[47] The same president who quotes the pessimist theologian Reinhold Niebuhr to warn against imperial hubris has also bought into the language of global security to justify his escalation of the war in Afghanistan with ambitious nation-building goals, to justify drone strikes and bombing campaigns, to rationalize the signature move of his period in office, his tightening of a ring of alliances to contain a growing China, and to urge for a punitive bombing of Syria to make an example of rogue states and bolster American credibility.

Globalism is not just made by and for Americans. A seminal moment was the "Chicago Speech" of British prime minister Tony Blair in April 1999. With a cosmopolitan, humanitarian, and internationalist twist, Blair articulated a transatlantic conception of security. As NATO bombed Serbia in the name of humanitarian intervention, Blair insisted that a new condition of interdependence had arrived, erasing the gap between values and interests, which should spur Western nations into activism abroad.[48] It was reworked as the foundational ideology of the NATO alliance and the transatlantic security community, a basis on which to maintain its purpose and identity in a post-Soviet world. The general secretary of NATO, Jaap de Hoop Scheffer, argued that the age of global risk made "passive" Cold War behavior like deterrence obsolete and required the Western alliance to go global, take anticipatory action beyond its region, reflecting "the need to look at security functionally, rather than geographically."[49] NATO secretary general Anders Fogh Rasmussen announced when promoting the alliance's 2010 *Strategic Concept* that we have entered an age of "globalized insecurity" of weapons proliferation and piracy, terrorism, and cyber attacks, where "no borders, and no oceans, could shield us from these kinds of threats."[50] In the name of this world view, NATO reinvented itself from stationary guardian defending a fixed territory known as the "West," to a mobile institution expanding a liberal ideology. It expanded all the way to the old Soviet borders and lifted the concept of the West from its geographical moorings. Russia's war with Georgia in the summer of 2008 was a reminder that this manifestation of globalization, Western penetration of its "near abroad," would not come without a fight.

The global village mentality links together utopian and dystopian assumptions. Allegedly, the very channels and devices of Western prosperity that circulate capital, ideas, technology, and people could also create pathways for violence and chaos as the delivery system for a new apocalypse that puts us all in the firing line. Just as pandemics and economic shocks respect no borders, neither do human agents. It is the "security paradox" for the chairman of the Joint Chiefs of Staff, for whom the worldwide commercial peace is making destructive technology "available to a wider and more disparate pool of adversaries" so that a single person with a computer can disrupt a city or a nation.[51] Addressing the US Congress on the eve of the invasion of Iraq in 2003, British prime minister Tony Blair portrayed a systemic virus that changed the rules of the game. Coming together as a species "provides us with unprecedented opportunity but also makes us *uniquely vulnerable* . . . the threat comes because in another part of our globe there is shadow and darkness . . . in the combination of these afflictions a new and deadly virus has emerged. The virus is terrorism whose intent to inflict destruction is unconstrained by human feeling and whose capacity to inflict it is enlarged by technology."[52] In this imagery, if the dominant image of the world is that of a village, the dominant image of threat is that of a contagion, or an epidemic of insecurity.

As Blair's words suggest, nuclear terrorism with its confluence of radical ideology and deadly technology is the ultimate embodiment of these fears. For those who believe we inhabit a dangerous globe that renders geography irrelevant, there is no graver prospect than a nomadic terrorist with no fixed address, aching for the afterlife and laying waste to a city.[53] Electronic warfare is also becoming a focus of fear. Last time, a grievous raid on home soil came in the form of planes converted into missiles. Next time, enemies could strike more insidiously than small groups slipping through the homeland security net, bringing on an electronic 9/11 or Pearl Harbor from anywhere with the cyber weapon, "with no boundaries or rules, costs little, and has monstrous potential," that could devastate power grids or worse.[54]

Globalism is an ideology of power as well as vulnerability. How states perceive threats and define the scope of their interests is partly a function of their capabilities and their sense of their own relative strength, generated not just by the command of vast resources, but by their ability to convert this material plenty into desired outcomes. Growing power tends to cause growing insecurity. The greater their relative strength, the more states tend toward a narcissistic view of themselves as central to everything.[55] If leaders sense that they cannot do much about a worrying development, they are less inclined to designate it as a grave danger. Yet the violent perils supposedly generated by globalization—weapons proliferation, catastrophic terrorism, or rogue regimes—are things US leaders of both parties have vocally identified as problems American power can address. Indeed, the appetite to find and eradicate threats all over the planet is made possible by the luxury of America's position and the imbalance of power in its favor. American rulers are able to identify global threats precisely because they do not have to focus their defenses against a major opponent that could threaten their homeland. They have a large nuclear arsenal, many allies, and face no major peer adversary or threatening coalitions. Being "top dog" tempts Washington to roam free, presuming to act from a position of overwhelming preponderance.

Globalism articulates itself in two ways, in terms of both the vulnerability of the shrinking world, and the power and reach of the West to tame it back into order. Popular culture reflects this dual assumption. The TV melodrama *24*, of the battle against terrorism, portrays super-militants and an intelligence apparatus hunting them down with almost godlike powers of surveillance. The mixture of fear and ambition was central to the Global War on Terror, an exercise not only in thwarting terrorism but in reconfiguring territories across the globe and altering the international system itself. As Donald Rumsfeld claimed in a note to the president weeks after 9/11, "if the war does not significantly change the world's political map, the US will not achieve its aim."[56]

These tendencies framed the debate over the most significant act of the War on Terror, the invasion of Iraq in March 2003. Typical of the mutual creation of alarm and confidence, the American political class perceived Saddam Hussein's tyrannical regime in Iraq as both an unacceptable threat and an easy target. In the buildup to war, an inflated specter of Saddam's supposed capacity for rapid assault with chemical weapons captured the public imagination. The British government reported in September 2002 that Saddam Hussein's Iraq had the capacity to launch chemical and biological weapons within forty-five minutes' notice.[57] London's assessments did not distinguish between tactical- and strategic-range weapons. The Chilcot Inquiry revealed that policymakers were incurious about the crucial distinction between tactical battlefield missiles and strategic long-range ones.[58] Tabloid newspapers interpreted the government's dossier to mean that Saddam could strike Britons with germ warfare missiles in Cyprus on forty-five minutes' notice, mistaking both the limited range of Saddam's weapons and the time it would take for them to reach their targets even if they were long-range.[59] In the public debate, Saddam's limited capabilities became "not a chemical weapon for use on the battlefield, but a weapon of mass destruction for use in an interstate war."[60] The government did not attempt to disabuse the public of this fear.[61] The issue here is not whether there was deliberate deception, but how easily a threat could inflate through a prism of fears about globalized insecurity, so that tactical and localized military capabilities could easily be confused with long-range ones. All of these fears the government promoted as it confidently assessed that a United States–led coalition could apply its power swiftly, cheaply, and decisively to remove a dangerously armed rogue state and liberate the country with minimal resistance, despite warnings to the contrary.[62]

In the American-led West and beyond, the global village myth works both as a strategic vision and an ideological claim about Western vulnerability, power, and authority. A world linked and shrunken is a world forever on the brink of chaos, crying out for a guardian to police it. Because this world can spread insecurity anywhere anytime, the West has no choice but to act as universal guardian, taming it back into order. Most restatements of America's claim to world leadership, most manifestos of an American liberal hegemony, and those explicitly arguing for an American empire are pervaded by the adjective "global" to denote the burden of responsibilities that must be shouldered by the superpower. America musn't pull back, globalists warn, as it has the strength to underwrite the world's security, and a retrenchment of global leadership would open dangerous vacuums. In this way, the word "global" is the watchword for America's imperial role.[63] America, supposedly, can only be secure in a world that it orders. Far from being an innocently objective account of obvious truths, the language of globalism is a warrant for the superpower to throw its weight around.

Globalism and its vision of a liberal, cosmopolitan world order frames itself as the better alternative to modern geopolitics, which suffers a bad press. Many of the leading geopolitical theorists were German intellectuals like Karl Haushofer (1869–1946) and Friedrich Ratzel (1844–1904), both associated with the causes of militarism and imperialism. Tainted by association, ever since it has stood accused of being too close to the cold monster of the state, and of preaching an amoral, instrumental view of people as extractive resources. Hitler's regime deployed Haushofer's writings as an intellectual resource for its project of carving out an Aryan empire. Geopolitics lived on in the Cold War in the Soviet-American competition for the balance of industrial and material power, remapping the world as a single battlespace, and it revived again as a subject of scholarly analysis in the 1980s.[64] But it never fully broke free of suspicion. As a critic warns, "few modern ideologies are as whimsically all-encompassing, as romantically obscure, as intellectually sloppy, and as likely to start a third world war as the theory of 'geopolitics.'"[65] Arguing for a better cosmopolitan path, another argues that the history of geopolitics is a history of "bad ideas—sometimes mad ideas—that have led countries to wars and recessions."[66]

But the antigeographic ideology of globalism is also lethal and dangerous, not least because it is so convinced of its own enlightenment. Its roots lie in an ideology that resists the idea of limitation, namely liberalism.

Kantians with Cruise Missiles: Globalism and the Liberal Tradition

Aside from its fixation with technology, globalism has its political-intellectual roots in the liberal tradition.[67] By the liberal tradition in this context, I refer to the working out in world politics of the system of "liberal values" that lies at the center of the battleground of American politics. I focus here on the Wilsonian version of liberalism that seeks to institute peace by spreading liberty, at the point of a bayonet if necessary. Liberalism combines ideals of individual liberty, free markets, democratic representation, and equality of opportunity and offers a set of ideas that penetrates the rhetoric and practices of America's strategic behavior abroad. It also offers an account of national security and how it can be pursued. It draws on Immanuel Kant and his program for "perpetual peace" in a liberal pacific union of republics made gentler by commerce and popular rule, a vision of peace through the eradication of authoritarian regimes that the revolutionary Thomas Paine also proclaimed.[68] Globalism resonates in American public life not because it is a new account of a new condition, but because it draws on traditions of American security thinking that unite the sometimes-squabbling members of the Wilsonian family.

Liberals are a heterogeneous lot and don't all sign up to radical measures to achieve security by spreading liberty. Many are more averse to the use of force and drawn more to international institutions, the strengthening of global governance, or the tranquil effects of commerce. Some draw different conclusions from globalization theory, arguing that commercial interdependence penalizes war to the point where it is futile. But their account of security prepares the ground and supplies the rationale for visionary world-ordering and continual war. They agree that the state of interdependence and proximity makes parties like Al Qaeda or rogue states more dangerous, because they have new access and can inflict more damage. According to the very liberal Princeton Project on National Security, today's world of weapons proliferation, of chaos-spawning failed states, and catastrophic violence "seems a more menacing place than ever."[69]

The liberal tradition contains the seeds of ideologically driven belligerence. As Loius Hartz argued, liberalism tends to desire the extermination of the illiberal.

Translated into a doctrine of strategic internationalism, it drives a desire within the United States to spread liberalism beyond its borders. The tradition teaches that America is a fragile republic that can be secure only in a world transformed in its image and thus hospitable to its way life. This can be achieved only if American institutions are replicated abroad, and through the spread of the "open door" of free markets. Thus it tilts toward the pursuit of what historian Charles Beard called "perpetual war for perpetual peace," where war is not abolished but charged with an ambitious mission, becoming more terrible.[70] As one's security is tied to the domestic good order of other states, the mere presence of nonrepublican states is dangerous and places them beyond the protection of sovereignty. Those states must be moved coercively if necessary into the light in order to bring about the peace that for Kant was republican, but for today's liberals is democratic and capitalist.

Iconic in this tradition is President Woodrow Wilson (1856–1924) and in particular the world view he articulated in entering World War I against the Central Powers. Wilson's own record had its contradictions. "Wilsonianism" can be invoked to support revisionist attempts to spread liberal values or to support a restraining status quo system of collective security.[71] Wilson's own faction was caught in the tension between the desire to replace a system of power politics with a stabilizing and restraining system of collective security on one hand, and the crusading, revolutionary conviction that ultimate peace was only possible with the overthrow of autocratic, militaristic regimes.[72] Our concern here, however, is not the internal consistency of those beliefs. Important here is his political legacy. "Wilsonian" here refers to the instinct to make the world safe for American democracy through ideological expansion. The most climactic, recent moment of liberalism as a strategic doctrine was the formulation and application of the Bush Doctrine. That doctrine in the Wilsonian tradition takes a liberal view of the sources of foreign policy, in the character of regimes themselves, and a liberal view of the solution, namely enforcing a democratic peace. This gives America a large stake in the type of government that rules other states.[73] President George W. Bush himself consciously placed his attempt to lead the "advance of freedom" in the Greater Middle East in the same genealogy of Woodrow Wilson's Fourteen Points and Franklin Roosevelt's Four Freedoms.[74] The rhetoric of removing rogue states and implanting democracy at the heart of the Middle East made Iraq "Woodrow Wilson's War."[75]

This way of defining the national interest helps explain why enlightenment republics like the United States might be peaceful in their relations with other liberal states, but historically show a strong appetite for conflicts with authoritarian regimes.[76] It helps explain why a sizable chunk of self-professed American liberals initially supported the United States–led invasion of Iraq, from Paul Berman to Hillary Clinton to the *Washington Post*. Clearly other motivations may have played a role, not least that the war was initially a popular cause. But thanks to the shared Wilsonian inheritance, it was ideologically easy for hawkish Democrats from the party of Wilson, Roosevelt, Truman, and Johnson to reconcile themselves to Bush's war. The continuity of Wilsonian instincts about American security in mainstream American politics is demonstrated in the only rigorous counterfactual analysis of the pressures that would have been brought to bear on a Democratic president Al Gore in similar circumstances.[77]

How does liberalism relate to geography? Because of its absolutist tendencies, liberalism is at odds with the principle of geographic limitation. As an attitude as well as an ideology, it is impatient with the notion that America should temper its idealism, rank its interests around regions with greater and lesser importance, and work within the constraints of geography. It fuses with the ideology of American exceptionalism, which has an ideal of infinite possibility married to great expectations of technology, from America's conquest of its frontier to its exploration of space. Apprehension about new technologies only strengthens this tendency. The mixture of competing ideologies with new weapons means that nothing and nowhere is strategically marginal, and threats can materialize anywhere and anytime. The flat world imagined by liberalism trumps the divided and interrupted world of geography, classically conceived. And it finds expression not only in Washington's National Security Strategies and in a wider discourse about contemporary security. In the visual aids produced by the World Economic Forum's annual *Global Risks* report, with its digitalized maps highlighting points of financial vulnerability, climate catastrophe, and resource scarcity designed to show that the world grows increasingly complex and interdependent. With this catastrophic imagery, a state of "liberal terror" arrives.[78]

So globalism draws on the pathologies of liberalism. Applied to questions of security, it has the following lineaments. It seeks a state of absolute security. Because it sees threats are viral and systemic, liberalism is prone to regard ideological competition as extremely dangerous and to favor a logic of eradicating threats over a logic of constraining and living with them. Its concept of security is deterritorialized, limitless, and ideologically intense. Equating security with the pursuit of a planetary monoculture of shared liberal democratic values, it cannot abide pluralism except on its own terms. Liberalism is insensitive to the issue of costs and limits, either overestimating American strength or formulating ambitious goals without appreciating how they exceed scarce resources. The belief that their security is everywhere on the line tempts states to embrace the precautionary principle.[79] The West cannot wait and must strike first. George W. Bush argued that "if we wait for threats to fully materialize, we will have waited too long," and his vice president formulated a "1 percent doctrine," that any degree of threat was intolerable and justified the radical application of power and resources.[80] That turned out to be scarce. The liberal security mindset alters even the sense of time. A condition of neither wartime nor peacetime becomes the norm, but a state of emergency and continuous military operations. Because the enemy is amorphous, and conflated with a generic "contagion" of threats, there is no precise concept of victory to delimit the struggle, and no end in sight.

Indeed, an American strain of liberal imperialism lies at the heart of globalist visions of the world. This is not the place to rehearse in depth the issue of whether America is an "empire." On one hand, America's power-political behavior differs from classical empires. After its obviously imperial continental expansion, it was mostly averse to formal conquest and annexation and lacked the "earth hunger" of European and Asian empires. On the other hand, there are modes of empire beyond swallowing foreign lands and grabbing acreage. Imperial "logic" can be found in America's pattern of rule through intermediary clients, its exercise of prerogatives that it would deny to other powers, such as sponsoring coups to overthrow regimes from Iran to Haiti, and its hub-and-spoke model of relations with states in its orbit, where the asymmetry of power blurs the line between persistent influence and indirect rule.[81]

While that debate persists, America's globalist ideology looks, sounds, and walks like the imperialist duck. By invitation and by choice, the United States appoints itself guardian of world order. It claims a unique historical mission or even a mandate of heaven. It exercises a selective disregard for others' sovereignty. And it accepts with a low threshold continuous intervention and violence on its peripheries, or in the euphemistic words of one commentator, "forward-leaning interventionist garden-tending."[82] Advocates of an American role as constant gardener explicitly or implicitly call for continued Western hegemony, instead of a balance of power. A balance of power is a state of equilibrium created by self-restraint and denying excessive greatness to any player. It accepts limitations that implicitly accept the continued existence of potential competitors. Hegemony, by contrast, is the pursuit of an unchallengeable imbalance that is favorable to the top dog. Part of the War on Terror was a clearly stated reaffirmation of America's commitment to primacy and peerless military might to back it up.

Through this imperial looking glass, globalism carries an anxiety about credibility. America has long been moved by "credibility" fears, the belief that the state should show commitment even to minor conflicts in order to avoid looking soft and to sustain international prestige. Seeing the world as a single battlespace and as a theater judging the performance of states to determine their credibility, failure anywhere affects one's position everywhere. Along with an inflated sense of borderless threat, and exaggerated assumptions about ability to project power, this feeds directly into policy decisions that are unexpectedly costly at best, and self-defeating at worst, from Korea to Vietnam to Iraq.[83]

Historical scrutiny demonstrates that the fear that the superpower must actively show "resolve" everywhere to ensure its security is often misplaced. On-looking states mostly do not judge a state's willingness to defend its core interests based on their action in previous crises, such as peripheral wars, but rather on judgments about its stake and capabilities in present ones.[84] Credibility is a real commodity. But it draws on practical capabilities that states can bring to bear in the here and now, and on perceptions of the balance of interests in a crisis. Enemies and rivals are sensitive to the difference between peripheries and areas of high strategic value. Defeat in Vietnam did not persuade Moscow that the United States would abandon Western Europe, any more than the Soviet Union's bleeding in Afghanistan meant the Warsaw Pact was a paper tiger. The very allies America hoped to impress with their commitment in Vietnam advised Washington against extending the war. When America has used force in the name of showing resolve, the results are disappointing if judged by that standard. The Korean War to curb Kim Il Sung did not dissuade the power bids of Gamal Abdel Nasser nor Ho Chi Minh. Intervention in Panama did not prevent Saddam Hussein's attempt to swallow Kuwait. Throwing back Saddam's adventurism in the Gulf did not put off Slobodan Milosevic or, indeed, Osama bin Laden. When Vladimir Putin last wielded force to strong-arm a state in Russia's backyard, it was in Georgia during the second term of George W. Bush, a president not known for his reluctance to draw America's sword and who intended his Iraq adventure to remind the world of America's willingness to show strength.

Anxious about order and chaos, globalists want it both ways. They frame the world as chaotically interconnected but exonerate the West from being part of the creation of that chaos, seeing it only as a stabilizing guardian, bringing order into chaos with little regard to blowback or unintended consequences. The recent embrace of the notion of "prevention" reflects that mentality.[85] It presumes that in such an "uncertain" world of "unknowns," somehow the West has the foreknowledge to anticipate where and how insecurity takes root and how to forestall it. It understands threats more as external forces rather than the product of tragic interactions. Terrorism, for instance, it deems dangerous because of its sheer capacity to inflict damage directly, not because of its capacity to bait target communities into reacting in costly, self-harming ways.

Like any state, no single ideology dictates America's policies. Presidents who articulate strong liberal principles can also violate their own nostrums, hence Washington's friendship with authoritarian regimes from Uzbekistan to Saudi Arabia. But liberalism is a powerful strain that is endlessly recalled. While not consistently observed in practice, it poses a powerful and recurrent logic. Indeed, for a country that has many ways of war, this logic defines its "way of strategy."[86] It has remained the standard by which doctrines and actions are judged, the basis on which military adventures are promoted, and in times of shock, a mantle the political class lays claim to and a powerful means for mobilizing the American people. Globalism represents more than a set of fears to be stoked by cynical politicians. It flows from what the historian Michael Howard and today's followers of the jurist Carl Schmitt identify as a form of politics based upon permanent emergency in a threatening globe, a "liberal way of war" for world-ordering purposes that cannot end in space or time because it pursues security through the creation of liberal subjects, leading to crusading doctrines such as a "war to end war" or a "war on terror."[87] To place liberal norms at the core of calculations about war is to do more than intend "relief to the displaced and the dispossessed and prevent mass murder." It is to wield force, an inherently illiberal process, to eliminate the illiberal roots of bad things.[88] And if the existence of the illiberal is a cause for war, there is always another demon to fight.

Going Too Far: Imperial Overstretch and American Uniqueness

The debate about historical security materialism, about agency and structure, technology and terrain is also about the horizons of America's "global" role and whether it, too, can go too far. As the phrase implies, "going too far" in the application of power abroad is partly a territorial concept. The vocabulary of self-defeating behavior suggests so. Consider British historian Paul Kennedy's phrase "imperial overstretch." Since classical antiquity, observers troubled by the fragility of power have linked it to territorial space as the marker of limits. If there is a tragic vision of politics that unites the likes of Thucydides, Carl von Clausewitz, and modern political realists such as Hans Morgenthau, it is that strong nations go through a cycle of accumulated success, the abandonment of limits, self-defeating behavior, and ruin.[89] In that tradition, the fear of decline is closely linked to the fatal crossing of lines. America's two wars in the Gulf, beginning in 1991 and 2003, brought these issues into sharp focus.

The theme of geographical transgression that weakens empires has never gone away. Paul Kennedy touched a nerve in Washington when he argued that the rise and fall of great powers was due to a failure to balance power and commitments, economic vitality and military expenditure, and that America was no exception in its susceptibility to these patterns.[90] At that time, American fears of decay were spurred by post-Vietnam reversals, economic eclipse by a booming Japan and West Germany, and increasing debt. These fears prompted an argument about how great powers "fell," and whether the United States is exempt from the patterns to be found in history. Kennedy's study was a "long-cycle history" and stressed the equation of material forces at moments of power transition. He warned of unsustainable imbalances in the long haul, such as overconsumption and undersaving, deindustrialization, the costs of maintaining hegemonic military power, and the "termite" erosion of economic foundations. By saying that the United States might be subject to the same problems as empires past, this offended the spirit of American exceptionalism, the notion that because of its uniqueness, America is exempt from the limitations suffered by previous great powers.[91] To believers in the enduring Pax Americana, warnings against material overstretch implied the emotive concept of decline, not merely the passing of the "unipolar moment" but of American civilization. And the very notion of decline, in the words of a former ambassador to China, is "un-American."[92]

The Persian Gulf wars that began in 1990 and 2003 restaged the debate about American overreaching and uniqueness, and whether overstretch is something that just happens to other powers. As well as long-term erosion, theorists of overstretch argued that imprudent wars could accelerate the fall.[93] In this context, debate returned to a text written by general from classical Athens, another power sure of its singularity. Thucydides's history of Athens's Peloponnesian war against Sparta and in particular, Athens's disastrous Sicilian expedition (415–13 BC) drew attention, as Americans turned for clues to the fate of Athens, America's surrogate as a democratic empire.[94] The Sicilian expedition has never been far away from American anxieties about overstretch. Hans Morgenthau, concerned about strategic blunder, likened it to America's Vietnam War.[95]

Thucydides's history meditates on the transgression of boundaries. He states that things went badly wrong for Athens after the unruly *demos* deviated from the advice of their dead leader Pericles, not to expand the empire during the war.[96] Pericles's design was to deny Sparta the kind of war that it wanted and to wear it down, while mounting raids in retaliation, avoiding Sparta's strength of pitched land battle, and exploiting Athens's ability to stay out of reach via its fortifications and its navy.[97] This strategy exploited the discretion of a naval power to ride out its enemy's predations, and thus not dance to its tune. This was a hard case to make. Pericles had to dissuade Athenians from the urge to take the Spartans head-on or end the war prematurely through a negotiated peace. By prolonging the war in return for a greater chance of victory, the strategy demanded that citizens forsake Homeric glory, endure suffering, and not engage the invading force.[98] The strategy demanded a level of civic consciousness that Athenians could not sustain without an elite guardian. Worse, Pericles was killed by his own strategy, as the resulting influx of people into Athens caused the plague that killed its architect. Restraint is possible but elusive, and subject to the passions and ambitions that war triggers.

As Thucydides portrayed it, Athens was unguided by a steady hand, and in 415 BC its democracy was corrupted by money and lured into disaster by promises of a quick, cheap win. Thucydides's account of the expedition is replete with anxiety about distance. Most Athenians were unaware of the size of the island of Sicily and its population when they voted for the expedition and failed to grasp the magnitude of the task. In the speech Thucydides puts in the mouth of Nicias, opposing the invasion in the Athenian Ekklesia in 415 BC, distance figures in several ways. Athens's design was really on the whole of Sicily, a "huge undertaking." Even if they succeeded, this would add a hard burden, to hold down "a distant and populous island." Athens would risk the awe they were held in by Sicilian Greeks if they failed, as "respect increases with distance and when reputations are not put to the test," and the hope for wealth from the campaign is a "disastrous allure of distant promise." Athens is "now dicing with the greatest danger it has ever risked." Athens should vote against the war, preserving "the present boundaries between them and us, which have proved effective barriers, the Ionian Gulf for the coastal route and the Sicilian Sea for an open crossing."[99] He is voted down. His opponent Alcibiades promises an easy victory and makes a "credibility" argument. Failure to intervene will embolden Sparta. The state should remain warlike to avoid internal friction that peace would bring. The expedition ends with the destruction of the expeditionary force. It triggers revolts in the empire and tilts the conflict in Sparta's favor by bringing in the Persian Empire on its side. Sicily did not finish off Athenian power, which fought on for another nine years. But it was a disastrous inflection point.

States at the height of their powers have the choice of restraining themselves from opportunities to cross fatal lines before overreaching. But as Thucydides brooded in his portrayal of post-Periclean Athens, this is difficult to sustain. America's own twelve-years-long debate about the outcome of the Gulf War (1990–91) drives home the point. Having seen off the Soviet Union without a head-on clash, the United States had smashed Saddam Hussein's forces from the air and in a mere one hundred hours of ground fighting. Yet despite public support in favor of continuing the fighting, President George H. W. Bush halted it. He resisted the chance to march on Baghdad or even continue to destroy Saddam's Republican Guard divisions. Bush and his advisers recall that they feared the unintended consequences of mounting an invasion across the Iraq-Kuwait border, fragmenting Iraq into civil war, and attracting violent resistance, fears that proved well founded after the invasion of 2003. They also wanted to restore public faith in America's ability to use force without quagmires.[100]

Ever since, critics accused Bush of a "missed opportunity" to destroy, rather than merely contain, a threat. They assailed Bush's restraint as unheroic.[101] Tactical victories, they charged, should have been pressed to the only satisfactory strategic outcome of regime change in Baghdad. It would have been easy, following Gen. Norman Schwarzkopf's dubious claim that American forces would have been "unopposed, for all intents and purposes," a claim both wrong in its intelligence assessment and breathtaking in its neglect of the wider political situation.[102] They assumed that that war is only worthwhile when it politically transforms a situation and annihilates a threat. This threw out a whole tradition of using war as a limited tool to rein back threat, contain a problem, with attention to costs and wider considerations. The actual outcome represented substantial "negative" gains. Not only did intervention undo an aggressor's conquest and annexation of a neighboring state, it also aborted Saddam's nuclear program, preserved the balance of power in the Gulf, reduced Baghdad's capacity to threaten its neighbors, curtailed his ability to put his foot on the world's energy windpipe, and all while sustaining the UN mandate and international alliance. Bush was partly the victim of his own public framing of the war. He had likened Saddam to Hitler, encouraging others to perceive greater stakes in the conflict, and had hoped aloud that defeat would induce his overthrow.[103] But his decision-making was based on a tragic conception of war as a chaotic force that could easily slip out of control, that must be limited to achievable goals, and that was more suited to reversing a wrong than creating a better world. The Iraq-Kuwait border represented not just a sovereign divide but a Rubicon beyond which combat would transform the politics of the war. Bush's critics reflected a "heroic" conception, not only of warmaking, but of the horizons of American power. Democratic armies should go all the way to destroy evil. That was the verdict of Victor Davis Hanson, whose idealist account of liberating feats of arms was read and admired by Bush the younger.[104] In his attempt at a limited intervention that stopped at a border, Bush the elder had placed the United States on a footing that would present dangerous temptations. Saddam's surviving regime was a lasting cause of anxiety and an opportunity that was hard to resist when fears of globalized insecurity again intensified.

Grounds for Suspicion

Five suspicions about globalism, in theory and practice, drive this study. First, as it is often articulated, globalism assumes as a premise what it needs to prove. Proponents mistake their hypothesis of a process of shrinkage for an obvious, self-evident objective fact. In their conceit that globalization is a "universal condition" as inexorable as the weather, rather than a force made and unmade by human choices, globalists fail to consider in any depth where it comes from, who makes it, whether its effects are constant, and how far is it resisted.[105] To infer from the internet, air travel, or the range of weapons a process of irresistible strategic shrinkage brought on as an independent, self-propelling force is to mistake *geography*— structural preexisting conditions—with the dynamism of human geopolitics.

Great powers may fancy that the global strategic orders they construct are the natural order of things, preordained and independent of politics.[106] But historically, such orders, with their trading protocols and monetary regimes, sea lanes, commercial routes, and control of raw materials, are designed and imposed by the strong. The opening of Asian markets was a by-product of violent coercion, imposed on China through the Opium Wars, and on Japan by Commodore Matthew Perry with the threat of naval bombardment in 1853–54. Today's economic order emerged when the United States flexed its muscles to dismantle the architecture of the exhausted British Empire, replacing its imperial preference system, the stirling bloc, and the pound's status as reserve currency with United States–designed institutions (the International Monetary Fund and World Bank) and the dollar. In the world of security, as in the world of economics, globalization is "a choice, not a fact."[107]

Second, the remedies offered by globalism are as disturbing as the disease they claim to address. Several wars have been fought in the name of curbing the terrors of globalization, and these have been disappointing adventures. The course and outcome of these wars and the "forward strategy of freedom" suggest that globalism is suspect not only in its execution but at its core, as an account of the West's power to secure itself by pacifying and transforming the global village.

On their own terms, the liberal wars in Afghanistan begun in October 2001 and Iraq in March 2003 have fallen well short of achieving the desired goals at an affordable cost. The war in Libya, launched in March 2011, was far cheaper in dollars and resulted in no US casualties, but also yielded disastrous results. Even those who would justify these wars as defensible moves will admit that the costs borne by America and those they sought to liberate have wildly exceeded expectations. Whether these costs are "worth it" or exceed the value of the object is a value judgment. But the liberal wars of our era have proven to be unsustainable.

The war in Afghanistan was the first of the "9/11 wars," fought to secure a terrorized America by democratically liberating a people from the Taliban theocracy that sponsored Al Qaeda. Beyond the disruption of a terrorist network, the United States–led coalition attempted to transform the poor country into a strong, centrally governed liberal state. The ambitious remedy of liberal pacification has been more expensive than forecast, with a return of only meager gains. Almost thirteen years of war have cost the United States $700 billion, over two thousand deaths, and over nineteen thousand wounded. According to the United Nations Assistance Mission in Afghanistan, it has caused at least fourteen thousand civilian casualties since they began counting in 2007.[108] Transparency International judges Afghanistan to be one of the world's three most corrupt nations.[109] The country remains fractured and ruled by a weak kleptocracy whose writ hardly runs beyond Kabul, where power is wielded by a resurgent Taliban, warlords, and the Haqqani criminal network. According to the National Intelligence Estimate, for all the blood and treasure spent, the gains made by international and indigenous Afghan forces are fragile and could quickly be lost after the coalition's departure.[110] Repeatedly, policymakers and commanders declared that the decisive defeat of the Taliban is at hand.[111] Repeatedly, they have fought back. As it draws down, the United States now seeks negotiation with the Taliban. The war has made life more difficult for Al Qaeda by making the country more violently inhospitable for it. This could have been pursued with more limited means, such as counterterrorist raiding, international intelligence collaboration, and old-fashioned police work.

The war in Iraq was the central project of the Bush Doctrine, launched in the name of eliminating a threat that embodied the dangers of a globalized world. The United States–led coalition overthrew a regime already weakened by sanctions in its ability to threaten its neighbors, and that had already ended its chemical and biological weapons research. In an anarchic aftermath, as intelligence warnings anticipated, the occupation unleashed communal bloodletting in a country already divided along sectarian and other lines, killing at least 100,000 people and at its height spreading the use of abduction and torture to levels beyond even the Saddam era. The occupiers got caught in a war of attrition against guerrillas and in the crossfire of criminal violence and civil war. The war presents a steep price tag, fiscally and strategically. Almost 4,500 US troops were killed, as well as at least 3,400 US contractors, and more than 32,000 troops were wounded, including thousands with critical brain and spinal injuries.[112] American society must now underwrite the costs of long-term treatment and disability benefits. Washington underestimated the costs of invading and occupying Iraq. Revelations of torture handed propaganda victories to adversaries, bruising America's reputation as a benevolent leader. White House budget director Mitch Daniels was dismissed after forecasting in December 2002 that it would be no more than $60 billion, a mere fraction of the estimated cost, while Deputy Secretary of Defense Paul Wolfowitz claimed that Iraq through its oil revenues could finance its own reconstruction.[113] But according to the Nobel Prize–winning economist Joseph Stiglitz and former secretary of commerce Linda Bilmes, the costs, direct and indirect, of the Iraq War will exceed $3 trillion when factoring in care for the wounded and long-term support for veterans, interest on money borrowed to pay for the war, restoring military capabilities frayed by Iraq, and higher oil prices.[114] The unanticipated fiscal drain of continuing operations has helped retard economic growth and run up dangerous budget deficits. As a measure of misallocation, two weeks of operations in Iraq cost more than it would take to triple the Nunn-Lugar nuclear weapon control program in the former Soviet Union, a measure that helps forestall nuclear terrorism.[115] For Iraq, the ultimate course is still unknown. Iraq has a constitutional government but is governed by an increasingly authoritarian regime that has alienated Sunni Iraqis, that has ties to Iran, an adversary empowered by the war.[116] Sectarian conflict persists and reaches new crescendos. Revelations of torture handed propaganda victories to adversaries, bruising America's reputation as a benevolent leader. The Iraqi security state, supposed to be one of the good legacies of the war, proved brittle in the face of the Islamic State of Iraq and Syria (ISIS) uprising in 2014.

The United States waged a war in Libya from March to October 2011. Washington justified "Operation Unified Protector" as a liberal intervention not only to protect Libyan civilians from a predatory ruler, Col. Muammar Qaddafi, but to also thwart refugee flights across borders, curtail tyrannical violence against dissidents, and uphold the democratic impulse of the Arab Spring. Initially conceived as a discrete measure to impose a no-fly zone, the war escalated into one of regime change. Now a fledgling state struggles to govern as the country has fallen under the sway of militias and criminal gangs.[117] This has suspended most of the country's oil production. The chaotic transition has empowered Islamists, who attacked the American embassy. The capital has seen assassinations of ministers and bombings of embassies. As reports of Médicins Sans Frontières and Human Rights Watch affirm, victorious rebels rounded up, dispossessed, and tortured sub-Saharan African immigrants indiscriminately. A war that was supposed to prevent a humanitarian catastrophe, dissuade tyrants from persecuting civilians, and advance international security has brought in a new order of torture and abuse and has not deterred rulers from Bahrain or Syria from violent repression. The overthrow and killing, once again, of a regime that had already abandoned its WMD program has provided an eloquent example of why it makes sense for insecure regimes to pursue a nuclear deterrent. These are poor dividends.

A state of constant war for liberalism and democracy abroad has damaged it at home. Wilson's liberalism in the First World War suggested the pattern, as the war to make the world safe for democracy also entailed the imprisonment of dissidents, suppression of free speech, and the Espionage and Sedition Acts. But this at least was within a conflict with a defined opponent that was terminated. Should a war become amorphous and permanent, the danger is graver. The Global War on Terror led to the announcement of a state of exception, the declaration of an ongoing emergency that permits the state to do largely as it pleases, extending its power against traditional restrictions. Against a threat deemed to be borderless, global, and severe, the state has arrogated to itself unchecked powers that erode the very freedoms the state claims to be advancing. Any balance sheet of the liberal wars of this century must include the assault on civil liberties. As well as extraordinary rendition and torture, this encompasses the erosion of habeas corpus, unwarranted domestic wiretapping, and the rise of sweeping extrajudicial state surveillance. These have come partly through the National Security Agency, whose extensive data sweeps were unsanctioned by Congress and were recently judged by the President's Review Group as excessive and unnecessarily indiscriminate.[118] State intrusion also comes through the FBI and its powerful instrument of a "national security letter" that can be issued without judicial oversight and that forbids disclosure. This is not to argue that there is no role for surveillance, espionage, and intrusion. But in pursuing absolute security from "global" threats, rulers lost sight of the difficult balance between liberty and security. Constitutionally, the War on Terror accelerated the creation of an imperial presidency, whereby the executive arrogates from the legislature the power to determine questions of war and peace, breaching what was supposed to be the coequal constitution sharing congressional and presidential responsibility for foreign policy, and weakening the legislature's checking and balancing role.

The embrace of a limitless concept of strategic interests opens the way to a continual program of armed intervention with utopian goals, on the logic that defeating terrorism "requires putting boots on the ground and engaging in nation building."[119] In the words of John Nagl, practitioner and theorist of small wars and fellow of the Center for a New American Security, "Sept. 11 conclusively demonstrated that instability anywhere can be a real threat to the American people here at home. Defeating instability through effective counterinsurgency operations is therefore a core mission of the Defense Department." Accordingly, the only effective way to defeat terrorism is to develop soldiers able "not just to dominate land operations, but to change entire societies."[120]

In fact, there are many measures short of ill-conceived COIN (counterinsurgency) campaigns that can disrupt violent threats against the United States from afar. Military occupations are not, historically, optimum antidotes for addressing instability, either away or at home (as France found in Algeria, Israel in Lebanon, and the Soviet Union in Afghanistan). In the long haul, interventions have a poor record. They tend to lengthen rather than shorten civil wars, make them more bloody rather than less, and rarely promote stable democratic evolution.[121] Except in atypically favorable conditions, wars followed up by rebuilding missions are costly, likely to fail, and in the case of Afghanistan and Iraq, a diversion from other important investment possibilities.[122] And there is a darker implication here. If security relies on "defeating instability," and "anywhere," then Nagl and his fellow small-wars advocates offer a doctrine of permanent revolution and continual war. "Counterinsurgency" may appeal as a gentler and kinder style of security-seeking, with its doctrine of securing populations and winning their support through "clear, hold, and build," but it perpetuates the militarization of diplomacy. Those who argue for this way to security share the premise that Western security is tied to the political interior of weak states, and that threats somewhere are threats everywhere. It still takes troops on the ground to clear and hold ground before rebuilding can be done. This process is bloody and meets resistance. In pursuit of absolute security, the embrace of global counterinsurgency would put America and its allies on a footing of endless emergency.

Third, globalism reflects a narrow and atypical experience of the world. We should not be innocent of the class politics of globalization rhetoric. To speak of the obliteration of boundaries is to speak in the language of the postnational cosmopolitan elite. They regularly fly, consume foreign luxury products, accumulate wealth from capital flows, and look down on localized identity as a relic of a bloody tribal century gone by. Most people do not enjoy such a deterritorialized existence. The vast majority of the world's population have never flown.[123] Only 3 percent of people live outside their country of birth. Only 2 percent of students attend a university outside their homeland. Less than 1 percent of all American companies have any foreign operations. The bulk of stock-market investment is in companies that are headquartered in the investor's home country.[124] Seeing the world through the lens of the consumer and tourist leads to the false conflation of one form of access and mobility with another. John Maynard Keynes predicted that modern consumers would order products by phone, travel cheaply anywhere, and invest globally.[125] But it does not follow that today's warmaking is effortlessly borderless. Insecure humans still crave the control of soil and battle their neighbors for it. As Ken Booth says, "globalization has not eliminated the most basic foot-slogging struggles over the possession of land. The violence in Israel/Palestine has shown this every day for many years."[126]

Fourth, globalism is suspect because of its reductionism. Its proponents abruptly dismiss alternative views as "isolationist" or nostalgically parochial. They frame the debate as a false choice between building resilient communities in an interconnected world versus the retreat to "a well stocked cabin in the woods."[127] This rhetorical ploy works as a slur in mainstream American politics, as leading figures from both political parties accuse each other of the isolationist heresy.[128] Advocates of an American grand strategy of primacy accuse the Obama administration of a retreat even for its limited and tentative measures of retrenchment and multilateral burden shifting.[129] Commentators brand as "isolationist" recent opinion polls showing public fatigue with wars abroad in an age of financial meltdown. This is logically flawed. To favor restraint and doing less is not to choose isolation. Opposition to wars such as those in Iraq, Afghanistan, Libya, or Syria does not equate to blanket opposition to trade, immigration, alliances, or engagement in general.[130] Washington does not have to choose whether to be global or insular. There is a wide middle ground, such as coexisting with other states in a more multipolar world. Globalism erases any sense of the intermediate spaces between those poles, making it harder to calibrate means and ends. The isolationist slur is also ahistorical, drawing on a crude view of history where America emerged from an insular dark age and saw the global light. It was never Washington's grand strategy to isolate itself from the world.[131] A periodic reluctance to enter formal commitments is not the same thing as a commitment to isolation. The United States has a long history of activism in its own claimed hemisphere, in Central and Latin America. From its founding, it was embroiled in struggles with European imperial powers such as Spain, Britain, and France. Even in the interwar era, the United States consistently exerted itself well beyond its water's edge.

Finally, globalization theory as it is applied to security questions ignores countervailing tendencies in international politics. In economics, skeptics strongly challenge globalism.[132] The teleology of a closed world becoming more open in a globalized (post-) modernity is historically false. Economies have integrated—and disintegrated—before. The advanced industrialized world in the period 1870–1914 was economically integrated to an extent comparable with today, whether measured in terms of foreign direct investment or merchandise exports as a proportion of GDP. This is significant because it shows that globalizing processes can be made and unmade, and that it is not an inevitable by-product of new, uncontrollable forces beyond the state. Indeed, according to the assessment of DHL, the worldwide mail service, flows of trade, capital, and people that make up global "connectedness" have declined since 2007.[133] Today, capital mobility is not producing a massive shift of investment and employment from advanced to developing countries. Foreign direct investment is highly concentrated among the advanced industrial economies, the quartet of Europe, Japan, North America, and China, and the Third World remains marginal in investment and trade. Major states still exert powerful governance pressures over financial and trading markets. Even states that preach the rhetoric of a borderless, connected world do not always practice it, jealously guarding their sovereignty when they choose.[134] Armed movements in Somalia, Spain, or Syria covet and fight for state power precisely because the state retains important powers, to tax, levy troops, set the terms of trade, and make laws. Globalization can generate economic interdependence, and interdependence can be a disincentive to war. But even the notion that interstate clashes make world markets unacceptably vulnerable, one argument used to support the case for US hegemonic leadership, may be overstated. The only general study of the issue suggests that even in times of high interdependence, neutral parties—especially great-power neutrals with large and flexible economies—prove to be resilient in reordering their economic arrangements. Historically, they not only ride out others' clashes but even benefit.[135]

It would be false to frame the issue in binary terms as one of state sovereignty versus globalization. The better view is that state sovereignty is more of an agent and architect than a victim of globalization. Globalization relies on state enforcement from property to contracts, from transport hubs to currencies.[136] Global capitalism depends on the infrastructure and functions provided by the state, the airports, seaports, or telecommunication arteries of transport and production.[137] Even the internet, so often assumed to be a borderless and therefore subversive force in international relations, is a domain where states often get their way. They lock in advantages in fields from intellectual property to content regulation, so that online activity reflects more than undermines offline power structures.[138] Even border-crossing technologies work also as instruments of state power. States harness social media to monitor and suppress dissidents, just as the printing press was harnessed by the Counter-Reformation.[139]

If markets don't reflect the expectations of globalization theory, neither does another important aspect of the sovereign state, its ability to govern the movement of people. Today we see the reassertion of the state through the revival of walls, an ancient mechanism of territorial control, sovereign authority, and interior defense. Human-made territorial buffers appear in the shape of concrete barriers, metal fences, and landmines, electronically enhanced and complemented by other kinds of barriers such as biometric passports, surveillance cameras, and no-fly lists.[140] Russia reinforces its border with the Ukraine border with barbed wire, and after its clash with Georgia in 2008, built walls surrounding the annexed territories in Ossetia. Fortifications line the US-Mexican border, the West Bank of Israel/Palestine, and the India/Kashmir border.[141] The United States erected fortifications in Baghdad, where the "winning of the people" involved the walled separation of communities, signaling a return of a classical practice in counterinsurgency and urban control. Militarily, states that could be on the receiving end of missile attacks rediscover the value of underground defenses. Today's nomads and travelers face a level of scrutiny that their ancestors would have found absurd. Their forbears did not need travel visas and massive diasporas were more possible. States process travel documents and passports that cost on average more than a tenth of the average annual income. In this regime of gatekeeping, people remain nationalized subjects.

Taken together, these suspicions suggest that there is something flawed not only about globalism's empirical claims about what is happening and why, but its underlying assumptions about human agency and the spaces where violent struggle takes place.

Conclusion

The global village has become the West's dominant mental cartography. Human minds carry psychological maps. They are prone to reimagining the globe in ways that suit assumptions about their security interests as they define them. Maps themselves are designed to simplify, and mistaken for purely objective reflections of the world, they can breed both inordinate fear and confidence. When Prime Minister Benjamin Disraeli worried in 1877 about Ottoman Turkey's threat to British India, Lord Salisbury cautioned against shrunken mental maps: "A great deal of misapprehension arises from the popular use of maps on a small scale.

. . . The distance between Russia and British India is not to be measured by the finger and thumb, but by a ruler. There are between them deserts and mountainous chains measured by thousands of miles, and these are serious obstacles to any advance by Russia, however well planned such an advance might be."[142]

Today, actual maps that fit a television, computer, or mobile phone screen may also mislead. Though their architects, like many ambitious cartographers since the Renaissance, aspire to create visualizations of the globe that "mirror the earth in a transparent act of representation," their maps too are subject to choices about what goes in and stays out.[143] By placing a representation of the globe in one's hand and giving off the illusion that the beholder can revolve it at will with an omniscient eye, they give little guide to the problems of costs incurred over space, the sheer effort, for instance, of merely sustaining operations and feeding material to embattled Western armies in the Hindu Kush. The question of how to map the world in times of security crisis has come up before in the choices faced by US policymakers. The next chapter turns to that history.

Notes

1. Alan Henrikson, "Distance and Foreign Policy: A Political Geography Approach," *International Political Science Review* 23:4 (2002): 437–66, 454.
2. Both cases Robert Jervis discusses, "Cooperation under the Security Dilemma," *World Politics* 30:2 (1978): 167–214, 194.
3. John Mearsheimer, *The Tragedy of Great Power Politics* (New York: W. W. Norton, 2001), 40–42.
4. Mearsheimer, *The Tragedy of Great Power Politics*, 265.
5. Daniel M. Gerstein, *Securing America's Future: National Strategy in the Information Age* (London: Praeger Security International, 2005), 23.
6. John Patch, "Fortuitous Endeavor: Intelligence and Deception in Operation Torch," *Naval War College Review* 61:4 (2008): 73–97, 75.
7. As critics of the "stopping power" theory suggest, Christopher Layne, "The 'Poster Child for Offensive Realism': America as a Global Hegemon," *Security Studies* 12:2 (2002): 120–64, 124–27.
8. See Barry Posen, "Command of the Commons: The Military Foundation of U.S. Hegemony," *International Security* 28:1 (2003): 5–46, 8.
9. On the tendency of states to see insular and maritime powers as less threatening than land powers, see Jack S. Levy and William R. Thompson, "Balancing on Land and at Sea: Do States Ally against the Leading Global Power?," *International Security* 35:1 (2012): 7–43; on the sterilizing effect of water on others' views of American power, see Joshua Shifrinson, "The Other Shield of the Republic: Geography and American National Security," unpublished paper, International Studies Association, 2014. I thank Joshua for sharing his paper.
10. Which is Posen's term for those areas where adversaries could hope to thwart the United States with force: "Command of the Commons," 22–42.
11. Michael I. Handel, "The Evolution of Israeli Strategy: The Psychology of Insecurity and the Quest for Absolute Security," in *The Making of Strategy: Rulers, States, and War*, ed. Williamson Murray, MacGregor Knox, and Alvin Bernstein (Cambridge: Cambridge University Press, 1994), 534–79, 534–35 537–38.
12. On the typology of war aims and the constraints around war aims of pure brute force, see Patricia L. Sullivan, *Who Wins? Predicting Strategic Success and Failure in Armed Conflict* (Oxford: Oxford University Press, 2012), 132–33.
13. Robert Jervis, *The Meaning of the Nuclear Revolution* (Ithaca, NY: Cornell University Press, 1989), 5–6, 28; Stephen Van Evera, "A Farewell to Geopolitics," in *To Lead the World: US Grand*

Strategy after the Bush Doctrine, ed. Melvyn Leffler and Jeffrey Legro (Oxford: Oxford University Press, 2008), 11–36, 12–14.

14. Nicholas J. Spykman, "Geography and Foreign Policy II," *The American Political Science Review* 32:2 (1938): 213–36, 236.

15. Stephen J. Blank, *Russia in the Arctic* (Carlisle, PA: Strategic Studies Institute, 2011).

16. As defined by Daniel Deudney, "Geopolitics as Theory," *European Journal of International Relations* 6:1 (2000): 77–107, 78, 80, 89.

17. Hans Weigert, *Generals and Geographers: The Twilight of Geopolitics* (London: Oxford University Press, 1942), 23.

18. Robert D. Kaplan, *The Revenge of Geography: What the Map Tells Us about Coming Conflicts and the Battle against Fate* (New York: Random House, 2012).

19. Kaplan, *Revenge of Geography*, 28, 192, 94.

20. Daron Acemoglu and James Robinson, *Why Nations Fail: The Origins of Power, Prosperity and Poverty* (New York: Crown Publishers, 2012); Niall Ferguson, *Civilization: The Six Killer Apps of Western Power* (London: Penguin, 2011).

21. Anne-Marie Slaughter, "Power Shifts: The Revenge of Geography by Robert D. Kaplan," *New York Times*, October 5, 2012.

22. Josh Rogin, "Anne-Marie Slaughter Accuses Obama of Prioritizing Oil over Values," *Foreign Policy*, March 16, 2011.

23. For Slaughter's Wilsonian views and their application to problems in international security, see "Problems Will Be Global—And Solutions Will Be, Too," *Foreign Policy*, August 14, 2011; "Good Reasons for Going around the U.N.," *New York Times*, March 18, 2003; *The Idea That Is America: Keeping Faith with Our Values in a Dangerous World* (New York: Perseus Books Group, 2007); "Congress, Support Obama on Syria," CNN, September 4, 2013; G. John Ikenberry, Thomas J. Knock, Anne-Marie Slaughter, and Tony Smith, *The Crisis of American Foreign Policy: Wilsonianism in the Twenty-first Century* (Princeton, NJ: Princeton University Press, 2009); for critiques, see José E. Alvarez, "Do Liberal States Behave Better? A Critique of Slaughter's Liberal Theory," *European Journal of International Law* 12:2 (2001): 189–90; David Rieff, "Without Exception: The Same Old Song," *World Affairs* 170: 3 (2008): 101–8; "'Save Us from the Liberal Hawks," *Foreign Policy*, February 13, 2012.

24. Douglas Hurd, *The Arrow War: An Anglo-Chinese Confusion 1856-60* (London: Collins, 1967), 56.

25. G. John Ikenberry, "The Illusion of Geopolitics: The Enduring Power of the Liberal Order," *Foreign Affairs* 93:3 (2014): 80–90.

26. Jared Diamond, *Guns, Germans and Steel: The Fates of Human Societies* (New York: W. W. Norton, 1997).

27. Seminal works in this stream are Gearóid Ó Tuathail, "Problematising Geopolitics: Survey, Statesmanship and Strategy," *Transactions of the Institute of British Geographers* 19:3 (1994): 259–72; "Understanding Critical Geopolitics: Geopolitics and Risk Society," *Journal of Strategic Studies* 22 (1999): 107–24; Derek Gregory, *The Colonial Present: Afghanistan, Palestine and Iraq* (Oxford: Blackwell, 2004); A. Godlewska and N. Smith, eds., *Geography and Empire* (Oxford: Blackwell, 1997); David Livingstone, *The Geographical Tradition: Episodes in the History of a Contested Enterprise* (Oxford: Blackwell, 1993).

28. Paul Kennedy, *The Rise and Fall of the Great Powers: Economic Change and Military Conflict from 1500 to 2000* (London: Fontana, 1989), 111.

29. As Jeffrey D. Sachs argues: "Government, Geography, and Growth: The True Drivers of Economic Development," *Foreign Affairs* 91:5 (2012): 142–50, 145.

30. Herodotus, *The Histories*, 9.122.

31. Aeschylus, *The Persians*, Opening Chorus (trans. Robert Potter); see also Herodotus, *Histories* Book VII. The symbolism is discussed in Tom Holland, *Persian Fire: The First World Empire and the Battle for the West* (London: Little, Brown, 2005), 213, 242.

32. Charles de Montesquieu, " Considerations about the Causes of the Greatness of the Romans and of Their Decadence" (1734).

33. Halford Mackinder, "The Geographical Pivot of History," *The Geographical Journal* 23 (1904): 472.

34. Eduard Mark, "From Roosevelt to Truman," Roundtable, September 10, 2007, 33–34, 5, at www.h-net.org/*diplo/roundtables/PDF/FromRoosevelt toTruman-Roundtable. pdf4.

35. Arden Bucholz, *Moltke, Schlieffen and Prussian War Planning* (New York: Berg, 1991), 164–65.

36. Karl Marx, *Grundrisse* (trans. Martin Nicolaus, New York: Penguin, 1973), 524; discussed also in Daniel H. Deudney, *Bounding Power: Republican Security Theory from the Polis to the Global Village* (Princeton, NJ: Princeton University Press, 2007), 200. On this body of ideas, see also Duncan S. A. Bell, "Dissolving Distance: Technology, Space, and Empire in British Political thought, ca. 1770–1900," *Journal of Modern History* 77:3 (2005): 523–62.

37. Mary Kaldor wrote of "a myriad of transnational connections . . . the distinction between internal and external . . . or even between local and global are difficult to sustain." *New and Old Wars: Organized Violence in a Global Era* (Cambridge, UK: Polity, 1999), 2; Richard Falkenrath, Robert D. Newman, and Bradley A. Thayer, eds., *America's Achilles' Heel: Nuclear, Biological, and Chemical Terrorism and Covert Attack* (Cambridge, MA: MIT Press, 1998); James A. Russell and James J. Wirtz, *Globalization and WMD Proliferation: Terrorism, Transnational Networks, and International Security* (London: Routledge, 2008), 8, 12, 164; David Lambach and Tobias Debiel, "State Failure and State Building," *Routledge Handbook of Security Studies* (2012), 159–68. The "new wars" literature is deftly punctured by Mats Berdal, "The 'New Wars' Thesis Revisited," in *The Changing Character of War*, ed. Hew Strachan and Sibylle Scheipers (Oxford: Oxford University Press, 2011), 109–34.

38. As Hew Strachan observes, "Strategy in the Twenty-First Century," in Hew Strachan and Sibylle Scheppers, *The Changing Character of War*, 503.

39. Ulrich Beck, *Power in the Global Age: A New Global Political Economy* (Cambridge, UK: Polity, 2005), 89.

40. Mikkel Vedby Rasmussen, *The Risk Society at War: Terror, Technology and Strategy in the Twenty-First Century* (Cambridge: Cambridge University Press, 2006), 3, 197.

41. James Gow, *Defending the West* (Cambridge, UK: Polity, 2004), argues that the stakes for the West are existential: "the rules must change, if the West is to survive," because the world has gotten smaller and interconnected to the point where problems in one place can easily disrupt from afar, 6, 59, 61, 62; Philip Bobbit, *Terror and Consent: The Wars for the Twenty-First Century* (London: Penguin, 2008), 12.

42. Robert Cooper, "Why We Still Need Empires," *Observer*, April 7, 2002; *The Breaking of Nations: Order and Chaos in the Twenty-first Century* (New York: Atlantic Press, 2003).

43. As of 2010, American defense spending made up approximately 45 percent of the global total. International Institute of Strategic Studies, *The Military Balance 2011* (London: Routledge, 2012), 473.

44. M. Geyer and C. Bright, "Global Violence and Nationalizing Wars in Eurasia and America: The Geopolitics of War in the Mid-Nineteenth Century," *Comparative Studies in Society and History* 38 (1996): 651–53; Michael Evans, *The Continental School of Strategy: The Past, Present and Future of Land Power* (Land Warfare Studies Center, 2004), 102–15.

45. Charles Krauthammer, "The Unipolar Moment," *Foreign Affairs* 70:1 (1991): 23–33.

46. As Adam Elkus describes it, "Globalization, Strategic Distance, and Policy," *Red Team Journal*, July 22, 2010, http://redteamjournal.com/2010/07/globalization-strategic-distance-and-policy/.

47. "Remarks of Senator Barack Obama to the Chicago Council on Global Affairs," April 23, 2007, cited at https://my.barackobama.com/page/content/fpccga/; President of the United States, *National Security Strategy* (Washington, DC: The White House, May 2010), 7–8.

48. Tony Blair, "What I've Learned," *The Economist*, May 31, 2007; Owen Bowcott, "Tony Blair: Military Intervention in Rogue Regimes 'More Necessary Than Ever,'" *Guardian*, September 1, 2010.

49. Jaap de Hoop Scheffer, "Managing Global Security and Risk," IISS Annual Conference at the International Institute for Strategic Studies Annual Conference, 2007, at www.nato.int/docu/speech/2007/s070907a.html.

50. "NATO—Managing Security in a Globalized World," Speech by Secretary General of NATO Anders Fogh Rasmussen at the Catholic University of Lisbon, Portugal, July 2, 2010, www.nato.int/cps/en/natolive/opinions_64814.htm. For further discussion of how NATO globalized its security interests, see Andreas Behnke, *NATO's Security Discourse after the Cold War:*

Representing the West (New York: Routledge, 2013), 162–91; Patrick Porter, "Hooked on Security: Keep NATO, but Curb Its Appetite," *The World Today* 66:10 (2010): 12–14.

51. Gen. Martin E. Dempsey, "Nation Faces Security Paradox," *American Forces Press Service* April 13, 2012, at www.defense.gov/News/NewsArticle.aspx?ID=67921.

52. My italics. " Transcript of Blair's Speech to Congress," CNN, July 17, 2003, http://edition.cnn .com/2003/US/07/17/blair.transcript/.

53. See the warning of Adm. Giampaolo di Paola, chairman of NATO's Military Committee: "Globalization also means that the security challenges have no boundaries, have no geographical location. . . . If you combine terrorism and proliferation, believe me, you get the scariest security challenge that we can think of." "NATO's Strategy Concept, the New Security Environment, and the NATO-Russia Partnership," July 23, 2010, www.nato.int/cps/en/natolive/opinions_69879.htm.

54. Clifford S. Magee, "Awaiting Cyber 9/11," *Joint Forces Quarterly* 70:3 (2013): 76–83, 76; Alex Spilius, "Cyber Attack Could Fell US within Fifteen Minutes," *Telegraph*, May 7, 2010; Richard A Clarke and R. Knake, *Cyber War: The Next Threat to National Security and What to Do about It* (New York: HarperCollins, 2010); Sen. Charles Schumer warned, "Terrorists . . . could gain access to our power plants, our air-traffic-control systems, our utilities and our banking systems, which translates into rolling blackouts, dead phone lines, and wiped-out bank accounts. Frankly, I fear we're on the verge of a digital Armageddon." "Is the Net Vulnerable to Terrorist Attacks?," at http://webserver.computoredge.com/online.mvc?zone=sd&issue=2435&article=in 2&session=.

55. On the relationship between power and fear in international relations, see Christopher J. Fettweis, *The Pathologies of Power: Fear, Honor and Hubris in US Foreign Policy* (Cambridge: Cambridge University Press, 2013), 24–94; Karl W. Deutsch, *The Analysis of International Relations* (Englewood Cliffs, NJ: Prentice-Hall, 1968), 88.

56. Secretary of Defense, Memorandum for the President, September 30, 2001, at http:// library.rumsfeld.com/doclib/sp/272/2001-09-30 to President Bush re Strategic Thoughts. pdf#search="political map".

57. *Iraq's Weapons of Mass Destruction: The Assessment of the British Government* (September 2002), 4, 17.

58. Remarkably, Prime Minister Tony Blair told the House of Commons he had been unaware that the controversial "45-minute" claim in the government's September 2002 Iraq dossier referred only to tactical battlefield weapons, and not long-range ballistic missiles. "Blair Admits Misunderstanding '45-Minute Claim,'" *Sydney Morning Herald*, February 5, 2004.

59. "Brits 45 Mins from Doom," *The Sun*, September 25, 2002.

60. Chilcot Transcript: *Iraq Inquiry*, Oral Evidence, Wednesday, November 25, 2009, Subject: Weapons of Mass Destruction, 24, lines 19–21.

61. "Saddam Hussein's Weapons Mirage," *The Economist*, January 31, 2004, 13.

62. According to those experts who briefed them, both Prime Minister Blair and President Bush did not take seriously warnings about the difficulties of reconstructing and politically reforming a post-Saddam Iraq. For the UK case, see the account of Jonathan Steele, *Defeat: Why They Lost Iraq* (London: I. B. Taurus, 2008), 18–19, 172; for the United States, see George Packer, *The Assassin's Gate: America in Iraq* (New York: Farrar, Straus and Giroux, 2005), 113–14; Bob Woodward, *State of Denial* (New York: Simon & Schuster, 2006), 256.

63. The word "global" or one of its variants (such as "globalization") is deployed fifty-three times in forty-four pages by Stephen G. Brooks, G. John Ikenberry, and William Wohlforth as they make the case for continuing a forward-leaning strategy, "Don't Come Home America: The Case against Retrenchment," *International Security* 37 (2012): 7–51; President Obama's recent *Defense Strategic Guidance* uses the word "global" thirteen times in eight pages.

64. Leslie W. Hepple, "The Revival of Geopolitics," *Political Geography Quarterly* 5 (1986): 21–36.

65. Charles Clover, "Dreams of the Eurasian Heartland: The Reemergence of Geopolitics," *Foreign Affairs* 78:2 (1999), 9–13, 9.

66. So argues Brian Blouet in his survey of geography in twentieth-century world politics, framing the issue as a contest between the reactionary geopolitics of the Old World and the cosmopolitan open globalism of the New. Brian Blouet, *Geopolitics and Globalization in the Twentieth Century* (London: Reaktion, 2001), 197.

67. On the liberal tradition and its relationship with US diplomacy, see Louis Hartz, *The Liberal Tradition in America* (San Diego, CA: Harcourt, Brace, Jovanovich, 1955), 12; Robert Osgood, *Ideals and Self-Interest in America's Foreign Relations: The Great Transformation of the Twentieth Century* (Chicago: University of Chicago Press, 1953), 51–52, 53–56, 104; David M. Kennedy, "What 'W' owes to 'WW,'" *The Atlantic* 30:5 (2005): 36–40; Colin Dueck, *Reluctant Crusaders: Power, Culture, and Change in American Grand Strategy* (Princeton, NJ: Princeton University Press, 2006), 57–58, 147–48, 164–67; Michael C. Desch, "America's Liberal Illiberalism: The Ideological Origins of Overreaction in U.S. Foreign Policy," *International Security* 32:3 (2007): 7–43; Christopher Layne, "Wilson's Ghost: Spreading Freedom around the World Will Destroy It at Home," *The American Conservative* 4:4 (February 28, 2005): 9–11; Lloyd E. Ambrosius, "Woodrow Wilson and George W. Bush: Historical Comparisons of Ends and Means in Their Foreign Policies," *Diplomatic History* 30 (2006): 509–43.

68. Immanuel Kant, "Perpetual Peace," *Kant's Political Writings* (1795), trans. H. B. Nisbet (Cambridge: Cambridge University Press, 1970); Thomas Paine, *The Rights of Man* in *Complete Writings*, ed. Eric Foner (New York: Oxford University Press, 1995), vol. 1, 342. For a study of the relation between varieties of liberalism and war, see Michael W. Doyle, *Ways of War and Peace: Realism, Liberalism, and Socialism* (New York: W. W. Norton, 1997), 205–301, esp. 251ff.

69. G. John Ikenberry and Anne-Marie Slaughter, *Forging a World of Liberty under Law* (Princeton Project Papers, September 27, 2006), 11.

70. Beard coined the phrase in a conversation that then became the title for a revisionist historical critique of expansive postwar foreign policies: Harry Elmer Barnes, ed., *Perpetual War for Perpetual Peace* (Caldwell, ID: Caxton, 1953), viii.

71. What exactly Wilsonianism is, and its vision of a liberal world order and how it could be achieved, has been interpreted in different ways. Some present it as a basis for the promotion of liberal democracy or collective security, others as the commitment to international institutions and law: "Wilsonianism: The Dynamics of a Conflicted Concept," *International Affairs* 86:1 (2010): 27–48, 28; G. John Ikenberry, Thomas J. Knock, Anne-Marie Slaughter, and Tony Smith, *The Crisis of American Foreign Policy: Wilsonianism in the Twenty-first Century* (Princeton, NJ: Princeton University Press, 2008).

72. Ross Kennedy, *The Will to Believe: Woodrow Wilson, World War One, and America's Strategy for Peace and Security* (Kent, OH: Kent State University Press, 2009), xii, 222–23.

73. Robert Jervis, "Understanding the Bush Doctrine," *Political Science Quarterly* 118:3 (2003): 365–88, 367.

74. "From the fourteen points to the four freedoms to the speech at Westminster (Ronald Reagan), America has put its power at the service of principle." Speech in Whitehall, November 2003, G. W. Bush, "Both Our Nations Serve the Cause of Freedom," *New York Times*, November 20, 2003.

75. Michael C. Desch, "Woodrow Wilson's War," *The National Interest* 99 (1999): 87–96.

76. See the discussion of Scott Burchill, *The National Interest in International Relations Theory* (New York: Palgrave, 2005), 112–14; for the historical belligerence of democratic regimes, see Steve Chan, "Mirror, Mirror on the Wall . . . Are the Freer Countries More Pacific?," *Journal of Conflict Resolution*, 28:4 (1984): 617–48.

77. Frank Harvey, *Explaining the Iraq War* (Cambridge: Cambridge University Press, 2012).

78. Brad Evans sketches in greater detail this logic, *Liberal Terror* (Cambridge, UK: Polity, 2013), 15–16, 36–37, 40; World Economic Forum, *Global Risks 2012*, 10.

79. After armed Islamists took hostages in Algeria and staged an uprising in Mali, Britain's prime minister David Cameron in the House of Commons claimed that Al Qaeda in the Maghreb and other North African terrorist groups pose a "large and existential threat," warned that they "thrive in ungoverned spaces," and that "parts of Mali have become a safe haven for Al Qaeda," declaring that if it is not confronted "the threat there will grow and we'll face it as well." When asked about the merits of containment as an alternative strategy, Cameron argued that the country's aim was "not containment but trying over time to completely overcome them." *Hansard*, January 21, 2013, columns 37–38; James Forsyth, "David Cameron Redoubles His Commitment to Interventionism," *Spectator*, January 21, 2013.

80. Office of the Press Secretary, "President Bush Delivers Graduation Speech at West Point."

81. On the "American Empire" debate, see Daniel H. Nexon and Thomas Wright, "What's at Stake in the American Empire Debate," *American Political Science Review* 101:2 (2007): 253–71.
82. David Brooks, "The Autocracy Challenge," *New York Times*, May 29, 2014.
83. On each war as a point of overextension, see Jeffrey Record, *Wanting War: Why the Bush Administration Invaded Iraq* (Dulles, VA: Potomac, 2010), 3–4; Peter Beinart, *The Icarus Syndrome: A History of American Hubris* (New York: Harper, 2010), 120–21,172–87, 337–65.
84. For critiques of the domino principle and credibility fears, see Daryl Press, *Calculating Credibility: How Leaders Assess Military Threats* (Ithaca, NY: Cornell University Press, 2007); Ted Hopf, *Peripheral Visions: Deterrence Theory and American Foreign Policy in the Third World, 1965–1990* (Ann Arbor: University of Michigan Press, 1994); Jonathan Mercer, "Bad Reputation: The Folly of Going to War for Credibility," *Foreign Affairs*, August 28, 2013; Robert H. Johnson, "Exaggerating America's Stakes in Third World Conflicts," *International Security* 10:3 (1985/6): 32–68; Jerome Slater, "Dominoes in Central America: Will They Fall? Does It Matter?," *International Security* 12:2 (1987): 105–34.
85. For the commitment to prevention, see Lecture, Chief of the Defense Staff, Royal United Services Institute (RUSI), December 18, 2013, at http://www.rusi.org/events/past/ref:E5284A3D06EFFD; Department for International Development, Foreign and Commonwealth Office, Ministry of Defense, *Building Stability Overseas Strategy* (London: July 2011).
86. As Michael Lind argues, *The American Way of Strategy: US Foreign Policy and the American Way of Life* (New York: Oxford University Press, 2006).
87. See the analyses of Michael Dillon and Julian Read, *The Liberal Way of War: Killing to Make Life Live* (New York: Routledge, 2009), 7–8, 85; Michael Howard, *War and the Liberal Conscience* (1978), 130; Benno Gerhard Teschke, "Fatal Attraction: Critique of Carl Schmitt's International Political and Legal Theory," *International Theory* 3:2 (2011): 179–227, 189–91.
88. For a milder defense of placing liberal norms at the core of calculations about war, see Lawrence Freedman, "The Age of Liberal Wars," *Review of International Studies* 31 (2005): 93–107, 107.
89. Richard Ned Lebow, *The Tragic Vision of Politics: Ethics, Interests and Orders* (Cambridge: Cambridge University Press, 2003).
90. Kennedy, *The Rise and Fall of the Great Powers* (1989).
91. On the debate ever since, see W. W. Rostow, "Beware of Historians Bearing False Analogies," *Foreign Affairs* 66:4 (1987): 863–68; Joseph Nye Jr., *Bound to Lead: The Changing Nature of American Power* (New York: Basic Books 1991); Samuel Huntington, "The US: Decline or Renewal?," *Foreign Affairs* 67:3 (1988): 76–95; Robert J. Lieber, *Power and Willpower in the American Future: Why the United States Is Not Destined to Decline* (New York: Cambridge University Press, 2012); Robert Kagan, *The World America Made* (New York: Alfred A. Knopf, 2012); Carla Norloff, *America's Global Advantage: US Hegemony and International Cooperation* (New York: Cambridge University Press, 2010); Christopher Layne, "Graceful Decline: The End of the Pax Americana," *American Conservative* 9:5 (2010): 30–33; Joseph Joffe, "The Default Power," *New York Times*, August 20, 2009; Fareed Zakaria, "The Future of American Power," *Foreign Affairs*, 87:3 (2008): 18–43.
92. Jeff Robinson, "Huntsman Says U.S. Decline Is 'Un-American' in First Speech," KCPW public radio, June 21, 2011, http://kcpw.org/blog/local-news/2011-06-21/huntsman-says-u-s-decline-is-un-american-in-first-speech/.
93. On the need to bring agency "back in" to the debate over imperial overstretch, see Dennis Florig, "Hegemonic Overreach vs. Imperial Overstretch," *Review of International Studies* 36 (2010): 1103–19.
94. Richard K. Betts, "Not with *My* Thucydides, You Don't," *The American Interest* 87 (2007): 140–43; J. P. Euben, "Thucydides in Baghdad," in *When Worlds Elide: Classics, Politics, Culture*, ed. K. Bassi and J. P. Euben (Lanham, MD: Lexington Books, 2010), 161–84; Lawrence A. Tritle, "Thucydides and the Cold War," in *Classical Antiquity and the Politics of America: From George W. Washington to George W. Bush*, ed. Michael Meckler (Waco, TX: Baylor University Press, 2006), 127–40; Richard Ned Lebow examines the shifting applications of Thucydides to American foreign policy and the attempt to reclaim him from the clutches of realpolitik: "International Relations and Thucydides," in *Thucydides and the Modern World: Reception,*

Reinterpretation and Influence from the Renaissance to the Present, ed. Katherine Harloe and Neville Morley (Cambridge: Cambridge University Press, 2012), 197–212.

95. As his student Richard Ned Lebow reports, *Tragic Vision*, 242.

96. Thucydides, *The Peloponnesian War*, Book 1:144, 2.65.

97. On Pericles's strategy, see Athanassios G. Platias and Constantinos Koliopoulos, *Thucydides on Strategy: Grand Strategies in the Peloponnesian War and Their Relevance Today* (London: Hurst, 2010), 42–59; Josiah Ober, "Thucydides, Pericles and the Strategy of Defense," in *The Craft of the Ancient Historian*, ed. John W. Eadie and Josiah Ober (New York: University Press of America, 1985) 171–88.

98. Robert Hariman, "Theory without Modernity," in *Prudence: Classical Virtue, Postmodern Practice* (University Park: Pennsylvania University Press, 2003), 1–35, 7–14, 8.

99. Thucydides, *History of the Peloponnesian War*, Book 6, Parts 8, 9,11,13.

100. George H. W. Bush and Brent Scowcroft, *A World Transformed* (New York: Vintage, 1998), 487.

101. Robert Divine, "Historians and the Gulf War: A Critique," *Diplomatic History* 19:1 (1995): 117–34; Brian Bond, *The Pursuit of Victory: From Napoleon to Saddam Hussein* (Oxford: Oxford University Press, 1997), 97; Michael R. Gordon and Bernard E. Trainor, *The Generals' War: The Inside Story of the Conflict in the Gulf* (Boston: Little, Brown 1995); Joshua Muravchik, "Losing the Peace," *Commentary* 94:1 (1992): 37–42; Angelo M. Codevilla, "Magnificent, but Was It War?," *Commentary* 93:4 (1992): 15–20; Donald Kagan and Frederick W. Kagan, *While America Sleeps: Self-Delusion, Military Weakness, and the Threat to Peace* (New York: St Martin's, 2001), 368–72; Robert Kagan and William Kristol, eds., *Present Dangers: Crisis and Opportunity in American Foreign and Defense Policy* (San Francisco: Encounter Books, 2000), 19.

102. On the debate, see Lawrence Freedman and Effraim Karsh, *The Gulf Conflict, 1990–1991: Diplomacy and War in the New World Order* (Princeton, NJ: Princeton University Press, 1993), 413–40, for the Schwarzkopf claim, 404.

103. "If History Teaches Us Anything, It Is That We Must Resist Aggression: Address by President Bush on the Situation in the Middle East," *Washington Post*, August 9, 1990; William A. Dorman and Steven Livingston, "News and Historical Content: The Establishing Phase of the Persian Gulf Policy Debate," in *Taken by Storm: The Media, Public Opinion, and U.S. Foreign Policy in the Gulf War*, ed. W. Lance Bennett and David L. Paletz (Chicago: University of Chicago Press, 1994), 69.

104. Victor Davis Hanson, *The Soul of Battle: From Ancient Times to the Present Day, How Three Great Liberators Vanquished Tyranny* (New York: Anchor, 1999), 410–11; Rone Tempest, "Right Way to Farm the Classics," *Los Angeles Times*, February 25, 2004; Laura Secor, "The Farmer: Classicist and Raisin-Grower Victor Davis Hanson Argues That the USA Needs a Dose of Ancient Greece's Warrior Culture. White House Hawks Are Listening," *Boston Globe*, May 25, 2003, D1; Barton Gellman, *Angler: The Cheney Vice Presidency* (New York: Penguin, 2008), 249–50.

105. See the criticisms of David Harvey, *Cosmopolitanism and the Geographies of Freedom* (New York: Columbia University Press, 2009), 57–58; "universal condition," from Andrew Moravcsik, "The New Liberalism," in Christian Reus-Smit and Duncan Snidal, *The Oxford Handbook of International Relations* (Oxford: Oxford University Press, 2008), 234.

106. As Peter Beinart argued, "An Illusion for Our Time," *New Republic*, October 20, 1997.

107. From Jeffery Frieden: "It is a choice made by governments that consciously decide to reduce barriers to trade and investment, adopt new policies toward international money and finance, and chart fresh economic courses." *Global Capitalism: Its Fall and Rise in the Twentieth Century* (New York: W. W. Norton, 2006), xvi.

108. United Nations Mission in Afghanistan, *Afghanistan: Annual Report, Protection of Civilians in Armed Combat* 2012 (2013), 1.

109. Transparency International, *Corruption Perceptions Index 2013* (Berlin, 2013), 2.

110. Ernesto Londono, Karen De Young, and Greg Miller, "Afghanistan Gains Will Be Lost Quickly after Drawdown, U.S. Intelligence Estimate Warns," *Washington Post*, December 28, 2013.

111. Rory Stewart lists the continued announcements of imminent decision in Afghanistan: *The Guardian*, October 8, 2011. For a discussion of overoptimistic assessments of the war, see Tim Bird and Alex Marshall, *Afghanistan: How the West Lost Its Way* (New Haven, CT: Yale University Press, 2011), 147–48.

112. The figures of American casualties are taken from Brown University "Costs of War" project, at http://costsofwar.org/, and the US Department of Defense, www.defense.gov/news/casualty.pdf.

113. Elizabeth Bumiller, "Threats and Responses: The Cost; White House Cuts Estimate Costs of War with Iraq," *New York Times*, December 31, 2002; Dan Murphy, "Iraq War: Predictions Made, and Results," *Christian Science Monitor*, December 22, 2011.

114. Joseph Stiglitz and Linda Bilmes, *The Three Trillion Dollar War: The True Cost of the Iraq Conflict* (New York: W. W. Norton, 2008); Martin Wolff, "America Failed to Calculate the Enormous Costs of War," *Financial Times*, January 11, 2006; John Duffield and Peter Dombrowski, eds., *Balance Sheet: The Iraq War and U.S. National Security* (Stanford, CA: Stanford University Press, 2009).

115. Amy F. Woolf, *Nunn–Lugar Cooperative Threat Reduction Programs: Issues for Congress* (Washington, DC: Congressional Research Service, 2002); also cited in Biddle, *American Grand Strategy*, 25.

116. Toby Dodge, "State and Society in Iraq Ten Years after Regime Change: The Rise of a New Authoritarianism," *International Affairs* 89:2 (2013): 241–57.

117. On Libya's state since the war, see Amnesty International, *Annual Report 2013—Libya*, May 23, 2013, at www.refworld.org/docid/519f518c47.html; Médicins Sans Frontières, "Detainees Tortured and Denied Medical Care," January 26, 2012, www.msf.org/article/libya-detainees-tortured-and-denied-medical-care; Patrick Cockburn, "Special Report: We All Thought Libya Had Moved On—It Has, but into Lawlessness and Ruin," *Independent*, September 3, 2013.

118. *Liberty and Security in a Changing World: Report and Recommendations of the President's Review Group on Intelligence and Communications Technologies*, at www.theguardian.com/world/interactive/2013/dec/18/nsa-review-panel-report document.

119. Max Boot, "The Struggle to Transform the Military," *Foreign Affairs* 84:2 (2005):), 103–18, 104.

120. John A. Nagl, "A Better War in Iraq: Learning Counterinsurgency and Making Up for Lost Time," *Armed Forces Journal* (2006): 22–28; "Unprepared," *RUSI Journal* 153:2 (2008): 83.

121. Patrick Regan, "Third-party Interventions and the Duration of Intrastate Conflicts," *Journal of Conflict Resolution* 46:1 (2002): 55–73; Reed M. Wood, Jacob Kathman, and Stephen E. Gent, "Armed Intervention and Civilian Victimization in Intrastate Conflicts," *Journal of Peace Research* 49:5 (2012): 647–60; Jonathan Monten and Alexander Downes, "Forced to Be Free? Why Foreign-Imposed Regime Change Rarely Leads to Democratization," *International Security* 37:4 (2013): 90–131.

122. Amitai Etzioni, "The Folly of Nation Building," *The National Interest* 120, (2012): 60–68, 63; Michael J. Mazarr, "The Rise and Fall of the State Failure Paradigm: Requiem for a Decade of Distraction," *Foreign Affairs* 93:1 (2014): 113–22.

123. According to the Worldwatch Institute in 2006–7, only an estimated 5 percent of the world's population have flown. *Vital Signs 2006–2007*, 68.

124. Pankaj Ghemawat, *World 3.0: Global Prosperity and How to Achieve It* (Cambridge, MA: Harvard University Press, 2011); Rana Foroohar, "Why the World Isn't Getting Smaller," *Time*, June 19, 2011.

125. John Maynard Keynes, *The Economic Consequences of the Peace* (New York: Harcourt, 1920), 11.

126. Ken Booth, *Theory of World Security* (New York: Cambridge University Press, 2007), 14.

127. John Robb, "Contagion," *Global Guerrillas*, December 13, 2011; liberal hawk Paul Berman described the alternative policies to invading Iraq and Afghanistan as the "isolationist alternative," March 20, 2013, at www.newrepublic.com/article/112701/iraq-war-10th-anniversary symposium#berman; Bill Keller, "Our New Isolationism," *New York Times*, September 8, 2013.

128. Philip Rucker, "Mitt Romney calls for new 'American century' with muscular foreign policy," *Washington Post*, October 7, 2011; "John McCain Chastizes 2012 Republican Field for Isolationism," ABC News, June 19, 2011; Aaron Blake, "Kerry: Not the Time for Armchair Isolationism," *Washington Post*, September 4, 2013.

129. Peter Feaver, "Americans Are Heeding the Siren Song of Isolationism and Global Retreat": "Does Obama's Gamble Make Sense?," *Shadow Government*, March 18, 2011; "A Diminished President: A Diminished Global Power," *Shadow Government*, August 2, 2011.

130. Benjamin H. Friedman and Christopher Preble, "Americans Favor Not Isolationism but Restraint," *Los Angeles Times*, December 27, 2013.

131. Bear Braumoller, "The Myth of American Isolationism," *Foreign Policy Analysis* 6:4 (2010): 349–71, 354.
132. For these critiques, see Paul Hirst and Grahame Thompson, *Globalization in Question: The International Economy and the Possibilities of Governance* (Cambridge, UK: Polity, 1999); Samy Cohen, *The Resilience of the State: Democracy and the Challenges of Globalization* (London: Hurst, 2003).
133. Pankaj Ghemawat with Steven A. Altman, *DHL Global Connectedness Index 2012*, at http://www.dhl.com/content/dam/flash/g0/gci_2012/download/dhl_gci_2012_executive_summary.pdf.
134. The theory/practice gap and the continued centrality of the state and interstate relations is well demonstrated in the fields of multilateral institutions, defense spending and procurement choices, and territorial control: Norrin M. Ripsman and T. V. Paul, *Globalization and the National Security State* (Oxford: Oxford University Press, 2010), 49, 53, 161, 173.
135. Eugene Gholz and Daryl G. Press, "The Effects of War on Neutral Countries: Why It Doesn't Pay to Preserve the Peace," *Security Studies* 10:4 (2001): 1–57.
136. For a recent argument for the centrality of the state to globalization, see Leo Panitch and Sam Gindin, *The Making of Global Capitalism: The Political Economy of American Empire* (New York: Verso, 2013).
137. "Beyond State-Centrism? Space, Territoriality, and Geographic Scale in Globalization Studies," *Theory and Society* 29:1 (1999): 39–78.
138. See Daniel W. Drezner, "The Global Governance of the Internet: Bringing the State Back In," *Political Science Quarterly* 119:3 (2004): 477–98.
139. On this issue, see Evgeny Morozov, *The Net Delusion: How Not to Liberate the World* (London: Penguin, 2012).
140. As David L. Berkey argues, "Why Fortifications Endure," in *Makers of Ancient Strategy: From the Persian Wars to the Fall of Rome*, ed. Victor Davis Hanson (Princeton, NJ: Princeton University Press, 2010), 5, 77, 92n79; Edward Wong and David S. Claud, "US Erects Baghdad Wall to Keep Sects Apart," *New York Times*, April 21, 2007; Peter Andreas, "Redrawing the Line: Borders and Security in the Twenty-First Century," *International Security* 28:2 (2003): 78–111; Reece Jones, *Border Walls: Security and the War on Terror in the United States, India, and Israel* (New York: Zed Books, 2012).
141. As one member of the Pakistani militant group Lashkar-e-Taibi reported, "We cannot send jihadists into India in big numbers like in the past because of tight security at the Indian side." Frank Jack Daniel and Sanjeev Miglani, "As Afghanistan Endgame Looms, India-Pakistan Tensions Rise," Reuters, August 13, 2013.
142. *Hansard*, 234, June 11, 1877, 1564–65.
143. On the history of the pursuit of a universally accepted global map, see Jerry Brotton, *A History of the World in Twelve Maps* (London: Penguin, 2012), 434, for the quote.

CHAPTER 2

Wars for the World
The Rise of Globalism: 1941, 1950, 2001

American leaders—moved by a traditional missionary impulse, convinced of their global responsibility, full of the self-confidence that comes of success, fundamentally unhurt by war in a wounded world—eagerly reached for their mandate of heaven.

—DANIEL YERGIN, *SHATTERED PEACE*

To many globalists, America must act as the world's hegemonic leader and guardian without rival. This is needed all the more, they argue, because the world is shrinking dangerously. When and why did this ideology of the "shrinking world" take root? And why has it proven so attractive?

The rise of globalism is best explained as an interlocking of four forces: America's growing power, the impact of strategic shocks, the force of liberal traditions about the nature of American security, and the "pulling" dynamics of empire. Material and ideological factors, external conditions, domestic ideas, and historical contingencies reinforced one another in a feedback loop to place globalism in the ascendancy.[1] If America, in Robert Kagan's words, became a "behemoth with a conscience," its was a liberal conscience with all the ambitions and dangers it entails.[2]

First, there is the growth of American power, principally through World War II. As a result of the war, America experienced unprecedented industrial expansion. Its GDP doubled. Its industrial base unmolested by bombardment and blockade, it reached the highest per capita productivity in the world. It had the highest standard of living, domination of the world's gold reserves and the Bretton Woods economic system, exerted great influence through the dollar as reserve currency, and became the largest creditor and exporter. Its capacity to project power with long-range bombers and carrier task forces was unparalleled. It had an atomic monopoly. The precipitate rise in its strength relative to other states devastated by war enlarged Americans' sense of their interests, and therefore their fears.[3] It enabled "visionary world-making," where states feel that they can pursue security through expansion by reordering the international system.[4] This generated demand as well as supply. America's world role was an "empire by invitation, stimulated not just by domestic ideas but by international attraction."[5] There was worldwide demand for its loans, arms, expertise, and patronage. American globalism was partly made abroad.

Some frame this as a simple story of the wartime rise from isolationism into internationalism.[6] Yet even World War II did not decisively tilt the debate about US security interests. Postwar America was torn between the desire to draw back and fear of leaving behind a strategic vacuum. It took a wave of crises between 1941 and 1950 to stimulate Washington into new commitments and convert its evolving world view into concrete plans. Some look to the competition with the Soviet Union as the defining moment when a notion of defense from afar yielded to the "new god" of national security.[7] But fear of the Soviet enemy is not sufficient as an explanation. We also need to explain the delay between 1945 and 1950–51, the time it took for America's Cold War to intensify, globalize, and militarize as the Soviet Union recovered. And if globalism depended on the Soviet enemy, it would be hard to explain why the idea persisted after that adversary's fall. Globalism is a persistent ideology precisely because it does not depend on specific adversaries and lives on after their fall. It casts particular enemies as symptoms of a systemic problem that demands American benevolent hegemony as the solution.

It also took strategic shocks to stimulate a sense of global insecurity, events that Americans interpreted as highlighting their vulnerability and the extent of their security interests. Americans interpreted the attack on Pearl Harbor and the North Korean and Chinese invasions of South Korea as proof of a shrinking world. Reeling from these shocks, policymakers believed America vulnerable to the extent that its security depended upon events far beyond its region. John Lewis Gaddis sees a larger pattern. In response to such shocks from the burning of the White House in 1814 to the destruction of skyscrapers in 2001, America's characteristic reflex is to enlarge its security domain.[8] The violent "shock event" is a historical pillar of American defense and foreign policy.[9]

Shocks from abroad, however, were not received in a vacuum. Also important were older, inherited liberal traditions about the fragile republic that can only be secure in a world it shapes and protects. These ideas framed how elites define and measure threats. America's liberal ideology is an efficient contributing cause of expansion, though not a necessary one. America is hardly the first state to lunge too far. Illiberal states have an impressive record of self-defeating behavior. Other universalistic ideologies drove states to inflate threats, expand to eliminate them through anticipatory wars, only to suffer self-inflicted wounds.[10]

Before the ideology of the Pax Americana, there were the imperial and universalist creeds of Philip II's imperial Catholicism, Wilhelmine Germany's bid for world power, and Napoleon's exported revolution. Overstretch is an occupational hazard of the strong.[11] America was distinctive not because of its ideas, but because it married its universalistic creed to a high level of relative material strength. This ideology makes the strongest, most secure state in history feel ever more insecure. A glance at history suggests that power does not automatically lead rulers to adopt universalistic ideas. Powerful states that lack universalist ideologies, such as Bismarck's Germany and (for long periods) ancient Sparta, resisted the bid for hegemony when presented with opportunities.[12] But growing power creates temptation. Strong states that adopt a liberal ideology and have formidable means of power projection, like nineteenth-century Britain or twentieth-century America, find expansion hard to resist.

Fourth, there is the self-propelling dynamic of empire. The pursuit of security through expansion ironically breeds new insecurities. Insecurity and ambition drives expansion, but expansion creates new frontiers that breed further insecurity. Power instils fear, and hegemonic states expand their interests as they sense a greater stake in world order as it becomes their back yard. Though America does not pursue the same modes of empire as the European colonizers, it too has a restless global "turbulent frontier,"[13]

> stabilized only as a truce or expedient, apparently defensible only by patrolling beyond its markers and fortifications, not to govern, but, if need be, to destroy. The Ho Chi Minh Trail in Cambodia, the coca fields of Colombia, the chemical factories of Libya, the mosques of Qum and the madrassas of Peshawar, the unguarded nuclear stockpiles of Central Asia, the reactors of North Korea . . . they will always be dangerous, always beyond normal negotiation, always within imagined military possibility.[14]

The horizons of a world power, in other words, exert a "pull" that unexpectedly draws great powers "into the politics of other polities."[15] In America's case, the dynamics of informal empire mixed with the anxieties of the Cold War to create pressure from the periphery to make fresh commitments.

Exactly how authentic are appeals to globalism is hard to tell. Real inner motives are often irrecoverable. Security elites do not always deploy ideas sincerely, but if globalism worked merely as a convenient pretext used for other secret motives, they must have been very secret. There is little evidence that the rhetoric of "war presidents" such as Harry Truman or George W. Bush were hollow, and some evidence to the contrary.[16] But this is less important than the rhetoric's own power. Even if hollow, as a rationalization it creates pressures to live up to it. As "self-perception" theory argues, people tend to act in accordance with the explanations they give.[17] The notion of a global battlespace was popularized in the shape of red lines, dominoes, and "terror." Once enunciated, those ideas took on a power of their own and became hard to abandon. Over time, the notion that America's security is tied to the replication of its institutions and values abroad became the "common sense" of its elites. It became the chief justification for expansion abroad, a totem to mobilize opinion around, and the ruling idea that defined security interests. Rulers have not always practiced what they preach. But it is consistently the standard they appeal to and by which they are judged.

This is also a history of antiglobalism. In the hour of America's rise as a superpower, an earlier generation of American political realists sought to place a prudent consciousness of distance, geography, and outer limits at the center of American diplomacy, and to find a middle ground between overreaching globalism and narrow isolation. The leading figures were Walter Lippmann, George Kennan, Nicholas Spykman, Hanson Baldwin, and Hans Morgenthau. All agreed with the premise that America's security interests went beyond the water's edge. But they also laid down a minority report against the developing orthodoxy of globalism. These intellectuals were part of the state's rediscovery of power politics, but also critics of it.

In each crisis, a division resurfaced between these figures and the foreign policy establishment of which they were part. Against the pursuit of hegemony and an unassailable level of national security via a favorable imbalance of power, they argued for a balance of power, the pursuit of an equilibrium of mutual restraint. Against exceptionalism and the belief that America's singularity gave it a transcendent historical role, they argued that American power was subject to the same historical forces that afflicted other strong states. Against monolithic thinking, they argued for ranking interests and distinguishing and dividing adversaries. Against ideological fundamentalism and the tendency to imbue the concept of the national interest with universal moral principles, they argued for prudent compromise and a tighter alignment of means and ends. And against the notion of a global battlespace, they argued for a more limited security domain. Against the belief that the United States was both so fragile as to warrant liberal crusades, yet so powerful as to be able to impose its will on the world, they argued that America was secure enough to coexist watchfully in a multipolar world and that the limits on its power would force it to. In different ways, they assumed what globalists rejected— that power tended to weaken across space, and that America could secure itself by building intermediate barriers without having to reorder the world. Not only was geography a dimension of power politics, but it was also a vital disciplining concept in statecraft through which what was vital (needed for life) could be distinguished from the peripheral. Thus emerged an American, classical realist critique of the liberal tradition and its global horizons, a critique continually remade.[18]

Dating Globalism

American globalism is not new. Expansive ideas about America's security interests have a long history.[19] The American strategic tradition can be seen as a struggle along a spectrum between two ideal types, "shapers" and "restrainers." To some, the republic can secure itself only by actively championing its values abroad and remaking the world in its image. Others are wary of entanglement abroad, arguing that America is better off embodying rather than spreading its values.

Washington once presumed against venturing forth internationally, at least beyond its own hemisphere. In his Farewell Address in September 1796, President George Washington regarded America's offshore separation from Europe, the center of great-power competition, as an asset that the new republic could exploit in order to rise peacefully.[20] By holding foreign states at arm's length, remaining solvent and protecting its sea approaches, the United States could use its "detached and distant situation" to buy time to grow and realize its strength, to the point where nations would respect its neutrality. Trading but avoiding entanglement would ensure discretion, "when we may choose peace or war, as our interest, guided by justice, shall counsel."[21] By staying at a remove, the republic adopted a strategy that would protect it not only against external threats, but also against an internal danger. It would relieve it of forming a vast army that would choke its liberty.[22]

Distancing was not yet a fait accompli. European powers still occupied the same continent. Rather than relying passively on the accident of geography, it would take adroit triangulation to maneuver the Spanish, French, and British out of the region. Extrication from foreign politics was hardly a tranquil process. America would create a navy to defend itself from the predations of the Barbary pirates, and the 1812 war was still to come. And not all Americans agreed. Ever since the debate over American neutrality in the Anglo-French wars onward, there was always a strain of opinion that American security was tied to revolutionary struggles abroad. But while the path was tortuous, the logic was clear.

Two centuries later, the balance of opinion had shifted. Strategists sensed that the United States as a superpower lacked the space and time it had once had. In 1988, a report written by a blue-ribbon commission for President Ronald Reagan noted that America's settled strategy was based on the forward deployment of forces, proximate to adversaries in Central Europe and on the Korean Peninsula, designed "to draw a line that no aggressor will dare cross."[23] In the nineteenth century the United States could hunker down in the Western Hemisphere, with years to mobilize before its late entrance into the great wars of the twentieth. They were now committed on the world's most dangerous front lines. Even now, those who favor retracting these commitments face an uphill battle. This is not what George Washington had in mind.

To understand globalism's ascent, it can be plotted around three crucial dates: December 7, 1941, June 25, 1950, and September 11, 2001. On each date, enemies inflicted a surprise attack on American interests, whether the Pacific Fleet anchored in Pearl Harbor, the thirty-eighth parallel line dividing South and North Korea, and, on 9/11, cities on home soil. In the wake of these shocks, Washington strategically reassessed its position, declared a world struggle, and went to war. These conflicts were not equal in terms of scale or type. But each was an occasion where the United States widened its strategic horizons and rededicated itself to a global project.

1941: Pearl Harbor and the Global Embrace

Imperial Japan's surprise strike on Pearl Harbor on December 7, 1941 ("12/7"), persuaded Americans that old geographic barriers were obsolete and that a new era of vulnerability had arrived. Americans concluded that new weapons, communication, and transport technologies had eclipsed distance. President Franklin Roosevelt invoked globalism to justify America's war against the Axis. Pearl Harbor showed that "we cannot measure our safety in terms of miles on a map any more."[24] New long-range capabilities, from naval aviation to air power, combined with predatory ideologies such as fascism and the overthrow of the European balance of power meant that American security could no longer be based on continental or hemispheric insulation. For the majority, the assault by a transoceanic predator demonstrated "that the rise of hostile states anywhere in the world could endanger our security."[25] A dominant Nazi Germany and Imperial Japan, it was feared, could threaten the homeland with encirclement, economic suffocation, or invasion. Great Britain played its part in feeding American fears, as British intelligence forged documents about Nazi plans for political subversion and the creation of satellite states in the Americas.[26] The fear of fifth columnists at home and the sighting of Japanese submarines off the west coast quickened the sense of enemies closing in.

World War II gave rise to the era of national security. This was an idea that would be institutionalized within American government and popularized in wider society. National security supplanted the more limited concept of "defense." Military "Rainbow" plans of the interwar period had little overall policy direction from the White House or the State Department, were separate and secretive from other branches of government, and the armed services had to guess the contours of national policy.[27] The disorder of the 1930s planted the seeds of an intellectual rediscovery of strategy as an intellectual discipline, and new weapons of greater range and lethality stoked fears in defense debate.[28] Edward Mead Earle at the Institute for Advanced Study at Princeton, along with Arnold Wolfers and Nicholas Spykman at Yale, led the academic embrace of the concept. But only after the United States formally entered the war did national security become an organizing principle for a new, complex bureaucracy. This would culminate in the formation of the Unified Command Plan of 1946 that placed large parts of the globe under geographically based military commands, and the National Security Act of 1947, establishing the National Security Council and the Central Intelligence Agency.[29] Once continental and hemispheric, America's conception of its outer defenses became extraregional.[30] "Security" now went beyond the material and territorial. "National security" as a term altered its etymology and associations, pointing to "the shrinkage of space and time."[31]

Hand in hand with the rise of national security came the renaissance in the institutionalized pursuit of strategy on a worldwide scale. Several converging forces drove this. These included the scale of worldwide war with its intercontinental alliances and multiple theaters of war, the need to synchronize campaigns with coalition partners, and the belief that combat in Asia, Europe, and Africa were united in what President Franklin Roosevelt called "a single world conflict" that put at stake America's "total security," demanding a "global strategy" that could only be comprehended by thinking in terms of five continents and seven seas.[32]

As well as reviving "big" strategy, a sense of the world war's connectedness drew attention to mapping and the relationship between space and power. A struggle of ideologies that spanned the globe led to a wave of American geopolitical thought. A range of thinkers recast Halford Mackinder's ideas about the struggle to control the world's pivotal "heartland" in light of the Allies' clash against the Axis powers and their drive to conquer Eurasia.[33] Some, though not all, of the geostrategists were émigré intellectuals who believed that in stepping into the conflict, the United States had to learn that its survival was inextricably linked to the struggle for vital territories and the need to deny predatory states like the Third Reich an empire that would unite German science with Russian manpower. Sometimes in collaboration with the state, these figures deliberately set out to transform the mental and actual maps of its population by raising "cartographic consciousness."[34] Edward Mead Earle and Harold Sprout helped produce an educational wartime map, the *Citizen's War Atlas* and a Brookings Institution study that argued for the prevention of any hostile powers or coalitions dominating the Eurasian landmass, which was adopted by the Joint Chiefs of Staff.[35]

How far the Axis powers genuinely posed a direct threat to the territorial integrity of the United States can be doubted. America remained a difficult target. It was a large landmass, not a small island. Invading and conquering from across two oceans was still difficult even after the inception of new technology. America had a strong protective curtain in its navy. Its surface fleet—joined also by Britain's while it remained on the board—dwarfed Germany's.[36] The Battle of Britain in 1940 was a marker for this argument. Hitler's inability to subdue let alone conquer

Britain, a closer and smaller island state, suggested that successfully attacking or transporting an invasion force across the Atlantic Ocean was a demanding logistical feat. America from its bases had interception reach to disrupt or deny any aggressor. Provided it maintained a sufficient coastal defense, it enjoyed a forbidding "home advantage" through shorter supply lines, the ability to shift its naval forces rapidly between oceans through the interior line of the Panama Canal, and the ability to apply its weight over a smaller distance. Far from conferring a decisive edge to the aggressor, new military instruments cut both ways. America could use it to widen rather than narrow its defended space.

That does not mean that intervention in the war was imprudent. But the argument for stepping in to fend off a direct security threat was overblown. Even if Nazi Germany conquered continental Europe and acquired nuclear weapons, the United States would have been able to strengthen its navy and air force as well as developing nuclear weapons of its own. It is likely that living with a nuclear Nazi Germany and an enslaved continental Europe with America on alert as a frightened "national security state" would have been more dangerous than the actual outcome, of a nuclear Soviet Union and an enslaved Eastern Europe with America on alert as a frightened "national security state." But it is a "closer call" than is often remembered.

Ironically, the course and conduct of World War II saw the revenge of distance. Space and weather were brutally important factors in Operation Barbarossa. Germany's high-tempo armored offensives and its ruthless and mobile onslaught to carve out "One World" could not conquer freezing temperatures, vastness, and poor roads. In the Battle of Britain, geography plus force also proved prohibitive. Field Marshal Wilhelm Keitel judged that a cross-Channel invasion represented nothing more than a "large river crossing."[37] But with Britain's larger surface fleet and air defense system, the English Channel turned out to be an obstructive moat and British airspace an expensive domain to contest. There had been prophecies that the strategic bomber was a distance-destroying and war-winning instrument. But in the European and Asian theatres of war, air power was a shield as well as a sword, used to defend as well as attack urban targets. B-29 Superfortresses or Heinkels meted out horrific violence, but took heavy losses in the process of striking thickly defended cities. In the Pacific war, breaking Tokyo's will exerted costs over space. Sheer distance—the 5,530 miles between San Diego and Tokyo—posed logistical difficulties. Pressing home the war against Japan required anchorage, land bases, and troop-staging posts. Tropical diseases caused more casualties than combat. Hopes that China could be a platform for attacking Japan were dashed once land air bases were overrun. Getting real estate for forward air bases in the Pacific required bloody battles over island fortresses like Iwo Jima and Okinawa that cost the invader losses that it could not repeatedly sustain.

However, America was still attacked in what seemed like unprovoked aggression. This brute fact overshadowed America's prewar escalating rivalry with Japan and the seriousness of anti-intervention arguments. It was only a short step from the notion of an unprovoked attack to the notion of an act of aggression on a diplomatically passive, "sleeping" America. This image of a "year zero" event was powerful as a way of rousing Americans to fight back. It also promoted an ever-growing concept of what the country must do to become secure. Though the war turned out to be a hard slog over lethally defended terrain, Pearl Harbor and its interpreters successfully redrew the map.

President Roosevelt loved maps and became the elite sponsor of the shrinking world ideology. He assigned himself the role of geography teacher in his national speeches, in his "fireside chat" in February 1942 telling listeners to get out their maps to see the scale of the war and their vulnerability.[38] Roosevelt had already articulated a new geopolitics, invoking the shrinking world in making the case for rearmament and conscription, for extending America's defensive perimeter from the Caribbean through the destroyers-for-bases deal into the Atlantic and as far as Greenland, and becoming the "arsenal of democracy." From his "quarantine" speech in October 1937 to Pearl Harbor and beyond, repeatedly he warned Americans of "a new range and speed to offense," that science's "annihilation of time and space" was stripping America of its insulation and destroying the "false teaching of geography" that "a distance of several thousands of miles from a war-torn Europe to a peaceful America gave to us some form of mystic immunity." Impregnable fortifications no longer existed, time was on the side of aggressors, and readiness and denying adversaries a foothold for attack was vital. As Nazi Germany expanded into North Africa, it had the power to occupy Spain or Portugal, positioning itself to seize the "island outposts of the New World," the Azores and Cape Verde Islands. "The war is approaching the brink of the Western Hemisphere itself. It is coming very close to home." Placing the new war in a familiar context, Roosevelt worried that "our Bunker Hill of tomorrow may be several thousand miles from Boston." In terms of the timetable of movement of "men and guns and planes and bombs," the voyage from Europe to San Francisco was effectively shorter than the voyage of Roman legions to Spain or Britain. The distance from the center of Europe to Santiago de Chile was shorter "than it was for the chariots of Alexander the Great to roll from Macedonia to Persia."

Alexander did not use chariots, which were not useful for transporting large armies across rugged terrain. Roosevelt's treatment of modern capabilities was also dubious. His depiction of military geography was a one-way street: He spoke of new weapons' offensive power and range, but not how these qualities could be exploited by defenses to make continental defense stronger rather than weaker. He spoke of modern air power's ability to reach the country, but not the harder task of winning air supremacy once they got there. And skeptics doubted that the United States with its large Atlantic fleet and air force would be bound merely to spectate as European conquerors ferried their forces over. But the point, though simplistic, was powerful. Modern transport accelerated conquest.[39]

The magazine mogul Henry Luce made the most memorable statement of the wartime rejection of prewar "defense" and the push for a more expansive view of America's security interests. As America was shifting from neutrality, materially aiding Britain and legislating the Lend-Lease program, Luce argued that the territorial concept of "defense" was to blame for the crisis. The new "American century" involved a struggle for a nonterritorial kind of security: "We are not in a war to defend American territory. We are in a war to defend and even to promote, encourage and incite so-called democratic principles throughout the world."[40] The son of Protestant missionaries with a deep attachment to China, Luce defined American war aims in ways that rejected limits. Expansion abroad must follow America's expansion over its own continent, especially as he told the Council of National Defense months before, "we felt the world closing in on us and it was essential for us to spread our way of life, which he called Democracy."[41] His media empire with its flagship magazines *Time*, *Life*, and *Fortune* delivered the message and printed the reshaped maps with their new North Pole projection. *Time* reached a mass circulation of a million copies a week by the end of 1942, and Life approach four million. About 750,000 copies of *Time* and 650,000 copies of *Life* were distributed free to American troops abroad, and 60 percent of US soldiers and sailors named *Life* their favorite magazine.[42] It was in the same colorful visual outlets where Americans could "see" illustrated the notion of a shrinking globe with red arrows threatening an embattled North American continent.

In maps as well as magazines, cartographers altered the image of America from a secure continent shielded by distance to a vulnerable island in a closed system world coming under the Axis triangular stranglehold. With the help of artist Richard Edes Harrison, the new paradigm of air-age globalism replaced the Mercator map, designed for maritime navigation and for the optic of the sailor, with the vertical map of the pilot, from a world divided by geography to a globe united as one linked monosphere, to persuade Americans that aviation "had fundamentally disrupted the nature of geography."[43] It also moved from the equator-based map to the North Pole–centered one, with the Arctic at the center suggesting the closeness of the United States and Japan or the Soviet Union. An Arctic-central map, and a consciousness of air power, added up to a dangerous proximity. The Eurasian battleground was next door, and planes could fly across the polar zone all year round. The frozen north was not an obstacle but an emerging line of approach.

If the world was shrinking strategically, for America's way of life to survive, it had to make sure that it retained access to a single world economy with its markets and raw materials, an access ensured by American military power. A hostile world that could penetrate America's region was also one that could strangle it commercially. So this was a war for the "open door policy." In the Wilsonian tradition, world order and America's survival in it relied on the interior politics and constitutions of its states, as well as the spread of free commercial markets that were vital arteries for American prosperity. While it aided Britain in fighting the war, Washington also dismantled its stirling bloc and imperial preference trading system, and pushed for an open world trading system of its own. The linked pursuit of military and economic hegemony took place through collaboration with geographers. The scholar Isaiah Bowman became "Roosevelt's geographer" and a vital link between public and scholarly geopolitics. Bowman argued for a new kind of economic globalism with America as its pivot, a single system of American "military and economic supremacy" to replace economic blocs, reflecting his belief that "no line can prevent the remote from becoming the near danger."[44] This reached the president's desk in October 1940. The Council on Foreign Relations in March 1940 recommended that the Monroe Doctrine territories expand to include Greenland as a part of America's hemisphere, and a point that would place an occupier within bombing range of North America. Roosevelt then invited Bowman to talks before announcing America's policy to create military bases there. Roosevelt also consulted Bowman in a secret meeting in April 1941 with Adm. Harold Stark, chief of naval operations, in which Bowman helped Roosevelt define the new hemispheric boundaries. For Frederick Schuman, the first American scholar to translate and explain Karl Haushofer's concept of "geostrategy," it was "an age in which technology has made all the planet one neighborhood, one marketplace and one battlefield."[45]

What Luce put in missionary terms, what cartographers portrayed on maps, and what geostrategists theorized was paralleled in defense planning by the Joint Chiefs of Staff. It took longer for the military establishment to get on board with global conceptions of security. Within their ranks were advocates of a narrower hemispheric defense and a "Pacific first" strategy rather than investing blood and treasure in multiple fronts.[46] "Pacific first" was formally made by the Joint Chiefs of Staff, with support from large segments of public opinion. The move from a more limited geographic concept of defense to a one of global security happened incrementally and the issue of how wide and where to plot America's true frontiers was contested.[47] But there was a shift. The Joint Board (that was replaced later by the Joint Chiefs of Staff) assessed in January 1941 that the United States could "safeguard the North American continent and probably the western hemisphere, whether allied with Britain or not."[48] Yet the war aims laid down by the Victory Program of September 1941 with the imprimatur of Adm. Stark, and army chief of staff Gen. George Marshall, went far beyond the concern for basic self-defense, looking to the "establishment in Europe and Asia of balances of power which will most nearly ensure political stability in those regions and the future security of the United States," widening this still further by including "so far as practicable" the "establishment of regimes favorable to economic freedom and individual liberty."[49] For the upper echelons of the military, a future war for self-preservation had expanded into a war for the world.

What did this mean in terms of concrete policy? The debate can be tracked within the Joint Strategic Survey Committee that advised the chiefs, whose strategic assessments presidents often called upon. In several areas, the successive studies of the military show America's widening strategic horizons. Consider what the Joint Chiefs of Staff said about the future employment of US armed forces, written under the war's shadow:

> Forseeable new weapons emphasize the necessity for keeping a prospective enemy at the maximum possible distance, and conversely of projecting our advance bases into areas well removed from the United States, so as to project our operations, with new weapons or otherwise, nearer the enemy. The over-all effect is to enlarge our strategic frontier. Further, the possibilities inherent in new weapons make it vital that we obtain accurate and prompt intelligence as to the progress of foreign nations in such developments. . . . Emphasized is the necessity of not permitting the first major blow to be struck against us.[50]

The desire for greater security created a paradox. Enlarging the frontier meant keeping the enemy at a distance from America's heartland, their bases organized as "an unbroken series of essential stepping stones to the primary and peripheral bases in order to obtain security in depth."[51] Not only must the "customary conception of Atlantic and Pacific defense boundaries" be secured, but as the chiefs warned in their report on US requirements for postwar air bases in November 1943, given the advent of "feasible sub-Arctic flight" would also have to be expanded to include the northern approaches ranging from Alaska to Greenland to Iceland.[52] In response, Roosevelt went even further—the outermost western defensive line should also include the Marquesas and Tuamotu Group of islands that within ten years of air-power development could be bases that menace the western coast of the Americas.[53]

At the same time, pushing out the frontline to keep enemies distant meant getting closer to them. It meant ensuring access so that future adversaries were within range, which meant developing a base and client system to project power from afar. In time, the distinction between core heartland and peripheral advanced forces would fade. US positions on those peripheries would be judged not just as the infrastructure of power projection in outlying areas, but as vital measures of American credibility and as front lines in a dangerous world battlespace where all adversaries were effectively nearby.

If America's defensive perimeter was to stretch beyond its region, it would have to be organized through practical mechanisms. These would include a global basing system, air transit rights, an international intelligence network, and long-range military reach. Even while the war was being fought, the acquisition of bases for the postwar period was "a matter of the very greatest importance."[54] The emergence of weapons of ever-greater power with new delivery systems such as long-range heavy bombers and rockets made bases a vital outer line of defense that had to be negotiated and locked down before the end of hostilities.[55] Shortly after the war, the Joint Chiefs of Staff judged that in a future war between major foreign powers, America was bound to be involved, and the potency and range of modern weapons reduced the invulnerability that geography had once ensured. This made deterrence vital, but also "making all preparations to strike the first blow if necessary" while avoiding "any misguided and perilous idea of avoiding an aggressive attitude to permit the first blow to be struck against us."[56] This was fatalism. If it was assumed that America could not hope to avoid major power wars, then hitting a potential enemy first outweighed the task of avoiding war.

The advent of the atomic bomb late in the war made the internal debate sharper and more urgent still about the right location of its defensive perimeter. Unlike other weapons, there was no known defense against it, and it had instantaneously destructive power that posed severe dangers to America's coastal concentrations of industry and populations. It could be resisted only by intercepting its delivery systems (at that stage aircraft bombers) in flight. This accentuated the demand for forward bases, well advanced in the Atlantic and Pacific Oceans and to the shores of the Arctic. This was before the introduction of intercontinental ballistic missiles, which would restage the debate about the need for forward staging posts. The argument for a "system of mutually supporting advanced bases extending far out from the homeland" would continue to generate justifying arguments, from intercepting physical threats to preventing a collapse of psychological dominoes. The more the world seemed to compress time and space and make geographical barriers obsolete, the greater the demand for an extended military presence to give America a chance for "adequate warning, interception and destruction of an attacking force."[57]

Exactly how deep should America's defense-in-depth extend? This was for a time unsettled. Within the Joint Strategic Survey Committee, Gen. Stanley Embick tried and failed to counter the push for an American base in Iceland, as well as urged accommodation with the Soviet Union over pressing its own security interests for access to the open sea. Seizing forward bases unilaterally that were inessential for American national security was indefensible, and they could create a security dilemma and make the difficult coming negotiations over Germany harder by "arousing Russian suspicion as to Anglo-American intentions." Embick lost that fight. In a further measure of how American horizons had stretched, Assistant Secretary of War John McCloy's representative replied that Embick's dissent "presents a rather restricted concept of what is necessary for national defense."[58] Here two views of American security collided. The minority view regarded Iceland as part of a wider effort at a negotiated postwar settlement, with an eye to how a wary Soviet Union with legitimate interests of its own might regard American accumulation of forward positions, a problem that in turn could threaten the security of both. The majority view, however, saw Iceland as an "absolute safeguard in security," equating security with the competitive maximization of one's own advantage.[59] The Joint Chiefs in July 1945 rejected Embick's minority position about Soviet base demands. Their growing fears in the same month of July 1945 were evident in their study of American-Soviet relations for President Truman, that the Soviet Union was not a traditional great power with legitimate security needs that could be accommodated, but a predatory and revolutionary actor that was driven by ideology, on the move to seize control of satellites, a threat that must be countered.[60] By October, the breakdown of talks at the London conference, their view was bleaker still. Recent failures sharpened fear of a hungry expansionist radical power whose appetite would only be whetted by conciliation, and even Embick now argued for confronting Moscow.[61]

The insistent need for postwar advanced bases did not just spring from fear of the Soviets. Earlier on, the Joint Chiefs of Staff envisaged international peace enforcement by wartime allies against "any incipient disturber of world peace." Competition was also apparent with the British, who "are directing covetous eyes toward some islands" that may be "forfeited to British control" lest steps were taken to ensure access to "insular bases vital to our economic and military security on possible transoceanic air routes." Independently of any one future enemy, an emerging aim of the war was to maintain "continued supremacy in military and commercial aviation."[62] Military planners followed Washington's vision that American security depended not only on a vigilant homeland defense, but on a favorable balance of power abroad and the prevention of any state generating overwhelming offensive combat power.

Thus two strands of globalist fear emerged from World War II. Partly it was technological, the fear that new weapons and means of transport and communication obliterated distance. And partly it was geopolitical, the fear that the collapse of former buffer states in Europe and the shift to bipolarity was bringing the United States into collision with a Soviet rival that also represented a new kind of actor on the world stage, a revolutionary revisionist power. At the close of the war in Europe, the first meeting of the Red Army and the US Army at the banks of the Elbe River on April 25, 1945, was the occasion of fear as well as rejoicing. With the Nazi threat that had they had collaborated around collapsing, the glue that had held the wartime coalition was coming unstuck and the powers were eye-ball to eyeball.[63]

Added to these two fears would come a third, the fear of "dominoes" falling.[64] From the "hot war" of actual combat to a cold war of more protracted and indirect security competition where successes were harder to measure, American makers of strategy came to define it partly as a psychological struggle where single con-frontations anywhere on the map were global tests, every enemy probe was now a "Munich moment" that potentially posed a general crisis that could unravel alli-ances and embolden enemies. But it would take further shocks to reach this point.

Between Globalism and Isolation: The Realists at War

Contrary to binary portrayals of the American debate as a struggle between inter-nationalists and isolationists, prominent realists who supported American inter-vention offered a more sober and measured case than the government for the nature of the threat and what was at stake.[65] Hanson Baldwin and Nicholas Spykman, two geopolitical thinkers sensitive to what changing military capabilities could actu-ally achieve, argued that a future Eurasian Axis superpower would not necessarily be an immediate military threat, but a longer-term threat in terms of the even-tual shift in the material balance of power that would create a climate of insecurity inauspicious for America's way of life.[66] Baldwin, a former naval officer and mil-itary analyst for the *New York Times*, believed America's stake in the conflict was important but indirect. The fear of closed of markets and a clash of economic sys-tems, as well as a general spiritual struggle of morals and ideals, was the only issue really worth the fight. He assessed the prospect of a direct military threat to the American homeland to be a "bogey." The present war might result in a grinding stalemate. Even in a worst-case scenario of an outright Axis victory, potential divi-sions within the signers of the Tripartite Pact and resistance in occupied territories meant that "if Hitler wins, his troubles may only be beginning." Even if an ascen-dant Axis overcame alliance frictions, the strain of oceanic distance on military operations added to America's relative strength, placed limits on the combined fleets of Germany, Italy, Russia, and Japan, with their restricted operating range operating far from their bases, to the point where "a direct invasion" from Europe or Asia was virtually impossible within the next ten years. Air power without effective seaborne assault could not hold or consolidate territory. In the medium term, the adversary might offer the nuisance of isolated bombing raids, submarine operations off the coast, or hit-and-run surface attacks, but these could not con-quer. And the vast logistical complexity of invading America even after a success-ful landing made it even more forbidding.[67] He criticized Roosevelt's dystopian view of offensive air power as one-dimensional, agreeing with army assessments that the development of modern planes increased rather than decreased American security and made the continent impregnable to seaborne invasion.[68] His wartime fear was that America would fall into an extreme state afterwards, either becoming a garrison state inhospitable to liberty, or becoming complacently utopian and failing to make preparations to deflect the fast, long-range attacks of tomorrow.

Baldwin's views would change only decades later. Vietnam and the nuclear missile age led him later to embrace both Roosevelt's vision of a technologically shrunken globe and a fear that would mark Cold War strategic debate, that of falling dominoes and threatened credibility as a postgeographical notion of American security. Baldwin's sensitivity to the offense-defense balance meant that he left open the possibility that antiballistic missile technology, lasers, or submarine detection might give the edge back to defense once more.[69]

Yale geographer Nicholas Spykman wrote one of the first in-depth studies of the spatial dynamics of American security, conceiving distance not as space between points, but as an interaction of space, technology, and the balance of forces. He believed Washington should intervene in the world war to prevent an economic strangulation. At the same time, he doubted claims that the Axis juggernaut could roll on from Europe via West Africa to Washington. Spykman recognized that America's hemispheric defenses presented great obstacles to transoceanic aggression. Land-based aircraft, naval defense, as well as interior communication lines made conquest of the American continent harder. The refuelling and logistical needs of mechanized armies created added problems for long-range attack. Even if aggressors somehow seized staging posts in South America without being destroyed by American air and naval power, it was not obvious how easily mechanized forces could strike through the buffer of the Amazonian rainforest. Provided states equip themselves with the ability to guard space, and especially in relation to America's security from East Asian adversaries, "distance is protection in all forms of warfare, even the most modern."[70] Spykman's fears related more to strategically vital raw materials and America's economic survival, rather than a military clash of continents.[71] He argued that America should focus its extraregional behavior on the vital "rimlands" of Europe and Asia, radiating its power inland to protect the peripheral approaches to America's position, and to shape the balance of forces abroad.[72] Spykman advocated not global American dominion, but a favorable balance of power pursued through a conscious "balancing" role that ensured neither Western Europe nor East Asia were dominated by a hostile state or coalition. Thus he advocated a "forward defense" and, presciently, a protective policy toward a defeated Japan. Spykman formulated an American role between hemispheric defense and global hegemony. His blueprint anticipated the doctrine of anti-Soviet containment as later conceived by the diplomat George Kennan, who looked to an eventual polycentric rather than unipolar world.

Spykman and Baldwin supported intervention while resisting inflated claims that the Axis aggressors posed a clear and present danger. Walter Lippmann offered a different warning against overstretch. Less mindful of the nature of weapon systems and the demands that cross-ocean invasion would make on invading forces, Lippmann strongly supported the argument that a victorious Axis could directly threaten the United States militarily. For his role in the wartime debate, Lippmann is remembered for popularizing the view that American security "depended upon the balance of forces outside the Western Hemisphere," a theme that reflected his enduring fear of the growth of German naval power and the dangers it entailed.[73] But Lippmann warned against other kinds of self-inflicted wounds.

Lippmann feared that America would win the war but lose the peace. In failing to balance its power and commitments, it would be newly endangered abroad and divided at home. The pathology of overstretch and withdrawal was a cycle in American history.[74] A former Wilsonian who had broken ranks with that tradition, for him, America's prewar failure had not been isolationism but insolvency, the failure to align power and interests with a surplus of power in reserve. Isolationism is a tradition that seeks security through isolation and detachment from foreign commitments.[75] By contrast, insolvency sprang from a failure to retain coherence between the nation's power and its political interests.[76] Hence he stressed "it is just as important to define the limit beyond which we will not intervene as it is to convince our people that we cannot find security in an isolationist policy."[77]

In attempting to circumscribe America's war aims, Lippmann focused on maritime peripheries, following not the tradition of Halford Mackinder and its emphasis on control of the Eurasian heartland, but the navalist Alfred Thayer Mahan in his view of the oceans as a commercial conveyer belt and as a highway that could propel aggressors to America's vulnerable ocean flanks. Lippmann was drawn to seapower and the coastal centers of industrial-military strength. American security interests extended to the coastlines of the Atlantic basin and the Pacific islands, which were also the outer limits of its domain.[78] Before the war, America had courted insolvency by acquiring far-flung interests, a large share of the earth's land surface, outweighing its power to protect them. In the Western Pacific after the Spanish-American War, it acquired commitments that it neither liquidated nor secured. It had conceded Japanese naval superiority in Asian waters and refused to place adequate defensive forces in the Philippines.[79] Now, by reaching outside its hemisphere, America in its newfound crusade might be on course for a fatal collision with the Soviet Union. No longer would American-Russian relations be steered by "the historic fact that each is for the other a potential friend in the rear of its potential enemies." America's widening frontier, enfolding the German, Japanese, and British "buffer zones," would collide with the widening

Soviet perimeter. Once again, unless statesmen could "with cold calculation organize and regulate the politics of power," they risked "a cycle of disastrous wars followed by peace settlements which breed more wars."[80] As he warned of postwar tragedy in world politics in his book *U.S. War Aims* of July 1944, the Allies had won major victories at Midway, El Alamein, Guadalcanal, Tripoli, and Tunisia, the German Sixth Army had been destroyed at Stalingrad, and the Allies had prevailed in the Battle of the Atlantic. Victory was merely a fleeting political opportunity. After victory, America should avoid the twin impulses of isolation and empire, and instead stick to territorialized goals, which should include a negotiated distance from the Soviet Union with whom it would have to live. Lippmann would advocate bilateral withdrawal from Germany, and agreed Soviet and American spheres of influence with buffers between them as a concrete measure.

The realists of mid-century did not conceive of space as a purely physical thing. For geography to yield security gains, it would have to be harnessed by a prudent foreign policy. States had to distance themselves. Foreign policy, not the oceans, was the true "shield" of the republic. In his critique of the false promise of "free security" guaranteed by oceans in themselves, he argued for a geographically defined defensive perimeter protected by favorable power balances, coalition diplomacy, and naval strength.[81] Nature would not guarantee insulation. But as the next pivotal crisis showed, the argument for territorially limiting the national interest was getting harder to make.

1950: The Turbulent Frontier

As it emerged from world war, America found itself in a novel position with no obvious precedents to guide it. Americans had not known such levels of relative international power, had not co-dominated a bipolar world with an ideologically hostile superpower rival, and had not received so many requests for help. After an internal debate, the US security elite decided not only to maintain the extended defensive perimeter it created in the war, but to extend it. In pinning down a date where this decisively happened, a good candidate is 1950. This year saw a renewed embrace of globalism when America might have taken different routes. It was the year when a preexisting strategic doctrine of anti-Soviet "containment" transformed strategic debate for decades. This section examines the internal debate within the new machinery set up to advise the government on foreign affairs, the Policy Planning Staff (PPS) of the State Department, and the wider struggle around its signature Cold War document of April 1950, NSC 68, "United States Objectives and Programs for National Security."[82]

In the terms outlined by the diplomat George Kennan in 1946–47, America and its allies would keep the Soviet bear in a cage.[83] The adversary was ultimately self-destructive and while contained would eventually collapse, mellow out, or change within. America could bound the threat and curtail its ability to operate, wait patiently for it to wither into an irrelevance or nuisance, without exhausting or overextending itself. Stalin's Soviet Union was aggressive, neurotic, and expanding, but also strongly motivated for survival, and could be blocked and curbed if the United States presented it with forbidding situations. Sensitive to the variation in importance of different regions, Kennan argued America should focus on denying Soviets the crucial military-industrial centers of Japan, the Rhine Valley, the United Kingdom, and Western Europe.[84] The concept of containment was a protean one capable of different interpretations. It took the Korean War and the fears it aroused to motivate Washington to develop containment into a blueprint for strategic commitments of worldwide breadth, and for the doctrine to grow out of all recognition.

US diplomatic history between 1945 and 1950 was fluid. There were competing pressures on American resources and conflicting conceptions of its role in the world.[85] America had widened its strategic horizons as its power grew. This was a utopian moment fertile for ideas about reordering the world. Yet this confident new colossus might have come home. Even during the war, presidents Roosevelt and Truman had been sensitive about the public's willingness to accept the blood price of intervention, and looked to limit American casualties. Roosevelt assured Stalin at the Tehran conference in late 1943 that US troops would be home two years after the end of the war.[86] His alliance bargaining recognized the reality of Stalin's orbit in Eastern Europe, made a fait accompli by the Red Army's seizure of eastern European states. The hesitancy of the new president, Harry Truman, made the picture more uncertain. In the first years of peace, Washington came under domestic pressure to pull back or limit its commitments and hold down defense expenditure. Anticommunists urging the defeat of the red menace were more domestically oriented. In the November 1946 congressional elections, Republicans pledged to lower taxes, cut deficits, and reduce inflation, demanding a strong perimeter strategy before denying Truman the resources to support it. Within government, Secretary of Defense Louis Johnson argued for an austerity drive on defense budgets. Alternatives to a strategy of containing the Soviet Union were entertained, such as continuing the wartime alliance, accommodating to some extent Soviet demands, and collective arms control or even the sharing of nuclear secrets. Secretary of War Henry Stimson in April 1945 argued that the United States should recognize the legitimacy of Soviet security goals and accept Soviet hegemony in Eastern Europe, as "our respective orbits do not clash geographically."[87] There was a strain of more classical, balance-of-power and spheres-of-influence opinion.[88]

American conceptions of the Soviet Union's nature as a diplomatic state split into what Daniel Yergin calls two "axioms." The Yalta axiom regarded Stalin's regime as a traditional great power with legitimate interests trying to secure itself within the international system. In this view, Stalin was a brutal totalitarian at home and in his near abroad, but was a cold and calculating czar in his international dealings. The Riga axiom, conversely, linked the regime's domestic practices with its external statecraft. It regarded the Soviet Union as an ideological monstrosity, a revolutionary revisionist state "powered by a messianic drive for world mastery" with whom accommodation was impossible.[89] Within a few years of the defeat of the Axis, the United States would regard the USSR not as a partner but an opponent. The case for containing this rival defeated the alternatives of conciliation and collaboration.

But the antagonism between the two superpowers took time to harden. The globalism enunciated during the war might have slackened. And before 1950, an alternative and more limited version of containment grew. What changed and why?

It would be tempting to pinpoint the decisive shift to President Truman's "Recommendations on Greece and Turkey" on March 12, 1947, what became known as the "Truman Doctrine," made as Truman drummed up support for embattled anticommunist governments in Greece and Turkey.[90] The doctrine pledged American help to any community resisting communist aggression, seemingly oblivious to limits. It built upon the logic of the memorandum of Clark Clifford endorsed by Truman in September 1946, urging US support for "all democratic countries any way menaced or endangered by the USSR."[91] It reflected fear of a vacuum opening around an aggressive Soviet Union. Britain's request in the spring of 1947 that America take over responsibility for protecting Turkey and Greece from communist subversion suggested that Roosevelt's vision for a postwar order jointly protected by the four policemen was not viable. The Truman Doctrine made in response turned "obligations to Greece and Turkey into what appeared to be a world-wide commitment to resist Soviet expansionism wherever it appeared."[92] One of the architects of postwar strategy, Paul Nitze, identified the year of the Marshall Plan, the Truman Doctrine, and the National Defense Act as pivotal.[93] As Secretary of State James F. Byrnes claimed in late 1946, America's domain had enlarged from the Monroe territories to the Eastern Mediterranean, as "Greece and Turkey are our outposts."[94]

The Truman Doctrine with its ambitions was an important stepping stone conceptually. Kennan warned that it could be read as a "blank check" and advised the government to clarify that they were aiding Greece and Turkey because they met criteria of severity and cost-effectiveness, and that aid was informed by the needs of "political economy" where goals were related to the expenditure of effort.[95] By ignoring territorial limits, the Truman Doctrine seemed to subvert the principles of containment intended by its intellectual father. Dismayed by the unbounded character of the doctrine, Kennan regretted that his version of anti-Soviet containment that he had argued for in 1946–47—nonuniversal, pragmatic, selective, primarily economic and civic, a restrained curtailment of Soviet expansion—was ambiguous and lent itself to misinterpretation. In the hands of mandarins, it became militarized, universal, and crusading.[96] The doctrine also provoked Lippmann's more public critique of Washington's pathologies. As Lippmann argued, globalism both literally and metaphorically denied a "middle ground." It imposed a reductionist logic whereby the strategic choice is limited to a false binary of parochial isolation versus enlightened internationalism, without the more measured dialectic of ends and means. As antagonism hardened with Moscow, eleven months after the Truman Doctrine was proclaimed, Lippmann grieved that a reductionism overshadowed American debate, imposing false choices between "isolation or globalism":

> There is no place in this ideological pattern of the world for adoption of limited ends or limited means, for the use of checks and balances among contending forces, for the demarcation of spheres of influence and of power and of interest, for accommodation and compromise and adjustment, for the stabilization of the status quo, for the restoration of an equilibrium. Yet this is the field of an efficient diplomacy.[97]

Demarcation and adjustment—these implied a territorial element, a mutual negotiation of space. Lippmann matched Hans Morgenthau's critique of the crusading impulse in the "new" American diplomacy.[98]

Kennan warned and Lippmann lamented, but the containment strategy that seemed universal in theory remained restricted in practice. The North Atlantic Treaty Organization was initially mainly a symbolic institution designed to reassure Europeans not to appease the Soviet Union and to resist communism at home. There were not yet large American forces in Europe, and West German rearmament was not on the table. Defense budgets were still relatively low compared to the soaring levels they reached later. While the Truman Doctrine seemed without limit, there was still a preference for ranking interests along the terms that diplomat George Kennan advocated. Against divided opinion, the Truman administration under fiscal pressure decided not to intervene to oppose the Chinese communist revolution of 1948. Not only was Washington reluctant to raise the costs it was willing to pay to meet its ambitious rhetoric. It had not yet embraced the most radical version of globalism, the notion that the world was "so interconnected" that communist gains in one area would have reverberations everywhere. "Strongpointers" still carried the fight to "perimeter" strategists.[99] Advocates of a strongpoint strategy, such as Secretary of State George C. Marshall and Kennan, argued that limited means should dictate the adoption of limited ends in proportion, and that America should focus its strategy around strongpoints.

Perimeter strategists such as Paul Nitze and the "China Lobby" pressed for Washington to rank Asia strategically equal with Europe, arguing that national security was indivisible, that ends should determine means, and that the United States should erect and defend a perimeter around the Soviet Union. "Domino" thinking had not yet conquered the classical geopolitical distinction between the vital and the peripheral.

To be sure, successive crises before 1950 increased the perception of threat. The communist coup in Czechoslovakia in February 1948, the Berlin Blockade of 1948–49, and the Chinese revolution convinced American policymakers that Stalin would not confine his brutal authoritarianism to his own borders, and that Stalinism was an epidemic spreading into Asia. There was fear of communist parties coming to power through the will of impoverished working classes. (Indeed, mass susceptibility to the appeal of Marxism-Leninism in Western and Southern European democracies, not direct Soviet military challenge, was Kennan's deepest fear.) If that wasn't enough, Stalin's first nuclear test in August 1949 indicated that America's trump card, its nuclear monopoly, was a wasting asset.[100] It was this shock that galvanized Truman to ask for a comprehensive strategic review.

But the Korean War is the best candidate for the shock that drove the United States back to globalism.[101] Just as Truman's review was under way, the Korean War (1950–53) erupted with two shocks. First, North Korean forces smashed across the dividing thirty-eighth parallel line in June, overcame the South's forces, and moved through Seoul, almost capturing the whole peninsula. The second shock was China's intervention in November 1950, which came after the seemingly triumphant United States–led UN forces had hurled back the invaders and then did some invading of their own, crossing the partition line despite unheeded warnings of a Chinese counterstroke. Within months, after UN forces marched toward China's borders, were driven back once more. The Korean War threw into a sharp relief the problem of how to define America's true frontiers in a fluid period, and the tension between territorial and psychological/ideological conceptions of containment.

Americans might once have seen this peninsula as inconsequential territory. Before 1950, security elites worked hard to define their perimeter, partly to balance it with limited resources. In East Asia, the question had been the extent of proper commitment beyond Japan, its protectorate and the cornerstone of America's role as guarantor of the peace in the region. The Joint Chiefs of Staff initially planned on withdrawing from Korea on the assumption that it would be an expendable front within a more general war. Their study in 1947 judged that Korea had "little strategic interest" from the "standpoint of military security" in maintaining bases and troops there.[102] But the accumulation of fears since then created a climate in which they were predisposed to link this regional clash with a general threat. The crisis on that peninsula globalized and militarized the idea of containment.

It moved Washington to match the rhetoric of 1946–47 with dollars and concrete commitments, to raise means to meet ends.

In this context National Security Council (NSC) 68 was produced. By the end of 1950, Truman approved NSC 68 as a statement of policy to be followed and proclaimed a national emergency.[103] NSC 68 identified a worldwide Soviet design that must be thwarted. It marked the consolidation of an orthodoxy, the translation of that orthodoxy into a vast material commitment, and the marginalization of alternatives. The crisis made preexisting arguments for "ramping up" the norm, while persuading others of globalism's tenets. Tying US security interests to the peninsula and inserting ground troops to recapture it marked a crescendo of the expansion of American security interests that had begun in 1941. Not only did the document sound an alarm about the Soviet threat. It also embodied the theory of a "small world," linking it to the need for American rearmament and world hegemony. Not a balance but a preponderance of power was needed. The root problem was not empowered Bolshevism, but a condition of disorder: "In a shrinking world, which now faces the threat of atomic warfare, it is not an adequate objective merely to seek to check the Kremlin design, for the absence of order among nations is becoming less and less tolerable. This fact imposes on us, in our own interests, the responsibility of world leadership."[104] That disorder was born of the profound change in the distribution of power, which had moved away from the collapse of European empires and toward the two superpowers, the radical nature of the Soviet Union, and the coming of "increasingly terrifying weapons of mass destruction." A reversal anywhere was intolerable.[105] In this nuclear competition, as well as the danger of a surprise attack launched by Moscow, was the temptation to engage in piecemeal aggression with the confidence that America dare not respond until directly attacked. This posed the risk of America underpreparing, and worse, its allies losing their determination. To meet the peril of a "shrinking world of polarized power," NSC 68 recommended a robust, militarized, and global containment strategy.

NSC 68 was not as simplistic a document as critics sometimes allege.[106] It acknowledged the problems of its own strategy. By strengthening itself, its architects recognized, the United States might strain public support or invite the Soviets to risk a general war. But, it reasoned, the risks of underpreparation and inaction were worse. It was driven partly by a reasonable anxiety about America's overreliance on nuclear weapons and its lack of other options in a crisis after its underinvestment in conventional military forces. Given that America had struggled to hold back the initial invasion in Korea even when committing virtually all of its combat-ready troops as well as a large share of its air force and navy, the document reflected fears about America's capacity to sustain a wider strategy of containment even if its answer was to increase costs rather than scale back commitments.

It came after a period when policymakers can be forgiven for their alarm at some of Stalin's behavior and inflammatory rhetoric. It was not absurd to fear that the Korean invasion was part of a Moscow-backed design. Policymakers did not have access to the archives that demonstrate how distantly and cautiously Stalin had preapproved the assault and limited his liability if things went wrong.[107] Truman was responding not only to voices of restraint, but was resisting those who urged a more radical strategy of rollback and preventive war. Even critics had been ambivalent about where precisely America should draw its lines.[108]

For all this, NSC 68 promoted a globalist outlook that lowered sensitivity to costs and limits. It was the triumph of perimeter over strongpoint strategists. It stressed will and assumed the country's great latent capacity. It even omitted specific financial estimates, one reason Truman's response was initially cautious. It promoted an undifferentiated view of America's security interests as a vast encircling perimeter. It unmoored America's strategic vision from the geographically based discipline of weighing and ranking interests. It advanced a "symmetrical" form of containment in which Washington was bound to respond to any communist thrusts and regarded the world as a linked battlespace. By framing American strategy around the pursuit of the perception of strength, for audiences at home and abroad, it opened the way to overstretch. And its apocalyptic tone made prudential compromise and self-restraint harder to achieve. This conditioned Cold War strategy to come. It was different from Kennan's more indirect definition of the threat as a Soviet political economy that could win over desperate masses at the ballot box, his more differentiated emphasis on areas of greater and lesser importance, and his more restrained strategy for dealing with it. If Kennan conceived containment ultimately as a form of self-restraint, of a contraction of American ambitions and creating power balances to avoid overextension, NSC 68 did the reverse.[109] The defense budget almost quadrupled in 1950 from $13 billion to $48 billion.

The Korean War set a pattern of fear leading to overconfidence, or panic followed by hubris. In mid-September 1950, Gen. Douglas MacArthur's inspired gamble, the Inchon landing into the rear of the advancing North Korean army, seemingly turned the tide. It generated a momentum that widened America's war aims and touched off a debate about whether to keep going. In NSC 81-1, Truman authorized General MacArthur to go beyond the defense of the status quo aim of preserving South Korea to reunify the peninsula. This placed the United States–led United Nations on a collision course with China. United Nations forces neared the Yalu River that divides North Korea from China and presented Mao Zedong with the prospect of an ideologically hostile foreign force poised at the border. MacArthur dismissed intelligence reports warning that this move would widen the war and bring in Mao's forces, massing at the border. Kennan's advice that

Truman publicly commit not to cross the thirty-eighth parallel also met with charges of appeasement. This hubris mounted precisely at the time when the terrain of northern Korea in the freezing winter stretched America's forces. Thanks to the optimistic assumptions of X Corps headquarters, the First Marine Division found itself exposed on one flank 70 miles from the Eighth Army and its northern and southernmost battalions separated by 170 miles and far from its supply base. For them this was not a triumphant advance but a dangerous journey into "Indian Country" that became more rugged and expansive as it went on.[110] As cold warriors celebrated triumph, US troops were exposed in long, vulnerable supply lines, extreme weather, and an enemy fighting from its home base. China invaded and hurled US forces into retreat. MacArthur and his supporters urged a more aggressive course still, arguing that America carry the fight into China by blockading ports, bombing installations, and even sponsoring an invasion by Chinese nationalists from Taiwan.

MacArthur derailed the Truman administration's effort to negotiate a ceasefire with China once the once Eighth Army had retaken Seoul on March 15 and approached the thirty-eighth parallel, threatening China that if it did not abandon Korea, the United States would assault its homeland. MacArthur's arguments for ending the war by escalating it, for abandoning the territorial limit of the thirty-eighth parallel, exhibited a mixture of swagger and alarm. In the House of Representatives on April 5, Republican leader Congressman Joseph Martin (MA) quoted MacArthur's letter that "here in Asia is where the Communist conspirators have elected to make their play for global conquest . . . if we lose the war to communism in Asia, the fall of Europe is inevitable."[111] The same China that he once dismissed in a meeting with Truman at Wake Island in October 1950 as weak, lacking air power, and unlikely to intervene, that was a childlike state that could be cowed into submission, he now presented as a fanatical aggressor poised to overrun Asia and inspire a communist takeover of Europe.[112]

The push to widen the war reflected globalism's stress on both America's fragility and power. America's growing strength enabled its officials to enlarge the scope of US vulnerabilities. The Truman administration was once preoccupied with budgetary limits and a fear of economic fragility that encouraged a reluctance to recognize new threats where resistance seemed unaffordable. But at the close of the 1940s, a new economic orthodoxy within government rose that would dovetail with Paul Nitze's view that the crisis was one of limited political will rather than limited means. Not only could the economy take more deficit spending and rearmament, but these were positive stimuli to growth. Empowered by this sense of mounting material strength, policymakers could entertain visions of the enemy as a superthreat, often a monolithic one, hardly constrained by geography, emerging from a chaos that America must resist.[113] By adopting a heightened belief in the state's power to eliminate threats quickly and decisively, they could take on board a more ambitious perception of what the threat was. Capabilities—or perceived ones—informed how they defined their interests.

NSC 68 marked the deterritorialization of the reigning American concept of national security. Secretary of State Dean Acheson in his infamous Press Club Speech on January 12, 1950, had tried to draw the line of America's sphere. Defining America's Far Eastern "defensive perimeter" from the Aleutian Islands to Japan, then on to Okinawa and the Philippine Islands, he stated that South Korea's defense was foremost up to the people and the UN. This merely repeated the position of the Joint Chiefs of Staff at the end of 1949 and General MacArthur's speech of March 1, 1949.[114] But drawing lines while mobilizing public opinion around universal claims was a difficult kind of political gymnastics. The search to define limits created a problem for the Truman administration, the gaps between words and deeds. Indeed, the rhetoric of globalism held a power of its own. It entrapped those who used it into making commitments that they had not originally intended, to project toughness at home and internationally. Acheson warned the Senate Foreign Relations Committee in July 1950 that "this is a situation where it is very important not to have our words run ahead of what we do."[115] The president had already rhetorically sold the population and Congress on an unbounded armed struggle, setting a standard by which he was harshly judged. The Chinese revolution in 1948 and the first detonation of the Soviet atomic bomb in 1949 led to accusations of weakness and betrayal. The administration became the victim of its earlier rhetoric, trapped "in the strategic images that it had earlier propagated amongst the public to gain support for its policies."[116] Acheson would admit that one motive for Korea was to prove a beleaguered president's anticommunist credentials, to outflank domestic critics and neutralize the charge of being "soft" on communism. Defining and sustaining clear and limited war aims was difficult given the competing demands of alliance bargaining, the pulse of the battlefield, the drive to escalate from General MacArthur, and presidential rhetoric that made compromise hard to accept.[117] It made possible the ascent of Sen. Joseph McCarthy's demagoguery that poisoned foreign policy debate. Lippmann's prophecy was realized, as strategic failure and domestic rancor mutually fed one another. The wages of this were the expansion of the war beyond the thirty-eighth parallel and conflict with China, "one of the greatest mistakes in our history."[118]

For realist critics, mass politics in an urban, industrial age was distasteful. In their lamentations, there was more than a whiff of ahistorical nostalgia for a time when elite guardians made strategy in colder blood.[119] But they were surely right to worry about the derangement of strategy during the Korean War by the demagoguery of American democracy. This problem inspired Hans Morgenthau's first major work on the concept of the national interest. In his critique of the Truman doctrine and NSC-68, he charged that Truman had fallen prey to a pathology in American democracy, the urge to present otherwise sound policies (aid to "key regions" such as Greece and Turkey to shore up the European balance of power) in extravagantly idealist language, in turn leaving statecraft in disarray. The articulated doctrine disfigured the policy substance. Applied consistently, the Truman doctrine failed to distinguish between what was desirable and what was essential, making democracy promotion as important in Korea as in France, failing to explain why Panama mattered more than Poland. As a statement designed for domestic consumption, the doctrine was a poor guide to political action.[120] This mattered because of the breadth of the territory involved. A blanket commitment to democracy promotion as the solution to an inflated problem would leave forces stretched thin across a vast perimeter. Used as a tool for mobilizing public support, globalism set an agenda that was hard to escape:

> You have falsified the real issue between the United States and the Soviet Union into a holy crusade to stamp out Bolshevism everywhere on earth, for this seemed a good way of arousing the public: now you must act as though you meant it. You have presented the Chinese communists as the enemies of mankind, in order to appease the China lobby: now you must act as though you meant it. You have told the people that American power has no limits, for flattery of the people is "good politics": now you must act as though you meant it.[121]

This warning was prescient. Lobbies would exploit the fear of globalized insecurity to create pressure for intervention. This would persist as a problem. Morgenthau reformulated the problem as one of containing Russian imperialism. The Soviet Union posed a challenge that needed more than aid and radio broadcasts to counter. But it was not so limitless as to warrant preventive war or universal commitments. The alternative was preparing for the worst militarily along with an accommodating diplomacy. America would reach that point later, but only after multiple crises, standoffs, and near misses.

Like other skeptics, Hanson Baldwin was concerned for limits. Baldwin regarded Korea as a "sideshow" from the main effort, the need to focus on Western Europe plus the revival and mobilization of European and Japanese manpower. He was especially fearful of the domestic political consequences of the extension of the Cold War into Asia. To end the war in Korea, paradoxically, might require drastic action. The globalization of the Cold War and the pursuit of "absolute security" would turn America into a garrison state, even an insolvent one, depleting its capacity to wage the struggle in the "long pull."[122] He concluded that the war had to be ended through escalation, and that this might mean the bombing of enemy positions in Manchuria and the blockade of the Chinese coast. But preventative war or "rollback" could radicalize Western Europe and Eastern Asia and lose the values America defended. Isolation was imprudent, given the "live" frontiers on the sea, in the air, and on land. Baldwin was losing faith in his wartime belief in America's capacity to defend itself. He warned of "space-devouring, ocean-spanning aircraft and missiles and submarines that can cross the oceans submerged and launch atomic-headed missiles against our coastal cities."[123] Yet like Kennan, he argued that geography still defined American interests and those that counted as vital.[124] The only responsible course was to help create a balance of power and fill opening vacuums, while shifting burdens to allies including the arming of South Korea's forces combined with American withdrawal, and German rearmament and unification.

Another point of division between dissenters and NSC 68 was over the question of geopolitical context. Kennan and Lippmann agreed that the tragedy of the postwar antagonism had geopolitical roots, namely the new proximity of two powers that had historically been separated and buffered by other powerful states, that war "eliminated this separation and placed their respective military forces in close proximity to each other in the center of Europe and the northern Pacific."[125] This could only be addressed by renegotiating the space between them. But this was at odds with the prevailing consensus in Washington. NSC 68 stripped the Soviet Union of influences in space and time except the ideological-cultural ones Marxism-Leninism and Russian great-power mentality. It was driven by a desire for world domination. Its behavior owed little to the insecurity created by the new structure of vulnerable frontiers, the devastation of the struggle against Operation Barbarossa (1941–45), and postwar Western encirclement. Kennan saw the Soviet Union and identified an adversary that was vulnerable to its own internal contradictions, and that could be countered selectively. But at the hands of the PPS, the adversary was a superthreat in a zero-sum global battlespace whose every move must be resisted.

NSC 68 also marked the rise of monolithic thinking, recasting communism as a unified whole. Policymakers had earlier divided on whether to see the communist world as one of disparate states that could be split and divided against one another (such as Tito's Yugoslavia or later, Mao's China). The Korean War strengthened the monolithic view.[126] It was, for Paul Nitze, a single game of chess. Moscow might "move some pawn, disclosing an interlocking threat of such magnitude that we would only retreat and exchange pieces on a wholly unfavorable basis."[127] It was through the Korean War that American cold warriors redefined and Asianized visions of the enemy, morphing from Soviet communism to a world threat mobilized in a Sino-Soviet bloc.[128] Not only did this close off potential opportunities for splitting enemies. It also added to anticommunist fear the terror of a mobile, ceaseless Asian horde unconstrained by geography. Descriptions of the Chinese–North Korean forces as reborn medieval Mongols suggested an opponent whose aggression was limitless against which the barriers of US air and naval power counted for little.

Korea introduced an important expression into the American lexicon, the "falling domino" principle and the fear of globalized insecurity. Defeat or setback in any clash would erode credibility everywhere and lead to cumulative insecurity. As Korea escalated, it was not just a matter of securing advance bases as buffers and staging posts from which to deter or intercept attacks on themselves or their allies, or as a platform to launch their own. Securing America became reputational as well as territorial, a matter of shoring up credibility worldwide by demonstrating political will to resist communist expansion wherever it probed. Articulated most famously by President Dwight Eisenhower in April 1954, warning of the ripples that the fall of Indochina would cause, its roots lie with Truman, who announced in a radio speech that "if aggression were allowed to succeed in Korea, it would be an open invitation to new acts of aggression elsewhere."[129]

Consider the contrast with World War II. The war had given rise to threat perceptions that were primarily material, involving the balance of combat capabilities, industrial power, and territory. To match the elevated war aims of the United Nations, Washington widened the physical geography of America's domain and identified the outposts of American security ever further away from home. But as George Marshall told the House Committee on International Relations in 1948, the strategy of wartime zeroed in on the problem of resource limits, which required America to define a hierarchy of interests and theaters.[130] In the Cold War, however, policymakers judged that psychological impression was now a measure of security.

The logical consequence of that fear was the belief that America must fight wars even in areas that might otherwise be inconsequential for the sake of its reputation as a security guarantor for its friends and an adversary for its enemies. "Dominoes" did not just reflect a belief in the fall of contiguous regimes or countries to communism. It also referred to the broader collapse of confidence that failure could trigger, such as the fear that withdrawal in Vietnam could induce allies such as West Germany and Japan to appease the Soviet Union.[131] Reversal in a remote region could generate a cumulative threat. Credibility as an indivisible commodity became Washington's concern for much of the Cold War. As Dean Rusk later warned, America "can be secure only to the extent that our total environment is secure." If the world was a single theater watched by an audience that judges American resolve from every one of its confrontations, every crisis became a moral test rather than a discrete problem. Though flawed, it was believed. If interests were on the line everywhere, the logic pointed to endless war. Doctrinally America was on the road to embroilments in Central America, the Middle East, and most consequentially of all, Vietnam.

The clash in Korea may have ended in stalemate. But it represented a decisive victory for globalism and its attendant framework for decisions in Washington: of perimeter defense, the domino principle, preponderance rather than balance, and the vision of an essentially strong adversary. Post-Korea Cold War strategy did not always have the same intensity that informed NSC 68. But even in President Eisenhower's "new look" attempt to scale back costs, America's defense spending was exponentially greater than before the Korean War. The norm of American strategy was continuous intervention, a ratcheted-up global military presence, the overthrow of regimes abroad, and periodic arms races.

This did not end with the Cold War. The Soviet Union's sudden collapse did not trigger a major revision of America's grand strategy in its essentials, or the "global village" myth on which it rested.

2001: Under Open Skies

Between 1989 and 1991, America suffered a strategic shock that few had foreseen, the bloodless collapse of the Soviet Union. Within Washington, Cold War victory offered an opportunity to consider what should replace the master concept of "containment." Should America come home to benefit from its "peace dividend," maintain the status quo, or extend its hegemony?[132] As it turned out, the most striking feature of the interregnum between the end of the Cold War and the Global War on Terror is not change but continuity, the persistence of American grand strategy in its essentials despite the radically changed landscape. The disappearance of the Soviet Union did not prompt a fundamental revision of American statecraft by either the Bush I (1989–93) or Clinton administrations (1993–2000). Precisely because the view of an interdependent global village predated the Cold War, after the Soviet Union's fall America could remain committed to a grand strategy of primacy and the world of the "open door." The ambition to shape world order was not enemy-specific but grew out of an interaction between the growth of American power and an expansive view of America's security needs.

There were calls for major retrenchment, a new more modest grand strategy, and for America to come home. But proponents of American hegemony won the debate. The Pentagon's leaked Defense Planning Guidance document (1992) reaffirmed the globalist logic of US grand strategy after the Cold War.[133] It formulated America's role as the overseer and protector of regions that could become military-strategic rivals, identified an extensive set of commitments, from the Arabian Peninsula and Persian Gulf to South Africa. Its blunt wording caused offense, but its core policy prescriptions were followed in the decade to come.

There have been nontrivial differences between (and within) each administration on questions of tactics, techniques, and the role and legitimacy of international institutions and allies in pursuing this strategy, and the distribution of burdens and costs. A leaner hegemony with expanded alliances, economic growth, and minimal number of body bags was Clinton's evolving formula. While Clinton reduced the defense budget, administration officials rejected the case for retrenchment of grand strategic commitments, on the basis that new threats had "no borders."[134] When it identified threats, it was willing to coerce states challenging its concept of world order. Clinton threatened preventive war against North Korea, dispatched the Pacific Fleet to ward off China's muscle-flexing against Taiwan, bombed Serbia to coerce its regime to cease ethnic cleansing in the Balkans, bombed Iraq in the cause of nonproliferation, bombed the Sudan in the cause of counterterrorism, and applied "shock therapy" economic reforms to Russia and the former Soviet Union. Clinton privately dismissed grand strategy as an artificial retrospective label more used in memoirs and academia than in government.[135] For an apparent absence of grand strategy, his critics charged him with being vacuous.[136] But objectively he tailored and consolidated a strategy in which the United States secures itself by remaking the world in its own image, a pattern that links most of his moves abroad. If we think of grand strategy not necessarily as a conscious or programmatic plan but as a logic of how to relate the state's interests with its power, the Bush I and Clinton years should be seen not as a vacuum of random drift, but as the consolidation of assumptions about America's role in the post–Cold War era.

What were those principles? Euphemized often as "leadership," it was the pursuit of continuing primacy or hegemony. Through this strategy the United States fashioned itself as the guardian of world order through a global military presence in which it continues to garrison much of the world, a network of permanent alliances and client states, and a pervasive spying and surveillance system, all underwritten by the Bretton Woods financial order and the dollar as the world's reserve currency. This strategy aims well beyond overcoming adversaries. It seeks to secure America by spreading a democratic and market ideology that remakes the world in America's image. By becoming the anchor of world security, America attempted to forestall the reemergence of a multipolar world of competitive power politics. It looked to deter or overmatch enemies, reassure friends and potential rivals, and remain the sole benevolent superpower with its domestic liberalism secure in a liberal globe. This strategy has as its interlocking parts dissuasion (to prevent potential rivals from challenging); reassurance (to act as guarantor, underwriting the security of allies and partners to persuade them not to pursue military self-reliance that could create rival power centers); coercive nonproliferation (to prevent the spread of nuclear and WMD capability); integration, where the United States promoted its political model through democratization and its economic model, giving potential future peer competitors such as China an equity stake in the "Washington consensus" of market capitalism and free trade; and especially with the "Bush Doctrine," anticipatory war and muscular democracy promotion.

The next violent strategic shock that brought an opportunity for reappraisal was the terrorist attack of September 11, 2001. Some lesser assaults had anticipated this major assault on the homeland, such as the bombing of US embassies in Kenya and Tanzania, the strike on the USS *Cole*, and an earlier cruder attempt to blow up the World Trade Center in New York. But none alarmed Americans like the far bloodier and more spectacular 9/11 atrocity. In response to this shock and the first year of America's fightback, the United States reembraced globalism in the form of the Bush Doctrine. How it defined and proposed to defeat the terrorist threat will be considered in the next chapter. Here it is important that the latest shock was another occasion where the president and most of the political class reiterated the repertoire they had inherited. Enemies with global reach struck a sleeping America. To meet the threat, America must decisively eliminate both the assailants and the ideological forces that underpinned them, and reorder the world to do so. Remarkably, President George W. Bush had only recently been elected after campaigning on a platform of humility and skepticism about America's role as the world's policeman. He had shown no interest in the Middle East prior to 9/11, in democratization, or Islamist terrorist threats, and was hostile to nation-building projects. Yet after 9/11, as a way of comprehending and addressing the shock of hostility from outside, he embraced globalism with a vengeance.

President Bush wrote in his diary on the evening of 9/11 that "the Pearl Harbor of the twenty-first century took place today."[137] Pearl Harbor, like the attacks of 6/25 and 9/11, quickly became a "code" for several assumptions about how the conflict started and what it said about American insecurity.[138] And like 9/11, Pearl Harbor entered the collective consciousness as a lesson in the reality of constant peril and the penalties of naive isolation.[139] Enemies from afar could force a sleeping America into a fight. Commemorations of the event portrayed a passive America, naively inattentive to foreign affairs, being assaulted out of the blue by an aggressor, a shock that educated Americans and left their "geopolitical innocence in ruins."[140] As interpreted events, these surprise attacks teach Americans about the proximity of dangers and the lesson that predators must be fought because they are within range. As his subsequent doctrines and policies would show, this instinctive response referred not only to a shocking assault, but also to what it meant about America's vulnerability in the world and what it should do about it.

The Pearl Harbor code is bad history. All three attacks, in 1941, 1950, and 2001, originated not just in the ideological zealotry of the assailants, but came out of preexisting and growing conflicts. In all three, the United States was not minding its own business. As such, the code with its distorting portrait of diplomatic prehistory does a bad job of explaining how conflicts originate, with its clear divide between war and peace rather than a continuum of conflict. Contrary to myths that isolationism led to Pearl Harbor, America was not dormant before December 7, 1941. Washington was already in an escalating conflict with Japan over the question of China. From July 1941, its embargo on raw materials and oil, and asset freeze placed a stranglehold on Japan. This presented Tokyo with the choice between abdicating its imperial ambitions or challenging American power. America's war originated not primarily in a failure of appeasement in Europe, but in a failure of deterrence and coercion in the Pacific. American prewar diplomacy did not generate Japanese expansionism in continental Asia. But it did make possible America and Japan's clash in the Pacific. Likewise among European powers, America had been actively involved, from the Washington Naval Treaty to the Dawes and Young plan for German reparations. Far from standing remote from world politics, President Franklin Roosevelt well before the shooting war deliberately courted conflict with Germany through an undeclared war in the Atlantic. He duplicitously presented the "*Greer* incident" of September 1941—where a German submarine fired on a pursuing American destroyer—as the sign of imminent Nazi aggression against America, "a rattlesnake poised to strike," to justify rearmament and widening America's defense perimeter.[141] These moves may have been prudent. But importantly for the argument about whether the shrinking world would force war on America, Roosevelt's moves were part of an active, conscious diplomacy in which the president knowingly stepped into struggles thousands of miles away. America's increasing involvement in the war was a political choice, not a fate preordained by weapon systems in the hands of hostile states. The world had not mechanically globalized to threaten America.[142]

The continuity of this code can be seen in the comparison of Clinton's and Bush's *National Security Strategy*, of 1999 and 2002 respectively. Written in different circumstances, Bush's document is more forceful. But both embrace the same principles. These are American exceptionalism, democracy promotion to further US security interests, the importance and liberating force of American military power, anticipatory "preventive" war neutralizing threats before they get worse, the preference for coalitions of the willing rather than multilateral consensus, and a stress on the intersecting threats of rogue states, terrorism, and WMDs. Defenders of the Bush Doctrine make a similar point. The substance of the Bush Doctrine is historically unexceptional. It echoes principles articulated from Roosevelt and Truman to Reagan, "regime change and the spread of stable, liberal democracy to address the real root cause of aggression as the ultimate goal in the war on terror."[143] Drawing on this tradition, Bush offered a similar antidote to the threat of this new breed of catastrophic terrorism. The antidote was pacification through global liberal order underwritten by American power.

Just as it was central to President Clinton's "enlargement" project and the bombing campaign against Serbia in 1999, globalism lay at the core of the more aggressively unilateralist Bush Doctrine and its signature project, the war in Iraq. The logic of a war without borders in a "new condition" of globalization informed the *National Security Strategy* of 2002 and the Bush Doctrine of American primacy, anticipatory war, and democracy promotion.[144] That administration depicted today's threats as proximate and stateless and warned of the confluence of radical ideologies and dangerous technologies.[145] As Iraq imploded in communal bloodletting and American troops met guerrilla resistance, Bush asserted in his second inaugural address that the "survival of liberty in our land increasingly depends on the success of liberty in other lands."[146] This was merely the most absolute and strident version of a theme that his predecessors and his successor sounded. Neither have they rebutted the most grave policy implication of this world view, namely the need to anticipate and eliminate threats early and at long range (or "destroying the threat before it reaches our borders").[147]

Bush laid down his doctrine both in the *National Security Strategy* of 2002 and in a speech to the United States Military Academy at West Point on June 1, 2002.[148] After 9/11, Bush offered a strikingly imperial vision: "We will defend the peace by fighting terrorists and tyrants. We will preserve the peace by building good relations among the great powers. We will extend the peace by encouraging free and open societies on every continent." As the speech as a whole made clear, the "peace" should be seen not as a neutral condition of an absence of violence, or keeping things peaceful. The peace Bush outlined meant a liberal order where America maintained unchallengeable military strength, reserved the right for preemptive war against materializing threats, and actively spread American institutions abroad. Peace in this design would be guaranteed by arms, under a Pax Americana where America claims a right to supremacy that other nations should follow.[149] It refers not to a minimal peace as the absence of war, but an ultimate peace created by the spread of democracy. In 2002, it referred to a "democratic peace," drawn from a contested theory in political science that modern liberal democracies rarely clash because of their shared, peace-producing values. This the Bush administration explicitly adopted as one rationale for the Global War on Terror. In this logic, peace would come only once America had released consensual, constitutional government into the world after toppling terrorists and tyrants—through war if necessary. Such an order until its completion offered not peace but a sword.

The Bush Doctrine was the product of both a shock and the president's changing opinion of security. Neoconservative intellectuals—as well as liberal hawks—within and outside the administration prepared the ground. The neoconservatives are sometimes portrayed as aberrations. But they have deep ideological roots in traditions of crusading liberalism and form the most muscular wing of the Wilsonian tradition. "Neocons" look to rescue the United States from entropy at home and danger abroad through a return to the politics of heroic greatness.[150] Concerns for stability or the status quo, they charged, are for "tired old Europeans and nervous Asians." America as the "most revolutionary force on earth" needed a "suitably glorious objective."[151] Like their liberal cousins, they argue that US security depends on idealistic internationalism backed by strength. They reject alternatives to hegemony, such as containment, power sharing, or accommodation of other powers. Their "primal scene" and code for political action are the failures of interwar appeasement and capitulation at Munich, the supreme emergency of Nazi Germany leading to Holocaust and catastrophe. Like their forebear Leo Strauss, a philosopher who fled Nazi Germany, they see the world "in terms of continual, potentially existential threats."[152] Unlike other Wilsonians, they see less value in legitimizing American hegemony through international institutions. They assume a preponderance of power and usually characterize failures as failures of will rather than capacity or competence. In the realm of foreign policy, theirs is a consciously revolutionary outlook. Embracing a doctrine of permanent revolution and seeing the military as America's most powerful revolutionary instrument, they are less the reactionaries than the Jacobins of our time.

Part of the neoconservative vision is a rejection of distance as a conditioning force on American statecraft. American statecraft allegedly should be based not on narrow material concepts of the national interest, but on America's historical mission to extend the ideology of America to the world. In seeking to remoralize America's conception of its interests, they cast geographically conscious realism as a legacy from Old Europe that foreign-born proponents of old diplomacy had foisted on the nation. They regard the likes of Lippmann, Spykman, Morgenthau, Kissinger, and even Kennan, a diplomat who spent much of his life abroad, as outsiders. They dismiss territorial conceptions of the national interest as "a grid of ground, sea lanes, industrial centers" and "strategic choke-points" as alien to American traditions.[153] They lament the moments where strategists felt bound by limits such as the restrictive Weinberger-Powell Doctrine on when to go to war. To legitimize their vision, Robert Kagan in particular interprets the founding fathers not as pragmatic, balance-of-power statesmen but as dangerous, hawkish idealists. In his words, America was born as a "Neocon nation."[154] While some argue that the world has changed so profoundly as to negate the traditional advantages of being an offshore power, Kagan argues that defining interests geographically has never been an authentically American instinct.

The rewriting of history to recast realism as wholly un-American is both suspect and ahistorical. Geographically based realism, or the geographical limitation of the national interest, is not alien to American traditions. An austere

balance-of-power politics was strong in the early republic.[155] Critics of
Morgenthau's plea for the sober analysis of the national interest with power at the
center accused him of offering an "American version of German Realpolitik."[156]
Yet he invoked American forerunners for his own cause from the country's first
decade, such as Thomas Jefferson on his evolving belief in the value of European
power balances, Alexander Hamilton for his realization of the importance of
power, and John Quincy Adams as the architect of the Monroe Doctrine, creating America's hemispheric dominance and distance from European squabbles.
The figures of an earlier generation, from Baldwin to Lippmann to Spykman to
Kennan to Morgenthau, were not bearing an unnatural strain of Old World power
politics. They revived in the twentieth century an instinct for power and its limits
that can be traced to the early republic.

This battle would be joined most intensely over the invasion of Iraq in March
2003. The Iraq War was the attempt to turn the Bush Doctrine into practice.
Launched primarily as a counterproliferation war, to disarm a rogue state, the
cause of that war became more ambitious over time, culminating in Bush's claim
that the war would spearhead his "forward strategy" of carrying out the democratic
liberation of the "Greater Middle East," reimagining the Arab-Islamic political
landscape as a pathological place it could transform at will, eradicating terrorism,
relying on authoritarian allies, and deepening its geopolitical penetration all at the
same time.[157] In a parallel way, debate about this war in 2002–3 restaged the clashes
of 1941 and 1950 between globalists and realist skeptics. Realist opponents of the
Iraq venture and of Bush's wider strategy drew on essentially the same critique as
their intellectual forerunners.[158] As they argued, to pursue universal democracy,
a worldwide democratic peace, or similar utopian projects was to court disaster
and invite blowback. To pursue unchallengeable hegemony was self-defeating.
Once more, both sides held different assumptions about the extent of American
power. Given early progress in the war in Afghanistan since the autumn of 2001,
Iraq hawks assumed America had the capacity to extend the Global War on Terror
to a new front. Realists, by contrast, argued that this was a dangerous diversion
from the struggle against Al Qaeda and might also bog down US forces against violent resistance and complex urban warfare. Where globalists saw a world-historical
opportunity in which America could apply its preponderance of power, realists saw
another climactic moment of triumphalism when calamity beckoned.

Conclusion

Looking back, how can we account for the ascendancy of globalism? The "pre-
global" conception of American security interests was not decisively overturned
until the middle of the twentieth century, in the period from 1941 to 1950. The
interlocking of shocks, growing power, the dynamics of empire, international

demand, and a well-organized lobby for activism persuaded makers of American strategy that they inhabited a dangerous, small world and that they could reshape it. This tradition teaches policymakers that America is a singular and therefore vulnerable superpower, that it can only be safe in an open-door world of absolute security, and that territoriality and space are less of a guide to America's security interests than more amorphous values and psychological perception.[159] Globalism became the dominant working theory of American statecraft.

At "hinge" moments, it took other forces to translate the theory into action. The impact of shocks is part of the story. On two of the three moments, a president had to be persuaded via a shocking event. Before Korea, an unsure Truman had been torn between the warring impulses of Cold War escalation and financial austerity. Similarly, before 9/11 the diplomatic novice Bush showed little sign of internationalist activism, and it took a major terrorist attack to give globalists a positive reception. In an environment of high-threat perception, extensive consultation of defense experts, and the memory of strategic shock at Pearl Harbor and then Korea, there formed an "internationalist" elite class. Disagreeing in some areas, they united around the proposition that in the smaller world, developments far away could vitally affect national security. Their outlook represented the mating of two forces: the combative world view of geopolitics, with its vocabulary of flanks, outposts, "shatter belts," and heartlands (which they divorced from a stress on limitation and constraint), with the heightened, moral, and idealistic terms of the Wilsonian tradition.[160] Globalism got a seat in a network of American institutions, think tanks, major foundations, and universities. Embedded in this way, it became a powerful world view to be deployed in debate and to justify behavior, from the strengthening of state power to military intervention to the enlargement of alliances.

And at each critical point, globalism was advanced by effective officials within government who outflanked opponents. The likes of Paul Nitze and Dick Cheney were able to impose their agenda within government and marginalize dissidents. In 1950 the State Department with its globalist agenda overshadowed Defense, as Nitze's PPS of the State Department sidelined the dissenting secretary of defense and co-opted the Pentagon into the writing of NSC 68. In 2001 and beyond, Donald Rumsfeld's Pentagon would outmaneuver Colin Powell's dissenting State Department.[161]

But the embrace of globalism was not preordained. It never held a monopoly over American diplomatic behavior. At crossroads moments, those arguing for the continuation or expansion of commitments had to fight for it before carrying the day. As the record shows, American security elites on several occasions contemplated a different course, when interludes of retrenchment and burden shifting could have set them on a different path. There have been moments when despite the pressure to escalate and expand from within and outside, presidents have opted to draw the line, restrain the projection of power before reaching the point of overstretch, and pull back. American governments have at times ranked and distinguished vital from peripheral interests, and sought great-power coexistence rather than unipolar dominance.

At each turn, a group of political realists has argued for the importance of distance both as a conditioning force and as a disciplining restraint on the extravagant designs of globalism. The likes of Lippmann, Kennan, Spykman, and Baldwin framed world politics as a tragedy about the limits of power rather than a morality play. Their critique of liberal idealism and its disregard for territoriality is not a relic of twentieth-century "great debates" about the nature and purpose of American power, but part of a clash between "shapers" and "restrainers" that continually returns to the surface. Their resistance to globalism has been mostly a losing struggle, but the argument has not ended.

Just as globalism was only one possible path then, it does not have to be permanent now. It is still open to scrutiny. As we will see, even on its own turf it fares badly under interrogation.

Notes

1. For a sophisticated alternative argument about the interaction of external pressures and domestic ideas, see Benjamin Miller, "Explaining Changes in U.S. Grand Strategy: 9/11, the Rise of Offensive Liberalism, and the War in Iraq," *Security Studies* 19:1 (2010): 26–65.
2. Robert Kagan, *Paradise and Power: America and Europe in the New World Order* (New York: Vintage, 2004), 41.
3. See further Paul Kennedy, *The Rise and Fall of Great Powers* (New York: Random House, 1989), 357–60.
4. I borrow the phrase "visionary world making" from Nicholas Kitchen, "Systemic Pressures and Domestic Ideas: A Neoclassical Realist Model of Grand Strategy Formation," *Review of International Studies* 36:1 (2010): 117–43, 141.
5. As Geir Lundestad argued, "Empire by Invitation? The United States and Western Europe 1945–1952," *Journal of Peace Research* 23:3 (1986): 263–77.
6. According to Stephen Ambrose's popular narrative account, the twin shocks of the Pearl Harbor attack and Nazi Germany's overthrow of the balance of power in Europe united government and defense intellectuals in their conversion to global security commitments far beyond the water's edge. Stephen Ambrose, *Rise to Globalism: American Foreign Policy since 1938* (London: Penguin, 1971, 2011).
7. According to James Der Derian, it took the Cold War to overthrow the national identity of a nation set apart from others with a bounded notion of "defense" and create the "new god" of national security, "as distance, oceans and borders became less of a protective barrier to alien identities, and a new international economy required penetration into other worlds." James Der Derian, "The Value of Security: Hobbes, Marx, Nietzsche, and Baudrillard on Security," in *The Political Subject of Violence*, ed. Mick Dillon and David Campbell (Manchester, UK: Manchester University Press, 1993), 94–113, 109.
8. John Lewis Gaddis, *Surprise, Security and the American Experience* (Cambridge, MA: Harvard University Press, 2004), 13: "For the United States, safety comes from enlarging, rather than contracting, its sphere of responsibilities . . . by taking the offensive, by becoming more

conspicuous, by confronting, neutralizing, and if possible overwhelming the sources of danger rather than fleeing from them. Expansion, we have assumed, is the path to security."

9. See Richard K. Betts, *Surprise Attack: Lessons for Defense Planning* (Washington, DC: The Brookings Institution Press, 1982); Charles F. Parker and Eric K. Stern, "Blindsided? September 11 and the Origins of Strategic Surprise," *Political Psychology*, 23:3 (2002): 601–30.

10. Stephen Van Evera, "Foreword," in *American Foreign Policy and the Politics of Fear: Threat Inflation since 9/11*, ed. A. Trevor Thrall and Jane E. Kramer (Abingdon, UK: Routledge, 2009); Robert Gilpin, *War and Change in World Politics* (New York: Cambridge University Press, 1981); Geoffrey Parker, *The Grand Strategy of Philip II* (New Haven, CT: Yale University Press, 1998). On typologies of self-defeating behavior, see Charles Kupchan, *The Vulnerability of Empire* (Ithaca, NY: Cornell University Press, 1994), 3–8; on anticipatory wars, see Matthew J. Flynn, *First Strike: Preemptive War in Modern History* (New York: Routledge, 2008).

11. John Lewis Gaddis, *The United States and the End of the Cold War: Implications, Reconsiderations, Provocations* (New York: Oxford University Press, 1992), 215.

12. As Michael Desch argues, "America's Liberal Illiberalism: The Ideological Origins of Overreaction in US Foreign Policy," *International Security* 32:3 (2008): 19.

13. Robert Jervis, "The Compulsive Empire," *Foreign Policy* 137 (2003): 83–89.

14. Charles S. Maier, *Among Empires: American Ascendancy and Its Predecessors* (Cambridge, MA: Harvard University Press, 2006), 128.

15. Paul MacDonald, "Peripheral Pulls: Great Power Expansion and Lessons for the American Empire," International Studies Association, International Studies Association, 2004, 9.

16. In his letters to his wife, President Harry Truman wrote of his fears of Soviet expansion and the need to mobilize to prevent it. See Robert H. Ferrell, *Dear Bess: The Letters from Harry to Bess Truman, 1910–1959* (New York: W. W. Norton & Co., 1972), 550–51. The evidence suggests that it really did take the shock of 9/11 to persuade President Bush, who had previously been hostile to nation building and military adventures, that the world was increasingly dangerous and that an armed ideological offensive was needed. See Andrew Flibbert, "The Road to Baghdad: Ideas and Intellectuals in Explanations of the Iraq War," *Security Studies* 15:2 (2006): 310–52, 315–16. Neoconservatives within or close to the Bush II administration confirm that the president only entertained their ideas after 9/11: Michael Elliot and James Carney, "First Stop, Iraq," *Time*, March 31, 2003, 177; Jeffrey Goldberg, "Breaking Ranks," *The New Yorker*, October 31, 2005; George Packer, *The Assassins' Gate: America in Iraq* (New York: Farrar, Straus and Giroux, 2006), 37–65.

17. See Daryl Bem, "Self-Perception Theory," in *Advances in Experimental Social Psychology*, vol. 6, ed. Leonard Berkowitz (New York: Academic Press, 1972), 1–62; used by Robert Jervis to interpret the Bush Doctrine: Robert Jervis, "Understanding the Bush Doctrine," *Political Science Quarterly* 118:3 (2003): 365–88, 365.

18. Brian C. Schmidt and Michael C. Williams show how these lines of critique were echoed in the Iraq War debate of 2002–3: "The Bush Doctrine and the Iraq War: Neoconservatives Versus Realists," *Security Studies* 17 (2008): 191–220.

19. James Chace and Caleb Carr, *America Invulnerable: The Quest for Absolute Security from 1812 to Star Wars* (New York: Simon & Schuster, 1988); Jonathan Monten, "The Roots of the Bush Doctrine," *International Security* 29:4 (2005): 112–56.

20. See the exegesis of the speech, and the debates that formed it, by Felix Gilbert, *To the Farewell Address: Ideas of Early American Foreign Policy* (Princeton, NJ: Princeton University Press, 1961).

21. President George Washington, *Farewell Address to the People of the United States* (Senate Document No. 106-21, Washington), 26–27.

22. A similar logic was anticipated in *Federalist* No. 8, authored by Alexander Hamilton in 1787, which spelled out that America's insular geography relieved it of the need for a vast military establishment that would threaten liberty. With a "powerful marine," this would "supersede the necessity of a numerous army within the kingdom." *Federalist* No. 8: *The Consequences of Hostilities between the States*, November 20, 1787.

23. Commission on Integrated Long-Term Strategy, *Discriminate Deterrence* (Washington, DC: Government Printing Office, January 1988), 5.

24. Franklin D. Roosevelt, "Fireside Chat," December 9, 1941, *Public Papers and Addresses of Franklin D. Roosevelt*, vol. 10 (New York: Random House, 1938–50), 528–29.

25. John Lewis Gaddis, *Surprise, Security and the American Experience* (Cambridge, MA: Harvard University Press, 2004), 69; Robert Osgood, *Ideals and Self-Interest in American Foreign Relations* (Chicago: University of Chicago Press, 1953), 429–30.

26. See Richard Aldrich, *Intelligence and the War against Japan: Britain, America, and the Politics of Secret Service* (Cambridge: Cambridge University Press, 2000), 100; Thomas E. Mahl, *Desperate Deception: British Covert Operations in the United States, 1939–44* (Washington, DC: Brassey's Inc., 1999), 155–76.

27. Fred Greene, "The Military View of American National Policy, 1904–1940," *The American Historical Review* 66:2 (1961): 354–77, 354–55.

28. As David Ekbladh argues, "Present at the Creation: Edward Mead Earle and the Depression Era Origins of Security Studies," *International Security* 36:3 (2011): 107–41.

29. Ronald H. Cole, Walter S. Poole, James F. Schnabel, Robert J. Watson, and Willard J. Webb, *The History of the Unified Command Plan 1946–1993* (Washington, DC: Joint History Office, Office of the Chairman of the Joint Chiefs of Staff, 1995), 11–13.

30. Daniel Yergin, *Shattered Peace: The Origins of the Cold War and the National Security State* (New York: Houghton Mifflin, 1978), 193–220; Bill McSweeney, *Security, Identity and Interests* (Cambridge, UK: Cambridge University Press, 1999), 19; Melvyn Leffler, "The American Conception of National Security and the Beginnings of the Cold War," *The American Historical Review* 89:2 (1984): 346–81; Louis Morton, "Germany First: The Basic Concept of Allied Strategy in World War 11," in *Command Decisions*, ed. Kent R. Greenfield (New York: Harcourt, Brace & Co. 1960), 11–47; Michael S. Sherry, *Preparing for the Next War: American Plans for Postwar Defense, 1941–45* (New Haven, CT: Yale University Press, 1977).

31. See Michael Sherry, *In the Shadow of War: The United States since the 1930s* (New Haven, CT: Yale University Press, 1995), 35–36, 39, 65.

32. See Hew Strachan, "The Lost Meaning of Strategy," *Survival* 47:3 (2005): 33–54, 40; Letter, President Franklin Roosevelt to Ambassador Joseph C. Grew, January 21, 1941, President's Secretary's Files, Diplomatic Correspondence, Box 43, Japan, January–September 1941, Franklin D. Roosevelt Library.

33. Halford Mackinder, "The Round World and the Winning of Peace," *Foreign Affairs* 21 (1943): 598–605; Nicholas Spykman, *America's Strategy in World Politics: The United States and the Balance of Power* (New York: Harcourt, Brace and Company, 1942); Nicholas J. Spykman and Helen R. Nicholl *Geography of the Peace* (New York: Harcourt, Brace and Company, 1944); Hans Weigert, *Generals and Geographers: The Twilight of Geopolitics* (New York: Oxford University Press, 1942); Robert Strausz-Hupé, *Geopolitics: The Struggle for Space and Power* (New York: G. P. Putnam's Sons, 1942); Edward Mead Earle, "Power Politics and American World Policy," *Political Science Quarterly* 58 (1943): 94–106.

34. Mark Polelle, *Raising Cartographic Consciousness: The Social and Foreign Policy Vision of Geopolitics in the Twentieth Century* (Lanham, MD: Lexington Books, 1999), 119: "The shock of Pearl Harbor and the subsequent American involvement in a truly global war brought forth the need to raise America's cartographic consciousness. Such consciousness was deemed a necessary part of the war effort by political geographers and other commentators on geopolitics because of their belief in the need to reorient Americans to the exigencies of a new age in international affairs; a new age that would see the US assume superpower status."

35. Edward Mead Earle Papers (EMEP), Princeton University Library, Princeton, NJ, Box 29, "Project for a Global War Atlas," November 24, 1942; Harold Sprout, "Revised Prospectus for a War Atlas," n.d.; Sprout to Chester Kerr, November 19, 1942; Earle to Kerr, October 4, 1943; "A Security Policy for Postwar America," March 8, 1945, 3, Albert C. (Coady) Wedemeyer Papers, Hoover Institution of War, Peace and Revolution (HIWPR), Stanford University, California, Box 90, Folder 5.

36. In 1940, Germany's surface fleet had 2 armored ships, four battleships, 6–8 cruisers, 2 aircraft carriers in production, and 50 destroyers and torpedo-boats, compared to America's 15 battleships, 6 aircraft carriers, 18 heavy cruisers, 19 light cruisers, and 163 destroyers. *The Statesman's Year-Book: Statistical and Historical Annual of the States of the World for the Year 1941* (London: Macmillan, 1941), 511, 970.

37. Cited in Williamson Murray, "Some Thoughts on War and Geography," in *Geopolitics, Geography and Strategy*, ed. Colin S. Gray and Geoffrey Sloan (London: Frank Cass, 1999), 205.

38. "This war is a new kind of war. It is different from all other wars of the past, not only in its methods and weapons but also in its geography. It is warfare in terms of every continent, every island, every sea, every air lane in the world. That is the reason why I have asked you to take out and spread before you a map of the whole earth, and to follow with me the references which I shall make to the world-encircling battle lines of this war." President Franklin Roosevelt, "Fireside Chat," February 23, 1942, *Public Speeches and Addresses.*

39. For Roosevelt's claims: *Public Papers and Addresses of Franklin D. Roosevelt*, vol. 8, "Annual Message to the Congress," January 4, 1939, 2–12, 2–3, 7; "The President Urges the Congress to Pass Additional Appropriations for National Defense," January 12, 1939, 70–74; vol. 9, "Radio Address before the Eighth Pan American Scientific Congress," Washington, DC, May 10, 1940, 184–87, 186; "We Stand Ready Not Only to Spend Millions for Defense, but to Give Our Service and Even Our Lives for the Maintenance of Our American Liberties," Message to the Congress Asking Additional Appropriations for National Defense, May 16, 1940, 198–212, 198–200; "The President Again Asks for Additional Appropriations for National Defense," July 10, 1940, 286–91, 289; vol. 10, 1941: "We Choose Human Freedom," A Radio Address Announcing the Proclamation of an Unlimited National Emergency, May 27, 1941, 181–94, 185, 189. For skeptical appraisals of Roosevelt's selective claims about technology and geography, see John A. Thompson, "The Exaggeration of American Vulnerability: The Anatomy of a Tradition," *Diplomatic History* 16:1 (1992): 23–43, 30; "Conceptions of National Security and American Entry into World War II," *Diplomacy and Statecraft* 16 (2005): 671–97, 684; Bruce M. Russett, *No Clear and Present Danger: A Skeptical View of the United States Entry into World War II* (New York: Oxford University Press, 1997).

40. Henry R. Luce, "The American Century," *Life*, February 17, 1941, 61–62.

41. Minutes, Meeting of Policy Committee of Cultural Relations Division of Coordinator's Office, September 27, 1940, Henry Luce Papers [henceforth HLP], Library of Congress [henceforth LC], Box 33, Folder 2.

42. Alan Brinkley, *The Publisher: Henry Luce and His American Century* (New York: Vintage Books, 2010), 282.

43. Alan K. Henrikson, "The Map as an 'Idea': The Role of Cartographic Imagery during the Second World War," *The American Cartographer* 2:1 (1975): 19–53, 38–39; Susan Schulten, "World War II Led to a Revolution in Cartography. These Amazing Maps Are Its Legacy," *New Republic*, May 20, 2014.

44. On Bowman and his impact on the geopolitics of the Roosevelt era, see Neil Smith, *American Empire: Roosevelt's Geographer and the Prelude to Globalization* (Berkeley: University of California Press, 2003), 27, 290, 322–24, 326–27; the council published the report, "Iceland and Greenland: An American Problem," *Foreign Affairs* 18 (1940): 742–46.

45. Frederick L. Schuman, "War for Time and Space," *Saturday Review of Literature*, June 27, 1942, 4; "Let Us Learn Our Geopolitics," *Current History* 2.9 (1942): 161–65. In the same year, the scholar of geopolitics Hans Weigert wrote of "an earth that is rapidly becoming politically, economically, and perhaps even culturally a closed unit." Weigert, *Generals and Geographers*, 59.

46. Mark. A. Stoler, "The 'Pacific-First' Alternative in American World War II Strategy," *International History Review* 2:3 (1980): 432–52, 434, 436–37.

47. See Mark Stoler, "From Continentalism to Globalism: General Stanley D. Embick, the Joint Strategic Survey Committee, and the Military View of American National Policy during the Second World War," *Diplomatic History* 6:4 (1982): 303–20.

48. ABC Staff Conversations, January 21, 1941, Steven R. Ross, ed., *American War Plans*, vol. 3 (New York: Garland Publishing, 1992), 309, discussed also in Thompson, "Conceptions of National Security," 680.

49. "Victory Program: Estimate Army Requirements," section II, para. 4, in Albert C. (Coady) Wedemeyer Papers, Box 76, folder 6–7, Hoover Institution of War, Peace and Revolution (HIWPR), Stanford University, Stanford, CA.

50. Joint Chiefs of Staff (henceforth JCS), National Archives (henceforth NA) ser. CCS 381 (5-13-45), JCS 1518 Record Group (RG) 165, box 145, "Strategic Concept and Plan for the Employment of United States Armed Forces," October 11, 1945.

51. Ibid.
52. JCS 570/2, RG 218, Box 270, "United States Military Requirements for Airbases, Facilities, and Operating Rights in Foreign Territories," Appendix A, November 2, 1943.
53. JCS 360 12-9-42 Sec. 2, "Memorandum for the Joint Chiefs of Staff, Subject: U.S. Requirements for Post-War Air Bases," November 23, 1943.
54. JCS, NA, RG 218, Box 270, "Air Routes across the Pacific and Air Facilities for International Police Force," November 15, 1943.
55. JCS, NA, RG 218, Box 270, Memorandum for the President, "United States Military Requirements for Airb,ases, Facilities and Operating Rights in Foreign Territories," November 2, 1943.
56. JCS, NA, RG 218, Box 299, JCS 1496/3, "United States Military Policy," September 20, 1945.
57. JCS, NA, RG 165, Box 145, "Over-All Effect of Atomic Bomb on Warfare and Military Organization," August 18, 1945.
58. JCS, NA, RG 165, Box 143, Sec. IV, Case 115, Memorandum, Lt. Gen. S. D. Embick to Mr. J. D. Hickerson, June 9, 1945; Memorandum, Harrison A. Gerhardt [on behalf of John McCloy] for General Hull, June 16, 1945; Joint Strategic Survey Committee, "Position That Should Be Taken by the U.S. Relative to Probable Russian Proposals Relative to the Straits, and (2) the Internationalisation of the Kiel Canal," July 4, 1945. That McCloy was reputed to be one of the "wise men" who held a "central place in the national security establishment": Walter Isaacson and Evan Thomas, *The Wise Men: Six Friends and the World They Made* (New York: Simon & Schuster, 1986), 192, is further evidence of how the expansion of America's strategic presence and the need for absolute security had become the dominant position.
59. JCS, NA, RG 165, Appendix A, JCS 1015, Discussion [attached to Memo for Assistant Secretary of War re: U.S. Base Facilities in Iceland].
60. Walter S. Poole, "From Conciliation to Containment: The Joint Chiefs of Staff and the Coming of the Cold War, 1945-1946," *Military Affairs* 42 (1978): 12–16, discussing JCS 1545, October 9, 1945, CCS092 USSR (3-27-45), sec. 1.
61. JCS 1545, October 9, 1945, CCS092 USSR (3-27-45), sec. 1. For the final JCS reports, see *Foreign Relations of the United States* (henceworth *FRUS*): *Berlin*, 2:649-50, 1420–22, and *FRUS*, 1945, 5:96–97.
62. JCS, RG 218, Box 270, "Planning and Developing U.S. Controlled Air Routes," September 20, 1943, Capt. F. B. Royal, USN, Deputy Secretary, Joint Chiefs of Staff.
63. On the mixed feelings of this moment, see John Lewis Gaddis, *The Cold War* (London: Penguin, 2005), 5–6.
64. The domino theory is "the notion that the outcome of contests in the periphery would produce a chain reaction affecting vital interests." From the preface to Robert Jervis and Jack Snyder, eds., *Dominoes and Bandwagons: Strategic Beliefs and Great Power Competition in the Eurasian Rimland* (New York: Columbia University Press, 1991).
65. Even Edward Mead Earle, one of the civilian experts closest to government who actively agitated for preparatory rearmament and supported Roosevelt's pursuit of defense in depth and buffer states on the Atlantic seaboard and the Asian mainland, argued that direct invasion was only a remote prospect posed by the Axis threat, which proceeded more by subversion, "flanking maneuvers," and gradual encirclement: "American Security: Its Changing Conditions," *Annals of the American Academy of Political and Social Science*, 218 (1941): 186–93; Edward Mead Earle *Against This Torrent* (Princeton, NJ: Princeton University Press, 1941), 18; for his prewar agitation for rearmament, see Earle Papers, Box 37, "Copy of Telegram" to the White House from "undersigned residents of the community of Princeton New Jersey," December 14, 1940. In a similar vein, he argued in 1943 in a secret assessment that while a victorious Soviet Union would be a geopolitical heavyweight, it would be constrained in attempting to project itself beyond the Eurasian heartland, due to America's superior alliance-building ability among the "oceanic nations": "The Emerging Power Position of the Soviet Union," August 17, 1943, in Earle Papers, Box 32.
66. Hanson Baldwin, *Defense of the Western World* (London: Hutchinson, 1941); Nicholas Spykman, *America's Strategy in World Politics: The United States and the Balance of Power* (New York: Harcourt, Brace and Company 1942).
67. Baldwin, *Defense of the Western World*, 43, 45, 73.

68. Hanson Baldwin Papers, Library of Congress, Box 6, "Footnotes to Battle," text later incorpo-
    rated into Baldwin, *The Price of Power* (New York: Harper, 1947)
69. Hanson Baldwin Papers, Library of Congress, Box 7, Speech, "A Long View of Strategy:
    United States Global Strategy," address delivered during the Sixteenth Annual Global Strategy
    Discussions, June 11, 1964 (Newport, RI: US Naval War College, 1964), 9–11, 29.
70. Nicholas John Spykman, *America's Strategy in World Politics: The United States and the Bal-
    ance of Power* (London: Transaction Publishers, 1942, 2007 edition), 215–30, 392–94, 397,
    391, 404–6, "threat of invasion," 432, 442–45, "distance," 441, grand strategic recommenda-
    tions, 460–70.
71. For a reappraisal of Spykman's "economic strangulation" thesis, see Robert J. Art, "The United
    States, the Balance of Power, and World War II: Was Spykman Right?," *Security Studies* 14:3
    (2005): 365–406.
72. I borrow this phrasing from James R. Holmes and Toshi Yoshihara, "An Ocean Too Far: Offshore
    Balancing in the Indian Ocean," *Asian Security* 8:1 (2012): 1–26.
73. See Thompson, "The Exaggeration of American Vulnerability," 31.
74. As I argue elsewhere, Patrick Porter, "Beyond the American Century: Walter Lippmann and
    American Grand Strategy, 1943–1950," *Diplomacy and Statecraft* 22 (2011): 557–77.
75. Bear Braumoller, "The Myth of American Isolationism," *Foreign Policy Analysis* 6: 4 (2010): 349–
    71, 354.
76. "The correct name for the policy of keeping the commitments without enlarging our power
    and our alliances is not isolationism, but insolvency." Walter Lippmann, *US Foreign Policy*
    (Boston, MA 1943), 69–70.
77. Letter, Lippmann to Hugh R. Wilson, April 8, 1943, Box 110, Folder 2251, Reel 99, Walter
    Lippmann Papers (henceforth WLP), Yale University Library, New Haven, CT.
78. Alfred Thayer Mahan, "The Problem of Asia," in *The Problem of Asia* (New York: Little, Brown
    and Company, 1900), 133. America's defenses "extend across both oceans and to all transoceanic
    lands from which an attack by sea or by air can be launched." *US Foreign Policy*, 94–95.
79. D. Clayton James, " American and Japanese Strategies in the Pacific War," in *Makers of Modern
    Strategy: From Machiavelli to the Nuclear Age*, ed. Peter Paret (Princeton, NJ: Princeton
    University Press, 1986), 703–35, 708, 711.
80. *US Foreign Policy*, 145, 101.
81. Similarly, the political realist Hans Morgenthau argued that the original isolation of the United
    States "was not a gift of nature to be preserved by doing nothing" but "rather the result of an
    intelligent and deliberate foreign policy to be achieved by hard thinking and hard work." Hans
    Morgenthau, "What Is the National Interest of the United States?," *Annals of the American
    Academy of Political and Social Science* 282 (1952): 2.
82. NSC 68, "United States Objectives and Programs for National Security," April 14, 1950, *Naval
    War College Review*, 27:6 (1975): 51–108. For the "state of the art" on the scholarship about NSC
    68, see Ken Young, "Revisiting NSC 68," *Journal of Cold War Studies* 15:1 (2013): 3–34.
83. George F. Kennan, "The Sources of Soviet conduct," *Foreign Affairs* 25:4 (1947): 566–82.
84. As the Korean War still raged, he argued that America's solemn duties abroad were to NATO
    and Japan, beyond which America as a strategic innocent reached the limits of its capabilities:
    American Diplomacy (Chicago: Chicago University Press, 1951), 178.
85. On these conflicting pressures and ideas, see Melvyn Leffler, "The Emergence of an American
    Grand Strategy, 1945–1952," in *The Cambridge History of the Cold War*, vol. 1, ed. Melvyn
    Leffler and Odd Arne Westad (Cambridge: Cambridge University Press), 67–90, on the domes-
    tic pressures against increased commitment, see 75–76; Melvyn P. Leffler, *A Preponderance of
    Power: National Security, the Truman Administration and the Cold War* (Stanford, CA: Stanford
    University Press, 1993); Campbell Craig and Fredrik Logevall, *America's Cold War: The Politics
    of Insecurity* (Cambridge, MA: Harvard University Press, 2009).
86. Warren F. Kimball, *The Juggler: Franklin Roosevelt as Wartime Statesman* (Princeton, NJ:
    Princeton University Press, 1991), 97–99.
87. Diary entry, April 16, 1945, cited in James Chace and Caleb Carr, *America Invulnerable: The
    Quest for Absolute Security from 1812 to Star Wars* (New York: Summit, 1988), 231.
88. Robert L. Messer, "Paths Not Taken: The United States Department of State and Alternatives to
    Containment, 1945–46," *Diplomatic History* 1 (1977): 297–319.

89. Yergin, *Shattered Peace*, 11.

90. On this issue, see John Lewis Gaddis, "Was the Truman Doctrine a Real Turning Point?," *Foreign Affairs* 52 (1974): 386–402.

91. The Clifford memorandum promoted preparation for atomic/biological war with the Soviet Union and a rollback strategy. Report, "American Relations with the Soviet Union," Clark Clifford ["Clifford-Elsey Report"], Naval Aide File, September 24, 1946, Truman Library. It is reprinted in Arthur Krock, *Memoirs: Sixty Years on the Firing Line* (New York: Funk & Wagnalls, 1968), 419–82.

92. Gaddis, *Strategies of Containment*, 22.

93. Paul Nitze Papers, LC, Box 193 Folder 4, Speech, Governor's Conference on World Affairs, Topeka Kansas, December 4–5, 1953.

94. NA, RG 107, Minutes of the Meeting of the Secretaries of State, War, and the Navy, December 18, 1946, April 23, May 1, 1947, RG 107, Robert P. Patterson Papers (RPPP), safe file, box 3.

95. Policy Planning Staff (PPS) Paper, "Policy with Respect to American Aid to Western Europe," May 23, 1947, Part IV, " Clarifying Implications of 'Truman Doctrine,'" in *FRUS 1947*, vol. 3, 224–30.

96. George F. Kennan, *Memoirs 1925–1950* (Boston: Little, Brown, 1967), 356.

97. Walter Lippmann, "The Rivalry of Nations," *The Atlantic*, February 1948, 17–20, 19.

98. "Compromise, the virtue of the old diplomacy, becomes the treason of the new; for the mutual accommodation of conflicting claims, possible or legitimate within a common framework of moral standards, amounts to surrender when the moral standards are themselves the stakes of the conflict." Hans J. Morgenthau, *Politics among Nations: The Struggle for Power and Peace* (New York: Alfred A. Knopf, 1948), 271.

99. On the strongpoint-perimeter debate, see Douglas J. Macdonald, "The Truman Administration and Global Responsibilities: The Birth of the Falling Domino Principle," in *Dominoes and Bandwagons: Strategic Beliefs and Great Power Competition in the Eurasian Rimland*, ed. Robert Jervis and Jack Snyder (New York: Columbia University Press, 1991), 112–44.

100. As Marc Trachtenburg describes it, "A Wasting Asset: American Strategy and the Shifting Nuclear Balance, 1949–1954," *International Security* 13:3 (1988): 69–113.

101. On the importance of Korea to the escalation of the Cold War, see Robert Jervis, "The Impact of the Korean War," *Journal of Conflict Resolution* 24 (1980): 563–92, especially 573–74 on the dominoes question; Colin S. Gray, "Harry S. Truman and the Forming of American Grand Strategy in the Cold War, 1945–1953," in *The Shaping of Grand Strategy: Policy, Diplomacy and War*, ed. Williamson Murray, Richard Hart Sinnreich, and James Lacey (New York: Cambridge University Press, 2011), 210–53.

102. Memorandum, State-War-Navy Coordinating Committee to the Secretary of the Joint Chiefs of Staff, September 15, 1947, *FRUS 1947* 6: 789, 817–18.

103. On December 16, 1950, Truman issued Proclamation 2914, "Proclaiming the Existence of a National Emergency," in *Public Papers of the Presidents of the United States: Harry S. Truman, 1950*, 746–47.

104. NSC 68, "A Report to the National Security Council," Executive Secretary, April 14, 1950, *Naval War College Review*, 27:6 (1975): 51–108, section B.

105. Paul Nitze had argued in February 1950 for the "dominoes" logic that any USSR move entailed high stakes that affected the United States directly or indirectly, which he feared could lead to mutual misperception and war. "Study Prepared by the Director of the Policy Planning Staff," February 8, 1950, *FRUS* 41:2, 145–47.

106. For harsher judgments, see "Sounding the Tocsin: NSC 68 and the Soviet Threat," *International Security*, 4:2 (1979): 116–58, 139; George R. Mitchell and Robert P. Newman, "By 'Any Measures' Necessary: NSC-68 and Cold War Roots of the 2002 National Security Strategy," in *Hitting First: Preventive Force in US Security Strategy*, ed. Gordon R. Mitchell and William W. Keller: (Pittsburgh, PA: University of Pittsburgh Press, 2006), 70–90.

107. Kathryn Weathersby, "To Attack or Not to Attack? Stalin, Kim Il Sung and the Prelude to War," *Cold War International History Project Bulletin* 5 (1995): 1–9.

108. Lippmann initially proposed a neutral buffer zone in Eastern Europe, then the following year, he accepted it as a Soviet sphere. He initially favored the unification of Korea in vague terms, then opposed a land war to enforce it. He had once regarded Japan as an advance base of American

power, writing in March 1948 in the wake of the Soviet Prague coup that it should be built up as part of a holding strategy: the Japanese islands were the "main base for action in eastern Asia" and that America should build up the power to "dominate Soviet Siberia." By December 1950, he rejected the notion that America could occupy Japan, because its forces would be vulnerable to a Soviet atomic strike, because a Pacific battle would be too vast, and because Korea demonstrated the costs of land commitments. Now America should switch to a maritime and carrier-centric strategy of sea denial from a more contracted Pacific perimeter from Alaska, Hawaii, and Guam to the Philippines. See Lippmann, "Today and Tomorrow," *The New York Herald Tribune* (July 20, 1950); Lippmann to Adm. Forrest P. Sherman, April 5, 1948, WLP, Box 102, Folder 1936, Reel 91, 105. Lippmann to Douglas Southall Freeman, December 19, 1950, WLP, Box 72, Folder 826, Reel 62.

109. For Kennan and Lippmann's critiques of the Truman Doctrine and NSC 68, see John Lewis Gaddis, *George F. Kennan: An American Life* (New York: Penguin, 2011), 263, 275, 278, 396–98; "Containment: A Reassessment," *Foreign Affairs* 55 (1977): 876–77; David Mayers, *George Kennan and the Dilemmas of US Foreign Policy* (New York: Oxford University Press, 1990), 122–23; George Kennan, "Measures Short of War," in *Measures Short of War: The George F. Kennan Lectures at the National War College, 1946–47*, ed. Giles D. Harlow and George C. Maerz (Washington, DC: US Government Printing Office, 1991), 3–21, 13–16; Richard J. Barnet, "A Balance Sheet: Lippmann, Kennan and the Cold War," in *The End of the Cold War: Its Meaning and Implications*, ed. Michael J. Hogan (Cambridge: Cambridge University Press 1992), 113–26; Ronald Steel, *Walter Lippmann and the American Century* (Boston, MA: Little, Brown and Company, 1980), 450–78.

110. From Cameron Craig, *American Samurai: Myth, Imagination, and the Conduct of Battle in the First Marine Division, 1941–1951* (Cambridge: Cambridge University Press, 1994), 229n59.

111. Gary R. Hess, *Presidential Decisions for War: Korea, Vietnam, and the Persian Gulf* (Baltimore, MD: Johns Hopkins University Press, 2001, 2nd ed. 2009), 67.

112. "Substance of Statements Made at Wake Island Conference," October 15, 1950, Harry S. Truman Administration File, Elsey Papers; as Bruce Cumings puts it, MacArthur cast Asians as "obedient, dutiful, childlike, and quick to follow resolute leadership."

113. On the economic dimension of the hubris at the time, see Peter Beinart, *The Icarus Syndrome: A History of American Hubris* (New York: HarperCollins, 2010), 122–23.

114. See also James Chace, who reminds us of the balancing act Acheson was trying to pull off with this speech, *Acheson: The Secretary of State Who Created the American World* (Cambridge, MA: Harvard University Press, 1998), 222–23.

115. "Statement by the Secretary of State," July 24, 1950, Senate Foreign Relations Committee, *Reviews of the World Situation, 1949–1950* (Washington, DC, 1974), 321. Cited and discussed in Stephen Casey, "Selling NSC-68: The Truman Administration, Public Opinion, and the Politics of Mobilization, 1950–51," *Diplomatic History* 29:4 (2005): 655–90, 668.

116. Charles A. Kupchan, *The Vulnerability of Empire* (Ithaca, NY: Cornell University Press, 1994), 423.

117. Stephen Casey, *Selling Korea: Propaganda, Politics and Public Opinion 1950–1953* (New York: Oxford University Press, 2008), 205–33.

118. Lippmann to Millard Tydings, January 22, 1952, WLP, Box 106, Folder 2093, Reel 95; on McCarthyism and its relationship with strategic failure, Lippmann to Alan G. Kirk, April 26, 1950, WLP, Box 82, Folder 1234, Reel 72.

119. For critiques of this world view, see Barton Gellman, *Contending with Kennan: Toward a Philosophy of American Power* (New York: Praeger, 1984), 157; Bruce Kuklick, *Blind Oracles: Intellectuals and War from Kennan to Kissinger* (Princeton, NJ: Princeton University Press, 2007); Joel H. Rosenthal, *Righteous Realists: Political Realism, Responsible Power, and American Culture in the Nuclear Age* (Baton Rouge: Louisiana State University Press, 1991), 32–36, 121ff.

120. Hans J. Morgenthau, *In Defense of the National Interest* (New York: Alfred A. Knopf, 1951), 115–21, 182–83, 69–70, 88–89.

121. Ibid., 239–40.

122. Baldwin Papers, LC, Box 6, Hanson W. Baldwin, "What's Going to Happen Next?," October 19, 1951; on "absolute security," see Baldwin, "Budget Arms Set-Up Hit," *New York Times*, January 16, 1949.

123. Baldwin Papers, LC, Box 6, "What Kind of Defense?," May 12, 1953.
124. "Concentration means a clear view of the objective toward which a nation's main effort should be directed; it means economy force, or reduction of peripheral or side-show commitments to a minimum. . . . Viewed against the yardstick of these principles of strategy, Korea is a sideshow. . . . If Russian Communism could be sent reeling to the eastern reaches of the Pripet Marshes and behind the Dniester, the victory would be far more decisive than any retreat of the Northern Korean Communists to the Thirty-Eighth Parallel." Cited in A. J. Liebling, "The Oracles of Mars Continued," *The New Yorker*, October 28, 1950, 80–87, 82.
125. George Kennan, *American Diplomacy* (Chicago, IL: University of Chicago Press, 1951), vii–viii, 170, 178. As Kennan was one of the figures who reintroduced Halford Mackinder's concept of the Eurasian Heartland into American public life, classical geopolitics and the gravitationally decaying effects of extending power over distance were abiding concerns of his. He would later note how "the effectiveness of the power radiated from any national center decreases in proportion to the distance involved." George Kennan, *Russia and the West under Lenin and Stalin* (Boston, MA: Little, Brown & Co. 1961), 261.
126. As the chairman of the National Security Resources Board put it to the National Security Council in July 1950, "the invasion of South Korea came as a surprise and shock . . . to the people around this table, whose job it is to keep the President correctly advised. . . . There are further shocks which must be absorbed, the possible consequences of which it is our duty to present to the President. First is the now unmasked great and growing combined military strength of Soviet Russia, and such of its willing and ambitious satellites as China and North Korea." Statement by the chairman of the National Security Resources Board, *FRUS*, July 6, 1950, 338–41, 338.
127. Paul Nitze Papers, Library of Congress, Box 193, Folder 4, "Certain Foreign Policy Alternatives 1949–1953," Address by Paul H. Nitze at Conference of Business Economists, October 17, 1953.
128. As Tarak Barkawi demonstrates, "'Small Wars,' Big Consequences and Orientalism: Korea and Iraq," *Arena*, no. 29/30 (2008): 59–80.
129. "Radio and Television Report to the American People on the Situation in Korea," September 1, 1950, at www.trumanlibrary.org/publicpapers/index.php?pid=861.
130. US House of Representatives, *US Policy in the Far East*, 165, cited and discussed in MacDonald, "The Truman Administration and Global Responsibilities," 122.
131. As Michael Lind illustrates, *Vietnam: The Necessary War; A Reinterpretation of America's Most Disastrous Military Conflict* (New York: Simon & Schuster, 1999), 38–41.
132. For the grand strategic debate of the 1990s, see Eugene Gholz, Daryl G. Press, and Harvey M. Sapolsky, "Come Home America: The Strategy of Restraint in the Face of Temptation," *International Security* 21:4 (1997): 5–48; William Kristol and Robert Kagan, "Toward a Neo-Reaganite Foreign Policy," *Foreign Affairs* 75:4 (1996): 18–32; Pat Buchanan, *A Republic, Not an Empire: Reclaiming America's Destiny* (Washington, DC: Regnery, 1999).
133. "Excerpts from Pentagon's Plan: 'Prevent the Emergence of a New Rival,'" *New York Times*, March 8, 1992; Patrick E. Tyler, "U.S. Strategy Plan Calls for Insuring No Rivals Develop," *New York Times*, March 8, 1992.
134. The National Security Council talking points prepared for President Clinton in January 1996 reflect the assumption of a borderless world and its need for American oversight as peacemaker (though not policeman): "Can't Be Isolationist: After Cold War, Some Say We Should Pull Back. They're wrong. Threats we face have no respect for borders: ethnic, religious hatred . . . rogue states . . . nukes . . . terror . . . crime . . . drugs." "Foreign Policy Talking Points," January 18, 1996, Anthony Lake Papers, Library of Congress, Folder 4.
135. Strobe Talbott, *The Russia Hand: A Memoir of Presidential Diplomacy* (New York: Random House, 2002), 133.
136. John Lewis Gaddis, "What Is Grand Strategy?," Karl Von Der Heyden Distinguished Lecture, Duke University, February 26, 2009, 2; Robert J. Lieber, *Eagle Adrift: American Foreign Policy at the End of the Century* (New York: Longman, 1997).
137. Bob Woodward, *Bush at War* (New York: Simon & Schuster 2002), 33.
138. John W. Dower, *Cultures of War: Pearl Harbor, Hiroshima, 9–11, Iraq* (New York: W. W. Norton, 2010), 4–14, 74–87, 111–15.

139. Bruce Kuklick, *Blind Oracles: Intellectuals and War from Kennan to Kissinger* (Princeton, NJ: Princeton University Press, 2006), 12–14.

140. "Remembering Pearl Harbor," *Newsweek*, November 25, 1991.

141. Franklin Roosevelt, "When You See a Rattlesnake Poised to Strike, You Do Not Wait until He Has Struck before You Crush Him," Fireside Chat to the Nation, September 11, 1941, in *Public Papers and Addresses of Franklin D. Roosevelt* (New York, 1938–1950), vol. 8, 384–92; John M. Schuessler, "The Deception Dividend: FDR's Undeclared War," *International Security* 34:4 (2010), 133–65. If Hitler had aggressive designs against the United States, an ultimate "clash of continents," the fragments of evidence suggest that he was probably thinking long-term rather than immediate. He tried to postpone a war with America, instructing his naval forces to show restraint and trying to eliminate Britain from the war, because he feared a premature war against that flanking giant before he had completed and consolidated his other gains. It may have been wiser to forestall that growing threat in 1941 rather than react later (and in that case deception may have been an important part of motivating Americans to agree), but that was a very different argument from Roosevelt's warning of imminent danger. On this issue further, see Saul Friedlander, *Prelude to Downfall: Hitler and the United States 1939–1941* (London: Chatto & Windus 1967), 310–11; Milan Hauner, "Did Hitler Want a World Dominion?," *Journal of Contemporary History* 13:1 (1978): 15–32, 24–5; Marc Trachtenberg, "Preventive War and U.S. Foreign Policy," *Security Studies* 16:1(2007): 1–31.

142. Similarly, though American accounts of North Korea's June invasion of 1950 represented it simply as an attack undertaken against a passive South Korea to expand Soviet communism, recent scholarship indicates that the South Korean regime of Syngman Rhee was also actively trying to reunify the peninsula with the backing of some officials in the Truman administration. See Campbell Craig and Fredrik Logevall, *America's Cold War: The Politics of Insecurity* (Cambridge, MA: Harvard University Press, 2009), 115.

143. Kaufman (2007), 127; see also the discussion by Frank Harvey, *Explaining the Iraq War* (New York: Cambridge University Press, 2012), 303.

144. President of the United States, *National Security Strategy of the United States of America* (Washington, DC: US Government Printing Office, September 2002), 31.

145. Weeks after 9/11, Bush's deputy secretary of defense, Paul Wolfowitz, spoke of the "globalization of terror, in which rogue states and terrorist organizations share information, intelligence, technology, weapons materials and know-how." According to Bush's secretary of state Condoleezza Rice, a new age of state failure accelerates worldwide flows of havoc, creating a perilous world of "global pathways that facilitate the spread of pandemics, the movement of criminals and terrorists, and the proliferation of the world's most dangerous weapons." Paul Wolfowitz, "Building a Military for the 21st Century," Prepared Statement for the House and Senate Armed Services Committees, October 3–4, 2001 (Washington, DC: US Department of Defense, 2001); Condoleezza Rice, "The Promise of Democratic Peace," *Washington Post*, December 11, 2005.

146. President George W. Bush, Second Inaugural Address, *Washington Post*, January 21, 2005, at www.washingtonpost.com/wp-dyn/articles/A23747-2005Jan20.html.

147. President of the United States, *National Security Strategy*, 2002, 6.

148. "Text of Bush's Speech at West Point," *New York Times*, June 1, 2002.

149. As Ali Parchami argues, *Hegemonic Peace and Empire: The Pax Romana, Britannica and Americana* (London: Routledge, 2009).

150. For sophisticated accounts of an often crudely understood political movement, see Michael C. Williams, "Morgenthau Now: Neoconservatism, National Greatness, and Realism," in *Realism Reconsidered: The Legacy of Hans Morgenthau in International Relations* (New York: Oxford University Press, 2007), 216–41, 217–27; Jacob Heilbrunn, *They Knew They Were Right: The Rise of the Neocons* (New York: Doubleday, 2009).

151. Michael Ledeen, "American Power—For What?," *Commentary* 19:1 (2000): 36.

152. Daniel Lieberfeld, "Theories of Conflict and the Iraq War," *International Journal of Peace Studies* 12:2 (2005): 12.

153. Robert Kagan and William Kristol, "National Interest and Global Responsibility," in *Present Dangers: Crisis and Opportunity in American Foreign and Defense Policy*, ed. Robert Kagan and William Kristol (San Francisco, CA: Encounter Books, 2000), 3–24, 23–24.

154. Robert Kagan, "Neocon Nation: Neoconservatism c. 1776," *World Affairs* (Spring 2008): 13–36; *Dangerous Nation: America in the World 1600-1900* (New York: Atlantic, 2006). Likewise, for Michael Lind, pessimistic *realpolitik* and the obsession with power balances and geopolitics was advanced by an old guard of émigré intellectuals, Central European realists who had fled the Old World and based themselves in American universities, such as Nicholas Spykman, Hans Morgenthau, Henry Kissinger, and, later, Zbigniew Brzezinski. Michael Lind, "Immigrant Intellectuals and American Grand Strategy," *The Globalist*, April 4, 2003.

155. Norman A. Graebner, "An American Tradition in Foreign Affairs," *The Virginia Quarterly Review* 65:4 (1989): 600–18; Christopher Fettweis, "Dangerous Revisionism: On the Founders, 'Neocons' and the Importance of History," *Orbis* 53:3 (2009): 507–23.

156. Christoph Frei, *Hans Morgenthau: An Intellectual Biography* (Baton Rouge: Lousiana State University Press, 2001), 219.

157. On the geopolitics of the "Greater Middle East" initiative and its contradictory goals, see Dona J. Stewart, "The Greater Middle East and Reform in the Bush Administration's Ideological Imagination," *Geographical Review* 95:3 (2005): 400–24, 415.

158. Prominent realists placed a paid advertisement in the *New York Times*, "War with Iraq Is Not in America's National Interest," September 26, 2002; on the grand strategic debate and the parallels between realists of 2002 and their forbears: Brian Schmidt, "Offshore Balancing Yesterday and Today," unpublished paper, International Studies Association, March 2011; John Mearsheimer, "Hans Morgenthau and the Iraq War: Realism versus Neoconservatism," opendemocracy.com, posted May 19, 2005.

159. See Christopher Layne, "'Liberalism and American Overexpansion," International Studies Association, Honolulu, 2005.

160. As Michael H. Hunt illustrates, *Ideology and US Foreign Policy* (New Haven, CT: Yale University Press, 1987), 150–51.

161. On Nitze's outmaneuvering and sidelining of Secretary of Defense Louis Johnson, see Nicholas Thompson, *The Hawk and the Dove: Paul Nitze, George Kennan, and the History of the Cold War* (New York: Henry Holt, 2009), 111.

CHAPTER 3

Lost in Space

Al Qaeda and the Limits of Netwar

Now, shadowy networks of individuals can bring great chaos and suffering to our shores for less than it costs to purchase a single tank.

—*National Security Strategy of the United States of America, 2002*

There is a chain of terror that comes from the Pakistani and Afghan mountains right to and across Europe and can end up very easily on the streets of Britain.

—Prime Minister Gordon Brown

We lost cities and afterward, villages, and the desert became a dangerous refuge. We got away from people and found ourselves in a wasteland desert.

—Abu Tariq (Al Qaeda emir), Anbar Province, Iraq

Today's terrorism, observers often warn, is borderless.[1] Thanks to the pathways of access created by globalization, violent radicals can spread insecurity like an epidemic, meaning that the eruption of extremism anywhere is now a direct threat, even to strong and wealthy nations far away. But how far is this true?

To probe the question, this chapter reexamines the role of distance in the evolution of the militant Islamist network Al Qaeda (AQ). In the debate about globalization and distance, AQ is an important test case for the debate about globalization and war for three reasons. First, it is significant as an agent in its own right because of its perceived global reach and deadliness. Originating in the politics of the Arab-Islamic jihadist movement, in fatwas it declared war on the United States, in August 1996 and February 1998. On September 11, 2001 ("9/11"), it successfully struck the superpower in its heartland across an intercontinental range. 9/11 was the most consequential strategic event since the end of the Cold War and the most destructive and spectacular strike on American soil since Pearl Harbor. It set off a widespread chain reaction, triggering a war in multiple theaters against multiple adversaries that has lasted over a decade.

Second, AQ deserves attention because it is said to reflect a more profound trend, a systemic change in international relations. It is, some claim, the symptom of the subversive power of globalization and its threat to the status quo, the unipolar liberal world order guarded by the United States and the very structure of territorial states. In the words of AQ's early assessment, 9/11 was a world-historical event, "the great superpower of America" was "thunderously attacked in its homeland," an event that spelled the "death certificate" for the "leader of the new world order" by an enemy "hard to detect, infiltrate, and strike."[2] As well as shaking the world's most powerful state, the attack seemed to signal a momentous stage in the evolution of war itself, marking the privatization of the means of destruction into the hands of actors who now had a dangerous level of access.

Third, we should study AQ because it is a revealing "easy" test of globalism where that theory should perform well. *Prima facie* this seems to be a case of war in the global village, made possible by "shrinking technological, economic, and geographic space," to some "the first major war in the age of globalization."[3] In most theories that assert the erosion of distance and the shrinking world, AQ takes center stage. Though nourished on medieval nostalgia for a lost empire, AQ used the tools and pathways of modernity to take war to the "far enemy," exploiting rapid communications, cheap travel, and digital finance.

But if, on a closer look, the most reputedly "global" terrorist network to date is still substantially constrained by distance, then we should think again about the theory and its policy implications. To reexamine AQ, this chapter uses opensource material such as reports, strategic documents, and public media. It also draws upon archival sources, namely the declassified and translated AQ documents at the Conflict Records Research Center at the National Defense University, Washington, DC, and the declassified letters captured in the raid on Osama bin Laden's compound in Abbottabad, Pakistan, in May 2011 and released to the Combating Terrorism Center (CTC) at West Point. These internal documents reflect AQ's self-audit and reveal the ways in which the pressures of war are brought to bear on AQ and how it tries to adapt. Analysis of captured documents must contend with the problem that they are fragments. But, as I argue, the fragments fit. They consistently reveal the impact of a changing operating environment, as well as internal debate and power struggles within an increasingly disjointed jihad. Strikingly, AQ's self-assessments are more sober than many Western theories about them.

How should we define AQ? Experts disagree over how exactly to define and conceptualize it. The issue of what AQ exactly "is," in terms of morphology, message, and structure, and in particular the extent to which it has mutated from a centralized hierarchy into a franchise network, is subject to ongoing debate.[4] It is broadly agreed that Al Qaeda, translated as "The Base," is a transnational, armed

Islamist movement forged in reaction to the Soviet Union's war in Afghanistan (1979–89). It then took up arms in Muslim struggles ranging from Chechnya, Bosnia, and the Philippines to Kashmir and Afghanistan. Its overriding aim is to restore what it sees as a pure Islamic nation, the *Umma*, replacing human law with divine Sharia law, and to create a worldwide theocratic state ruled by a supreme clerical leader, an Islamic caliphate. It seeks to purge corrupting foreign powers from Muslim nations and expel the "Crusader-Zionist" interlopers from the Middle East. AQ is a Salafist jihadist movement that authorizes the killing of civilians. Strategically, AQ theorists position themselves as "knights" acting as a vanguard at the head of a broader movement. Taking the jihad to the "far enemy," they use inspirational violence in order to mobilize the Muslim masses into a revolt that bleeds the United States into abandoning the Arab-Islamic world, and that overthrows the nearer enemies, America's "apostate" client regimes such as those ruling Saudi Arabia and Egypt. In his original fatwa declaration of war in 1996, the wealthy founder of AQ, Saudi Osama bin Laden (1957–2011), laid out a three-tiered plan to expel Western forces from the region and sever their relationship with Israel, undermine infidel pro-Western Arab regimes (the near enemy), and unite the Muslim world under a theocracy.[5] Especially after the US invasions of Afghanistan and Iraq, an attritional struggle of bleeding the United States through the "management of savagery" became central to AQ's strategy.[6]

How exactly AQ evolved since then has caused confusion. For the purpose of this chapter, I take as a starting point Jason Burke's triptych, where AQ functions through an interplay of three levels: as a hard core of its leader, deputy, and lieutenants; as a broader network of cadres, containing mujahideen from training camps or wars who returned to home countries; and a loose outer movement of those who identify with AQ ideology and act on its messages, sometimes independently without direct association and sometimes through direct contact. AQ has collaborative relationships with other groups in its orbit, such as AQ in the Maghreb, in the Arabian Peninsula, Jemaah Islamyah in Southeast Asia, and Boko Haram in Nigeria, and criminal bodies such as the Haqqani network. The leaders of affiliate groups have sworn *bayat* (loyalty) to AQ's leader and bin Laden's successor, Ayman al-Zawahiri. This continuous interaction of different levels of jihad follows the logic laid out by the group's veteran intellectual and teacher, Abu Musab al-Suri.[7] AQ is not a static movement. As we will see, the fluidity of the AQ network under the pressures of war is an important part of the story. A militant cause that is part idea and part coalition, AQ is contested terrain. Its founder's losing struggle to reassert control over it tells us a lot about how the force of distance constrains his supposedly "borderless" movement.

This chapter argues that after the 9/11 attacks, the US security elite (along with academic observers, some of whom are close to policymakers) perceived and framed AQ as a first-order threat on that basis, that it was a mobile enemy unconstrained by geography, that it heralded a deeper condition of globalized insecurity that empowered new agents of war and made sovereign states fragile, and that demonstrated the need for a renewed Pax Americana. But on closer inspection, AQ is doubly constrained by a distance-decay effect. First, the closer it comes to its principal enemy, the more the active shielding of space constrains it. "Going long" from its core territory attracts increasing state hostility, making distance as much of a resistant barrier as a carrier, and reduces the ease of AQ's operations. Losing a secure core territory has also made life more complex and difficult for AQ. Second, decentralizing or dispersing over space purchases increased survivability at the cost of reduced cohesion, command and control, and capability. These effects have consequences for AQ's power and reputation, and ultimately have fragmented its jihad. Territoriality and its dynamics lie at the heart of Al Qaeda's origins, evolution, and subsequent misfortunes.

To argue for the enduring power of geopolitical constraints is not necessarily to argue that the jihadist wave is spent. To be sure, AQ lives on and reinvents itself. Militant neojihadism in its different and shifting forms persists. Groups linked with it remain active especially in the arc from North Africa to the Middle East and South Asia. A radical offshoot of AQ, the Islamic State in Iraq and Syria (ISIS), is a strong force in the embattled territory straddling Syria and Iraq, where it has recently captured cities. Its fate in this latest "front" is unknown. At the same time, there are fresh signs that the movement once again is splintering into rival groups with local agendas, and it would be unwise to speak of ISIS's ascent as though it is just a product of "ungoverned space," unrelated to the 2003 invasion of Iraq and the sectarian client regime it left behind.[8] As sectarian divisions intensify in Syria, different Islamist factions laying claim to AQ's banner turn on each other, so a cycle of reinvention, resurgence, and self-destruction may be repeating.[9] AQ and other guerrillas of the information age, as well as lone wolves, can still inflict atrocity, as was shown on the streets of Boston in the United States and Woolwich in the United Kingdom. But this is not a question of persistence and whether the movement can be eradicated. It is a question of capability and reach, the extent of the threat it poses, and whether it can be contained. I argue here that the operating environment is increasingly hostile and difficult for them. Resilient nation-states have reduced AQ's ability to inflict mass casualty terrorism on Western soil. The mounting difficulties of projecting power over space mean that AQ is not an intrinsically major challenge to the security of its "far enemy's" way of life. In the West, almost all attempts fail, and those that succeed are crude and nothing like the possibilities that 9/11 suggested. AQ poses a major threat mostly to the extent that America misperceives and inflates the problem to the point where Washington can be baited into imprudent responses. To borrow from

Fawaz Gerges, AQ's power as an agent of catastrophic terrorism lies mostly in the extent that "it continues to have a hold over the Western imagination, in part because the West will not let it go."[10]

9/11 and Netwar: Home and Away

According to Stephen Walt's landmark study of how states define their interests, proximity plays an important role in threat perception. As well as its hostility, the perceived "nearness" or "farness" of an actual or potential enemy shapes calculations about their capacity to threaten.[11] In the era of transnational terrorism marked on 9/11, policymakers concluded that their enemies were effectively nearby. They had struck from within America and seemingly had gotten into the country with little trouble. AQ's attack gave the idea of a "borderless world" renewed potency as a way of explaining violent disorder. Seemingly out of the blue, Saudi and Yemeni militants with a base in Afghanistan, an impoverished country far away, struck hard against Western power in its Manhattan financial heartland and the Pentagon, America's military nerve center. Its fourth plane-missile was only a midair brawl away from America's seat of government. The assault shocked Americans, but not just because of the spectacular violence of the event. The shock, and the call to arms, also flowed from a visceral sense that the American homeland had once been basically secure—even immune—in its physical insulation from international threats and a desire that this security be restored.[12]

There is nothing inevitable about declaring global war as a response to a terrorist attack, "and there was no automatic path from the Twin Towers to Baghdad. September 11, like all political events, did not speak for itself. It required interpretation, and it did not have to lead to a War on Terror."[13] The United States has been subject to attacks before (albeit on lesser scales and different targets) without responding with an ambitious war, such as the bombing of the Marine barracks in Beirut in 1983. States do not uniformly treat urban terrorist attacks as acts of war that merit the status of war. And even if some military response was politically inevitable and domestic politics created pressure for retaliation, the George W. Bush II administration made choices about how to define the enemy and the scope of its response.

Washington did not regard this as a catastrophic "one-off." It regarded 9/11 not as an aberration that marked the upper limits of the enemy's powers, but as a foretaste of worse attacks that portended a profound change in the way American national security could be threatened.[14] The administration depicted today's threats as proximate and stateless and warned of the confluence of radical ideologies and dangerous technologies.[15] In response, Washington did not just declare war against a specific adversary in a climate of bellicose public opinion. It made a point of declaring hostilities against all terrorists of global reach.[16] It declared war on terrorism itself, which amounted to a struggle against a tactic rather than a specified opponent, a project that lacks geographical limitation.

The United States also had "rogue states" in its sights and went on to wage war against Saddam Hussein's regime in Iraq. At first, America defined this front in the War on Terror primarily in terms of counterproliferation, to counter the imminent security threats linked to the spread of weapons of mass destruction (WMDs). With the course of events, ideas about pacifying threatening states through democratic modernization became more central, and the vision of the war grew symbiotically with the pulse of the battlefield. Bush in his Second Inaugural Address declared the ultimate goal of securing America by ending tyranny on earth. As Iraq imploded in communal bloodletting and American troops met guerrilla resistance, Bush asserted that the "survival of liberty in our land increasingly depends on the success of liberty in other lands."[17] The ambition was to transform the conditions that bred fanaticism through which a range of disparate enemies could link up, including rogue states and terrorist and criminal networks. The war became a conflict ultimately not against specific adversaries but against a deeper condition of insecurity exemplified by the men who had brought the fire to New York and Washington, as well as Bali, Madrid, and London.

Geopolitics was at the center of how the Bush administration and the wider foreign policy establishment interpreted the shock. The government's strategic documents, from the president's *National Security Strategy* (2002) to the Pentagon's *Quadrennial Defense Review* (2006), upheld the logic of a "new condition" born of globalization.[18] Building on the premise of a dangerous new world and America's mission to reorder it, the Bush Doctrine was born, a muscular and idealist doctrine that embraced unilateralism, anticipatory war, and democracy promotion. Countering terrorism rose to the first rank to become the "fifth pillar" of US grand strategy.[19] This led to the investment of trillions of dollars in related defense spending and homeland security, as well as a strengthening of state power, a curtailment of civil liberties, and a spread of secret prisons. The bedrock assumption for all these measures was that America lives in a deteriorating security environment that is more volatile than earlier eras. A logic of eradication, or "rollback," dictated that the United States could not live with the new insecurity but must stamp it out. A premise of the emerging Bush Doctrine, reaffirmed by Obama, was that against irrational Islamist foes and their allies, alternative strategies such as containment or deterrence—which looked to competitive coexistence rather than extermination of threats—were obsolete.[20] Paradoxically, Washington's self-image was that it was a state both uniquely threatened and uniquely powerful.

The premise that the United States could not safely coexist with failed states was shared across the political mainstream. Susan Rice, the Democratic foreign policy hand, argued that Bush was "wise to draw attention to the significant threats to our national security posed by failed and failing states."[21] Hillary Clinton spoke of "the chaos that flows from failed states" that are "invitations to terrorists to find refuge amidst the chaos."[22] President Barak Obama has distanced his administration from aspects of the Bush wars, renouncing open-ended military commitments on the ground and torture in favor of an expanding hunt-and-kill program. But Obama too claimed that the world has shrunk, that remote developments can quickly threaten vital interests, and that America should strive to remain the hegemonic guardian of world order.

Collective historical memories shaped immediate responses to the event. To make sense of the appearance of proximate enemies like the hijackers of 9/11, two memories predominated, Imperial Japan's attack on Pearl Harbor in 1941 and the frontier wars of the eighteenth and nineteenth centuries. Comparisons with Pearl Harbor were immediate.[23] Rhetoric of the War on Terror revived the Pearl Harbor–era vocabulary of a passive, innocent "sleeping giant" awakened to its destiny by an unprovoked aggression that is symptomatic of a dangerously small world. The perceived shrinking of the world allegedly meant that there was no longer policy discretion and that war could force itself on the United States. But this time, not only did the enemy have intercontinental reach. Compared to Imperial Japan's Combined Fleet, it was a more insidious threat, as a diasporic movement with followers everywhere, posing a threat that could incubate at home and strike with ease. The Department of Defense concluded that the US homeland and international security had merged, so that "we can no longer think in terms of the 'home' game and the 'away' game. There is only one game."[24]

In speeches and media coverage, interpreters of 9/11 also revived memories of another moment of vulnerability to nearby enemies, the fear of the surprise attacks in the Old West in the "wilderness era" of frontier violence between native and white Americans. These resonated because they were embedded in popular culture.[25] As US soldiers found themselves amidst communal bloodletting in Iraq while struggling against a resurgent Taliban in the Afghanistan-Pakistan war, the fearful spoke of a violent frontier threatening the vulnerable homestead but mapped this onto the fatal terrains of Arabia and Central Asia.[26] American security was implicated on the turbulent peripheries that forever threatened the core. Perceived through the lens of Pearl Harbor, or the frontier wars, again Americans feared the problem of predators who could overcome the barriers of space. The frontier had gone global.

The corollary of these visions of dangerous vacuums in need of policing is that the United States had an imperial mandate to restore order to "Indian country."[27] The coming together of transnational terrorism, grinding expeditionary wars, and anxieties about global perils to national security restaged the issue of empire explicitly in American strategic debate, which took an "imperial turn." The Bush administration disliked the language of formal empire but still acted according to the premise that "in a fragmenting, postmodern world, where small bands of fanatics based in crumbling polities could cause havoc and mayhem elsewhere, imperialism with American characteristics was the only real answer."[28] This was problematic, as 9/11 had as much to do with America's active geopolitical presence in the Gulf than its absence in Central Asia.[29] Nevertheless, the perceived need for a reassertion of American hegemony as the antidote to terrorism took hold.[30] Ideas and ideology intervened to translate 9/11 into an unlimited global war, based on an instinctive reading of American strategic history that interpreted violent threats as symptoms of a global village that needed taming.[31]

This logic was codified by the 9/11 Commission that interpreted 9/11 as a brutal lesson in the need for a "global strategy":

> National security used to be considered by studying foreign frontiers, weighing opposing groups of states, and measuring industrial might. To be dangerous, an enemy had to muster large armies. Threats emerged slowly, often visibly, as weapons were forged, armies conscripted, and units trained and moved into place. Because large states were more powerful, they also had more to lose. They could be deterred.

Now threats can emerge quickly. An organization like Al Qaeda, headquartered in a country on the other side of the earth, in a region so poor that electricity and telephones were scarce, could nonetheless scheme to wield weapons of unprecedented destructive power in the largest cities of the United States.

In this sense, 9/11 has taught us that terrorism against American interests "over there" should be regarded just as we regard terrorism against America "over here." In this same sense, the American homeland is the planet.[32]

This analysis, built partly on the testimony of academic terrorism experts, offers a shallow view of strategic prehistory before 9/11 and a flawed account of AQ.[33] Before 9/11, deterrence at times failed to deter. Life was full of surprises and intelligence failures, from Japan's sudden attack on Russia in 1904 to the shock of the Arab strike on Israel in 1973. Nations did not necessarily lumber slowly into place with ample warning. Even if they did arm and prepare over time, it was often unclear whether mobilization was defensive. Some struck in the dead of night with small amphibious forces, as did Argentina over the Falklands in 1982. The Cold War, which the 9/11 Commission blithely portrays as a period of stability and certainty, was haunted by fears that the nuclear deterrence system would fail through accident, surprise attack, or inadvertent escalation. Al Qaeda did not emerge quickly but originated in the late 1980s, more than a decade before 9/11.[34] Its hostile intentions against America were on record and its capabilities were visible in multiple prior attacks. The notion that an attack on urban targets by a known adversary represented an unimaginable "black swan" event is not only baseless but is a misleading alibi. It relieves policymakers for their culpability in a failure to act on intelligence warnings. As the commission's own inquiries show, the CIA gave repeated warnings to incurious policymakers between 2000 and 2001 with the system "blinking red."[35] 9/11 was a preventable attack that could have been curtailed primarily through competent homeland policing, rather than an eruption from a turbulent security environment the existence of which must be uncritically assumed.

In 2001 Al Qaeda's weapons did not wield "unprecedented destructive power." The weapons were mobile phones, box-cutters, and commercial airliners. Damage inflicted on 9/11 was not unprecedented in scale or quality. Contrary to the commission and the president's review panel report into National Security Agency (NSA) surveillance, the use of crude weapons aboard a plane on 9/11 did not demonstrate the danger of weapons of mass destruction.[36] Compared to carrying and using an edged weapon on a plane, detonating a nuclear device is vastly more difficult. Modern nukes typically are equipped with security safeguards and the equivalent of self-destruct devices. And, as we shall see, contrary to the implicit claim about the irrelevance of distance, the fate of AQ afterwards shows that it makes a great deal of difference strategically where armed force is generated and projected from.

These distortions matter. The commission's simplistic periodization of history accentuates the message that 9/11 marked a divide in history, in which a stable world became smaller and deadlier, demanding the West's global vigilance. Thus the rhetoric of the commission goes beyond a claim about how the world is. By prompting fears of borderless superthreats, the 9/11 attacks called forth a process of "geopolitical re-scripting and geographical remaking," which recreated an expansive vision of security that claims the planet as America's security domain.[37]

If 9/11 brought forth a view of a new form of terrorism that was symptomatic of globalized insecurity, we should examine these claims in greater depth.

Global Guerrillas and System Viruses

Ever since the 9/11 attacks, prophets of the death of distance have regarded AQ as the manifestation of a new type of information age fighter (or "global guerrilla") using new tools to outflank, devastate, and elude their backward nation-state adversaries. Before 9/11, a body of literature predicted that globalization would arm and shield terrorist networks and make them borderless in "post-sovereign" virtual communities, placing them beyond conventional battlefields and retaliation.[38] AQ is only the most well-known practitioner of "netwar," a form of war-making that empowers the traditionally weak against the traditionally strong, where the diffusion of capability and the networking of organizations gives them the edge against traditional unitary actors with command hierarchies, and where the "de-massification" of warfare means that large-scale material forces are no longer a precondition for success.[39] If globalization collapses space and reduces the costs and time for communication and the circulation of goods, capital, and people, new agents can forge a potent "nonterritorial network enterprise." It empowers nonstate actors against states and offers an ease of access, a connectivity, and a diffusion of knowledge through the internet, digital finance, instant communications, and cheap travel, as well as an ability to disperse and swarm without a clearly identifiable base that can be smashed.[40] AQ exemplifies a "new terrorism," standing at the intersection of radical ideology, deadly technology, and elusive networks.[41] Above all, it haunts states with the ultimate specter of radical groups acquiring weapons of mass destruction. President Obama identified nuclear terrorism as the number-one threat to American security.[42]

"Netwar" theorists share a common core of assumptions, that AQ's war is powered by globalization and represents a systemic shift in the balance of power between states and those who would subvert them. AQ threatens because the global reach and swiftness of its assaults on Western heartlands demonstrates the shrinkage of distance. It spearheads "a new breed of strategic agents . . . able to operate because globalization makes the world easily accessible to terrorists as well as traders."[43] Others argue that in a digital age, AQ is dangerous not because it can master territory, establishing bases and then moving quickly from "over there" to "over here," but because it is post-territorial. The information revolution allegedly enables new agents to forge a "nonterritorial network enterprise," a diaspora of extremists "without territory and without formal command structures" that elude the blows of nation-states.[44] As the "first guerrilla movement in history to migrate from physical space to cyber space," AQ showcases how the internet and instant communications empower insurgents to find education, inspiration, and organization.[45] Talk of bases and the concentration, command, and mobilization of material mass is therefore anomalous. They can avoid the hard slog of attending training camps by transferring knowledge and skills online, trafficking in an open-source bazaar of weapons, technical education, and financing, lowering the costs of access so that anyone with an internet connection can play.[46] Cyberspace is the platform for preaching and rhetorical incitement, the medium for today's "levée en masse" that generates an imagined community of worldwide jihadists.[47] And the information revolution facilitates a flattened form of organization in which AQ's franchises and affiliates operate as a network rather than a top-down hierarchy. Through its dispersal across space and cyberspace, AQ survives and feeds off the violent counteroffensives of its state adversaries.[48] Its "absence of a territorial base, a globalized field of contention shaped by new media and information technologies," enables it to exert power that resists crudely material estimations of capabilities, including the classically geographic.[49] The nonterritoriality of this invisible movement represents something "entirely new." It has "no geographical location; its membership is distributed across the globe and cyberspace." Against this invisible enemy, it is not possible to attack its "infrastructure," "to carpet-bomb al-Qa'ida's positions, or attack its soldiers."[50] Symptomatic of wider globalization, AQ's evolution mirrors today's transnational and borderless multinational corporations.[51] To approach it as a physical entity that can be curtailed or rolled back by using force to deny it state sanctuary, training camps, or other kinds of earthly "nodes" is an exercise in nostalgic thinking from the interstate wars of yesterday against jihadist networks that "transcend territorial space."[52] Territorial notions of conflict wrongly externalize and place "over there" a phenomenon of global jihad, with "the capacity to be, not somewhere else, but everywhere."[53] Lighter, agile enemies threaten to bring down states from their staging posts in the new technological domain, with cyberspace a "virtual safe haven." According to the preeminent theorist of netwar, John Arquilla, networks will persist until they have the capability to land nuclear blows, marking a confluence of medieval fanaticism and modern destructive technology, where concepts like "deterrence" and "containment" of aggression will blow away like leaves in the wind. The United States should adapt to this, "saving the world from darkness."[54]

Such views of Al Qaeda and its broader significance tie together several propositions that can be summarized as follows:

> As communications technology allows people and groups to organize on a global scale, and porous borders allow them to infiltrate countries and move weapons and materiel across national borders, terrorism should emerge as a truly global challenge. . . . In a globalized world, however, transnational terrorist groups have global reach and can carry out operations against multiple targets across the world with *relative ease* and, therefore, require a global effort to combat. Moreover, as goods move more easily across national boundaries, transnational terrorist organizations may be able to access the international black market for fissile materials (perhaps from a cash-starved Russia or ideologically motivated actors in Pakistan) and threaten devastating nuclear attacks. Given these *enormous stakes*, therefore, counterterrorism efforts should be occurring on a transnational basis, too, to meet the threat effectively.[55]

If netwar creates a radically new and proximate enemy, this naturally leads to demands for radical countermeasures. Since it can create staging posts in fragile or "failing" states abroad (as well as through domestic or "homegrown" agents), countering it demands measures beyond counterterrorist police work, including the surgical rescue of broken states, the suspension or curtailment of civil liberties, and even anticipatory war. It warrants an ongoing state of emergency and "exception" without a clear terminus. Neoconservative intellectual Charles Krauthammer argued there is no alternative to an ambitious drive to shift the strategic balance against Arab-Islamic radicalism, because Fortress America has "no moat—not after the airplane, the submarine, the ballistic missile—and as for the drawbridge, it was blown up on 9/11."[56]

Interpretations of what AQ "is" and how it relates to geography have evolved since 9/11. In the conflict that ensued, AQ has experienced the loss of its major prewar base in Afghanistan and its subsequent dispersal, its own wars in Afghanistan-Pakistan and Iraq, and in May 2011 the killing of its iconic leader. At critical junctures, events in the Global War on Terror have restaged the question of the movement's relationship with geography and what this says about its lethality, and whether therefore the United States–led coalition should scale back its efforts to more conventional counterterrorism, targeted killings, and intelligence-led police work. At each turn, the notion that AQ is a first-order or existential threat is maintained on the premise that it is dangerous because it is functionally "borderless," applying its armed force in a shrunken world. In 2009–10, as the Obama administration pondered whether to recommit itself to the war in Afghanistan with a "surge" of troops, one of the principal arguments deployed in its favor was "sanctuary denial." The return of the Taliban regime, some argued, would entail the intolerable return of Al Qaeda in some form to Afghanistan, a presence that would constitute a grave threat as it did before 9/11.[57] In his speech in December 2009 at West Point, President Obama claimed that it was "from here" (the "Af/Pak" region) that "we were attacked on 9/11" and that AQ could "operate with impunity" if the region "slides backward."[58] With each blow struck against the network—the loss of a central base in Afghanistan, the continual killing of their mid- to top-level leadership, the curtailing of plots and failure of the network to inflict any further complex mass casualty attacks on Western soil, the death of Osama bin Laden, and the marginality of AQ and its theocratic vision in most of the popular uprisings of the Arab Spring—alarmists warn against complacency and argue that the threat remains or is even getting worse.[59] It is difficult to discern in these bleak assessments any theory by which AQ could be said to be failing. To assert its nonterritoriality is often to assert its immunity to defeat. At its most ambitious, this approach regards the killing or elimination even of AQ's most talented, seasoned, and influential figures as strategically irrelevant. What matters above all is the subversive legend of Al Qaeda. Dead or alive, the likes of Osama bin Laden and Ayman al-Zawahiri will continue to inspire through their dark charisma. Killing them will merely martyr them. The network functions like an impersonal contagion, virus, or cancer that spreads through the world like it would through a human host.[60]

In this way, it lacks any obvious center of gravity that can be targeted, meaning that the accumulation of skill and experience by key figures hardly matters: "Bin Laden's death would not end or even cripple the radical Islamist movement. Fragments of his organization will spread, subdivide, and inject themselves into other parts of the worldwide Islamist network, like a metastasizing cancer that lives on with sometimes lethal effects even after the original tumor has been excised."[61]

Given what is at stake, just how deterritorialized is AQ?

Examining the "Netwar" Argument

Is the Al Qaeda terrorist network a "globalized" phenomenon, to the extent that distance is irrelevant or marginal as a measure of its capabilities? Is it the forerunner of a deeper phenomenon of "netwar," through which the armed militants of today and tomorrow operate as "dark networks" that reflect the "dark side" of globalization?

Let's begin with the first proposition, that AQ represents primarily an identity-based, nongeographical insurgent movement. This is at odds with what the architects and leading figures say about their movement. Whatever else it is, AQ's core has a strategic world view that is both instrumental and territorial. Its very name—translated as "The Base"—suggests a territorial dimension. So too does its main doctrinal innovation, exporting jihad to the "far enemy" to inspire an Islamic uprising against the "apostate regimes" in the Arab-Islamic world, to bleed its enemies out of the sacred lands, and to unite them under a territorially defined caliphate. AQ's theoretician of jihad, Abu Musab al-Suri, speaks of a struggle for the "Muslim heartland."[62] Granted, the motivations and meanings of terrorist violence are manifold, the emotional pull of martyrdom cannot be denied, and performance before an audience is an important part of AQ's brand and concept of revolutionary violence.[63] But the theorists and central figures of AQ also have demonstrably territorial goals and an instrumental view of violence. As chief theorist and now leader Ayman al-Zawahiri insisted, "if the successful operations against Islam's enemies and the severe damage inflicted on them do not serve the ultimate goal of establishing the Muslim nation in the heart of the Islamic world, they will be nothing more than disturbing acts, regardless of their magnitude, that could be absorbed and endured, even after some time and with some losses."[64] In AQ's designation of the United States as its prime enemy, the galvanizing event was a territorial one, the stationing of American troops in Saudi Arabia, the cradle of the faith, at the invitation of Riyadh in 1990 as part of Operation Desert Shield. Bin Laden's rationale for "guerrilla methods" also has a recognizable, material strategic logic. When declaring war in 1996, he justified AQ's asymmetrical tactics not as a means of enacting sacred violence theatrically for its own sake, but as a way of countering the enemy's strengths, because America's military might created an "imbalance of power."[65]

This is not to fall prey to one-dimensionally material interpretations. But elites within the movement at its inception and thereafter have been concerned with an ultimate goal that has a geographical dimension, the expulsion of adversaries, the triggering of Islamist revolution, the overthrow of America's client regimes in a vital region, and the restoration of a lost empire. To define success or failure through more nebulous notions of sustaining a narrative is to set the bar well below what the founders of AQ have consistently said they want to achieve in the long term.

What of AQ's "global" capabilities? A difficulty here is that academic literature on Islamist terrorism since 9/11 focuses mainly on motivation, sociology, and ideology, not on the more prosaic issue of skills and education, while political rhetoric largely takes the deadly capabilities of Islamists as a given. The oft-used phrase "global reach" is misleading. To be sure, AQ struck its "far enemy" on 9/11 and has inflicted attacks in a number of countries since. But power projection is not an undifferentiated constant. It is historically uneven, patchy, and unequally distributed. In the case of AQ and other militant jihadist groups, the space into which it applies its "reach" is susceptible to being fortified and obstructed by state hostility. Obtaining an airline ticket or internet link does not confer global strike capability. AQ is an international network, but in terms of capability it is not a global one. The debate in 2009–10 about the military "surge" in Afghanistan restaged this issue. Just how dangerous would an AQ sanctuary in Afghanistan or Pakistan be? But 9/11 was not inflicted directly from sanctuaries in Afghanistan. There was no straight line from the base in Afghanistan to Manhattan. Its success on 9/11 depended on intermediate critical spaces—forward operating bases—closer to its targets in the First World, such as flight schools in Florida and Arizona, and meeting rooms in Hamburg. And Obama's warning of an AQ operating with "impunity" presupposes an implausibly passive America. Even in a worst-case scenario in which the Taliban returned to power and hosted AQ, it is inconceivable that this would recreate the pre-9/11 situation. This time it would have the attention of a newly alert and hostile United States with public support for sustained military activity to disrupt international terrorism. Any large-scale organized presence of AQ in a fresh sanctuary would hardly be a secure base operating under the radar, instead being vulnerable to violent disruption.[66]

As the 9/11 Commission's investigations also make clear, to operate from its forward bases closer to targets in the West, AQ also required a whole range of steps within the United States that had to come together successfully. Consider the ways in which the plotters had to negotiate the operation and navigate through American space: They had to arrange visas and acquire new "clean" passports with the help of AQ's passport division in Kandahar; they had to clear customs to enter the United States (and on one occasion, two of the ringleaders had to persuade inquisitive US inspectors to admit them despite their student visas having expired); they had to get their flight training and pass; they had to learn English and develop competence in it; they sought practical assistance in buying cars, signing leases, and opening bank accounts from friends, contacts, and translators; and they had to arrange money wire transfers.[67] The overall pattern is not one of ease of operation, but of difficulty, not invisibility and independence, but a high degree of trust in and dependence on social relationships. If it was that difficult when the homeland defense system was relatively vulnerable and policymakers undersensitive to the threat, it is not hard to appreciate how much more difficult it would be to penetrate and attack on such a scale. AQ's own written guidelines to urban cells reflect the obstacles and demands of operating in cities, where cells must have legal documentation, cover, huge financial support, and training and must divide into smaller cells to survive and communicate only via physical "dead drops," pointing out that the state mobilizes most of its operatives in the cities that contain the most important state targets.[68]

Plots since then against targets on American soil have failed repeatedly. According to Risa Brooks, who draws on court records, official documents, and news reports, homegrown terrorists in plots from 2001 to 2010 have had difficulty finding a safe domestic sanctuary in which to operate, even from the early stages of plots. In twelve of the eighteen attempted plots she identifies, an agent or informant was involved at the formative stage, defined as the period "before weapons are acquired or specific targets are developed."[69] A similar pattern can be found in the Heritage Foundation's list of foiled efforts attempted by militants originating from home or abroad, derived from open-source records of trials and investigations; between 9/11 and April 2012, at least fifty publicly known terrorist plots have failed.[70] Most (forty-two) were homegrown efforts, or attempts made by American citizens, permanent legal residents or individuals radicalized largely while in the United States, though a number received assistance from overseas. Only in a minority of cases was the attempt known to be initiated from abroad. And these cases show repeatedly successful surveillance, espionage, infiltration, and sting operations by the FBI and local police, aided as well by informants.

Some illustrative cases show how in the process of preparation, organization, financing, and planning, would-be terrorists have been detected and disrupted. In December 2005, Michael C. Reynolds in his conspiracy to attack oil and gas refineries while waiting for a payment was exposed by an FBI agent posing as a collaborator. In August 2004, an undercover agent from the New York City Police Department's Intelligence Division infiltrated a group planning to bomb a subway in New York. Would-be guerrillas continually have suffered from their security being breached, from financial transfers being exposed, or from their online discussions (such as chat room conversations) being monitored, such as the foiled plot to attack underground transit links between New York City and New Jersey in July 2006, and a sting operation that uncovered a plot to bomb an office tower in Dallas in September 2009.[71]

From these cases, several patterns can be seen. It is now appreciably more difficult to carry out a complex, mass-casualty attack on American soil. The operating environment is more hostile. Entering the United States is more difficult. Border staff are more alert and watch lists exist. Intelligence sharing between law enforcement and intelligence agencies has been enhanced. Aviation security has hardened significantly.[72] And crucially, the role of local informants shows that civil society also intervenes. Neojihadist terrorism, especially of the long-range variety that requires successful movement of people and materials across borders, is effectively (though not perfectly) disrupted by international police work, border control, the building of databases, intelligence sharing, airport security, and support for regional powers like Pakistan.[73] There may be a "chain of terror" between the mountains of Pakistan and Britain's streets, but it can be broken at many points between. By getting the attention of the state and creating a consensus in public opinion supportive of robust counterterrorism measures, the very success of 9/11 foreclosed (or made far more difficult) future attacks of similar magnitude. In this way, terrorism on a catastrophic scale paradoxically has a self-canceling quality. And this makes the space again a barrier as well as a carrier. Also apparent is the doubled-edged nature of technology. The same tools emerging in the age of globalization credited with empowering nonstate actors like AQ can also empower their adversaries. Information technology can facilitate decentralization and networking, but it can also place them at risk of having their communications overheard, putting them on a visible grid to be watched and intercepted. Information technology can also be used to create databases, collate and distribute intelligence, and map insurgent groups.[74] The power to broadcast can come at the expense of discretion, as it did for Adel Daoud, a teenager arrested in Chicago in September 2012 planning to bomb a Chicago bar but who was monitored and fooled by an undercover agent after he got the FBI's attention by posting material online about killing Americans in violent revenge.[75] Globalization, in other words, has not turned the homeland into a permissive operating environment.

For AQ, the double-edged dangers of emerging technologies have been felt at the highest level. Strikingly, Osama bin Laden, whom some observers had characterized as a hi-tech cybernetic figure who inspired the jihad from behind encrypted software, lived in a remarkably low-tech fashion. This was revealed by the state of his compound as it was discovered in Abbottabad.[76] To avoid detection, he avoided the internet himself. His compound wasn't wired for it. He had no phone. He relied on couriers to communicate. He dared meet only a few donors personally. Such was the pressure from US intelligence and military forces that he had trouble sending the simplest communications.[77] The information superhighway wasn't a freeway. Against prepared defenders, it was a dangerous two-way zone of hostility where he could be hunted.

Carrying out attacks against Western targets is also more difficult than "netwar theories" imagine, because it requires hard-won skills that usually can be attained only by physically traveling across distance to be trained face-to-face with others. Training and education is one site where the intimacy of modern war reasserts itself. Theories of AQ that stress its ideological orientation and the ease of joining the violent jihad tend to lose sight of the more prosaic problem that for private agents as much as nation-states, the use of force to achieve a goal remains a matter of practical military skill. Several capabilities are vital to the tradecraft: operational security, weapons acquisition or manufacture, financing, fraud, and the acquiring of false identification documents.[78] A significant proportion of terrorist-type attacks involve explosives rather than firearms. Both require some practical knowledge, but explosives are more demanding to learn how to assemble, transport, and detonate. As acquiring training abroad in camps becomes more difficult and dangerous, "lone wolf" assailants can succeed in relatively low-tech attacks (such as the Fort Hood shootings) but have struggled to inflict more complex bombings. Consider the Times Square bombing attempt in May 2010, featuring "a very crude device that is at the bottom of the food chain when it comes to explosives" prepared by one who "lacks a formal training in explosives."[79]

Among contemporary jihadists, there has been a high level of variation of capability. Mohammed Atta, the 9/11 ringleader, stands at the far end of the spectrum, with months of training and assistance from AQ leaders. He was a highly talented engineering student with meticulous ways. Those that have developed proficiency have normally sought out education by experienced hands. "Self-starting" or homegrown radicals mobilized by jihadist internet videos normally become lethal only when making in-person contact with hardened experts. Two of the bombers behind the 7/7 bombings in London in 2005, for example, and participants in the foiled attack on multiple airliners in August 2006 had been trained in countersurveillance and bombing at training camps in Pakistan.[80] Conversely, among the ranks of would-be holy warriors, there is considerable evidence for incompetence, testifying to the fact that becoming a capable militant is a matter of capacity as well as will.[81] Ultimately, effective terrorism relies upon hard-won skills, teamwork, and efficiency. It may be true, as Walter Laqueur argues, that "information on how to manufacture bombs . . . is now a click away."[82] But seasoned expertise, operational security, and group cohesion is not. The dilemma for aspiring trainees is that either they seek direct training usually through travel to dangerous war zones that are increasingly under surveillance, such as Waziristan, or they attempt to self-educate, which has a poor record of success. So as well as focusing on the sociology of radicalization, states should continue limiting the ability of radicals to obtain operational training.

This places limits on theories that the jihad can migrate to the internet. While the Web is no doubt an important site for fundraising, recruitment, and incitement, intimate contact with educators in a shared local space, as well as active experience, is a necessary (though not sufficient) part of acquiring skills that the internet cannot replicate. As Michael Kenney observes, while it is possible to transmit one type of abstract knowledge (*techne*) remotely across a virtual domain, experiential and practical knowledge (*metis*) is harder and more costly to attain.[83] His study of European Islamist militants reveals a body of people largely underskilled, bad at operational coordination, and bad at planning. Global guerrillas have in common with other military organizations the need for in-person and direct education. That is why, as Peter Bergen cautions, "just as the U.S. military doesn't conduct its training over the internet but at boot camps, it turns out that effective jihadist terrorists are generally the graduates of training camps or war zones, rather than the passive consumers of jihadist propaganda on the Web."[84] The generation of AQ leaders emerging from the war in Afghanistan regarded knowledge grounded in direct experience as the most important measure of a recruit. Captured teaching documents from the house of AQ ideologue Abu Haf in Kandahar defined war as "an experimental science learned through practice," urging future leaders of the jihad to continuous education through not only continuous study, but contact with "expert leaders" and actual command of a unit, "because good leadership can only be achieved through training."[85] This was one reason Osama bin Laden demanded that his subordinate commanders prove themselves first in actual warfighting in the most testing "fighting fronts" of Pakistan, Yemen, Afghanistan, Somalia, and Iraq. He wanted proof of practical capability as well as religious zeal.[86]

What is the role and significance of sanctuaries or safe havens for AQ? For those who do agree that physical sanctuary matters, the threat of AQ obtaining fresh safe havens is often raised uncritically, resting on a blanket typology of the "failed state" that is oblivious to the particular dynamics in each case. As Patrick Stewart notes, "analysts and policymakers alike have simply presumed the existence of a blanket connection between state weakness and threats to the national security of developed countries."[87] An argument has emerged since 9/11 that AQ and its like thrive in chaotic "ungoverned spaces," in weakly governed states that lack adequate levels of order and security. Due to the intolerable risks flowing out of fragile states, some argue, the United States must transform and strengthen those states in a far-reaching program of intervention and investment.[88] As the Global War on Terror reached a crescendo, this became the official position of the US government in its strategic documents.[89] The CIA has identified some fifty such zones worldwide. Others maintain that states are only of marginal importance, for example, that AQ does not require the sponsorship of a state to acquire chemical, biological, radiological, and nuclear (CBRN) weapons, but "can grow, amass strategic strength and survive without a country's active financial backing or central oversight."[90]

On the one hand, both subjectively and objectively secure physical havens and a sympathetic host state do matter to AQ as a site of training, organization, and the creation of intimate social and ideological ties.[91] Any armed struggle needs physical domains in which to recover, regroup, seek finance, and prepare. The coming of the internet hasn't removed the need for shielded space, or the communal intensity of actual congregation. That is why AQ worked hard to find a state patron in the Sudan and then Afghanistan, rather than hide itself in a power vacuum. Afghanistan before 9/11 was the place where AQ formed its plan to attack iconic targets in Washington and New York in 1996, where it gave the pilots their orders about target selection in 1999, where the ringleaders were groomed, and where the fifteen "muscle" hijackers were trained. It was where Khalid Sheik Mohammed schooled jihadists in the English language, fitness, and combat and firearms skills. AQ located its document forgery center at Kandahar airport for the production and supply of fake passports and travel documents. The greater and more complex the plot, the more the demand for actual space that is large yet discrete enough to prepare in.[92] AQ's internal documents speak of its pre-9/11 camps as the facilities for the "best training on Jihad activities" and the basis for separating promising from inadequate individuals, and which prepared the martyrs of 9/11.[93] AQ's chances of finding another sanctuary on that scale and convenience are slim. But the need for bases is why its affiliates continue to seek footholds from Pakistan to Yemen to Iraq as well as exploiting the internet.

Equally, as we have also seen, the mere existence even of an undisrupted sanctuary does not entail a secure or direct pathway to the heartland of AQ's "far enemy," more so now than before 9/11.[94] Like its adversary, AQ needs an intermediate chain of forward links to be able to project power. And once a base is subjected to the hostility of a state, it no longer automatically bestows a safe point of organization. Thanks to the killing and capturing program of the United States and its allies and partners since 9/11, AQ's members in the most embattled zones spend much of their time and resources trying merely to survive. Few locations function for long as an unmolested staging post for international terrorism. Though jihadists seek havens in Pakistan, for example, these are hardly secure. Bin Laden himself in late 2010 urged that some AQ members who could not keep a low profile relocate out of Waziristan given that it was becoming an unsafe haven. He noted the dangers of using cars, the gaze of America's aerial photography, the need for deputies to communicate only through letters, and for leaders to stay "in a faraway location lest lower leaders rise with less experience who would make mistakes."[95] While the wider effects of "drone" killings are open to debate and will be discussed in chapter 5, a continuous assassination and surveillance program dilutes its most talented figures and diverts their attention to operational security and survival. The Afghan-Pakistani border is no longer the place described by then-CIA director George Tenet in 2003 as "veritable no 'man's lands. . . where extremist movements find shelter and can win the breathing space to grow."[96] While clearly AQ does seek footholds in such states, those spaces are highly dangerous for them. Turbulent vacuums of power are generally unsafe for most people in them.[97] Because they can do little to protect or even monitor their sovereign borders, such states are generally more open to military countermeasures by US special forces, naval interdiction, or surveillance. Consider Somalia, feared as a new sanctuary in the making.[98] The United States has subcontracted the hunting of AQ in that country and offered bounties. It is also difficult to inhabit secretly, as a non-Somali's presence is usually quickly detected, and to ensure secrecy any outsider would need to be virtually housebound. If that doesn't make it difficult enough, terrorist networks would be vulnerable to the same predations of kidnapping, extortion, and assassination that endanger aid agencies there. For these reasons, terrorist groups need a baseline of political order and functioning infrastructure to operate securely from.[99]

Given these security problems, lack of infrastructure, and logistical difficulties, it is therefore no surprise that most effective terrorists do not come from "failed states" but from strongly governed states such as Saudi Arabia, and most failed states do not host many organizations that back terrorism.[100] Of the top twenty states identified by *Foreign Policy* as "failing" on its Failed States Index, only Sudan appears as a state sponsor of terrorism, and apart from Pakistan and Afghanistan, which no longer offer secure sanctuaries as before, most have little connection with terrorism.[101] AQ's franchises mostly do not seek bases in the most chaotic states of the world, such as in sub-Saharan Africa, compared to wealthier and more functional states in the Middle East. Weak statehood, indeed, may be incidental compared to other variables, such as proximity to a war or the permission of a "weak" state that exercises some sovereign control.[102] While it may be that some states afflicted by acute problems of governance are prone to terrorist attacks and may be more likely to have transnational terrorists within them, they are usually not reliable hosts for plotting complex large-scale attacks abroad.[103]

AQ's own documents reflect a concern for the geopolitical difficulties of balancing operational security and survival with access and effectiveness, all the way from decisions about where to seek bases down to the most practical tactical level of planning and executing operations.[104] Bases in "friendly" lands with shelters dug into mountains are needed for training, recovery, rest, and logistics, and a platform to sustain and broadcast jihad. Yet setting up a base in a friendly host country brings the difficulty of maintaining relations with an interfering patron state.[105] Internal documents suggest an ongoing interest by AQ figures in geographical terrain as they seek out locations for training camps and the nature of "the land: climate, topography, its resources, its suitability for guerrilla warfare."[106] Yemen appealed as a historic "fortified base" or "natural fortress" for operations in the Arabian Peninsula that had helped its inhabitants throw off raids by the Portuguese, British, and Ottoman empires that was more defensible than the flat desert lands of the peninsula, and because "everything is available in Yemen: weapons, ammunition, mountains, valleys, water sources, suitable areas for setting camps, sufficiently trained brothers."[107] The dynamic of moving between cities and remote locations such as mountains is a problem of adaptation that attracts much analysis. Earlier documents before the urban struggles in Iraq in particular link guerrilla survival with the seeking out of remote locations "over which the government forces have no control. Usually, these areas have difficult terrains such as mountain areas, forests, marsh areas."[108]

In challenging the assumptions behind more radical measures to combat terrorism, such as liberal wars or an overextended surveillance state, it is methodologically difficult to judge precisely how far other measures to forestall terrorist attacks are effective and to disentangle "effort" from "effect." By definition, it involves estimating what causes something not to happen. Do lesser, predominantly "law enforcement" measures work?

There are good reasons to believe that other more modest counterterrorism policing, combined with judicious raiding, is sufficient to contain AQ's capabilities to the extent that their reach and lethality are reduced to make them mostly a nuisance. Consider the role of intelligence. While public debate has focussed on either large intelligence failures or the more controversial activities of extraordinary rendition, torture, and wiretapping, more prosaic intelligence work has played a leading part in creating a more difficult environment for AQ to operate in. As we have seen, the detailed history of thwarted plots in the United States, made available in court cases, does suggest the importance of intelligence penetration and the cultivation of relations with local communities who may give or withhold information. In addition, enhanced liaison with foreign states and an increased capability to "track" suspects with targeters scanning and interpreting ever-more integrated data, such as signals intelligence or financial transactions, has increased the rate at which the United States is able to locate, seize, or kill AQ commanders.[109]

This is not just a matter of direct disruption, but of deterrence, or dissuading an adversary from taking an action that they otherwise would have taken by convincing the adversary that the cost the action will outweigh any potential gains.[110]

Deterrence can happen through cost imposition, such as retaliation, or through benefit denial. Contrary to the assumption that AQ and its imitators are fanatically oblivious to security countermeasures and beyond this interaction, they do respond dynamically to measures they do or think they will meet.[111] Even movements that glorify violent jihad contain supporters, organizers, and leaders who value their lives and can sometimes be influenced, and this applies too to the wider circle of potential enablers and facilitators. Foot soldiers who wish to sacrifice themselves can be deterred by the prospect of failure. Airport security and border control may largely function as theater, but nevertheless it seems to deter attacks or encourage smaller, stealthier, and cruder or less dangerous ones. Since the introduction of more stringent airport surveillance rituals, militants attempting to smuggle bombs aboard airliners build smaller, more concealable devices whose payload is less, to "trade reliability for concealment."[112] The 2001 "shoe bomber" and 2009 "underwear bomber" involved relatively unskilled men with small quantities of explosives that may not have been enough to inflict the damage they desired. That they boarded planes armed was hardly welcome news. But it does suggest that the creation of the perception of effective barriers incentivizes determined adversaries to adapt in ways that reduce their lethality. Similarly, the "Times Square bomber" tried to evade detection by purchasing inferior ammonium nitrate and fireworks to lower the profile of his purchases.[113] There is also incremental but suggestive evidence of cases where deterrence-by-retaliation and deterrence-by-denial got the desired reception. The enhanced fortification of a US base in Turkey persuaded an AQ affiliate to call off its attack there. Increased scrutiny of financiers after 9/11 reportedly persuaded some potential donors from funding militant groups.[114] Captured documents from Iraq suggest that aspiring suicide bombers are sensitive to and can be put off by the risk of tactical failure and botched planning.[115] And while the link cannot be established with certainty, given the other possible causes involved, there is a consistent correlation between countermeasures, such as the introduction of magnetometers as a routine practice of passenger screening or the increased fortification of embassies with a decline in aircraft hijacking attempts and a reduction in attacks on embassies.[116] The United States also has scored some notable victories in fracturing terrorist networks such as the Moro Islamic Liberation Front of the southern Philippines, whom it persuaded not to assist AQ, using a combination of carrots and sticks to get the MILF to distance itself and actively assist rounding up AQ members in its backyard.[117] Stronger defenses, of course, are probably not the only reason for the overall decline in the number and severity of attacks. But the evidence we do have suggests that the cumulative force of a more hostile public environment, greater intelligence gathering, more monitoring and interdiction of international financing, and tougher border and airline security have created a more difficult operating environment than before 9/11. It is harder for them to travel, raise money, move materials, gather safely, and stay off the radar.

As further proof of how jihadist groups respond to countermeasures in ways that reduce their lethality, consider also Justin Hastings's work on the difficulties of the Southeast Asian Islamist group Jemaah Islamiyah against constraints imposed on its operations by state power. Based on fieldwork and interviews with both jihadists and the authorities chasing them down, Hastings shows that transnational jihadists were better able to operate during periods of relative political openness, but that when their adversaries are roused into hostility, geographical borders again closed in.[118] When after 9/11 Jemaah Islamiyah's activities such as the 2002 Bali bombing aroused adversaries like Indonesia, Singapore, and Malaysia, the state tightened its control of the infrastructure of seaports, highways, and railroads that guerrillas rely upon to shift their guns, explosives, and contraband. Fighters adapted by switching their movements into the forbidding terrain of jungles, islands, and mountains. After 9/11, they traveled by plane less often and chose illicit routes. Basic logistical problems became more difficult, of assembling all of the "parts" of an operation in one place overall, "once the political window began closing," the group "became more vulnerable to interdiction as it struggled to cross international boundaries using illicit routes that hugged the landscape." The mobility conferred by modern technology was outweighed by the "lack of support from the dominant authority in an area."[119] This confirms the argument that terrorism in a hostile environment is harder than it looks. Secretly putting together the skilled people, the plot, and the materials and pulling off a sufficiently large and prominent operation without a mistake is difficult. Even 9/11 only just succeeded. AQ's guide to its own travelers warns of a "security war . . .from all governments, border entry points and airports," requiring greater levels of tradecraft in minimizing suspicions and in communications.[120]

All of the constraints on terrorism discussed above come together in the issue of WMD-armed or nuclear terrorism. Geographic obstacles complicate the task of building, securing, and transporting WMDs across space and make the nightmare of nuclear or biological terrorism particularly difficult to realize. Pulling off a bioterrorist attack entails a multistep process of obtaining, preserving, moving, and detonating the weapon, while employing specialist skills, maintaining secrecy, and moving through highly policed territory.[121] As John Mueller calculates, the atomic terrorist's task might involve a twenty-step process, from successfully obtaining HEU (highly enriched uranium), to assembling a team of highly skilled scientists and technicians, to smuggling of the improvised nuclear device weighing a ton or more, to the successful attack.[122] Both require the secure procurement, preparation, and secret movement of a heavy instrument through increasingly monitored space and across borders. What about the prospect of "rogue states" handing over

WMD capabilities to terrorist networks? This is obviously something worth minimizing through counterproliferation steps. But it is also more remote than both the Bush and Obama administrations warned, and this must be balanced against arguments for more high-cost preventative measures like war. In the only extensive study of the subject, Keir Leiber and Daryl Press show the flaws in the empirical and logical claims behind the fear of surreptitious nuclear weapons transfer to terrorist networks. Going on the high attribution rate by the state after attacks on American soil, the small number of countries that sponsor terror, the small number of groups that have a state sponsor, and given that only one state (Pakistan) has ties to such groups and has nukes or enough fissile material to make one, it is very unlikely that a group or a state sponsor could remain anonymous after an attack, so that passing weapons to terrorists would not relieve states of being subject to retaliation.[123] In other words, even if post–Cold War globalization may make nuclear materials more available to some states or networks, that does not make realistic an "anonymous" and unaccountable nuclear terrorist strike, either as an independent or proxy act.

Both versions of the arguments that AQ is deterritorialized are flawed, whether the claim that globalization places safe havens in direct striking distance, or the claim that the internet is a substitute for physical bases. Both of these notions are innocent of the politics of distance. The notion of a direct pathway between sanctuary and target loses sight of the transforming effects of state hostility upon space. The notion of the internet as a substitute sanctuary loses sight of the vital importance of real group dynamics and the role of intimate space in forging ties and teaching skills.

Networking and the Fragmentation of the Jihad

So far I have traced how distance constrains AQ's capabilities, from its ability to mount long-range catastrophic attacks, to its ability to train and reproduce effective agents. Distance also takes effect in another important way. The most significant strategic change that AQ underwent after the Global War on Terror began was to decentralize and disperse with the aid of technology. A core assumption of the "netwar" school is that geographically dispersed, transnational networks are superior forms of organization to hierarchies. Unquestionably, networks can confer advantages. By becoming more diffuse, an organization or movement can gain greater adaptability and resilience. It is harder to smash decisively. But the "network" literature "tends to assume away problems of distance."[124] Increased resilience and survivability tend to come at the price of command, control, and cohesion. Creating distance between fellow members can fragment a movement, erode trust, and make misunderstanding and conflict more likely than in colocated teams.

One practical sign of AQ's problems with command and control can be seen in its paperwork. For a network that is supposedly a phantom menace, either "virtual" or being managed on the back of an envelope, AQ is surprisingly bureaucratic. Whether in Afghanistan, Iraq, or Somalia, its accounting practices produce a vast paper trail of documents, from salary spreadsheets to job applications to documentation on each member, down to the smallest expenses.[125] It is one of the few ways of tracking and controlling its members who operate often remotely. Trips into the desert wear down Toyota Land Cruisers, as receipts for oil changes, batteries, filters, and new parts suggest. This is evidence that even for AQ, the enterprise is logistically intensive and a concern for accountability and discipline is strong. And the promise of "netwar" meets the difficulty that switching to the internet as a paperless, electronic body would make AQ more detectable and vulnerable.

At its peak, when it was capable of inflicting 9/11, Al Qaeda had not been a "virtual community." It had evolved through preexisting, intimate social bonds.[126] The movement relied on family members and friends for the storage and movement of funds. When it lost a secure territorial base in Afghanistan in the autumn fighting of 2001, in important ways Al Qaeda became less effective. Its loss of a safe central staging post for recruitment, forging social ties, and group cohesion was not only a contributing factor to the weakening of its capacity to inflict complex, mass-casualty attacks. It also moved AQ into a more incoherent and troubled state structurally from which there is no clear escape.

We can chart this breakdown from the published manuscript of the operative Fadil Harun in 2009, the "confidential secretary" of AQ central who was killed in Somalia in 2011. Harun wrote to distinguish AQ and its focus on major military and economic targets from the regional jihadist groups and their indiscriminate attacks on civilians. AQ in its training aimed to strip recruits of regional and ethnic agendas and turn them into "jihadists without borders." The arc of his story is the misfortune of what happens next. Like bin Laden, he laments the fall from the "original" AQ and the hijacking of a "lawful" and disciplined movement and the misuse of its banner by lesser, juvenile militants, the post-Taliban young men "who dispersed around the world." The internet he fears attracts a mindless enthusiasm for martyrdom without strategic judgment, whom he calls "jihadis. com." Such *takfiris* carried out "random," "monstrous" killings, for example, in the Islamic Maghreb. It is not easy to determine the reliability of his claims that attacks on civilians were the fault of wayward "brothers."[127] But the very fact that a member of the original inner circle felt compelled to write a work separating the brand from its most politically damaging followers and to assert "the sincerity and uprightness of al-Qaida's path" points to the problem. As Ronald Reagan quipped, if you're explaining, you're losing.

AQ suffers dilemmas that are attached to the process of networking.[128] There are drawbacks to its much-hyped franchising. As a "big tent" that attracts localized struggles, it exerts only limited control over its adherents. It draws to itself forces that it may not be able to discipline. It is a good demonstration of the terrorist's organizational dilemma and its principal-agent difficulty. The dilemma is that controlling violence, managing an organization, and disciplining members creates vulnerabilities, but taking measures to secure an organization from those vulnerabilities compromises its ability to control its violence in politically effective ways.[129]

The "security versus control" dilemma reached its most serious crisis point for AQ in Northern Iraq after Saddam Hussein was overthrown. Abu Musab al-Zarqawi (1966–2006), a Jordanian Islamist anointed by Osama bin Laden as the "Prince of Al-Qaeda in Iraq," became the head of Al Qaeda in Iraq (AQI). AQI stoked a sectarian war on Iraqi Shiites in particular with its assault on the revered golden dome of Samarra's Askariya shrine. It also waged a campaign of sectarian bloodletting and authoritarian intimidation, often without bin Laden's preapproval, that went on despite the written pleas of al-Zawahiri. Al-Zawahiri counseled that AQI should follow a focused, sequential strategy of first expelling the US occupying forces before establishing a Sunni emirate on captured territory.[130] AQ's senior leadership urged al-Zarqawi to confine his violence to Americans and refrain from undermining broad Islamic support for the resistance. But AQI attacked Shiites to foment a religious war as well as imposed a harsh Islamist rule on Sunni neighborhoods, a pattern of rigidity and sectarian brutality that his successor, Abu Hamza al-Muhajir (1968–2010), would continue. This helped trigger the "Anbar Awakening" from the autumn of 2006. Sunnis who had staged an insurgency against international forces had offered several times to negotiate ceasefires with US forces and this time successfully realigned with US forces against AQI. Having applied the theory of Abu Bakr Naji that sowing *fitna* (chaos) would motivate the local Sunni population to embrace the jihadists' arms as liberators and security providers, AQI's indiscriminate violence of bombings, kidnappings, and beheadings and in particular the bombing of hotels in Jordan gave it the reputation of predators more than providers.[131] A poll in Iraq in 2007 revealed 100 percent opposition to AQ attacks on civilians and 98 percent opposition to the group's efforts to recruit foreign fighters.[132] This was compounded by the fallout between AQ and local power figures over criminal fiefdoms and smuggling income.[133] Rather than making it more strategically effective, in one of its most valued battlegrounds in "the land with two rivers" that AQ wanted to be a pillar of the Islamic nation, decentralization generated unanticipated consequences by opening the way to an alienating sectarian violence that had always unnerved "AQ central." Abu Turab al-Jazairi, an Al Qaeda commander in Iraq, complained to the Qatari newspaper *Al-Arab* that only a third of his fellow jihadists in Mesopotamia were reliable and that "Al-Qaeda has been infiltrated by people who have harmed its reputation."[134] The Sunni rebellion against al-Zarqawi's brand of Islamism mixed synergistically with the US "surge" turned the tide against AQI and, for a time, lowered the level of violence that had climaxed in 2007.[135] This is hardly the end of the story of AQ's struggles in Iraq, but the disadvantages of operating as a global banner to which diffuse factions are drawn can be seen.

In many of its battlegrounds, a similar pattern of blowback can be found. AQ triggered condemnation in the Maghreb, as reflected in al-Zawahiri's open online meeting with critical Muslims in April 2008.[136] Jihadist websites featured posts protesting against a wave of killings, and jihadists on the ground warned that failure to channel the violence would mean that "people will start fighting us in the streets."[137] Confronted by a local affiliate in Algeria murdering Muslims over which he has little control, he defended its activities after the fact before an audience of dismayed fellow believers. In Saudi Arabia, after a wave of attacks in 2003–4, support for AQ collapsed, reinforced by state measures, from rehabilitation techniques seeking to cure young men of "deviant" beliefs to new regulations on formerly unmonitored religious charities and King Abdullah's public campaign against AQ propaganda. Even in Gaza, where the Palestinian nationalist group Hamas and AQ-linked groups at times collaborate, the two have also clashed repeatedly. Hamas in August 2009 denounced AQ attacks abroad, cracked down on foreign bin Ladenists declaring an "Islamic Emirate" in a southern Gaza town, and accused it of trying to tie the Palestinian nationalist cause to its global jihad, and launched raids against it.[138] Even in terrain AQ regards as central to its cause, it breeds hostility.

There have also been schisms and blowback at a theological level. In reaction to the predations of AQI, leading Muslim clerics who had once approved of defensive jihad, such as al-Zarqawi's former mentor Abu Muhammed al-Maqdisi, rebuked his methods and renounced his campaign. Sayyid Imam al-Sharif, also known as Dr. Fadl, was formerly the leader of the Egyptian group Al-Jihad and one of the founding fathers of Al Qaeda. This veteran renounced AQ's ways as both doctrinally wrong and politically futile, favoring instead more limited jihad, and challenged AQ's religious authority.[139] There may be good reasons to be wary of jihadist recantations, especially by those serving prison sentences. Regardless, in the wider struggle over ideas it is a blow against the legitimacy of AQ's jihad.[140]

For all its innovations and agility, AQ is ultimately self-defeating because it is not sufficiently unitary to achieve the most important requirement of strategy, the limitation of war. Gaining in terms of resilience, it has lost ground in terms of legitimacy and cohesion. It is hard to pose as the knight of Islam if AQ cannot stop its movement continually slaughtering Muslims. As a "big tent" that attracts localized struggles, AQ exerts only limited control over its adherents. It draws to itself forces that it may not be able to discipline. According to a Combating Terrorism Center Study in December 2009, Muslims are a large majority of the victims in attacks that AQ claims credit for.[141] This is not merely an inference from observation of AQ's behavior and wider reaction. It is also discernable within AQ's own audits. The difficulty of holding together a focused jihad as a vision that would unite Muslims is reflected in the internal debates within AQ about its targets and methods, and the continually debated issue of how decentralized execution of the jihad results in repelling rather than attracting fellow Muslims.[142] There is a recurrent internal critique by such AQ theorists as Abdelaziz al-Anzi, Ayman al-Zawahiri, and Abu Musab al-Suri that failure to "take the people's stance into consideration" would sacrifice sympathy and assistance and lead to isolation and failure, as did the Armed Islamic Group in Algeria in the mid-1990s. For the War on Terror era, figures from the upper echelons of AQ believed in a strategy of "America First." They warned against the diffusion of the jihad away from a struggle against America, and toward multiple wars against multiple adversaries. Particularly after the US invasion of Iraq, there were a number of exhortations to AQ franchises to focus their jihad as a war against America. A letter addressed to the leader of AQ in the Arabian Peninsula (AQAP), probably from either Atiyah Abd al-Rahman or Osama bin Laden, expressed concern about the new recruits' misunderstanding of the overarching strategy. It advised that rather than carrying the fight to the Yemeni state or security forces, AQ

> concentrate on its external big enemy before its internal enemy. . . . America is the head of the nonbelievers. . . . It is very important to remind all of our brothers about it with a note to the new generation, who joined the jihad road and were not advised about this issue . . . any work to directly defend the mujahidin group will be excluded from al Qaida's general politics policy because the muhjahidin group should be able to carry out its mission, which is striking American interests . . . our work and messages concentrate on exhausting and straining the America, especially after September 11. We will continue to pressure the Americans until there is a balance of terror, where the expense of war, occupation, and influence on our countries becomes a disadvantage for them.[143]

There is considerable evidence that regional AQ attacks that killed Muslims damaged its reputation and plunged it into a crisis of legitimacy. Bin Laden himself in September 2006 attracted criticism, accurately or not, for allowing a jihad to be conducted inside the Arabian Peninsula and particularly Saudi Arabia, where AQ's activities caused revulsion in a clamp-down by the state, which resulted in "tightening the security of all passage points that lead to jihad."[144] So much so that at least from 2010, bin Laden lamented that after the war expanded beyond Afghanistan, some of the overzealous mujahidin who spread out "became totally absorbed in fighting our local enemies" and inflicted poorly conceived attacks that unnecessarily killed Muslims, led to propaganda defeats, the "loss of the Muslims' sympathetic approach to the Mujahidin," a pattern that would lead to "winning several battles while losing the war at the end." Bin Laden argued on this basis for the recentralization of AQ's media operations and regional jihadist groups.[145]

The combined result of all these trends has been to turn a body that could once inflict a devastating strike across the world into a set of increasingly fragmented movements on many fronts that represent a chronic but not first-order level of menace. With the organization attrited and divided, its violence is not globally synchronized, is frequently crude and low-tech, its targets are mostly "soft" (nongovernmental) ones, its franchises and cells are mostly disrupted, and most of its attacks fail in Western heartlands.[146] In the words of one CIA expert, this leaves AQ "small, lethal, disjointed and miserable."[147] In this light, the shift to online incitement through *Inspire* magazine is less a sign of strength but of weakness and fragmentation. Rhetorical appeals for assaults may raise motivation but do not generate capability. Its polemics might attract sympathy but abandon the attempt to impose control or cohesion.

Though this analysis has focused particularly on AQ's group cohesion and military capability, this has a broader significance as it is symbiotically linked to its level of support, sympathy, and legitimacy. Misdirected violence has alienated and generated antibodies, as shown above. And continual failure to strike at a sufficient level of magnitude in turn has consequences for AQ's following. As the internal analysis of AQ's senior figure Abu Yasir had prophetically observed, "success, in most cases, attracts supporters. Failure and defeat, however, will most likely disperse supporters."[148] With the cumulative effect of fragmentation and blowback from misdirected violence, it is not surprising that in those Arab Spring uprisings that have been led primarily by civil society, as in Egypt and Tunisia, AQ has been politically marginal.

Conclusion

There is an "over here" and an "over there" after all. On closer inspection, theories of netwar lose sight of the more low-tech and mundane needs of any armed insurgent movement, while theories of a postmodern "global insurgency" focus disproportionately on the benefits of deterritorialization while losing sight of the tradeoffs involved. AQ is not postgeographic or simply a "global enemy that can strike anywhere at anytime. It must now contend with a heavily surveyed, policed, and disrupted space of border checkpoints, databases, and surveillance, of identity checks and aircraft photography, of informants and outsider infiltration, black sites and torture chambers, in some places a virtual "kill zone" of relentless drone strikes. The distance-decay effect still applies in multiple ways.[149] In adapting to the pressures of aroused state hostility, separation and decentralization across space may make their groups harder to smash, but only at a serious cost in group trust, command and control, and strategic cohesion. Today's "global guerrillas" are not the equivalent of a borderless contagion or system virus that moves easily and quickly. That metaphorical language is inaccurate and lends itself to threat inflation. Bounded by geography and the spatial dynamics of power, makers of "netwar" are very human.

After 2001, a networking effect was forced upon AQ by Western retaliation and had important results. In the evolving environment since then, AQ found the space around it increasingly dangerous and disruptive. Its lethality and effectiveness relies upon the control of actual territorial bases, as well as intimate and person-to-person social relationships and the localized acquisition of hard-won skills. Because terrorism is a military skill that relies upon face-to-face contact, and not an instant capability rapidly passed on through the internet, AQ finds it hard to replace its killed or captured talent and is made up of members many of whom lack core skills. AQ's subsequent internal schisms, fragmentation, and crisis of legitimacy can be partly traced to the dilemmas of distance.

AQ's presence in physical sanctuaries does not mean that its incubation in fragile states make it highly proximate and within easy striking range. And its presence in the cyber domain does not mean that it is a deterritorialized force immune from the decaying effects of distance. It does, in fact, rely on secure space, and there are many intermediate steps between its locations and its Western targets that can be broken, and it is vulnerable to being weakened through violent (and nonviolent) disruption.

What are the implications of these arguments for strategy? While I do not offer a programmatic list of concrete steps, we can draw from these arguments a broad logic for countering AQ. A prudent strategy must make the security gains worth the costs or weigh up the costs we are willing to incur in proportion to the magnitude of the perceived threat. This calculus in turn is affected by our assessment of the gravity of the threat.[150] The contest is between a logic of containment and of eradication or "rollback." Containment is more prudent because it recognizes that the adversary is self-defeating and its capabilities can be limited while it slowly becomes marginalized into a nuisance. It also recognizes that measures short of ambitious nation-building wars are sufficient to constrain AQ substantially. A containment strategy is mindful of not creating a cure that is worse than the disease, which in this case is nontrivial but hardly existential.

Eradication, by contrast, is a logic based on the unfounded assumption that AQ is a first-order threat because it is a borderless movement with global reach, that it cannot be coexisted with in any degree, and that a far-reaching war is needed to eliminate it. Stephen Biddle, arguing in favor of war in Afghanistan on different grounds, exposed the logic of armed nation building as a solution to terrorism as an approach that would lead quickly to strategic insolvency: "We clearly cannot afford to wage protracted warfare with multiple brigades of American ground forces simply to deny al Qaeda potential safe havens; we would run out of brigades long before bin Laden ran out of prospective sanctuaries."[151] Not only has the effort to pursue absolute security proven too costly. Based on the findings here, it is not needed.

Because this adversary is ultimately self-defeating, more incremental efforts will suffice to suppress AQ's lethality that stop short of trying to "fix" the interior political space of failed states. Some of these are eminently achievable, such as further investment in measures already under way, including training police and airport-security staff, drying up AQ's sources of funding, international intelligence-sharing, and the "Nunn-Lugar" program of securing and locking down of loose nuclear materials from the territories of the former Soviet Union, to make the threat of nuclear terrorism even more remote at an affordable price. It would also include more difficult measures such as carefully judged targeted killings that minimize the killing of civilians, a subject that a later chapter will explore in greater depth. The aim does not have to be eliminating safe havens, but ensuring that such havens that do exist are unsafe, isolating them, and disrupting the links in the long chain between AQ's footholds abroad and its striking power closer to Western heartlands.[152]

In responding to AQ, there needs to be a deeper debate about the causes of militant Islamism of the transnational type, whether and how far the United States is willing to alter its grand strategy to "drain the swamp" that produces it, and whether it is willing to endure the continual threat of AQ as a worthwhile cost of its forward military-strategic presence. In the meantime, more modest and unspectacular counterterrorism, standoff strikes, law enforcement, and counter proliferation measures are an effective and sustainable way of containing the movement while it slowly destroys itself.

The issue of threat perception is crucial, because AQ remains dangerous if Westerners still perceive it as a globalized superthreat. If it retains this aura, it can bait its adversaries into misperceiving the threat and overreaching. Realizing that the global guerrilla can be constrained by distance is an important step in guarding against overreaction and self-defeating behavior. To ignore distance as a dimension of the problem is to perpetuate one of the most serious errors of the War on Terror, the failure to measure risks and costs soberly. AQ may still have the capacity to pose lower-level and chronic security threats. But it does not pose a borderless threat of existential magnitude to its far enemies. A little proportionality is due.

Notes

1. For the purposes of this chapter, I define terrorism only to refer to armed force carried out to induce a state of terror and to inspire wider audiences for political purposes, along the lines suggested by Alex Schmid: "an anxiety-inspiring method of repeated violent action, employed by (semi)clandestine individual, group or state actors, for idiosyncratic, criminal, or political reasons, whereby—in contrast to assassination—the direct targets of violence are not the main targets." Alex P. Schmid, "The Response Problem as a Definition Problem," in *Western Responses to Terrorism,* ed. Alex P. Schmid and Ronald D. Crelinsten (London: Frank Cass, 1993), 8. That working definition does not resolve the problem that "terrorism" is essentially a term of political judgment about the legitimacy of violence, but I happily leave that debate to others.

2. Conflict Records Research Center, National Defense University, Al Qaeda and Associated Movements Collection (henceforth CRRCNDU-AQAM), undated review of 9/11 attacks, circa late 2002, AQ-SHPD-D-001-285, 1, 8; AQ-SHPD-D-000-042, handwritten notebook captured "in vicinity of Tora Bora," written after October 2001, 5.

3. Pascal Vennesson, "Globalization and al Qaeda's Challenge to American Unipolarity," in *Recalling September 11th: Is Everything Different Now?,* ed. James Burk (New York: Cambridge University Press, 2013), 232–61, 242; Kurt M. Campbell, "Globalization's First War?," *Washington Quarterly* 25:1 (2002): 7–14, 7. The author also too hastily accepted this interpretation of Al Qaeda and its relationship with globalization: Patrick Porter, *Military Orientalism: Eastern War through Western Eyes* (New York: Columbia University Press, 2009), 63.

4. Marc Sageman, *Leaderless Jihad* (Philadelphia: University of Pennsylvania Press, 2008); Bruce Hoffman, "The Myth of Grass-Roots Terrorism," *Foreign Affairs* 87:3 (2008): 133–38; Elaine Sciolino and Eric Schmitt, "A Not Very Private Feud over Terrorism," *New York Times,* June 8, 2008; Andreas Behnke and Chrisvtina Hellmich, eds., *Knowing Al Qaeda: The Epistemology of Terrorism* (Farnham, UK: Ashgate, 2012).

5. Osama bin Laden, "Declaration of War against the Americans Occupying the Land of the Two Holy Places," August 23, 1996, www.pbs.org/newshour/updates/military/july-dec96/fatwa_1996 .html.

6. That is the title of the online manual published in 2004, Abu Bakr Naji, *The Management of Savagery: The Most Critical Stage through Which the Umma Will Pass* (trans. William McCants, John M. Olin Institute for Strategic Studies, Harvard University, 2006).

7. Jason Burke, *Al Qaeda: The True Story of Radical Islam* (London: I. B. Tauris, 2003); Brynjar Lia, *Architect of Global Jihad: The Life of Al-Qaeda Strategist Abu Mus'ab al-Suri* (London: Hurst, 2007); "Al-Suri's Doctrines for Decentralized Jihadi Training," *Terrorism Monitor* 5:2 (2007).

8. In Syria, for instance, the al-Nusra front and ISIS (the Islamic State of Iraq and Syria) are reportedly clashing and have drawn the condemnation of "AQ central." See Michael Doran, William McCants, and Clint Watts, "An al Qaeda-Linked Group Worth Befriending," *Foreign Affairs,* January 23, 2014; "Al Qaeda Chief Annuls Syrian-Iraqi Jihad Merger," Al Jazeera, June 9, 2013.

9. As Seth Jones argues, "Al Qaeda Is Far from Defeated," *Wall Street Journal,* April 29, 2012.

10. Fawaz A. Gerges, *The Rise and Fall of al Qaeda* (New York: Oxford University Press, 2011), 3.

11. Stephen M. Walt, *The Origins of Alliances* (Ithaca, NY: Cornell University Press, 1990), 114.

12. As Stephen Biddle reflects, "Learning to Live with Insecurity in a Post 9/11 World," *Council on Foreign Relations,* August 30, 2011.

13. As Ronald R. Krebs and Jennifer K. Lobasz suggest, "Fixing the Meaning of 9/11: Hegemony, Coercion and the Road to War in Iraq," *Security Studies* 16:3 (2007): 409–51, 413.

14. I borrow this distinction from John Mueller, "Harbinger or Aberration? A 9/11 Provocation," *The National Interest* 69 (2002): 45–50.

15. Weeks after 9/11, Bush's deputy secretary of defense, Paul Wolfowitz, spoke of the "globalization of terror, in which rogue states and terrorist organizations share information, intelligence, technology, weapons materials and know-how." For Bush's secretary of state, Condoleezza Rice, a new age of state failure accelerates worldwide flows of havoc, creating a perilous world of "global pathways that facilitate the spread of pandemics, the movement of criminals and terrorists, and the proliferation of the world's most dangerous weapons." Paul Wolfowitz, "Building a Military for the 21st Century," Prepared Statement for the House and Senate Armed Services Committees,

October 3–4, 2001 (Washington, DC: US Department of Defense, 2001); Condoleezza Rice, "The Promise of Democratic Peace," *Washington Post*, December 11, 2005.

16. In his address to the Joint Session of Congress after the 9/11 attacks, Bush asserted that "our war on terror begins with al Qaeda, but it does not end there. It will not end until every terrorist group of global reach has been found, stopped, and defeated." President George W. Bush, "Address before a Joint Session of the Congress on the United States Response to the Terrorist Attacks of September 11," September 20, 2001, at www.presidency.ucsb.edu/ws/?pid=64731.

17. President George W. Bush, Second Inaugural Address, *Washington Post*, January 21, 2005, at www.washingtonpost.com/wp-dyn/articles/A23747-2005Jan20.html.

18. According to the *National Security Strategy* of 2002: "In a globalized world, events beyond America's borders have a greater impact than inside them. Our society must be open to people, ideas, and goods from across the globe. The characteristics we most cherish—our freedom, our cities, our systems of movement, and modern life—are vulnerable to terrorism. This vulnerability will persist long after we bring to justice those responsible for the September 11 attacks. As time passes, individuals may gain access to means of destruction that until now could be wielded only by armies, fleets, and squadrons. This is a new condition of life." President of the United States, *National Security Strategy of the United States of America* (Washington, DC: US Government Printing Office, September 2002), 31. According to the *Quadrennial Defense Review* of 2006, "throughout much of its history, the United States enjoyed a geographic position of strategic insularity. The oceans and uncontested borders permitted rapid economic growth and allowed the United States to spend little at home to defend against foreign threats. The advent of long-range bombers and missiles, nuclear weapons, and more recently of terrorist groups with global reach, fundamentally changed the relationship between US geography and security. Geographic insularity no longer confers security for the country." *QDR* 2006, 24.

19. Counterterrorism became a coequal pillar alongside (1) dissuading the rise of hostile peer rivals through overwhelming military superiority and diplomatic accommodation; (2) spreading democracy, spreading the "open door" of market capitalism and free trade; and (3) counterproliferation. See the discussion in Stephen Biddle and Peter Feaver, "Assessing Strategic Choices in the War on Terror," in *Recalling September 11th: Is Everything Different Now?*, ed. James Burk (New York: Cambridge University Press, 2013), 27–56.

20. Bush claimed that "after September 11, the doctrine of containment just doesn't hold any water," cited in David Dunn, "Myths, Motivations and 'Misunderestimations': The Bush Administration and Iraq," *International Affairs* 79:2 (2003): 279–97, 292; James Bone, "Ministers United over Saddam's Defiance," *The Times* (London), February 7, 2003; Obama claimed that the Soviet Union operated on a model that "we could comprehend . . . they don't want to be blown up, we don't want to be blown up, so you do game theory and calculate ways to contain . . . [but] certain elements within the Islamic world right now don't make those same calculations." David Mendell, "Obama Would Consider Missile Strikes on Iran," *Chicago Tribune*, September 25, 2004.

21. Susan E. Rice, "The New National Security Strategy," *Brookings Brief* 116 (February 2003).

22. "Senate Confirmation Hearing: Hillary Clinton," *New York Times*, January 13, 2009, 42.

23. On the evening of 9/11, President Bush wrote in his diary, "The Pearl Harbor of the twenty-first century took place today." Bob Woodward, *Bush at War* (New York: Simon & Schuster, 2002), 33; see John Dower's account of how the War on Terror built on an earlier mytho-historical code formed out of the shock of Pearl Harbor: *Cultures of War: Pearl Harbor, Hiroshima, 9–11, Iraq* (New York: W. W. Norton 2010), 4–14, 74–87, 111–15; see also David Hoogland Noon, "Operation Enduring Analogy: World War II, the War on Terror and the Uses of Historical Memory," *Rhetoric and Public Affairs* 7:3 (2004): 339–64.

24. Department of Defense, *Strategy for Homeland Defense and Civil Support* (Washington, DC: US Department of Defense, 2005), 40.

25. As Susan Faludi argues, looking at the proliferation of "Indian country" and "frontier" metaphors in post-9/11 political rhetoric and popular culture, *The Terror Dream: Fear and Fantasy in Post 9/11 America* (London: Metro Books, 2007), 13.

26. See Stephen W. Silliman, "The 'Old West' in the Middle East: US Military Metaphors in Real and Imagined Indian Country," *American Anthropologist* 110:2 (2008): 237–47; Michael A. Elliott, *Custerology: The Enduring Legacy of the Indian Wars and George Armstrong Custer* (Chicago: University of Chicago Press, 2007), 278–79.

27. If, as Max Boot argued, 9/11 was the result of "insufficient American involvement and ambi-tion," then the conclusion is momentous: "it takes an empire." Emily Eakin, "It Takes an Empire," *New York Times*, April 2, 2002.

28. Michael Cox, "Empire, Imperialism and the Bush Doctrine," *Review of International Studies* 30 (2004): 585–608, 590; see also Sebastian Mallaby, "The Reluctant Imperialist: Terrorism, Failed States and the Case for an American Empire," *Foreign Affairs* 81:2 (2002): 2–7.

29. AQ's war against America is directly linked to Washington's deep entanglement of the West in Gulf states, as apostate regimes. Specifically, a driving ideological force in AQ's jihad was America's support of Gulf client regimes loathed by the bin Ladenists, preceded by outrage at America's support for Israel's invasion of Lebanon. As Richard Betts argued, "it is hardly likely that Middle Eastern radicals would be hatching schemes like the destruction of the World Trade Center if the United States had not been identified so long as the mainstay of Israel, the shah of Iran, and conservative Arab regimes and the source of a cultural assault on Islam." Richard Betts, "The New Threat of Mass Destruction," *Foreign Affairs* 77:1 (1998): 26–41. On the causal links between America's geopolitics in the Gulf and AQ's war, see Peter L. Bergen, *The Longest War: The Enduring Conflict between America and Al Qaeda* (New York: Simon & Schuster, 2011), 18–21; Rohan Gunaratna, *Inside Al Qaeda: Global Network of Terror* (New York: Columbia University Press, 2002), 45; Max Abrahms, "Al-Qaeda's Scorecard: A Progress Report on al-Qaeda's Objectives," *Studies in Conflict and Terrorism*, 29:4 (2006): 509–29; Peter Bergen, "What Were the Causes of 9/11?," *Prospect* 126 (2006), at www.prospectmagazine.co.uk/maga-zine/whatwerethecausesof911/#.UvDQD7SdvSg.

30. According to the writer-adventurer Robert Kaplan whose work was holiday reading for President Bush, the War on Terror updated America's nineteenth-century mission of taming the frontier. Only this time, the Wild West equivalent was to be found across the planet, from Colombia to the Philippines. Robert Kaplan, "Indian Country: America's Military Faces the Most Thankless Task in the History of Warfare," *Wall Street Journal*, September 25, 2004, A22; *Imperial Grunts: The American Military on the Ground* (New York: Random House, 2005), 4; "Bush Reading Reveals History Fan," BBC News, December 28, 2005, at http://news.bbc.co.uk/1/hi/world/americas/4563804.stm.

31. On the role of intervening ideas in shaping the response, see Simon Dalby, "Calling 911: Geopolitics, Security and America's New War," *Geopolitics* 8:3 (2003): 61–86.

32. *The 9/11 Commission Report: Final Report of the National Commission on Terrorist Attacks upon the United States* (New York: W. W. Norton & Co., 2004), 362.

33. For example, the international authority on terrorism Magnus Ranstorp, then the deputy director of the Center for the Study of Terrorism and Political Violence at the University of St. Andrews, testified to the committee in April 2003 that "mass destruction terrorism on this scale has become a permanent 'clear and present danger,' symptomatic of a 'wild globalization,'" and that "terrorist acts can now be controlled by remote-control from any distance or remote cor-ner. The uniqueness of this new terrorism is that it has hijacked globalization through riding the so-called techno-web, creating infinite new vistas of communication and attack modes, lim-ited only by their imagination in the target acquisition and execution." "First public hearing of the National Commission on Terrorist Attacks upon the United States: Statement of Magnus Ranstorp to the National Commission on Terrorist Attacks upon the United States," March 31, 2003, at http://govinfo.library.unt.edu/911/hearings/hearing1/witness_ranstorp.htm.

34. Its founder publicly declared a jihad to expel foreign troops from Islamic lands in 1996: "Declaration of Jihad on the Americans Occupying the Country of the Two Sacred Places," in Peter Bergen, *Holy War, Inc.: Inside the Secret World of Osama Bin Laden* (London: Phoenix, 2002), 96–97.

35. Threat reports before 9/11 had surged from June and July, and in August 2001 Tenet had heard a briefing titled "Islamic Extremist Learns to Fly." The 9/11 Commission concluded that "in sum, the domestic agencies never mobilized in response to the threat. They did not have direc-tion and did not have a plan to institute. The borders were not hardened. Transportation sys-tems were not fortified. Electronic surveillance was not targeted against a domestic threat. State and local law enforcement were not marshaled to augment the FBI's efforts. The public was not warned." This is also the recollection of the former senior CIA analyst and national intelligence

officer for the Near East and South Asia Paul Pillar that "the 9/11 disaster occurred despite strong strategic warning," *Intelligence and U.S. Foreign Policy: Iraq, 9/11, and Misguided Reform* (New York: Columbia University Press, 2011), 279; "Think Again: Intelligence," *Foreign Policy* 191 (2012): 51–56.

36. *Liberty and Security in a Changing World: Report and Recommendations of the President's Review Group on Intelligence and Communications Technologies* (Washington, DC, 2013), 71.

37. As Alan Ingram and Klaus Dodds argue, "Spaces of Security and Insecurity: Geographies of the War on Terror," in *Spaces of Security and Insecurity: Geographies of the War on Terror* (Surrry, UK: Ashgate, 2009), 3.

38. See, for example, Victor D. Cha, "Globalization and the Study of International Security," *Journal of Peace Research* 37:3 (2000): 391–403.

39. As terrorism expert Brian Jenkins testified to the Senate Armed Services Subcommittee, 9/11 marked "a final long-term trend. Power—the power to kill, destroy, disrupt, alarm, and force nations to divert vast resources to protection against attacks—is descending to smaller and smaller groups." Brian Michael Jenkins, "Statement on Terrorism: Current and Long Term Threats," Senate Armed Services Committee on Emerging Threats, November 15, 2001 (Santa Monica, CA: RAND Testimony Series, 2001).

40. Jeffery B. Cozzens and Magnus Ranstorp, "The Enduring Al Qaeda Threat: A Network Perspective," in *Contemporary Debates on Terrorism*, ed. Richard Jackson and Samuel Justin Sinclair (London: Routledge, 2012), 90–97.

41. D. Tucker, "What's New about the New Terrorism and How Dangerous Is It?," *Terrorism and Political Violence* 13 (2001): 1–14; J. Arquilla, D. Ronfeldt, and M. Zanani, "Networks, Netwar and Information-Age Terrorism," in *Countering the New Terrorism*, ed. I. Lesser (Santa Monica, CA: RAND, 1999); Olivier Roy, Bruce Hoffman, Reuven Paz, Steven Simon, and Daniel Benjamin, "America and the New Terrorism," *Survival* 42:2 (2000): 156–72.

42. "The single-biggest threat to US security, short term, medium term, and long term, would be the possibility of a terrorist organization obtaining a nuclear weapon," Mr. Obama said. "This is something that could change the security landscape in this country and around the world for years to come." "US President Barack Obama Warns of Nuclear Terrorism," BBC News, April 12, 2010, at http://news.bbc.co.uk/1/hi/8614695.stm.

43. David C. Rapaport, "The Fourth Wave: September 11 in the History of Terrorism," *Current History* (December 2001): 419–24; Michael T. Klare, "Waging Postindustrial Warfare on the Global Battlefield," *Current History* 100:650 (2001): 433–37; Audrey Kurth Cronin, "Behind the Curve: Globalization and International Terrorism," *International Security* 27:3 (2002/3): 30–58; M. V. Rasmussen, *The Risk Society at War: Terror, Technology and Strategy in the Twentieth-First Century* (New York: Cambridge University Press, 2007), 3.

44. Mark Duffield, "War as a Network Enterprise: The New Security Terrain and Its Implications," *Cultural Values* 6:1 & 2 (2002): 158; John Mackinlay, *The Insurgent Archipelago* (London: Hurst, 2009), 6.

45. Steve Coll and Susan B. Glasser, "Terrorists Turn to Web as Base of Operations," *Washington Post*, August 7, 2005; Magnus Ranstorp, "The Virtual Sanctuary of Al-Qaeda and Terrorism in an Age of Globalization," in Johan Eriksson and Giampiero Giacomello, *International Relations and Security in the Digital Age* (London: Routledge, 2007), 31–57.

46. Timothy L. Thomas, "Al Qaeda and the Internet: The Danger of Cyberplanning," *Parameters* 23:1 (2003): 112–23.

47. Audrey Kurth Cronin, "Cyber Mobilization: The New Levée en Masse," *Parameters* 36:2 (2006): 77–87.

48. Jeffrey B. Cozzens, "Approaching Al-Qaeda's Warfare: Function, Culture and Grand Strategy," in Magnus Ranstorp, *Mapping Terrorism Research: State of the Art, Gaps and Future Directions* (London: Routledge, 2007), 127–64, 132: "The marriage of the network form to the information age permits networks to 'thrive like parasites on the advantages of globalization in creating crossnational networks—enhancing command, control and communication and sources of financial revenues—that enable them to survive, flourish and expand' in ways hierarchies cannot. . . . Networks [have] advantages over hierarchies, their marriage to globalization and function in the information age."

49. Marc Lynch, "Al-Qaeda's Constructivist Turn," *Praeger Security International*, May 5, 2006, 1; Alexander Spencer, "The Social Construction of Terrorism: Media, Metaphors and Policy Implications," *Journal of International Relations and Development*, 15:3 (2012): 343–419; Christopher Coker, *Globalization and Insecurity in the Twenty-First Century: NATO and the Management of Risk*, Adelphi Paper 345 (London: International Institute for Strategic Studies, June 2002), 40; see also Mona Harb and Reinoud Leenders, "Know Thy Enemy: Hizbullah, 'Terrorism' and the Politics of Perception," *Third World Quarterly* 26:1 (2005): 189–90. For Faisal Devji, this is an expression of Al Qaeda's weakness, not its strength: *Landscapes of the Jihad* (London: Hurst, 2005), 1–2.

50. Abdel Bari Atwan, *The Secret History of Al-Qa'ida* (London: Saqi Books, 2006), 265–66.

51. "Market state terrorism will be just as global, networked, decentralized, and devolved and rely just as much on outsourcing and incentivizing as the market state. . . . It is transnational, borderless, and prosecuted by virtual states (like al Qaeda) or by non-state actors (like the Colombian drug cartels) sheltering in weak states . . . it is the Internet that allows al Qaeda to communicate its strategy even while its leaders are in hiding, and despite the loss of its territorial base, which once would have meant defeat and marginalization but is now easily overcome." Philip Bobbit, *Terror and Consent: The Wars for the Twenty-First Century* (London: Alfred A. Knopf, 2008), 45–47.

52. Colin Flint, "Netwar, the Modern Geopolitical Imagination, and the Death of the Civilian," in *Denial of Sanctuary: Understanding Terrorist Safe Havens*, ed. Michael Innes (Praeger: London, 2007), 34–48, 48.

53. David Jones and M. L. R. Smith, "Whose Hearts and Whose Minds? The Curious Case of Global Counter-Insurgency," *Journal of Strategic Studies* 33:1 (2010): 81–121, 102; see also 84.

54. John Arquilla, "The New Rules of War," *Foreign Policy* 178 (2010): 60–67; John Arquilla and David Ronfelt *In Athena's Camp: Preparing for Conflict in the Information Age* (Santa Monica, CA: RAND, 1997), 6; according to Bruce Riedel, the former senior director for Near East affairs on the US National Security Council who would chair the president's review of policy toward Afghanistan and Pakistan in 2009, AQ poses a "deadly threat" because it could acquire in the black market a nuclear weapon from a sympathetic Pakistani officer, to be used against Israel or the United States. *The Search for Al Qaeda: Its Leadership, Ideology, and Future* (Washington, DC: Brookings Institution, 2008), 131, 155, 158.

55. As summarized by Ripsman and Paul, *Globalization and the National Security State* (New York: Oxford University Press, 2010), 30–31. For a similar formulation, see Fathali M. Moghaddam: "Globalization has fundamentally transformed the nature of security, given birth to new security threats, and brought about serious feelings of insecurity . . . increasing interconnectedness has resulted in globalized security, so that changes in security in one part of the world impact security in other parts of the world. It is no longer possible for a nation, even a superpower, to isolate itself and remain immune to security threats in other parts of the world . . . 'local' radicals can threaten distant targets, garner world attention, and force the international community to take them seriously. This is because electronic communications, rapid long-distance transportation, and long-range missiles with the potential to carry nuclear warheads, allow local radicals to operate internationally. As 9/11 demonstrated, it does not take a lot of resources for local hotheads to inflict serious damage against distant targets that are much, much larger and more powerful than themselves." *The New Global Insecurity: How Terrorism, Environmental Collapse, Economic Inequalities, and Resource Shortages Are Changing Our World* (Santa Barbara, CA: Praeger, 2010), 12–13.

56. Charles Krauthammer, *Democratic Realism: An American Foreign Policy for a Unipolar World* (Washington, DC: American Enterprise Institute, 2004), 4, 16–17.

57. Michael E. O'Hanlon and Hassina Sherjan, *Toughing It Out in Afghanistan* (Washington, DC: Brookings Institution, 2010), 4; Max Boot, "Obama Can't Downsize to Success in Afghanistan," *Los Angeles Times*, September 28, 2009.

58. "Remarks by the President in Address to the Nation on the Way Forward in Afghanistan and Pakistan," December 1, 2009, at www.whitehouse.gov/the-press-office/remarks-president -address-nation-way-forward-afghanistan-and-pakistan.

59. Katherine Zimmerman, "Al Qaeda Renewed: It Is Decentralized and Dangerous," *National Review*, December 26, 2013. Anthony Cordesman, from the Center for Strategic and Interna-

tional Studies, states, "AQ has had ten years to attain another leader, has formed strong and international cells and superfluous networks, and has found alternative sites throughout the world. AQ is still a large threat and the United States and its allies still have a long way to go in the war against terrorism." "One Year on from Osama bin Laden's Death: Implications for Counter Terrorism," *Asia Pacific Security Magazine*, May 3, 2012.

60. For one observer, it is "an ideologically driven collection of insurgents who act transnationally, are highly networked, and like a cancer, are adapting and metastasizing." John Hillen, "Developing a National Counterinsurgency Capability for the War on Terror," *Military Review* 87:1 (2007): 12–15, 13.

61. Paul R. Pillar, "Beyond Al Qaeda: Countering a Decentralized Terrorist Threat," *Washington Quarterly* 27:3 (2004): 101–13, reprinted in *Terrorism and Counterterrorism: Understanding the New Security Environment, Readings and Interpretations*, ed. Russell D. Howard, Reid L. Sawyer, and Natasha E. Bajema (New York: McGraw Hill, 2009), 492–502, 499. Pillar uses a similar logic to argue that physical sanctuaries hardly matter to AQ: "In the past couple of decades, international terrorist groups have thrived by exploiting globalization and information technology, which has lessened their dependence on physical havens. . . . Terrorists' real haven isn't on the ground, it's online," *Washington Post*, September 16, 2009.

62. CRRCNDU-AQAM, AQ-THEO-D-001-288, Abu Massab Al-Suri, book about the Yemenis' defense of the "holy places," 14.

63. These ideas have historical roots: Kenneth Payne, "Building the Base: Al Qaeda's Focoist Strategy," *Studies in Conflict and Terrorism* 34:2 (2011): 124–43.

64. Cited in Thomas G. Mahnken and Joseph A. Maiolo, eds., *Strategic Studies: A Reader* (London: Routledge, 2008), 2; see also Colin Gray, *Another Bloody Century: Future Warfare* (London: Routledge, 2005), 227–28; Youssef H. Aboul-Enein, "Ayman Al-Zawahiri's Knights under the Prophet's Banner: The al-Qaeda Manifesto," *Military Review* (2005): 83–85; Christopher Henzel, "The Origins of Al Qaeda's Ideology: Implications for US Strategy," *Parameters* 35:1 (2005): 69–80, 75–76.

65. Osama bin Laden, *Declaration of War against the Americans Occupying the Land of the Two Holy Places*, 1996, cited in Don D. Chipman, "Osama bin Laden and Guerrilla War," *Studies in Conflict and Terrorism* 26 (2003): 163–70, 163.

66. As Steve Metz argues, "America's Flawed Afghanistan Strategy," *Strategic Studies Institute* (August 2010), www.strategicstudiesinstitute.army.mil/Pubs/display.cfm?pubid=1014.

67. *9/11 Commission Report*, 215–53.

68. CRRCNDU-AQAM, AQ-SHPD-D-000-085, "Organization of Small Groups in the Cities."

69. Rosa A. Brooks, "Muslim 'Homegrown' Terrorism in the United States: How Serious Is the Threat?," *International Security* 36:2 (2011): 7–47, 28–29.

70. James Jay Carafano, Steve Bucci, and Jessica Zuckerman, "Fifty Terror Plots Foiled since 9/11: The Homegrown Threat and the Long War on Terrorism," *Backgrounder* no. 2862, April 5, 2012.

71. Spencer S. Hsu and Robin Wright, "Plot to Attack NY Foiled," *Washington Post*, July 8, 2006; USA v. Hosam Maher Husein Smadi, US District Court for the Northern District of Texas, D.C. No. 3-09-MJ-286.

72. As Steven Simon and Jonathan Stevenson argue, "Afghanistan: How Much Is Enough?," *Survival* 51:5 (2009): 47–67, 61.

73. Marc Sageman, "Confronting Al Qaeda: Understanding the Threat in Afghanistan and Beyond," *Testimony to the Foreign Relations Committee*, October 7, 2009, 18.

74. On these issues, see Martin J. Muckian, "Structural Vulnerabilities of Networked Insurgencies: Adapting to the New Adversary," *Parameters* 36:4 (2006–7): 22–23; "Is Imperial Rule Obsolete? Assessing the Barriers to Overseas Adventurism," *Security Studies* 18:1 (2009): 79–114, 89–90.

75. Michael Schwertz and Marc Santora, "Man Is Accused of Jihadist Plot to Bomb a Bar in Chicago," *New York Times*, September 15, 2012.

76. "To avoid detection, bin Laden had no internet, e-mail or phone lines that he could use to send them. The audio files were evidently stored on a CD or tiny thumb drive and passed from courier to courier until they reached As Sahab, Al Qaeda's media arm." "Without Internet, Phone, Osama Depended on Couriers," *New York Times*, May 8, 2011.

77. David Ignatius, "A Lion in Winter," *Washington Post*, March 18, 2012.

78. "Terrorism Tradecraft," *Stratfor*, October 2012, at www.stratfor.com/weekly/terrorism-tradecraft.
79. Sean Gardiner and Summathi Reddi, "Bomb Was Crude but Lethal," *Wall Street Journal*, May 3, 2010.
80. Bruce Hoffman, "Radicalization and Subversion: Al Qaeda and the 7 July 2005 Bombings and the 2006 Airline Bombing Plot," *Studies in Conflict and Terrorism* 32 (2009): 1100–16.
81. On the serial incompetence of most jihadists, see Daniel Byman and Christine Fair, "The Case for Calling Them Nitwits," *The Atlantic*, June 8, 2010.
82. Walter Laqueur, *The New Terrorism: Fanaticism and the Arms of Mass Destruction* (London: Oxford University Press, 1999), 263.
83. Michael Kenney, *Organizational Learning and Islamic Militancy* (Unpublished, Department of Justice, 2009); "Dumb yet Deadly: Local Knowledge and Poor Tradecraft among Islamist Militants in Britain and Spain," *Studies in Conflict and Terrorism*, 33 (2010): 911–32.
84. Peter L. Bergen, *The Longest War: The Enduring Conflict between America and Al Qaeda* (New York: Free Press, 2010), 205.
85. CRRCNDU-AQAM, AQ-SHPD-D-000-282, "Captured Document Discussing Lessons Learned from the Jihad in Syria," estimated date prior to 2002, 25; AQ-TRED-D-000-177, "The Art of Leadership," obtained from Abu Haf's house in Kandahar, date prior to 2002, 1.
86. Bin Laden, for example, doubted Anwar al-Awlaki, the American-born preacher who was a rising figure in the Yemen-located AQAP (al-Qaeda in the Arabian Peninsula). Bin Laden requested that al-Awlaki prove himself in battle. "We here become reassured of the people when they go to the line and get examined there," bin Laden said. Al-Awlaki was killed in a CIA drone strike in Yemen in September.
87. Stewart Patrick, "Weak States and Global Threats: Assessing Evidence of Spillovers," Center for Global Development, Working Paper Number 73 (2006), 5; for more in-depth critiques of simplistic assumptions about the relationships between "failed states" and international security, see Patrick Stewart, "Weak States and Global Threats: Fact or Fiction?," *Washington Quarterly* 29:2 (2006): 27–53; Charles Call, "The Fallacy of the 'Failed State,'" *Third World Quarterly* 29:8 (2008): 1491–507.
88. Ray Takeyh and Nikolas K. Gvosdev, "Do Terrorist Networks Need a Home?," *Washington Quarterly* 25:3 (2002): 97–108; Paul D. Miller, "Five Pillars of American Grand Strategy," *Survival* 54:5 (2012): 7–44, 24.
89. The *National Security Strategy* of 2002 claimed that "America is now threatened less by conquering states than we are by failing ones," 1; the *National Defense Strategy* of 2006 assigns the military to fortify the capacity of weak states to counter internal threats of terrorism, insurgency, and organized crime and address "ungoverned spaces": *National Defense Strategy of the United States of America* (March 2005); Secretary of Defense Donald Rumsfeld linked terrorist networks to "ungoverned areas": report on speech, from Jim Garamone, "Rumsfeld Describes Changing Face of War," *Armed Forces Press Service*, May 25, 2005.
90. Alejandra Bolanos, "The 'New Terrorism' or the 'Newness' of Context and Change," in *Contemporary Debates on Terrorism*, ed. Richard Jackson and Samuel Justin Sinclair (London: Routledge, 2012), 29–35, 31; anticipating this argument: A. Benjamin and S. Simon, "The New Face of Terrorism," *New York Times*, January 4, 2000.
91. On the importance of state sponsorship and sanctuary to AQ, see also Daniel Byman, *Deadly Connections: States That Sponsor Terrorism* (New York: Cambridge University Press, 2005), 2ff, 217.
92. On the role of the Afghan sanctuary, see Lawrence Wright, *The Looming Tower: Al Qaeda and the Road to 9/11* (New York: Penguin, 2006); Jim Arkedis, "Why Al Qaeda Wants a Safe Haven," *Foreign Policy*, October 23, 2009.
93. Conflict Records Research Center, undated report, "The September 11th Attacks or the Impossible Becoming Possible," 4, AQ-SHPD-D-001-285.
94. For critiques of "safe haven" arguments, see Michael Innes, "The Safe Haven Myth," *Foreign Policy*, October 12, 2009; John Mueller, "How Dangerous Are the Taliban? Why Afghanistan Is the Wrong War," *Foreign Affairs*, April 15, 2009.
95. Letter, October 21, 2010, Osama bin Laden to "Shaykh Mahmud," SOCOM-2012-0000015, in *The Osama Bin Laden Files* [henceforth OBLF], 112–13.

96. George Tenet, "The World Wide Threat in 2003: Evolving Dangers in a Complex World," testimony before the Senate Select Committee on Intelligence, February 12, 2003, at www.cia.gov/news-information/speechestestimony/2003/dci_speech_02112003.html.

97. Benjamin H. Friedman, "The Terrible 'Ifs': US Defense Policymakers Have Developed the Precautionary Principle," *Regulation* 30:4 (2008): 32–40, 37.

98. On the Somalia case, see Kenneth Menkhaus, "Somalia and Somaliland: Terrorism, Political Islam, and State Collapse," in *Battling Terrorism in the Horn of Africa*, ed. Robert Rotberg (Washington, DC: Brookings Institution, 2005), 39–41; Richard Jackson, "Critical Reflections on Counter-Sanctuary Discourse," in *Denial of Sanctuary: Understanding Terrorist Safe Havens*, ed. Michael Innes (London: Praeger, 2007).

99. Stewart makes this argument in one of the few sustained critical studies of the issue, *Weak Links: Fragile States, Global Threats and International Society* (Oxford: Oxford University Press, 2011), 62.

100. See Anna Simons and David Tucker, "The Misleading Problem of Failed States: A 'Sociogeography' of Terrorism in the post-9/11 era," *Third World Quarterly* 28:2 (2007): 387–401, 388–89.

101. As observed by Michael Mazarr, "The Rise and Fall of the State Failure Paradigm: Requiem for a Decade of Distraction," *Foreign Affairs* 93:1 (2014): 113–22, 116.

102. See the critique of Edward Newman, "Weak States, State Failure and Terrorism," *Terrorism and Political Violence* 19:4 (2007): 463–88, 481, 483.

103. There is a contrary view put by James A. Piazza, who argues that failed states are more likely to host terrorist networks that commit transnational attacks: "Incubators of Terror: Do Failed and Failing States Promote Transnational Terrorism?," *International Studies Quarterly* 52 (2008): 469–88. While Piazza's study indicates that transnational terrorists are present in and do operate from failed states, it does not follow from this frequency that the state "failure" is a positive advantage. The more qualitative study by Stewart Patrick, *Weak Links*, suggests that when they do operate from these states, it is more despite than because of their "failed" condition and that networks such as Al Qaeda prefer "corrupt but functional states, such as Kenya, where sovereignty provides some protection from outside interdiction." Stewart M. Patrick, "Why Failed States Shouldn't Be Our Biggest National Security Fear," *Washington Post*, April 15, 2011.

104. A guide to planning operations directs planners to consider the tradeoffs of open terrain providing no cover versus congested terrain slowing down movement, closeness to the target versus the safety of distances that make quick attack and withdrawal harder, and the exposure of daylight versus the obstruction of movement and difficulty of operating at night. CRRCNDU-AQAM, AQ-TRED-D-001-015, "Planning Outline Regarding Theoretical and Practical Steps to Be Taken Prior to Executing an Operation, Based on Military Rules and War Principles," estimated 2002, 4; CRRCNDU-AQAM, AQ-TRED-D-000-250, "Urban Warfare Combat Tactics," estimated date prior to 2002, also breaks down the benefits and drawbacks of the geography of urban combat, with its strengths of the ease of cover, protection, ease of movement and opportunities for mining and booby-trapping, and its weaknesses of short fields of fire, difficulties of communication and control, and obstacles to flexible maneuver.

105. CRRCNDU-AQAM, AQ-SHPD-D-000-119, "Basic Facts and Obstacles Faced for Jihad in Tajikstan and Afghanistan," undated but prior to 2002, 3, 12.

106. CRRCNDU-AQAM, AQ-TRED-D-000-974, "Report of Trip by Al Qaeda Leadership (Written by Saif Al-Islam in August 1994) to Somalia to Establish Training Camps, August 1994," 15.

107. CRRCNDU-AQAM, AQ-TRED-001-289, "Advice on How to Prepare for Jihad in Yemen," undated, translated September 23, 2008, 2; CRRCNDU-AQAM, AQ-THEO-D-001-288, Abu Massab Al-Suri, book about the Yemenis' defense of the "holy places," 18.

108. AQ-TRED-D-000-175, "Training Manual on the Organization of Guerrilla Warfare Units," dated prior to 2002.

109. Daniel Byman, "The Intelligence War on Terrorism," *Intelligence and National Security* (2013): 1–27, 12–17.

110. On the theory and practice of deterrence and terrorism, see Wyn Q. Bowen, "Deterrence and Asymmetry: Non-state Actors and Mass Casualty Terrorism," *Contemporary Security Policy* 25:1 (2004): 54–70; Matthew Kroenig and Barry Pavel, "How to Deter Terrorism," *Washington*

Quarterly 35:2 (2012): 21–36; Andrew R. Morral and Brian A. Jackson, *Understanding the Role of Deterrence in Counterterrorism Security* (Santa Monica, CA: RAND, 2009).

111. Brian A. Jackson et al., *Breaching the Fortress Wall: Understanding Terrorist Efforts to Overcome Defensive Technologies*, MG-481-DHS (Santa Monica, CA: RAND), 2007.

112. Brian Michael Jenkins, "How Do We Know If Security Measures Work against Terrorists?," *Inside Science*, January 27, 2014.

113. Peter Grier, "Why the Times Square Bomb Failed Spectacularly," *Christian Science Monitor*, May 3, 2010, discussed also in Brooks, "Muslim Homegrown Terrorism," 32.

114. These examples are taken from Kroenig, "How to Deter Terrorism," 26, 29.

115. These examples are taken from Morral and Jackson, *Understanding the Role of Deterrence*, 2–3.

116. There does remain debate about which measures are cost-effective, as one of the most critical studies finds that hardening cockpit doors is a cost-effective reduction of risk compared to more expensive and less impactful measures, such as the Federal Air Marshal Service: Mark G. Stewart and John Mueller, "A Risk and Cost-Benefit Assessment of United States Aviation Security Measures," *Journal of Transport Security* 1 (2008): 143–59, 154–58.

117. Robert F. Trager and Dessislava P. Zagorcheva, "Deterring Terrorism: It Can Be Done," *International Security* 30:3 (2005): 87–123, 111–18.

118. Justin V. Hastings, "Geography, Globalization, and Terrorism: The Plots of Jemaah Islamiyah," *Security Studies* 17 (2008): 505–30; Justin V. Hastings, *No Man's Land: Globalization, Territory and Clandestine Groups in Southeast Asia* (Ithaca, NY: Cornell University Press, 2010).

119. Hastings, *No Man's Land*, 84.

120. CRRCNDU-AQAM, AQ-INSE-D-000-976, "Instruction Book, 'Security of the Traveler,'" Containing Recommendations Regarding Personal Preparation, Documents, Cover Stories and Choosing Hotels," undated, written before 2002.

121. According to Milton Leitenberg, a successful bioterrorist attack requires that "one must obtain the appropriate strain of the disease pathogen. One must know how to handle the organism correctly. One must know how to grow it in a way that will produce the appropriate characteristics. One must know how to store the culture, and to scale-up production properly. One must know how to disperse the product properly." *Assessing the Biological Weapons and Bio-Terrorism Threat* (Carlisle, PA: US Army War College, Strategic Studies Institute, 2005), 46.

122. John Mueller, *Atomic Obsession: Nuclear Alarmism from Hiroshima to Al-Qaeda* (Oxford: Oxford University Press, 2010), 186.

123. Keir Lieber and Daryl G. Press, "Why States Won't Give Nuclear Weapons to Terrorists," *International Security* 38:1 (2013): 80–104.

124. See the seminal challenge to network theories by Mette Eilstrup-Sangiovanni and Calvert Jones, "Assessing the Dangers of Illicit Networks," *International Security* 33:2 (2008): 1–44, 28.

125. Associated Press, "Al-Qaeda Documents Show Obsession with Keeping Receipts, Down to a $0.60 Cake," *National Post*, December 30, 2013.

126. Nick Fielding, "How al Qaeda Utilizes Family Networks," presentation at Watson Institute, October 2003, cited in Thomas Biersteker and Sue E. Eckert, *Countering the Financing of Terrorism* (London: Routledge, 2008), 11.

127. Nelly Lahoud, *Beware of Imitators: Al-Qa'ida through the Lens of Its Confidential Secretary* (Combating Terrorism Center, West Point, June 4, 2012), 6, 8, 16, 58, 59, 73.

128. As I have argued, "Long Wars and Long Telegrams: Containing Al Qaeda," *International Affairs* 85:2 (2009): 285–305.

129. Jacob N. Shapiro, *The Terrorist's Dilemma: Managing Violent Covert Organizations* (Princeton, NJ: Princeton University Press, 2013), 37–38.

130. Letter, Ayman al-Zawahiri to Abu Mus'ab al-Zarqawi, July 9, 2005, 3, translated by the Combating Terrorism Center, at www.ctc.usma.edu/posts/zawahiris-letter-to-zarqawi-english-translation-2.

131. On AQ's self-defeating behavior in Iraq, see Frederick Wehrey, "The Iraq War: Strategic Overreach by America—and Also Al Qaeda," in *The Long Shadow of 9/11: America's Response to Terrorism*, ed. Brian Michael Jenkins and John Paul Godges (Santa Monica, CA: RAND, 2011), 47–54.

132. Faisal Gerges, *The Far Enemy: Why Jihad Went Global* (New York: Cambridge University Press, 2009), 301.

133. On criminal markets and the Anbar Awakening, see Austin Long, "The Anbar Awakening," *Survival* 50:2 (2008): 67–94, 77; Carter Malkasian, "A Thin Blue Line in the Sand," *Democracy* 5 (2007): 55.

134. *Al-Arab* (Qatar), February 12, 2008, cited in MEMRI (Middle East Media Research Institute) Special Dispatch Series 1866: "Al-Qaeda Commander in Northern Iraq: We Are in Dire Straits."

135. On the interaction of the "surge" with the Anbar Awakening, see Stephen Biddle, Jeffrey Friedman, and Jacob N. Shapiro, "Testing the Surge: Why Did Violence Decline in Iraq in 2007?," *International Security* 37:1 (2012): 7–40.

136. Peter Bergen and Paul Cruickshank, "The Unraveling: The Jihadist Revolt against Bin Laden," *The New Republic*, June 11, 2008.

137. "Instructions to Abu Osamah," CTC IZ-060316-02, at http://ctc.usma.edu/aq/pdf/IZ060316-02-Trans.pdf.

138. Tony Karon, "Behind Hamas' Own War on Terror," *Time*, August 21, 2009; "Hamas Eases Up on al Qaeda in Hopes of Securing Qatari Cash," *World Tribune*, November 6, 2013.

139. Lawrence Wright, "The Rebellion Within: An Al Qaeda Mastermind Questions Terrorism," *New Yorker*, June 2, 2008.

140. Nelly Lahoud, "Jihadi Recantations and Their Significance: The Case of Dr. Fadl," in *Fault Lines in Global Jihad: Organizational, Strategic and Ideological Fissures*, ed. Assaf Moghadam and Brian Fishman (New York: Routledge, 2011), 138–44.

141. Combating Terrorism Center, West Point, *Deadly Vanguards: A Study of al-Qaida's Violence against Muslims* (2009); Yassin Musharbash, "Al-Qaida Kills Eight Times More Muslims Than Non-Muslims," *Spiegel*, December 3, 2009.

142. On the history of this anxiety within Safai jihadist ranks, see Mark Stout, "In Search of Salafi Jihadist Strategic Thought: Mining the Words of the Terrorists," *Studies in Conflict and Terrorism* 32:10 (2009): 876–92, 884–85.

143. Letter to leader of AQAP, cited from OBLF SOCOM-2012-0000016, 122–24.

144. Letter, September 14, 2006, OBLF SOCOM-2012-0000018, 162–64.

145. Letter from Osama bin Laden to "Shaykh Mahmud," May 2010, OBLF SOCOM-2012-0000019, 170–71.

146. See Miles Kahler, "Collective Action and Clandestine Networks: The Case of Al Qaeda," in *Networked Politics: Agency, Power, and Governance*, ed. Miles Kahler (Ithaca, NY: Cornell University Press, 2009).

147. Glenn L. Carle, "Overstating Our Fears," *Washington Post*, July 13, 2008.

148. Undated letter, Abu Yasir, CRRC, AQ-SHPD-D-000-995.

149. As Adam Elkus illustrates, arguments for the strategic death of distance derive from and echo earlier thinking about the revolutionary implications of long-rage weapons during the Cold War: "Nukes and Credit Default Swaps," June 20, 2012, www.cnas.org/blogs/abumuqawama/2012/06/nukes-and-credit-default-swaps.html.

150. Stephen Metz, "Strategic Horizons: Al Qaeda's Comeback," *World Politics Review*, October 31, 2012.

151. Stephen Biddle, "Is It Worth It? The Difficult Case for Afghanistan," *The American Interest* 4 (2009): 4–11.

152. On isolation strategies and safe havens, see Kim Kragan, "The Strategic Dilemma of Terrorist Havens Calls for Their Isolation, Not Elimination," in *The Long Shadow of 9/11: America's Response to Terrorism*, ed. Brian Michael Jenkins and John Paul Godges (Santa Monica, CA: RAND, 2011), 113–20.

CHAPTER 4

Access Denied
Technology, Terrain, and the Barriers to Conquest

I n the last chapter, we saw that today's war maker does not necessarily have the global reach of the trader or tourist. The collapse of space and time may at times confer an ease of access on strategic actors. But their attention aroused, their adversaries can interrupt and reverse that space. This turned out to be the problem for Al Qaeda, an international armed movement often credited with revealing the obsolescence of geographical defenses. Its moment of "offense dominance" under open skies in the enemy's heartland was powerful but fleeting. The adversary's defenses grew ever stronger as it erected new barriers. What's more, the lack of a territorial heartland became a source of weakness as well as strength. AQ's main strategic move after being stripped of its bases in Afghanistan was to decentralize and network over space, but this helped cause the fragmentation of its jihad. The perception of a new era of empowered hostile militants with easy access to their First World targets was misplaced as a measure of the threat. On the other side, Washington underestimated the costs of fighting its own global war to eliminate threats.

This chapter continues the focus on "access," shifting focus to another important context: conquest and expansion, offense and defense. As well as critically reviewing the biography of an idea, that weapons erase distance, I examine the problem across the Taiwan Strait, where the fear of expansion and invasion is not a thing of the past. The question of whether globalization empowers the "offense" has particular salience to the rivalries and insecurities brewing around the contested maritime peripheries of the Asia-Pacific, where nervous states fear the prospect of interlopers bearing new offensive capabilities. Some American observers fear that if China's prodigious growth continues at the same rate, it could use its superior weight to impose itself on its neighbors in the Asia-Pacific. Implicit in these pessimistic predictions is the notion that without a counterbalancing American presence, an ascendant China would overcome military and geographic barriers to dominate other states and make East Asia "Chinese," perhaps even without firing a shot. In this picture, distance would count for little and offer scarce protection. This kind of assessment marginalizes water, in favor of a narrower estimate of the material power balance.

An important test of globalism and its dismissal of distance and its barriers is the issue of conquest. How well does globalism apply to the question of territorial expansion?[1] If the world is getting small to the point where the barrier power of distance is significantly weakened, then the geopolitical advantages that distance confers on defenders should count less. After all, globalism is a theory about the relationship between territory and human-made systems of weapons, communications, and information. It should have something to say about clashes over the control of territory, one of the oldest paths to war. A particularly important case in which to probe this issue is seaborne invasion, or amphibious conquest. I define this as the projection of ground forces from sea to land, independently of ports and airfields, against resistance, or the "successful penetration of a defended beach."[2]

Globalists' arguments suggest that barriers created by the human exploitation of terrain should now matter less. For their expectations to be valid, the offense-defense imbalance does not have to be absolute. As Keir Lieber argues, "what matters most for empirical evaluation is not whether the balance in any given period favors offense or defense in absolute terms—in fact, it is almost always easier to defend than to attack—but how and to what degree the balance has shifted in either direction."[3] Invading successfully across water separating two countries has probably always been more complicated than snap invasions across contiguous land frontiers, but if globalists are right, this difference should matter significantly less.

But beyond its uncontroversial insight that intercontinental ballistic missiles and other long-distance arms put enemies separated by thousands of miles within striking distance of one another, globalism in this context turns out to be a shallow account of how military instruments can be used to pursue policy aims. In short, it is a poor guide to war as a political act.

In this chapter, I revisit globalist claims about the impact of technology on space within the context of interstate warfare, suggesting an alternative argument. I then put these claims to the test with an important case for the collision of technology with geography: amphibious warfare, specifically an invasion of the Republic of China (Taiwan) by the People's Republic of China (PRC). The task of creating a scientific, falsifiable theory of the offense-defense balance I happily leave to others. Here, the more modest purpose is to show that in making sense of territorial expansion from water onto land, globalism does a bad job.

This chapter has three parts. First, I review the history of the notion that globalization creates offense dominance in the world of major military capabilities, and explain why those on either side of the globalization debate should be interested in amphibious warfare and the broader question of military expansion and conquest across water.

Second, I lay out two competing propositions, formulating as robustly as possible the globalist argument about what we should expect in the offense-defense balance in the context of clashes between states. I propose that "globalizing" innovations can have paradoxical effects, putting states in greater physical reach while still empowering defenses to the extent that defended terrain remains a barrier. In other words, military innovations widen as well as shrink space. Assertions that the world is a strategic village make simplistic "one-way street" assumptions about the function of weapons. They betray a deterministic view of technology bearing intrinsic "offensive" or "defensive" properties with little regard for doctrine, or ideas about how weapons should be optimally used. And they build on generalizations from the nuclear and missile revolutions that may not be applicable in other strategic contexts.

Next, to test this proposition, I conduct an estimate of a military scenario that weighs the military balance across the Taiwan Strait, based on existing hypothetical campaign studies and wargames literature about a hypothetical Chinese invasion of Taiwan.[4] This case involves an amphibious invasion of an island by a stronger state, aiming to seize control of the territory and force the inhabitants to do its will (in this case, to accept de jure reunification with the mainland on its terms), against a smaller defender that we can reasonably expect to resist. In this case, observers suggest that the relative power of the "defending" side has weakened. Those impressed by China's military modernization and in particular its capacity to project power doubt Taiwan's capacity to hold out against a Chinese invasion. While we cannot decisively judge the outcomes of a future conflict, we know enough about relative capabilities, about the conditions that are needed for an attacker to succeed in an amphibious assault, to make an informed judgment that could shed light on the future of the offense-defense balance and the duel between swords and shields across water.

Storming the Beach: Why Amphibious War Is an Important Case

Traditionally, the outcomes of conflicts can be explained partly by distance and the dynamics of fighting at home or "away." In armed conflict there is rarely a convenient neutral ground on which the stronger can simply apply their superior doctrinal and material strength against the weaker. The smaller on their home turf, with more at stake and positioned closer to the fighting and to their center of their power, can bleed and repel the greater. Geography and location can be exploited to counter or even equalize resource imbalances in favor of one side. This logic can work to the advantage of states living in the shadow of giants. In Australia's defense debate, the concept of deterrence via the threat of punishment is known as the "Beowulf option."[5] In a neighborhood of rising Asian powers, some argue that Australia need not become a giant to survive if a military threat appears on the horizon. It merely has to be able to rip a giant's arm off. Any interloper that threatens its maritime approaches can be punished by its array of submarines, advanced aircraft, and air defenses. Larger and richer states like China (or in time, Indonesia) conceivably could threaten its sea lanes or overrun its defenses with an overwhelming weight of force and numbers. But even under worst-case conditions where an isolated Australia had to fend for itself, it could hurt its much larger adversary. That prospect, Australian planners hope, would haunt the adversary's calculations and make it think twice.

This helps us answer the "David and Goliath" puzzle, of why states possessing superior material power historically do not necessarily prevail over weaker states, or why they sometimes do only with great difficulty. Traditionally, defenders fighting closer to home have enjoyed several advantages. Geographically, they know better the terrain to be fought over. They can prepare and fortify that terrain. Because they are on defense, local actors can disperse, hide, and shield their forces, their command-and-control centers, and their supply chain. The invader or aggressor must show their hand by initiating movement. Even the success of the offense creates problems for itself, as it stretches itself and increases the transaction costs of asserting itself over distance, while the defender can fall back on shortening interior lines.

Defenders fighting at home a stronger but distant adversary also often have a political advantage. Distance threatens the stronger party's political capacity to wage war against a materially weaker opponent. As it defines its interests and what it is willing to bleed for, the "farness" of the battleground may lead the materially stronger side to value the struggle less than its weaker opponent fighting at home. Conversely, their weaker opponents—the American revolutionaries, the Vietnamese communists, the Afghan Taliban—fighting for what they value closer to home have more of a dog in the fight.[6] In the Vietnam War, America's ability to transport troops unmolested to a South Asian theater did not erase the imbalance of interests that took hold once they got to that theater, or the imbalance of "cost-tolerance" whereby rising losses for an object of limited value distressed and polarized American opinion at home. As the costs mount on the periphery, those losses focus the attention of the public and elite decision makers in the metropole, leading them to ask just how much they value the cause and how much they are willing to sacrifice for it, to distinguish the vital from the merely desirable. Their appetite for continued war may fall. The policy debate shifts to one of acceptable costs, political transitions, timetables for withdrawal, and exits.

Historically, smaller states with sufficient strength, adequate doctrine, and the advantages of fighting at shorter range with enough political will have put up strong resistance. Consider the body-blows Japan inflicted at sea and on land against Russia in 1904–5, despite the fact that Russia enjoyed a greater economic weight by a factor of three to one. Recall Britain's difficulties in wresting back the Falkland Islands across eight thousand miles in 1982 from an Argentina economically weaker by a factor of six to one. Such was the logistical strain and time pressure on Britain's dwindling supplies that the task force commander called it a "close run thing."[7] Today, if America and China went to the mat over Taiwan, the United States would have the advantage of greater material weight and military firepower but would be fighting five thousand miles from its mainland. Conversely, China would be materially weaker, but fighting on its doorstep of the East Asian littoral zone. Not only does this create an asymmetry of effort, where the United States would have to expend more resources and energy to project power over a wider space. It also creates an asymmetry of interest. China would have more at stake in the region than America, so may accept higher costs and risks.[8]

None of this is a guarantee of victory to the weaker party. Doctrine and competence matter. Stronger sides fighting from afar with lower cost tolerance can still defeat weaker sides fighting for higher stakes at home.[9] To prevail, the weaker sides must avoid premature open battle, prolong the conflict and accumulate time as a commodity to wear down their opponents' will, and do well enough in strategic interaction so that they can make distance "count." If they can, stronger states attempting to impose their power against resistance across distance face the "ham omelette" dilemma. In a ham omelette, the chicken is involved, but the pig is committed.

How much have these dynamics changed–of distance, will, and the offense-defense clash? What is the net effect of today's weapons and the ways they can be used? How far can states still erect barriers to deter and defend against aggressors? Is the military-strategic balance shifting from between offense and defense, and to what extent? Can even outmatched states raise the costs on any predator to the point where victory would be Pyrrhic? Or has the age of the long-range missile, the aircraft carrier, the stealth bomber, and the satellite collapsed space? In terms of projecting power over space, do new tools make conquest—the seizing, occupation, or annexation of territory against a host population's will for an extended period—easier or harder? Just how strong are maritime shields today? By "maritime shields," I mean something more complex than mere "moats." I mean the use of man-made tools and doctrines to convert bodies of water and the coasts that join them into defensive terrain with the competent use of weapon systems including surveillance, air and coastal defenses, submarines, antiship missiles, mines, or anything that makes it harder to traverse.

The extent to which water properly exploited remains a barrier to expansion poses difficulties for globalist theories. As we have seen, globalists claim that the shrinkage of the world by revolutions in information, communications, transport, and weapon technology reduces the power of distance, to the extent that traditional distinctions between "home" and "away," or "over here" and "over there," lose their force and the defensive advantages of distance suffer. If they are right, if the world is strategically shrinking this much, this must pass a test: The "distance-decay" effect should be substantially reduced. Barriers that have traditionally obstructed expansionism, through the mix of terrain (such as water) and military capability should be weakening. If we presume, for the sake of argument, that other factors that might hinder expansion do not apply, if we hold all other factors equal, logically the conditions supposedly created by globalization should make conquest easier.

A decent yardstick for this issue is amphibious invasion. We should pay attention to amphibious invasion as a site of the debate for two reasons. First, it is an important test of theories about the shrinkage of distance by technology. More than most other kinds of combat, amphibious clashes pit defenders exploiting geographic barriers against invaders trying to overcome them. The history of modern amphibious assault is a mixed bag. There have been notable successes, but failures have been costly and at times calamitous, from Gallipoli to the Bay of Pigs.[10] This is partly because of the complexity of such operations. Conquest across bodies of water is harder than "snap" invasion across contiguous territory, because it involves the translation of forces at the point where land and water meet, from one medium into another under fire. For British strategist Basil Liddell Hart, "a landing on a foreign shore in the face of hostile troops has always been one of the most difficult operations of war."[11] The sea when it is an uncontested highway can be the swiftest and most efficient way of transporting weighty military forces. But it can also be a dangerous operating medium. When projecting into hostile land space, as opposed to a merely administrative "ferrying" of troops, bodies of water increase the cost and effort required to project power. Ships along with their cargoes of people and materiel have nowhere to hide, and without bases or ports have no refuge and can be sunk. What's more, moving from one medium to another is particularly hazardous. In the transitional moment of shifting men, supplies, and vehicles from sea to land, and shifting from the maritime phase to the land assault, ships bearing invading forces must come within range, stop, and disembark forces, a point where they and their cargo are vulnerable. It then entails fighting on land where the obstacles of its terrain come into play. Natural hazards such as surf, sandbars, and rocks must be negotiated. Dispersed and concealed defenders must be overcome. In a large-scale amphibious operation, an invader must not only seize air and sea superiority but then must insert troops onto land and sustain them with uninterrupted support.

This issue resurfaced around the anniversary of D-Day, and because of a difficult debate about the future of warfare and choices about defense spending. In the words of one skeptic, "at first glance, it might seem like the innovations in transportation and communication technology that have triggered globalization would make contemporary amphibious assaults easier." Some indeed argue that amphibious invaders have evolved their methods to overcome defenders' growing firepower before, such as coastal artillery, and could turn today's precision weaponry on defenders, to eliminate shore-based missiles and clear a path to the beach, with the help of helicopters, submarines, and airborne troops.[12]

We should pay attention to amphibious cases also because scenarios of cross-water invasion are plausible—though remote—contingencies that have got the attention of policymakers and planners. The case examined here causes concern at high levels of government. American strategic documents reflect worry about the security situation in the Taiwan Strait and the possibility of China resorting to forced reunification of Taiwan and examine the contingency of a Chinese invasion.[13] China officially declares that reunification is its objective and openly warns that unilateral Taiwanese declaration of independence would trigger war. More broadly, states and militaries in Asia worry about the prospects of armed conflict over disputed islands.[14] Power struggles are already under way in the South China Sea and Western Pacific, and these will probably involve contests over the control of islands. Projecting power from sea to land is particularly relevant to the Asia-Pacific–Indian Ocean region, where heightened tensions and rivalries and the race for new force-projection capabilities threaten stability. Wealthy and growing states eye one another nervously as they strengthen their armed forces. Maritime Asia has become Washington's geopolitical focus and is the stage for its "pivot" to the region. If the twenty-first century is becoming an Asian century, where the Pacific and Indian Oceans' rich resources, rising states, and critical sea lanes become the center of world geopolitics, it is across bodies of water that security interactions will play out.[15]

Perception of the relative ease of offense and defense matters also more broadly. It affects how states approach arms control, threat assessment, the allocation of scarce resources, and the wider context of diplomacy.[16] Even if there is no cross-strait clash, if China's military modernization continues to persuade observers that it could swiftly overwhelm Taiwan in a fight, that perception could tilt domestic Taiwanese opinion in favor of conciliation and away from expensive defense investment, in turn persuading others that it is not a horse worth backing. If both sides perceive that China holds a strong upper hand, that could add leverage to China at the bargaining table or conversely drive Taiwan further into America's arms. Likewise, perception of offense dominance is important for US-China relations. As some argue, the separation afforded by the Pacific Ocean and nuclear weapons ought to make both China and the United States feel rela-tively secure. But even if the environment ought to be recognized as benign, states can fall prey to their fears of others' power and their inflated views of their own. If states misperceive the offense-defense balance, if they exaggerate either their abil-ity to expand or their insecurity in the face of others' expansion, if America, say, inflates the military threat posed by China's growing military capabilities or vice versa, their sense of mutual insecurity may lead them to adopt overly competitive policies that drive one another into spirals of hostility.

Of course, the rising costs and falling utility of expansionism may not be due to defensive capabilities alone. If conquest is on the way out and becoming a mar-ginal feature of international relations, this may be stemming from other profound causes. We live in mercantile times, and we may be seeing the transformation of "strategic states" into "trading states," or warfare states into welfare states, that are "debellicized" and prefer peaceful commerce.[17] Economic changes make industry and territory less attractive spoils of war and lower the benefits of conquest by frag-menting production across countries and rewarding exchange and knowledge over force.[18] Financial markets with their influential credit agencies and unprecedented flow of capital may impose a discipline that discourages interstate war—though does not guarantee its extinction—erecting an additional economic barrier to mili-tary adventurism. And there may be a normative shift under way. Out of the distress of fascist imperialism in World War II and the defeat of European colonial empires thereafter, there may have emerged a norm against conquest, a shift in values away from bellicose expansionism and toward an internationally enforced preservation of the existing status quo of sovereign territorial frontiers.[19] The nuclear revolution and the memory of the Cold War also presents a fearful obstacle to conquerors, turning armed conflict toward other more indirect or more limited kinds of competition, such as proxy wars, raids or campaigns of coercion against lesser enemies, and arms races short of war or deterrence and war avoidance among the greater.

But even if we controlled for these alternative potential influences and none of them applied, conditions are still inhospitable for conquest. Even if humans valued soil more than Sony, even if industrial plants and populations were still attractive assets to seize, even if nations were primarily oriented toward security competition and war, even if the nuclear revolution had not happened, they would face a problem. Those who would use force in territorial disputes face a military-strategic obstacle posed by the conventional weapons when efficiently used: the apparent power of "shields" over "swords." This is not an absolute power that pre-cludes expansion, but sufficient power to inflict costs on invaders that most states would regard as prohibitive. In other words, in the unending cycle of offense ver-sus defense, the military-strategic balance for some time may favor weapon sys-tems used skillfully for defensive purposes against would-be expansionists.

We should regard technology as more than a mere instrument. The original meaning of technology embraces both materials (*techne*) and knowledge (*logos*) but today often is reduced to a synonym for materials alone. When it comes to the "offense-defense balance" debate, globalism misconceives the nature of "offense" and "defense." It falls prey to the old fallacy that weapons in themselves contain intrinsic properties that render them offensive or defensive. To conceive technology in this way is tempting empirically, as it offers the seductive prospect of a quantitatively measurable quantity. It is tempting politically: To characterize one's own capabilities as defensive and others' weapons as offensive is to claim greater legitimacy under the guise of objective categories. This is too narrowly materialist in its search for the key that will unlock the secrets to victory and defeat in modern war, inattentive to the social and interactive nature of war, and wrong in its designation of some weapons as essentially "offensive" and others as "defensive," when weapons are historically indistinguishable and more ambiguous in the way onlookers perceive them, so that what is intended as a defensive measure can easily look like a threat. Above all, weapons do not have intrinsically offensive or defensive properties. It is their purpose that determines their function.[20] Weapons do not make war, security communities do, and it takes ideas and doctrines, as well as successful interactions, for agents to use them smartly.[21] A tank, an electron, a submarine, or a missile is neither exclusively one nor the other. Capability is generated by both tools and doctrine, or the ideas that guide action and inform the use of force. At this level, human agency intervenes. As "broad" offensive-defensive theorists argue, rather than seeking out the "offensive" or "defensive" essence in weapon systems, it is better to identify offense and defense as different military-political activities with different aims and functions, where geography, doctrine, and relative levels of will play a part. The analyst's task is to measure and specify the relationship between these moving parts.

Technology and Terrain: Two Propositions

Consider two clashing propositions about the relationship between technology and terrain. The first is that the range, precision, and lethality of emerging technologies weaken geographical barriers and the defensive advantages to be found in terrain, and thereby create *offense dominance* that makes expansion easier. The independent (causal) variable is the globalization revolution in ICTW (information, communications, transport, and weapons), and the dependent (caused or outcome) variable is the defensive barrier quality of distance, understood as the exploitation of geography by the defender. In successive waves, the air-power, missile, and nuclear revolutions all diminish distance as a protective barrier. If "away" advantages now don't count, or count substantially less, then the conquest of weaker states by stronger states across bodies of water should be easier. By "easier" in this case, I mean that amphibious invaders ought to be able to neutralize the traditional advantages of defenders to the extent that the conflict is decided by their relative weight of combat power rather than by the skillful use of terrain. A world of offense dominance rewards "first strikes," preventative or anticipatory war, quick escalation, and opportunistic expansion and instead of forcing attackers to overcome obstructive terrain, places attackers and defenders on a level playing field.

From this perspective, a measure of America's global power is its ability to project power from far away.[22] For historian Jeremy Black, "the entire world is literally under the scrutiny of surveillance satellites, missiles and planes that benefit from midair refuelling can deliver warheads continents away, and units can be rapidly transported to and on the battlefield and, once there, can use real-time information to increase their effectiveness. Space no longer appears to be an encumbrance, let alone a friction."[23] Strategic air power and global delivery systems have revolutionary significance, pointing to "the implications of bombers that can take off from Missouri, drop their bombload on Kosovo, and land back in Missouri. In our rapidly shrinking world, where air power can now be projected around the world from any position, the geographical location of bases (and indeed geography itself) is becoming increasingly irrelevant."[24] Such claims do not tell us much about the ability to translate the ability to move forces physically across "banal distance," into the ability to achieve desired outcomes in the face of resistance. It is far from clear that merely dropping bombs on Serbia from another continent in 1999 was enough to dislodge its regime. And the location of bases turns out to be important even as they are becoming more vulnerable.

Some worry that the trend toward "instant warfare" at long range could generate crises in maritime East Asia. The "first strike" advantages of modern air and naval warfare against vulnerable command-and-control systems could present rival states with the temptation to use their capabilities before they lose them. If the side that moves first can knock out, blind, or disable the command-and-control nerve centers of their adversaries, wide bodies of water will no longer be "defense dominant."[25] British anxieties about the vulnerability of the Falkland Islands to Argentine conquest also presume that a first airstrike could be a decisive blow, taking out the vital runways on Mount Pleasant airfield "by lunchtime" and ensuring that a cross-seas invasion could succeed with relative ease. Former Royal Navy chiefs warn that after the scrapping of one of Britain's two aircraft carriers and its Harrier jets, Argentina is "practically invited to attempt to inflict on us a national humiliation on the scale of the loss of Singapore."[26]

The argument that globalization gives attackers the edge has implications beyond interstate warfare. Some argue that globalization reduces the barriers to expansion abroad. Military technologies from remotely piloted vehicles to Stryker brigade combat teams to modern medicine may assist occupation forces against the armed resistance of weaker irregular, guerrilla opponents.[27] And this at a time when "the rise of new transnational threats and the failure of the nation state model to contain them will generate significant pressures on the United States to respond in an imperial manner."[28] Far from the death of conquest, it is argued, new technologies in the hands of the powerful may mean that liberal empire strikes back.

The fear that weapons erase the barrier effects of distance has an older intellectual pedigree in the nineteenth and twentieth centuries. It draws on several strands. Strategic theorists have credited each new wave of mobile and "offensive" weapons with transforming the geopolitics of war. The steamship and the railway prompted prophecies of the death of distance. During and after World War II, so too did the air-power, nuclear, and missile revolutions. The Yom Kippur War of 1973 underlined the pace and intensity that guided missiles and mechanized ground forces lent to modern land battles.

But it was the middle part of the Cold War that gave rise to the most theoretical accounts of how missiles eclipsed distance. The year 1959 was good for such prophecies. Americans feared the vastly inflated "missile gap," which was wrongly believed to be growing dramatically in the Soviet Union's favor.[29] In that year, Bernard Brodie warned of the revolutionary impact of nuclear weapons combined with new delivery systems such as intercontinental ballistic missiles, innovations that gave little or no warning time and could inflict instant destruction on the target's heartland.[30] John Herz argued that the atomic weapon had altered the historic tendency for power radiating from the center to weaken over distance until it found equilibrium with opposing power: "Now that power can destroy power from center to center everything is different."[31] Thomas Schelling argued that nuclear weapons combined with new means of delivery meant that military victory on a front line against an opposing force was "no longer a prerequisite for hurting the enemy." He also noted the flip side of that coin, that a side destined to lose the war could also inflict "unendurable" damage, denying national leaders the promise of victory at acceptable cost.[32]

The year 1959 was also when the defense intellectual Albert Wohlstetter published his findings that America's nuclear deterrent, its early-warning radar systems, bombers, and forward bases were vulnerable to a shock Soviet attack.[33] The feared "missile gap" between America and the Soviet Union, and the range and instantaneity of modern weapons, could defeat the space that traditionally had given America time to respond. During the Vietnam War he extended his argument further. Amidst intensifying debate over Vietnam and America's ability to fight land wars in Asia, the concern for distance and its power was an illusion. The obsolescence of the old geopolitics did not just apply to nuclear relations, but to nonnuclear strength.[34] Long-haul transport of materiel was surprisingly cheap, rebutted the distance-decay effect, and ever more powerful transport and communications would reduce it further. Over decades, the enduring theme of Wohlstetter's career was the transforming effect of new military technology on the "security environment." Yet for a case where resistance grew with space, he needed to look no further than the Vietnam War that prompted his critique, where Chinese- and Russian-supplied antiaircaft artillery were inflicting casualties and limiting the scope of America's war, to resist US incursions into the region. Even if transport to the theater was faster and more effective, this was written at a time when Americans could naturally assume the ease of transoceanic travel, based on unchallenged Western dominion over space between its heartland and the-aters of war, when the United States dominated the Pacific and Indian Oceans as its lakes, and when carrier and expeditionary strike groups could sail with impu-nity through maritime backyards of Asian states. As Asian states acquire means of force projection and access denial, this is increasingly redundant, and American forward bases are potentially more vulnerable as targets themselves.

The person who first formulated in depth the notion of the "loss of strength gradient," Kenneth Boulding, also lost faith in his own theory. Revolutionary developments in military technology in the twentieth century seemed to put the gradient into decline.[35] Writing in the early 1960s when the missile age had arrived, he judged that states could now defeat their opponents through strate-gic air power as a self-sufficient instrument. With the luxury of hindsight, we can see that his disillusionment with his own theory was premature. Putting aside the complex arguments about what strategic bombing can and cannot achieve, it is clear that it often cannot straightforwardly subdue or overthrow an opponent as a self-sufficient weapon. "Bombing to win" has a decidedly patchy record.

Speculation that a distance-destroying revolution was at hand would inten-sify with the so-called Revolution in Military Affairs (RMA) after the Cold War. RMA theory saw new technologies, doctrines, and mindsets transforming war. By applying the innovations of the information age, America could dominate the modern battlespace. Wohlstetter inspired neoconservatives' faith that the revolu-tion in military technology could expand the possibilities of American might and widen its strategic horizons.[36] New innovations made his vision seem achievable, such as the Predator drone and the Joint Direct Attack Munition. To his support-ers, wars after the Cold War proved right his decades-long advocacy of precision, hi-tech military capabilities. In successive clashes, futurists plundered each con-flict for signs of what was to come: the Gulf War of 1990–91, the NATO-Serbia War of 1999, Afghanistan 2001, and then Iraq 2003.[37] To the hopeful, those con-flicts cumulatively suggested that precision munitions, information systems of rapid data transmission, stealth technology, and small, mobile ground forces could give America unparalleled lethality. America's panoptic gaze over the battlespace would dispel the "fog of war," see over the hill, and strike precisely with satellite-guided, air-delivered missiles from afar.

Time and space were central to the RMA. The slogan "speed kills" suggested that the overdog could outpace its opponents in the decision-making and coordination of the kill-chain. One conceit of the RMA was that the United States can be swift and mobile to the extent that distance hardly constrains its power and that it could subdue its enemies at will.[38] Part of the RMA is an ambition that technology trumps terrain. As well as the ability to conduct war precisely at great distances, it looks to a revolutionary change in which well-choreographed forces in command of flows of instant information can, in Stephen Biddle's words, "make terrain irrelevant" and can "see and destroy anything on the Earth's surface regardless of cover or concealment or intermingling."[39] For Adm. William Owens, former vice chairman of the Joint Chiefs of Staff, information technology would allow US forces the capability for the first time in the history of man to be able to "see" a very large strategic battlefield with great definition: "That means that twenty-four hours a day, in real-time, all weather, we could have the ability . . . to see every activity and facility which might be of interest to our warfighting, peacemaking or peacekeeping effort. . . . If we are able to view a strategic battlefield this way and prevent an enemy from doing so, we have dominant battlefield awareness, and we are certain to prevail in a conflict."[40] RMA proponents do not always make such absolute claims. But in common, they look to the possibility of a significant change in the relationship between tools and terrain that can tilt the balance meaningfully between offense and defense. Campaigning for office in September 1999, then-governor George W. Bush announced, "Our forces in the next century must be agile, lethal, readily deployable, and require a minimum of logistical support. We must be able to project our power over long distances, in days or weeks rather than months. Our military must be able to identify targets by a variety of means—from a Marine patrol to a satellite. Then be able to destroy those targets almost instantly, with an array of weapons."[41] After 9/11, Bush's declared aspiration was for a military transformed, which "must be ready to strike at a moment's notice in any dark corner of the world."[42]

RMA visionaries presumed that military dominance would naturally yield grand strategic dividends. Hawkish nationalists in the Bush administration believed America's military was so powerful that it could reorder the very international system as Washington wished, if only its leaders would realize.[43] Its displays of power could intimidate adversaries such as North Korea and Iran into capitulating. RMA enthusiasts regarded America's war in Afghanistan from October 2001 as a "signpost war." America had gone to war in a landlocked, mountainous country and overthrown the Taliban with only light losses. The United States wielded a supposedly new "way of war," marrying air power, cash, special forces, and indigenous troops as its spearhead. Apparent mastery of one of the world's most fatal terrains, the graveyard of empires, created confidence in US capacity to use force as instrument of policy. Traditionally, there is a tradeoff to be made when fighting over range. Attacking over greater distance brings more security, but at the expense of accuracy. Greater proximity brings less security but more accuracy. Optimists speculated that the revolution on display cheated the problem, as the United States securely killed the Taliban fighters with standoff precision blows, seemingly from nowhere.[44]

What looked like a quick victory in a single campaign season in Afghanistan in 2001 became a measure of America's ability not only to assert itself militarily, but the natural ease with which grand strategic results would flow. Invasion had birthed constitutional government and routed terrorists. As John Lewis Gaddis noted, "suddenly, it seemed, American values were transportable, even to the remotest and most alien parts of the earth. . . . If we can topple this tyrant, if we can repeat the Afghan Agincourt on the banks of the Euphrates, then we can accomplish a great deal."[45] Smashing the Taliban quickly in open combat would finish them decisively as a political force and open the way for a consensual liberation.[46] Excited onlookers after the fall of Kabul and then Baghdad proclaimed a new "American way of war."[47] The lurch from initial doubt to jubilation about speedy victory in Afghanistan emboldened the Bush administration about the prospects for invading Iraq without getting bogged down.[48] After being on the receiving end of an enemy's power projection over space on 9/11, the apparent low costs and pyrotechnic display of American power projection played well to Bush's interpretation of the meaning of 9/11: In a new world of fanatical opponents who struck without warning, America had to strike first.

It is precisely a flaw in the vision of revolutionary netwar that it conflates military speed with wider and low-cost political transformation. The RMA became a kind of "technological sublime," a vision of technological mastery of the environment fused with a belief in America's limitless destiny and in the realm of security, a belief that American pioneering ingenuity could transcend defense dilemmas that had long seemed eternal.[49] With the Taliban's subsequent revival and reinvention after their overthrow in November–December 2001, the limits of such visions were brutally exposed.

An Alternative View

There is another way of conceiving the relationship between technology and terrain, offense and defense. Theories of "offense-dominant" globalization are both conceptually and historically weak. Military technology and doctrine may make violent relationships between states more intimate, yet with regard to territorial disputes the net effect of military capabilities has been to stretch the strategic distance between states.

False prophecies of offense dominance have accompanied most major technical innovations since the pace of change accelerated from the industrial revolution. From a longer historical perspective, the debate about "swords versus shields"
echoes the cyclical fears that technical innovations have attracted over time. In the
historic offense-defense cycle, the net impact of technologies at critical moments
has been so double-edged as to be effectively neutral. Consider the railway, which
Halford Mackinder cast as the decisive instrument that would give birth to the primacy of land power over sea power and, as a result, create a new powerful Eurasian
heartland ripe for conquest. Yet looking back, we can see that the opposite claim
was also compelling. The father of German geopolitics, Friedrich Ratzel (1844–
1904), believed railways would favor defense, not offense, enabling states that were
attacked to concentrate to meet the threat. Events on the eastern and western fronts
of 1914–15 followed his forecast. Formidable force-to-space ratios and the difficulties of outflanking opponents supplied by rail demonstrated the defensive potential of capability. Other innovations also proved double-edged. New technologies
from the steamship to the plane created initial fears of their offensive potential,
such as the invasion scares of the nineteenth century in Europe, fed by the assumption that faster fleets could transport armies rapidly across the English Channel, or
that the same Channel was no obstacle to bombers. But over time, doctrine caught
up to the point where they could also be used as defensive assets.[50] In the Battle of
Britain (July–October 1940) geography plus force and doctrine proved prohibitive.
German field marshal Wilhelm Keitel had predicted that a cross-Channel invasion
represented nothing more than a "large river crossing."[51] But with Britain's larger
surface fleet and air defense system, the Channel turned out to be a strong barrier,
not a highway, and British airspace an expensive domain to contest. The Luftwaffe
were fighting far from their bases over hostile territory where, thanks to extended
radar, the defense had the advantage of surprise. Distance exerted its pressures
down to the tactical level. German fighter pilots far from their bases had less time
to stay in British airspace than defenders and were imprisoned if they were shot
down and survived. Against prophecies that the strategic bomber was a distance-
destroying and war-winning instrument, air power was a shield as well as a sword,
used to defend as well as attack urban targets. The "home and away" dynamic also
shaped the balance of interests. Britain's Fighter Command inflicted losses that
Hitler was unwilling to sustain, given that he wanted to preserve his air force for a
wider war.

Not only do most weapons offer defensive as well as offensive possibilities.
In the areas of supply and logistics, new instruments that promise accelerated
expansion also generate new problems for the aggressor. Two European invasions
of Russia are the extreme historical cases of lightening technology being pitted
against formidable geography.[52] Both Napoleon's invasion of 1812 and Hitler's of

1941 were designed to be short campaigns against the clock, to defeat the czarist or Red armies before the autumn rains and then winter came on. Between both episodes, the growth in army size and complexity had made the difficulties of provisioning and maintaining force in the face of ice, snow, and rain all the greater. Mobility was a problem for Napoleon's Grande Armée, but was an even greater difficulty for Hitler's mechanized (and on-foot) forces. More powerful machinery was also harder to maintain in freezing or muddy conditions. Recoil fluid and lubricating oil on weapons froze. Firing pins went brittle and broke. Tanks, vehicles, and horses were lost to mud. Soldiers were struck by hypothermia and trench foot. The further the Wehrmacht's lines stretched, the harder it was to resupply and maintain it with spare parts and filters. Just to keep vehicles operational they were kept running, consuming increasingly scarce fuel. In a vast territory with a poor transportation network the advantage fell to the defending Soviets. They were better prepared and conditioned for the cold and could replace their greater losses more readily than the overstretched Germans. Learning to exploit space to purchase time, the Soviet Union could bring its growing industrial strength and manpower to bear. After spectacular German victories, it seemed to one soldier, "General Winter has stopped us with his icy hand."

What about today and tomorrow? Undeniably, some states have an unprecedented capacity to inflict devastation or annihilation from afar. That is a meaningful thing if destruction is the aim in itself. But short of such absolute and rare ambitions, the coevolution of defensive power (weapon systems combined with doctrines of access denial) is making the use of the military instrument as a tool of expansion more difficult, not less. Today's condition is a paradoxical one of "fire without conquest," where the rising costs of expansion caused by increased firepower disrupt the linkages between military force and territorial expansion. The same tools that are physically shrinking the world may be strategically expanding it.

For America, this gives it security and constrains its power at the same time. As Christopher Layne argues, "far from shrinking the world grand strategically, for the United States, modern weaponry—naval and strategic airpower, intercontinental delivery systems, and nuclear weapons—has *widened* it."[53] That same logic that assists US territorial security when playing on defense also constrains American power on offense, and the capacity of even powerful air/maritime states to apply force across space or even to operate. In 1999 Paul Bracken argued that the coming of disruptive technologies from the ballistic missile to WMDs to tracking and reconnaissance grids to sea mines would transform East Asia into a zone of exclusion. Whereas in the past decades the United States as a maritime heavyweight could operate with relative ease, Asian states with weapons of increasing range and lethality would deny America the freedom to mass its forces and fight from its advanced bases by threatening those very bases. They would threaten America's ability to move its forces into the region. In short, they would turn the free thoroughfare into an obstructive battlespace, turn owned space into contested space, raising the stakes of any intervention. If Asia was entering a "crisis of room" as technology compressed time and space, from the outlook of Washington, the region strategically was getting further away.[54] Both American intervention and Chinese expansion would be constrained by crowded South Asian waters. As will be argued below, his analysis was prescient.

What of the claim that swords used in a "first strike" overpower shields? This is not necessarily the case. States may threaten each other's astral and cyber-dependent command-and-control systems with instant knockout blows. But in response to the offensive capabilities of the space age, states like China are bringing their defenses back down to earth. Since 1995, China has constructed an underground "great wall." Turning to the "passive defenses" of antiquity in updated form, it is moving some of its defenses into a complex of hardened sub-terranean facilities, hundreds of miles long, to increase their survivability, along with around forty "super-hardened" underground air bases that may be diffi-cult to destroy.[55] The Second Artillery Corps reports that it has dug an under-ground tunnel 3,107 miles long in Hebei Province of northern China to give China's nuclear weapons survivability and through which missiles, equipment, and personnel can be transported unseen.[56] Grounding defenses in the earth in this way would have both direct and subtle benefits. We can never know for cer-tain the offense-defense balance in this regard, given the secrecy that surrounds the covert development of "passive defense." But that secrecy in itself can cre-ate doubts about the feasibility of a first strike, lest the attacker miscalculate and overestimate the defender's vulnerability and invite retaliation. If attacks on Chinese satellites proved insufficient to blind its command-and-control system, a persistent adversary wanting to land a decisive hit would need to inflict attacks on Chinese soil itself. A terrestrial strike on the country's territory, as opposed to a celestial one, would raise the stakes considerably. And as we will see, the doubts and difficulties around first strikes that help China in these ways could also hin-der it when it is the overdog. Against adversaries that can project offensive power across all domains, their adversaries reinvent low-tech fortifications and "pas-sive defense." This is evidence against the claim that there is a deterritorialization under way that empties terrain of weight and creates a liquid world. This misper-ception is encouraged by the misleading "TV/video game effect," accentuated in the pyrotechnic displays of long-range firepower in the Gulf wars of 1991 and 2003, that offers seductive images of instant war.[57]

Just as it builds a great wall below the earth, China is also creating blue-water ramparts. Maritime East Asia today presents increasingly formidable barriers to expansion or even incursion. China's "Assassin's Mace" defense system, marrying submarines, antiship missiles, and information technology, is designed to expand its maritime periphery and raise costs on any force encroaching on its environment.[58] The military modernization programs under way in East Asia, through ballistic and cruise missiles, submarines, sea mines, and surveillance systems, are creating formidable exclusion zones. The range of China's preventive strikes against air bases is growing. China's buildup of access-denial and area-denial defense has extended its defensive perimeter out to a range of roughly 1,500 km (900 miles), the range of missiles and the combat radius of fighters and naval strike aircraft.[59] According to the Pentagon, the entire South China Sea and Malacca Strait will fall within the range of the PLA's antiship ballistic missiles, making it able to lock onto moving warships from hundreds of miles.[60] Modern ships rely on electronics as much as armor, so can be disabled or taken off the board through damage to radar aerials or missile launchers. This is both a constraint and a shield. The same maritime barriers between China and neighboring states that make it a "dragon in a bathtub" also give it the ability to stretch the strategic distance of the Pacific Ocean against interlopers.[61] The costs China could impose with its growing ability to sink American ships and strike its bases mean that an American president today would probably think twice before dispatching aircraft carrier battlegroups to the Taiwan Strait, as President Clinton did in 1996, to coerce China from conducting missile tests to intimidate Taiwanese voters. The risk such escalation would pose to US surface ships would now be greater. Throwing one's weight around in this way is now a more risky and complicated affair. Uncontested command of the seas, especially one hundred to two hundred miles from China's coast, is probably a thing of the past.

This is a debate about space and time, and the calculations about space and time based on information and secrecy. Changes in surveillance, intelligence, reconnaissance, and warning technology, therefore, are crucial to the issue. The improved ability to identify, track, and pinpoint enemy forces makes surprise attacks more difficult, provided the defender is paying attention to the oncoming military offensive. Satellite reconnaissance, sharp visual sensors, and rapid data crunching provide the wary observer with more warning time and make a large-scale offensive out of the blue, such as Pearl Harbor or the German assault through the Ardennes in May 1940, more difficult. Importantly, these new hi-tech "eyes" do not make failures of imagination impossible: Analysts can still misinterpret the movement of forces preparing to strike, whether at the borders of the Soviet Union in 1941 or the multiple warnings of Al Qaeda's activity in 2001. And concealment is still possible for defenders staying under cover. But for forces coming out of cover to strike, the hi-tech "eyes" available to their opponents mean that deception is harder to achieve and they are more likely to be ready. The pursuit of a Hannibalic feat of deception and shock annihilation, a "Cannae," has long obsessed militaries but may be more out of reach than ever.[62]

The paradoxical effects flowing from new weapons make themselves felt in the task of supplying war over land at sea. Ever more complex and powerful weapon systems make forward bases even more important. All combat operations rely on a system of delivery and more sophisticated technology demands more physical support. Jet fighters, tanks, and helicopters need constant maintenance and logistical backup. To wage war against Iraq in 1991, the United States amassed a gigantic quantity of supplies in Saudi Arabia. US sealift and airlift moved 9.7 million short tons, including two million gallons of drinking water and 22,000 vehicles.[63] For the United States to project power into Asia, it would need forward bases to project power and sustain military operations. Without those bases, it would have to exert far greater effort to fight its way into the region than China. Contrary to claims that the United States could simply abandon all forward-leaning bases and rely on the reach of its weapons, James R. Holmes and Toshi Yoshihara remind us that

> naval bases, then, are mundane yet indispensable. Nearly a century ago, Rear Adm. Bradley Fiske likened their purpose to "supplying and replenishing the stored-up energy required for naval operations." To stay with his physics simile, the fleet swiftly discharges its potential energy at sea. Smaller warships such as destroyers and frigates, which defend aircraft carriers and other "high-value units" against air, surface, and undersea attack, refuel underway every three to four days lest they exhaust their bunkers. A virtually inexhaustible fuel source drives nuclear-powered flattops through the water. Thirsty air wings nonetheless demand jet fuel to stay aloft, sustaining sortie rates typical of aerial combat. By no means does nuclear power liberate carriers from their bases. Submarines boast the greatest at-sea endurance in modern navies. During the Cold War, US ballistic-missile submarines routinely undertook seventy-day patrols. Even so, their crews still need food—and they must put into harbor periodically to load it.[64]

Yet as Yoshihara also recognizes, the sophistication of modern military technology that puts such a high premium on bases with their storage tanks, ammunition depots, or repair facilities also renders those bases increasingly vulnerable. China's increasing stocks of long-range ballistic missiles such as the DF-15 and the DF-21 missiles threaten to disable American naval and air bases in the "first island chain" of the western Pacific, in Japan and Okinawa, forcing the United States to operate from thousands of miles farther eastward, thereby depleting its forces' staying power.[65] Making America's forward bases more vulnerable and extending China's defensive perimeter would stretch time and space, especially considering the time it still takes to sail a carrier battle group from America's Pacific Coast, not to mention the heavy sustainment of food, fuel, and ammunition that carrier groups require. For America to project power without prohibitive costs into those regions, it would be forced to rebuild its military to strike from far over the horizon. This could place in jeopardy the operating assumption for generations, that the United States is a permanent resident with a secure forward presence in maritime Asia.

The dilemmas posed by distance, such as the imbalance of interests and the ability of well-organized defenders to exploit terrain, also affects the question of empire. Judging by recent wars conducted at long range, new technologies that enable the projection of firepower and supposedly tilt the balance in favor of empires have not overturned the problem that distance often makes it increasingly difficult for the side with the lesser stake in the conflict to keep slugging it out. This is the problem of the imbalance of will and interest. Over time in Iraq and Afghanistan, bloody attrition inflicted on Western expeditionary forces sapped public opinion in favor of the commitment and the political ability to sustain it. Because Americans could go home, and many (though not all) insurgents were fighting at home, the location of the war "over there" shaped political calculations about the effort being expended. The public increasingly did not believe that the costs were worth it, despite the repeated claims of their leaders that vital interests were at stake.[66] As he tried to shore up support for the war effort, President Bush attempted to turn the distance between Iraq and the United States into a reason to keep fighting there, claiming, "We are fighting these terrorists with our military in Afghanistan and Iraq and beyond so we do not have to face them in the streets of our own cities."[67] How this squares with his other claim of a borderless conflict against a global threat is not clear. Regardless, it did not prove persuasive enough to stop public support hemorrhaging. As costs mounted, presenting wars in Central Asia and the Persian Gulf as a vital existential struggle for the security of "our streets" at home became a hard sell.[68] When the fighting in Iraq reached its worst point in April 2007, 66 percent of those polled said the war was not worth it.

Even in an age of panoptic surveillance, of Google Earth and GPS, the very wars that supposedly showcased the RMA also demonstrated the ability of weaker defenders to defy attackers armed with precision standoff weapons and at times force them into more intimate combat. The RMA could not eliminate the difficulties of fighting in forbidding environments, such as fortified cities and mountains. In NATO's bombing of Serbia in 1999, what was supposed to be a three-day air campaign to coerce the regime of Slobodan Milosevic went for seventy-eight days and with camouflage, decoys, and effective concealment in forests, regime forces withstood 6,728 precision-guided munitions striking six thousand aim points.[69] That war repeated air power's traditional conundrum, the tradeoff that safer high-altitude bombing reduces effectiveness, making it harder to locate forces from ten thousand feet and identify the right targets. In this case, targets were hidden from patrolling aircraft with ease, and forces sheltered in Tito-era underground bunkers and diverted NATO bombers with decoy weapon emplacements, while bad weather disrupted laser-guided smart bombs.[70] Urban guerrillas have proven adaptive and resilient, whether as Somali gunmen exploiting the city environment in Mogadishu in 1993 or Chechnyan insurgents in Grozny in 1995. Skilled urban defenders can neutralize or reduce the advantages of a stronger side fighting from long range, presenting mutilayered defensive positions, "places where they can retreat, regroup and prepare to fight again. The urban environment neutralizes the key technical advantage of United States soldiers in ground warfare—the ability to locate and kill the enemy at ranges much greater than those from which the enemy can locate and kill them."[71]

Even in the one season highlighted for showing off the possibilities of stand-off precision strikes shows the flaws in its prophecies. At critical points, the interactive moves and countermoves of the combat did not make it easy for America to dispatch Afghan fighters remotely and precisely. Close-quarters combat played a much greater role, and fortified terrain proved more resistant, than the techno-fetishist accounts presumed. Jihadists confronted by revolutionary, hi-tech distanced bombing learned (or relearned) to disperse, conceal, and dig in, and by shielding themselves forced their invaders to fight up close. Air strikes and air assaults alone could not blast dug-in Al Qaeda fighters out of their reinforced mountain complexes at Tora Bora stockpiled with food and ammunition and defended from prepared firing positions.[72] The same fortified terrain had proven resilient against Soviet air assaults and air strikes in the earlier war. Even the hammer of dazzling air power needed an anvil of ground forces. If Serbia, Afghanistan, and Iraq are any guide, prospects for empires seeking expansion on the cheap are not good.

If new technologies spawn new difficulties that strain power projection, this applies also where armies hungrily devour supplies. Merely sustaining operations in Afghanistan, a landlocked and politically fragmented country, across thousands of miles exerts political costs that were not foreseen in the early triumphant phases of the war. Where once heat exhaustion afflicted invaders, air conditioning in Afghanistan and Iraq at the height of operations cost America $20 billion a year.[73] Faster vehicles and industrially produced food increase the weight of logistics required. Feeding body armor, meals, ammunition, and other materiel into the theater requires an expensive supply system. This occurs from the air, with great wear and tear on planes, or through land from the port of Karachi, which relies on the collaboration of entrepreneurs for the protection of convoys, injections of money that in turn finance warlords and insurgents. In 2008, 12 percent of all US supplies moving from Karachi to Bagram Air Base disappeared. Its other land route, through the Northern Distribution Network, relies on the consent of

Russia, giving it the means of geopolitical leverage over Washington. The change lies not in a seismic disappearance of geography, but in the shifting ways that distance reimposes limits on power.

Inevitably, those functions must then interact on a geographical stage. In this case, we are concerned with the capacity—constituted by physical ability and political will—to take and hold territory from the sea. I argue that one important case suggests that conditions in amphibious war are generally more favorable to defense. Applying force as a conqueror—and crucially, sustaining and supplying force—has in important ways become more costly rather than less. That cannot be an absolute law. For defenses to prevail, they must still perform well, or well enough. One potential flashpoint in international politics where the weaker side can and possibly is presenting a viable defense is over the Taiwan Strait.

Dangerous Straits: A Test Case

To restage the issues outlined above, I now examine a hypothetical scenario of a Chinese attempt to forcibly unify Taiwan with the mainland through a cross-strait invasion against resistance. An invasion by the PRC ROC on the islands of Taiwan is an illustrative case for the argument here. It involves the crossing of water onto land and thus enables us to pit technology against terrain in a clash between a major and minor state. It involves a materially larger side with ten times the number of troops, an absolute advantage in quantities of ballistic missiles and submarines, and a vastly greater defense budget, invading across a relatively narrow body of water against a smaller defender. We would expect there would probably be resistance by a defending side armed at least with a minimal level of modern capabilities (doctrine, technology, resources) and driven with a minimal level of political will to survive. And it is a useful case study because, unusually, it limits the importance of another variable that might cloud the issue, the question of the "ham omelette." From what we know, both sides regard the status of Taiwan as first-order in importance, if not equally so. The intervening factor of the "imbalance of interests" matters less in this case than in asymmetrical clashes across greater distances such as America's Vietnam War where the imbalance of interests played a decisive role. We can reasonably forecast that both sides would care very much about the outcome of a battle for Taiwan, to the extent that they would be willing to incur great costs to prevail. Exact pain thresholds are unknowns, but Taiwan could not safely assume that China would care so much less that its cost tolerance would be low and would have to ensure that its defense coped competently enough. This makes the interaction of technology and terrain more important to the issue.

To be sure, a war over Taiwan would be a remote contingency. Remote contingencies are common enough in history to be taken seriously. It is plausible enough as a scenario that it generates considerable attention in governments and militaries that worry that China may be willing to use force to press its territorial ambitions.[74] Even if it does not occur, perceptions of the changing military balance between the two could shape the calculations of Washington and Beijing, their contingency plans for a clash between one another, and their willingness to use force should the question of Taiwan trigger a wider conflict. Whether or not it could exploit terrain to mount a successful defense against an amphibious assault is also a matter of interest not only in the seas of East Asia but in the South Atlantic.

There are numerous sources available for this case. These include campaign analyses by Richard E. Bush and Michael O'Hanlon in 2007 and the RAND Corporation in 2009 and estimates by the Center for Strategic and International Studies and the US-Taiwan Business Council, all supplemented by a US secretary of defense appraisal in 2013 and by doctrine produced in open source by both the People's Republic of China and the Republic of China.[75] As well as official strategic documents, we can identify patterns suggested by the choices of weapons, training, and preparation Beijing and Taipei have made. Given the secrecy of defense plans and capabilities, a precise estimate is impossible. But this case is offered as an investigation of broader patterns in the offense-defense balance. To test the claim that a globalized world is an "offense-dominant" world, we can design a plausible worst-case scenario that favors the offense where we assume that areas of doubt "break" for the benefit of the invader.

What proposition exactly are we testing here? What would a "globalist" scenario look like? To specify: Historically an amphibious invasion usually requires three steps to succeed. The assailant must achieve air supremacy or such a dominant amount of air superiority that it can operate at will. It must capture a defensible beachhead so that it can securely insert its ground forces from sea to land and so that it can sustain and resupply them. And it must then turn its foothold into a "breakout" before the defender can focus its defenses on the point of entry and cut it off. For globalism to offer a robust account of what might happen, the invader should be able to neutralize and overcome the barriers created by terrain and human agency to the extent that the clash would unfold on a "level playing field" where the outcome would be determined by the material balance between the two sides and where terrain would count for little. Using its formidable first-strike advantages, China would successfully "jump the gun" with a bombing campaign that would suppress Taiwan's air defenses, interdict Taiwan's lines of communication and supply, gain strong advantage or even air and maritime supremacy, be able to supply and sustain combat operations, and after seizing a secure foothold on the island, break out and march on Taipei. With its strengthening access and area-denial capabilities that might seriously complicate any US intervention,

Beijing could plausibly threaten to fight a localized war against an isolated and overmatched island.

China with the military balance as it was would probably struggle greatly to mount a successful conquest of Taiwan without taking losses so serious that it would cost the loss of much of its invading ground force, possibly some severe damage to its maritime and air capabilities, and risk a protracted struggle that might widen into a struggle with other parties, namely the United States.

Context and Design

The PRC regards Taiwan as part of its sovereign territory. The ROC regards itself as an independent state though has not formally declared independence. Relations between both have eased in the most recent "detente." But their positions on the question are still irreconcilable and could again deteriorate. While mutual efforts to dampen down tensions and strengthen economic ties continue and Beijing expresses a preference for peaceful reunification, the PRC has never renounced its willingness to use force to compel reunification. Not only does China regard Taiwan as a matter of principle and territorial integrity. It also regards Taiwan as a vital part of its regional security architecture. Facing growing rivalries and tensions with United States–backed states such as the Philippines, Vietnam, and Japan, a United States–friendly Taiwan could become a threatening guard tower in a hostile "island chain," a potential base from which the United States could radiate power along its coastal periphery, and a barrier to any Chinese forward defense beyond the first island chain of the Philippines, Aleutians, Borneo, Kuriles, and Ryukus.[76] The question of Taiwan is also bound up in wounded memories of China's "century of humiliation." Taiwan could also offer a convenient pretext for war, and a glance at diplomatic history suggests that this is not a frivolous concern.

The Taiwan question may not come to outright invasion. There are other plausible ways China could use or threaten the use of force to pursue its aims. Achieving a favorable military balance without blood could be one, presenting the region and the United States with an altered picture that would lead to states in its shadow jumping on the bandwagon. China could deploy its military as part of a wider strategy of tightening the noose, through a military buildup, economic penetration, and the cultivation of political and commercial elites, deterring American intervention and isolating and weakening Taiwan to the point where it "has no choice but to cut the best deal it can with the mainland."[77] If it was more willing to compromise or fudge on the question of Taiwan's status, China could opt for a more consensual process of "Finlandization" by beckoning Taiwan into its orbit with the promise that in exchange for submitting to China on foreign policy matters, its internal affairs are its business, thereby demilitarizing the strait without formal unification.[78] And to discourage Taipei's unilateral secession,

China hopes that it could threaten to use its military power in many ways such as maritime blockade/quarantine, limited coercion to intimidate/exact political concessions, or a bombing campaign short of invasion. With these possibilities, it seeks to deter Taiwan with the threat of punishment. The prospects of a clash of some kind that would favor China are an important background in its diplomatic efforts to influence it to settle its long-standing status dispute on China's terms.[79] Even though invasion may not be a likely or desirable thing for both parties, China's ability to invade successfully is part of the picture. Ultimately the dispute centers on the control of territory. The ability to capture that territory must inform how the states involved view the problem.

For the sake of argument, the scenario presented here works in favor of the assailant to make it an "easy test" where globalist theory ought to perform well. We give the invading China optimum diplomatic circumstances, namely a purely localized war in which third parties do not intervene. For the defender, regional security arrangements and strategic ties to the United States come to nil. In a purely dyadic or two-sided contest, this takes off the table Taiwan's preferred strategy of holding the invader off until the US Navy enters the conflict as a relief force. Where expert observers suggest China lacks sufficient transport equipment, namely sealift and landing platform dockships to get troops ashore, or aerial refueling and logistics, we grant it these things, optimized in line with its short- and medium-term plans.[80] As we are weighing up the interaction of technology, geography, and doctrine, there is the need to "control" for other variables such as shortfalls in the invader's military capabilities. There is a fluidity about constantly evolving defenses in competitive rearmament, but for the purpose of analysis we grant China the platforms it would desire while restricting Taiwan to the equipment it currently has. We also exempt China from the rule of thumb where the attacker's army needs to outnumber the defender's manpower 3:1.[81] For China's forces to prevail, only a 1:1 manpower ratio is the necessary condition of minimal numerical parity (though not a sufficient condition) to seize and establish a beachhead. I assume that China restrains from nuclear strikes. Its primary aim is not to destroy or punish but conquer, to apply enough force to overwhelm Taiwan's defenses. I assume that both sides would be willing to fight. A supposed norm against conquest would not apply to China, while closer ties to the mainland and the emergence of a more reluctant younger generation would not lead Taiwan to capitulate without a struggle. Where in doubt, we give the benefit of the doubt to China.

So this is a case where in an "offense-dominant" world, the stronger party should find the balance shifting decisively in its favor. China cares as much, or almost as much, about the outcome as the defender. It regards the disputed territories as its sovereign possession. And it has the "first-strike" advantage. Neither side

has an appreciable advantage in recent military experience; both powers are relatively inexperienced at real armed conflict. In this scenario I control for shortfalls
in current inventory of equipment and for the outside intervention of stronger
party. In real life there are unknowns. We do not know the exact pain thresholds or cost intolerance of either side, precisely how many casualties and resource
losses China would be willing to suffer, and whether Taiwan would be willing to
fight to the death. So for the purpose of this analysis, we presume that once hostilities commence, the motivation for both sides is roughly equal.[82]

At the turn of the twenty-first century, assessments of China's ability to invade
Taiwan found strongly in favor of Taiwan. Beijing would probably lose the battles
in and for the air and the sea, and whether it could even transport significant numbers safely across the strait was in doubt.[83] Now, observers see a shifting balance.
The International Institute of Strategic Studies worries for the fate of Taiwan in the
event of a Chinese invasion. As it warns, "the capacity of such a small armed forces
[sic] to withstand a concerted Chinese offensive from across the Taiwan Strait is
doubtful. Moreover, a growing reluctance on the part of the US to furnish Taiwan
with the most advanced military equipment means that China is rapidly closing
the technology gap. Taipei is currently emphasizing the procurement of early-
warning and missile-defence systems to enable the island to withstand an assault
for as long as possible, with the goal of buying time for US intervention."[84] In other
words, Taiwan is so overmatched that its only hope would be to hold out until
the American cavalry rides to its rescue. This follows other similarly pessimistic
assessments in open sources. The US Department of Defense (DOD) identifies a
shifting military balance with China's acquisition of "over a thousand ballistic missiles, an anti-ship ballistic missile program, increasingly modern ships and submarines, combat aircraft, and improved C⁴ISR capabilities" that could negate the
factors that Taiwan has traditionally relied upon to keep the wolf from the door,
such as the "inherent geographic advantages of island defense" as well as military
advantages that are eroding.[85] If this assessment is right, it effectively means that
in one of the potential flashpoints of future war where defenders might hope to
exploit the advantages of their island, that technology (along with superior capability) will trump terrain. Even if Taiwan is defendable, as one recent assessment
argues, China is rapidly getting a qualitative and quantitative edge over Taiwan
and an increased ability to deter American intervention in a shooting war. This
in itself could give Beijing illusions of an easy victory and tempt it to reunify the
country by force.[86] China's military analysts have reportedly studied prior cases
of amphibious warfare intensively, especially the nearest comparable case of the
Falklands War of 1982. They conclude from this rough analogy that an invasion
of Taiwan would not be a doomed "million-man swim," but a feasible move where
it could hold other intervening powers off and mount a successful attack given the

right amount of training, deceptive feints, and assets such as sea transport, landing ships, and amphibious armoured vehicles.[87] In Taiwan, a computerized assessment in 2010 estimated that "China would capture the island's capital in just three days if the two sides went to war."[88] Such homegrown pessimistic forecasts may be intended to stoke fears for political purposes at home and abroad. Yet by feeding real fears that Taiwan might become a ripe target, that in itself would have consequences. Both the objective prospects for invasion and perceptions of it matter.

If, as the DOD warns, the cross-strait military balance is tilting in Beijing's favor, might this mean that it could in the near future overrun Taiwan? The wargames scenario was based on the assumption of conflict taking place now (at the time of writing, 2013), with a sequence of China's People's Liberation Army launching a bombardment before sending in airborne and ground troops. I organize this analysis around three phases: Phase 1, winning maritime air supremacy; Phase 2, seizing a foothold, achieving sustainability (secure resupply); and Phase 3, breakout.[89] These phases are identifiable in historical amphibious campaigns and around which China itself formulates its own doctrine for an invasion of Taiwan. China's doctrine for amphibious assault is its "Joint Island Landing Campaign" concept, which reflects these phases: "to break through or circumvent shore defenses, establish and build a beachhead, transport personnel and materiel to designated landing sites in the north or south of Taiwan's western coastline, and launch attacks to seize and occupy key targets and/or the entire island."[90] How would this fare today?

Seizing control of the air is an important precondition for modern amphibious campaigns. This can take the form of either *air supremacy* (complete control of the skies) or at least *air superiority* (enough control to prevent prohibitive interference by opposing air forces). Air supremacy is needed to suppress and interdict defending forces, to enable the invading forces to reach the shore and disembark while minimizing losses. Ideally, it facilitates the arrival and switch from sea to land and isolates the beachhead during the first critical and vulnerable stage in the assault.

For this first phase, we have available the detailed RAND study that draws on a "Monte Carlo" technique to model the likely success of the air strikes, a technique that allows for variation in the number and accuracy of strikes within the known numbers and range of the attackers' arsenal. These are probabilistic rather than absolute estimates that indicate the range of possible outcomes that accommodate the play of chance and the inherent uncertainties in the balance of both sides' performance. Their models accommodate variation in relative performance, given that neither China nor Taiwan has conducted intensive air warfare for over half a century, and given the uncertainty of just how inferior China's pilots are to Taiwan's, given the latter's greater annual flying hours and apparent superiority in training. They accommodate variations in the resilience of air bases and the number of sorties "red" and "blue" teams can fly per day. The estimates do point to some enduring dynamics that persist in this phase of the campaign.

Until the past five years or so, assessments were more doubtful of China's ability to suppress Taiwan's air defenses before storming the beaches to the extent that it would seize supremacy rather than just the edge.[91] But as both countries modernize their militaries, reducing the overall numbers of aircraft and replacing them with more powerful advanced aircraft, the gap in the "air and missile balance" may be widening in China's favor. According to later studies, China's present capability to neutralize Taiwan's air defenses, seize command of the skies over Taiwan, and exploit that command to disrupt Taiwan's other defenses is considerable, and it is ramping up that capability further.[92]

To execute this phase and rupture Taiwan's air defenses and their ability to operate, China would need to strike air bases, radar sites, missile batteries, space assets, and communication facilities. It would probably launch initial missile attacks, followed in the cleared airspace by a wave of fighter-bombers bearing precision-guided missiles (PGMs) and Harpy drones targeting Taiwan's air defenses. China now has a growing precision strike capability, with a growing arsenal of both short-range ballistic missiles (SRBMs) and fourth-generation fighter planes. The PLA Second Artillery Corps has deployed between 1,000 and 1,200 SRBMs on its southeast coast opposite Taiwan. RAND estimates that with targeted warheads, China could "cut every runway at Taiwan's half-dozen main fighter bases and destroy essentially all of the aircraft parked on ramps in the open at those installations," estimating that if the entire first wave of missiles were fired to attack the air bases with a missile accuracy rate of CEP (circular error probable) of forty meters, China would have a better than 90 percent chance of cutting all runways.[93] In their terms, the air war for Taiwan could essentially be over before much of the blue air force has even fired a shot.[94] It could follow up the initial bombardment with an air campaign in which it has roughly a 2:1 numerical superiority, fielding approximately seven hundred combat aircraft within range including five hundred advanced modern aircraft such as the Su-27, Su-30, J-10, and JH-7. China would hope that its first bombardment would have disabled much of the Taiwan Air Force's "fourth-generation" aircraft (F-16A/Bs, Mirage 2000-5s, F-CK-1A/Bs).

In terms of sheer force, China would have several advantages in this phase. Taiwan is developing its antimissile capabilities and ground-based air defenses, based on its own Tien Kung-II (Sky Bow) surface-to-air missile (SAM) system, and Patriot-III missiles. But its SAM batteries could only hope to take out a fraction of the incoming missiles. Currently Taiwan fields only three SAM batteries of PAC-2 antiballistic missiles.[95] Without an expanded and improved ballistic-missile defense system that could hope to withstand a ballistic-missile attack, the large volleys China could fire would probably overwhelm Taiwan's air defenses within minutes. Second, Taiwan's runways are vulnerable. It has only a small number at air bases that are within range of Chinese missiles, and if damaged could be disabled in the crucial time window.

There is no question that considered in a narrow sense with enough surprise, China could inflict a devastating first strike, achieving air superiority if not supremacy. It could establish an air dominance of some degree that would enable it to disable Taiwan's air defense infrastructure and take a large share of its air force out of action. Depending on Taiwan's preparations, it is unlikely that this first strike would destroy Taiwan's hundreds of combat jets in their entirety. Taiwan has invested in an early-warning network, developing an EWR station and mobile platforms such as upgraded Hawkeye planes (E-2T) as well as the radar sensors of remotely piloted vehicles.[96] Taiwan invests in early-warning radar from fixed and mobile platforms to give precious minutes to get planes out of hangars and off runways. Even a small amount of early warning would also give time to forewarn the civilian population. In that time, Taiwan could disperse its Apache helicopters and mobile artillery pieces, and perhaps some fixed-wing aircraft away from their bases to highway strips, and move multiple brigades (about a third of its active force) into defensive positions to defend its beaches with artillery.[97] Some of Taiwan's surface-to-air missiles, its Sky Bow III (Tien Kung III), stored in both underground shelters and on towed platforms, would probably survive, and these have a reported range of a thousand kilometers.[98]

But even if Taiwan was forcibly stripped of its SAMs and China could command the skies at low cost, in a wider context China faces a dilemma, a tradeoff between surprise and preparation. Whether it struck in 2009, 2014, or 2019, surprise and deception would come at the expense of preparedness and speed of engagement with large-scale forces, and vice versa. To inflict a surprise first strike that successfully suppressed Taiwan's air defenses to the extent that it achieved air dominance, China would need to do so from a standing start, and to avoid giving the game away would have to forgo a prior preparation of a large-scale invasion force into a cross-strait armada, to cross the one hundred nautical miles from its bases closest to the most plausible point of assault, the small number of locations on the northwest beaches of Taiwan. It could hardly amass this force invisibly if a watchful Taiwan was minimally alert and used its surveillance technology efficiently. The interval between the first strike and then preparation for the attempted invasion would afford a vital window of time for Taiwan to recover and prepare for the next phase, including the roughly seven hours it would take for a fleet traveling at fifteen knots to make the one-way crossing. Conversely, to prepare adequately with a buildup of force would sacrifice surprise, giving Taiwan days at least to disperse its forces, ensure the survival of large parts of its air force, and get its planes off the airfields. Taiwan's topography is such that there are only a few land-ing-friendly points along its five-hundred-mile coastline where a massed invasion could take place and where the defender could concentrate its forces. Consider the contrast with the Allied invasion of Normandy, where an amphibious assault could have taken place along a coastline twelve hundred miles long and without the surveillance assets of today. Since the invasion fleet would have to be a sizable one of a hundred assault ships loading vehicles, troops, and supplies, and since a fully loaded invasion fleet would take about seven hours going at fifteen knots in a one-way crossing of a hundred nautical miles at the closest point, it is inconceiv-able that Taiwan would not see the buildup or see them coming.

Given China's greater strength of numbers and firepower and the problem that Taiwan would simply be unable to outmatch it in crude material terms, a vital part of Taiwan's defense is the degree to which it has chosen prudent "doctrine" and how realistically it defines victory. Doctrine simply means ideas of force employ-ment. It scarcely determines outcomes and relies on execution but is needed to link technological means with strategic ends. Taiwan may not be able to outgun China materially, but as history suggests, well-prepared weaker defending sides can return fire conceptually by optimizing what they have to create an imposing defensive system. Taiwanese and international observers have intensively debated what it should do with its lesser resources in the face of an adversary whose rela-tive material strength is growing alarmingly. Several competing doctrinal options have been on the table. None of these are mutually exclusive but there are tradeoffs as each would draw resources from the others. They can be organized around two ideal-typical "poles," "classical defense" and "porcupine defense."

The classical defense grows out of Taiwan's traditional doctrine of defense against an invader. When it had the greater qualitative military edge, Taiwan defined victory in offensive terms, to win in a direct clash for control of the seas and skies, overpowering China's larger but less advanced forces. It also planned on interdicting China's approaching forces far from Taiwan's coast. Designed for a symmetrical, toe-to-toe clash, this approach was capital intensive and involved hi-tech conventional forces at the cutting edge. It sought to thwart Chinese invad-ing forces out at sea and in air space well beyond its islands, which would also be defended by a mass citizen army. Budgetary constraints, China's military mod-ernization fueled by economic growth, disenchantment with conscription, and a shift to an all-volunteer army have made this approach problematic. Today the model is reinvented in the argument that Taiwan should compete with China's modernization program with its own, lobbying hard for state-of-the-art aircraft such as the F-16C/D or the Joint Strike Fighter, as well as developing the ability to take a conflict via bombing the Chinese mainland with surface-to-surface mis-siles with extended range, which would also form a preemptive strike capability.

In a struggle that would entail clash of advanced machines, Taiwan would not give up its effort to compete in the same technological contest and match its quality with China's.

By contrast, the porcupine defense is more deliberately asymmetrical in the sense that it seeks to exploit the differences between invader and defender, differences of strategic objective, as well as differences in the type of forces being used.[99] Instead of an expensive modernization program that attempts to match the quality if not the quantity of China's forces, it looks more to a "passive defense" that would ensure that enough of Taiwan's forces could survive the initial onslaught. The porcupine approach invests more in the survivability of forces, their dispersal and concealment, the hardening of command-and-control systems, the repair of damaged assets such as runways, and resilience against electromagnetic and cyber attacks. It is a more army-centric doctrine that places more investment in fortifying ground-based infrastructure and training personnel for a land war. It emphasizes the exploitation of terrain. It is less reliant on American largesse and technology transfer. In an alternative version, a low-tech porcupine strategy could also extend out to sea, with guerrilla warfare in nearby waters waged by "swarms of light combatants."[100]

What we know of Taiwan's actual strategy mixes features from both models. This evidence that we have suggests that Taiwan is making prudent choices about how it allocates its resources and is redefining its objectives realistically. It draws from the porcupine logic the shift from ambitious to achievable strategic goals. Rather than seeking to defeat Chinese forces outright in a decisive Mahanian naval clash, its objective is to deny China an affordable conquest by raising costs on the invader to defend de facto independence. When it had the greater qualitative military edge, Taiwan defined victory in offensive terms—to win in a direct clash for control of seas and skies, overpowering and destroying China's larger but less advanced forces. It designed its defenses accordingly, around capital ships and advanced planes and matching its adversaries' investments. Judging by its own published doctrine, the *National Defense Report* of 2011, Taiwan recognizes that victory in these terms is no longer realistic and it is switching accordingly.[101] Taiwan now defines victory as ensuring the survival of enough forces and preventing land forces establishing a foothold on Taiwan.[102] Its *Quadrennial Defense Review* of 2013 also suggests a doctrinal shift, emphasizing the preservation of critical infrastructure to prevent being paralyzed by "sudden and high-intensity assaults" and the exploitation of Taiwan's advantages in space and time.[103] The same logic that enables China with today's tools to raise the costs of US intervention into its maritime space to unpalatable levels also enables Taiwan to do the same at a price more suited to its limited GDP expenditure on defense.[104] To turn the nautical approaches to the island into contested zones, it exploits "swarming" methods by preparing small attack craft armed with antiship cruise missiles as light guerrillas at sea.

There is evidence that Taiwan is putting these doctrinal decisions into practice.[105] Taiwan has built a hidden underground sanctuary inside a mountain near its Hualien air base on its eastern coast, a bomb shelter large enough to shelter two hundred fighters linked to the above-ground base by a 7,500-foot taxiway. At least since 2010, it has been hardening air field facilities, introduced a major hardened aircraft storage facility at Taitung in southeastern Taiwan, and is now addressing one of the weaknesses identified by RAND in 2009 by strengthening its Rapid Runway Repair crews to improve the survivability of runways at several air bases. It invests in mobile launchers for missiles and has acquired and now fields road-mobile missile launchers that can be dispersed and camouflaged, armed with rockets capable of firing at ships (such as the HF-3 supersonic antiship cruise missile) and Ray Ting 2000s with an artillery range of up to forty-five kilometers into China's mainland. To turn the point of amphibious landing into a shooting gallery, it is digging in with entrenched antiship and antiair missile sites. To make both the sea approach and the beachhead more perilous, it prepares sea and land mines, the former of which could be scattered by artillery tubes. And it prepares to wage a "war of the flea" out at sea with small, fast, and low-signature missile-armed ships (thirty-one Kuang Hua VI class boats) that are harder to locate and sink than heavier frigates and destroyers. They would be assisted by twelve maritime patrol aircraft. These lighter ships are armed with cruise and surface-to-surface missiles, thereby mixing the asymmetrical logic of the porcupine strategy with the active extended defense desired by the classical approach. There is some uncertainty about how effectively these could operate in a full-scale war, given their reliance on off-board radar and datalinks for targeting, which are located on vulnerable radar sites within range of China's missiles. Regardless, Taiwan has also diversified and expanded the number of smaller ships, increasing the size of its coastal patrol craft from fifty-one to sixty-one, a 20 percent increase (as of 2012) and arming seven patrol boats and a radar-evasive fast attack corvette with Hsiung Feng III (HF-3) ramjet-powered supersonic antiship missiles to increase the probability of a having a surviving naval defense off its coastline.[106] This prudently trades off Taiwan's ability to fight a high-seas naval battle for the ability to mount a defense closer to its littoral. Taipei has also developed the ability to push the defense line farther out from its coast through the alternative means of long-range missiles that enable the interdiction of enemy forces out at sea. If the "swarming" orchestration of smaller assets against larger forces is potentially a potent way for weaker states like Taiwan to threaten surface fleets with their large, expensively acquired capital ships, on the evidence we have, a prima facie overview suggests that Taiwan has developed both the doctrine and tools to carry it off.[107] Since RAND produced its estimate in 2009, Taiwan's increasing investment in and attention to building a passive defense by increasing the probability that its capabilities will be dispersed, concealed, and survivable is possibly the most significant development in Taiwan's preparation to counter the growing "missile" imbalance across the strait.

Even though there remains uncertainty about the success of any of these measures in a conflict, each of them adds a "layer" of defense that increases the probability that China will not be able to clear the seas and skies sufficiently to create a safe corridor for its invading forces to approach, and that Taiwan can punch back and inflict significant damage after the first barrage. Just as importantly, each extra layer of potential surviving defense adds uncertainty to China's calculations about the costs of invasion.[108] Through passive defensive measures, Taiwan would aim to keep its forces survivable: through mobility, redundancy, and the hardening and camouflage of its assets, as well as the stockpiling of food and fuel. These would not prevent large-scale damage to Taiwan's military and civilian property but could preserve enough combat power to keep material costs on a following-on invading force high. This doctrine properly applied would help it raise costs on the amphibious force as it approached and as it reached the shore in the following phases.

The "bottom line" in an amphibious campaign is the ability to transport enough troops to the point of invasion, and securely enough to land and supply them. Let us assume that China now possesses the hundred transport ships it aims to acquire. Going on a rough 1:1 manpower ratio, RAND in 2009 estimated that China would need to get at least two group armies, or roughly 60,000 troops, ashore, and that this would require 194 successful naval trips or sorties.[109] The difficulty for China is that unless its initial effort to suppress Taiwan's defenses and deflect its air and naval attacks succeeds almost perfectly, its ability to get enough ships across safely will be in jeopardy. Unless China could successfully neutralize Taiwan's ability to "thin the herd" by taking out its air bases, its fixed and mobile land-based missile launchers (such as RBS-17 coastal-defense missiles mounted on trucks), its missile-armed Apache helicopters, and its swarming fast-attack ships, its invasion will be in trouble.

To take one layer of defense alone: RAND estimates that if Taiwan's thirty-one Kuang Hua VI class fast missile boats, armed with four Hsiung Feng II ASCMs each, launch half of their payload, that would put sixty in the air, enough to inflict a disabling "mission kill" on perhaps twelve Chinese transport ships. Going on RAND's estimate that, distributed evenly, each ship represents 310 troops and six vehicles, twelve ships sunk or turned back would see off 3,700 troops and seventy-two vehicles, and prevent those ships from participating in the three extra sorties needed for the entire transport fleet to get 60,000 troops and their equipment across within a reasonable span of five days. If China would want each ship to attempt four sorties, twelve ships taken out of action before completing their first sortie would mean a total of 48 sorties denied of the 194 out of 400 needed to succeed.

In this first phase, the weight of forces would favor China, but the conditions of space and time would favor Taiwan. On the more optimistic end of the spectrum, Taiwan's early-warning system would succeed, giving it vital minutes to protect its forces from incoming strikes and preserving enough planes to contest the skies. Taking a worst-case scenario would also leave it with warning of another kind, even if the People's Liberation Army Air Force with saturation missile attacks and then fixed-wing attacks lands a knockout punch against Taiwan's air bases, following the failure of its early-warning system. Taiwan would be forced to use degraded air bases with a degraded capacity to generate air sorties. But to ensure deception and surprise, China would have to refrain from large-scale preparatory buildup of amphibious forces. The air attack plus the time it would take to build up invasion forces would place Taiwan on notice to mobilize forces for defending ground. If Taiwan had time and based on preparation could adopt a "layered" forward defense, it would look to "thin the herd" of China's amphibious forces at sea before defending at the water's edge. It would take aim primarily at its transport ships.

Let us suppose that despite the many problems the task would meet, China has seized the ability to cross the distance of a hundred nautical miles from the bases closest to northwestern Taiwan, neutralized Taiwan's sea and air defenses, and reached the coast bearing platforms to operate from, such as several Type 071 Landing Platform Dock ships with hangers and landing and vehicle decks, and vehicle decks, loaded with marines, vehicles, and helicopters, and over a dozen landing ships. The next task would be to forcibly enter terrain in the face of reinforced defenses while vulnerable, establish a beachhead, and continuously supply a very large military force across the ocean despite adversary actions.

In a worst-case scenario for Taiwan, where China successfully destroyed its air bases and runways, the defender would probably still be able to mount a robust defense that inflicted serious costs by creating a lethal zone at the point of "run-in" where the approaching forces must operate in plain sight, unmasked by electronic sensors.[110] Taiwan's coastline means that it could anticipate the approximate point of invasion. China's transport ships would enter a kill zone in which Taiwan would have roughly a twenty-minute window to fire Hellfire missiles at transports, or five minutes to fire at faster air-cushion landing craft. Then with a minimal surviving blend of Apache helicopters, dug-in and mobile artillery and missile forces and mines, Taiwan could be expected to turn the point of disembarkation into a shooting gallery and a chaotic traffic jam, even if it lacked control of the skies over the beach and even if its aircraft are pinned in shelters or immobilized by destroyed runways. If it would take two one-thousand-pound bombs, such as Joint Direct Attack Munitions, to destroy a warship, one hundred fired by a B-1B plane could disable fifty ships, or failing that, helicopters, ground launchers, infantry, and tanks could deliver Hellfire missiles over a short range of five miles. In this respect, RAND's estimate of 2009 still holds, only Taiwan has taken greater steps to ensure that its arsenal would survive the preliminary bombardment.

This is not the place for a precise forecast that ignores the play of chance and the effect of "unknowns," not least China's relative ability to mount cyber attacks against Taiwan's increasing preparations of cyber defense, an aspect of the conflict too secretive and untraceable to measure precisely in advance.[111] But on this analysis, the scenario is more difficult for the invader than the defender to the extent that the stars must align more or less perfectly for the attacker. The defender, Taiwan, would merely have to ride out the first bombardment well enough to be able to make an attempted invasion expensive.

A Supporting Case: The Falkland Islands

The estimate presented here, that the defense could and probably would present formidable obstacles, is not only consistent with estimates about other cases involving the weak exploiting geography against the strong, such as a future Sino-Vietnamese war.[112] It is also supported by more comparable amphibious cases like Mark Bell's recent careful assessment of a hypothetical Argentine invasion of the Falkland Islands.[113] The question of the offense-defense balance over the Falkland Islands is not an abstract question, at least in the minds of the owners. British defense chiefs draw up fresh contingency plans for an Argentine invasion.[114] The status of the Falkland Islands (or Malvinas) is an ongoing object of territorial dispute between the two countries that is intensifying and became a multilateral international wrangle when the South American trading bloc banned boats flying the Falklands flag from docking in their ports.

The Falkland Islands case is not a direct analogy with Taiwan. The stakes for the defender are different: For Taiwan it is about the defense of its heartland; for Britain the Falkland Islands are a faraway possession in the South Atlantic defended at first instance by garrison forces deployed far from their metropole. The scale is obviously different, as Taiwan would see combat between tens of thousands for control of a population of roughly twenty-three million. And the international political context is different, as a battle for Taiwan would be more likely to internationalize further and draw in third parties.

While hardly an exact parallel, it is the most prominent case of an interstate war involving a contested amphibious landing against resistance. Enough similar dynamics apply to make the comparison instructive. As with Taiwan, the invader would have to neutralize the defender's air defenses, seize a foothold, and get enough forces and materiel onto the territory. Looking at the range of outcomes at each stage of the invasion and the low probability that Argentina could successfully suppress Britain's air force and safely get enough troops landed, Britain would stand a decent chance of defending the Falklands from an amphibious assault (though it would struggle to retake them successfully on its own, projecting power from afar into the South Atlantic). Argentina would probably not be able to achieve the triple trick of neutralizing British air superiority, securely inserting troops via airdrop or beach assault, and getting enough troops into theater to attack the Mount Pleasant airfield within the time window it would need before Britain's Joint Rapid Reaction Force arrived from Ascension Island within thirty-six hours. Too many things would have to go perfectly for Argentina to take Britain's four Typhoons and Rapier Missile Installations out of action, especially given Argentina's lack of precision munitions, the number of hangars, and the size of the runways. But even if it got troops ashore safely via a secure "airhead," there would be numerous obstacles that derive from problems of space and time: A British nuclear-powered attack submarine lurks ready to pounce on seaborne forces, any invasion would give Britain time to fortify its base and call up its Falkland Islands Defense Force, and inexperienced commandos would likely have difficulty seizing control of the Mount Pleasant airbase against warned and prepared troops. Above all, as with China across the strait, Argentina would face the dilemma of surprise versus preparation. An attack to neutralize British air superiority beforehand would supply vital warning time, to both the defending garrison and the British government that could order its reinforcements to deploy. On the other hand, an attempt to seize initiative with a surprise invasion would face the serious risk of being destroyed by the intact Typhoon and Rapiers.

Importantly for the argument here, consider RAND's judgment about the Falklands War, the dangers of amphibious assault in the age of the antiship missile, and what it says about any future Chinese assault on Taiwan: "Distance matters." Had the British and Argentine militaries squared off on neutral ground or in European skies and waters, the outcome would have been a rout for the UK: In every dimension, Great Britain's armed forces were far superior to those of Argentina in 1982. However, the enormous distance that lay between Britain and the operational theater, which lay near the Antarctic Circle, meant that a mere fraction of the UK's military power—which was, by 1982, mainly configured for a short, violent war on the plains of nearby Western Europe—could be brought to bear in the Falklands. . . . The geographical advantage enjoyed by Argentina allowed its otherwise outnumbered and outclassed armed forces to make a go of it against the British."[115] The distance across the Taiwan Strait is physically less, but as this analysis indicates, China's offensive weapons have not turned it into neutral ground. Its technology has not transcended the dilemmas that previous estimates have identified: the tradeoff between preparation and surprise, the predictability of the point of invasion, the difficult vulnerable moment of translating ground troops from sea to land, and the ability of materially weaker sides to exploit time, space, and terrain. For China, no matter how rapid, precise, and large its military instrument, there would still be the dilemma of trading off time versus surprise, there would still be the problem that Taiwan's forces would probably have enough survivability to deny Chinese transports a safe passage to make enough sorties, and even if the approach succeeded, there would still be the vulnerability of the shore-to-beach transition.

Conclusion

If we really do inhabit a globalizing world where distance loses its force, that process should make conquest easier. This should be so to the extent that the outcomes of conflicts are generated by the balance of material forces, mediated far less by the effects of exploiting terrain than it would have been historically. But as this chapter argues, our era is different. Across bodies of water, it is one of fire without conquest. New weapons with their range and lethality have the capacity to increase distance and erect new barriers to interlopers. Space, therefore, is better conceived as an interplay of political will, capabilities, and geography. As I have demonstrated here, the history of the continual shifting balance between sword and shield, and the tendency of states to measure the stakes involved according to the "nearness" or "farness" of the war, casts doubt on strategic visions where technology erases the dilemmas of distance or creates unambiguous "offense dominance." We are seeing the emergence of a period of access denial. These issues are pressing in maritime East Asia, where the strategic implications of new weapons shape the rivalries and mutual fears of rising powers. An illustrative case where offensive technology would meet the exploitation of time, space, and terrain for defensive purposes is the cross-strait military balance and the prospects for a Chinese invasion.

The estimate here suggests that amphibious assaults, projecting ground forces from sea to land, against a determined adversary making prudent doctrinal and technological choices remains complex and demanding. There is little doubt that in a war that the United States stayed out of, China would probably eventually prevail at least so far as neutralizing Taiwan's air force and navy, if not simply sending repeated waves of ground troops if it could keep enough sea and airlift capability. But it would be costly, protracted, and geopolitically dangerous.

The problems flowing from the increasing striking range of defenders is reflected also in the projections of future campaigns by the US Marine Corps, the world's premier amphibious force. Its "Expeditionary Force 21" concept predicts that ever-longer-range capabilities, such as precision-guided missiles, along with widely available and cheap sensors like nautical radar, "will force the fleet to stay at least 65 nautical miles offshore, a dozen times the distance that existing Marine amphibious vehicles are designed to swim."[116]

Of course, this is about more than capabilities. There is no certain way to measure the political will of either side in a neat cost-benefit calculus. To itself and its hostile larger neighbor, Taiwan represents something bigger politically than just an island with resources, and the history of the issue is drenched with emotion. We can estimate, however, what an attempted conquest would entail and the kinds of costs and risks that the invader would be wise to consider. The longer the struggle were to continue, the greater fear of it escalating and drawing in other powers. Taiwan's objective would be to pose the question to China of just how large a sacrifice it was prepared to make to achieve its objectives. Despite the eroding defense advantages and closing gap between China's and Taiwan's forces, Taiwan could still inflict grave, possibly prohibitive costs on the invader. China's increasing air-power "edge" and strengthening cross-strait strike and invasion capabilities would not be enough to negate the possibility of exploiting geography to the defender's decisive advantage. Taiwan's objective, within reach of its capabilities, would not be to sink/destroy China's navy and air force but make adventurism very expensive, to the point where successful conquest would set its military back years if not decades. This confirms the recent warning of RAND that "forced entry" via large-scale, over-the-shore amphibious assault against resistance is obsolete for many environments.[117] The same logic that enables China with today's tools to raise the costs of US intervention into its maritime space to unpalatable levels also enables Taiwan to do the same at a price more suited to its limited GDP expenditure on defense.

What does all this mean in the bigger picture? It should both caution and reassure US policymakers. Taiwan can present an ominous defense against an invader without America going to the trouble of ramping up its security assistance and arms trade with Taiwan, and the deterioration of relations with China that this may create. Taiwan's vulnerability is easily exaggerated. In terms of its ability to conquer, a rising China is not as strategically threatening as sometimes assumed. This is also important for the wider security environment. Contrary to some observers, it is not clear that Beijing has an appetite for limitless expansion, or that China's strategy of "peaceful rise" is comparable to that of the Third Reich. But even if China does increase its appetite and make a bid for region-wide supremacy, now or in the future, conditions are not promising for a would-be conqueror. East Asia is not a power vacuum open to the predations of a single aggressor like Nazi Germany or Imperial Japan, but a region crowded with states developing their own formidable defensive maritime-air capabilities to deter and respond to one power's adventurism.

The other side of that coin is that American military power is more greatly constrained than before. If it is true that that the home defender enjoys advantage against cross-sea invader, so too does China's geographic and strategic position make life increasingly difficult for America as an Asia-Pacific power. China's greater proximity to Taiwan in West Pacific or East Asian waters combined with its growing capacity for access and area denial threatens America's ability to intervene at acceptable cost and more broadly therefore to maintain its credibility as a security guarantor. It is harder for America to function as the guardian of the Pacific region if its ability to operate there is strained and it can no longer act as though the sea lanes were its uncontested lake. This poses difficulties to America's "Air-Sea Battle" concept. Washington's "pivot" toward Asia is "a foreign-policy enterprise by which US joint forces concentrate for action in remote theaters. The military must mass strategically significant quantities of manpower and armaments in a contested theater like the Far East, surmounting both transoceanic distances and regional antagonists' attempts to veto intervention."[118] The increasing range and lethality of weapon systems coupled with the determination of states to defend themselves means that paradoxically, the growing capacity of states to strike over range has also empowered defenders to an unusual degree.

We are left with a paradox. On the one hand, today's war-making tools with their reach seem to have collapsed distance in a physical sense. On the other hand, as this chapter demonstrates, it seems prima facie that the conquest of territory against defenders with a minimal level of capability mostly no longer pays. The greater reach and lethality of weapons today empowers defenders as well as attackers, and at least in the case of attempted territorial expansion across bodies of water, there remains an overall imbalance that favors defenders if they are willing and competent enough to resist. The likely costs of conquest most of the time makes it prohibitively difficult. Measured in these terms, for would-be conquerors and for those who would ride to the rescue of the conquered, the world has never been so large.

Notes

1. I define expansion as "threatening or using force to seize part or all of the territory controlled by another state." I draw this from M. Taylor Fravel, "International Relations Theory and China's Rise: Assessing China's Potential for Territorial Expansion," *International Studies Review* (2010): 505–32, 537.
2. I base this definition on M. H. H. Evans, *Amphibious Operations: The Projection of Sea Power Ashore* (London: Brassey's, 1990), 9.
3. Keir Lieber, "Grasping the Technological Peace: The Offense-Defense Balance and International Security," *International Security* 25:1 (2000): 71–104, 75.
4. An operational estimate is a tool of campaign design that according to British doctrine offers the commander Joint Force Command (JFC) "a *theory of change* of how the operation will achieve the desired end-state and the information effect that is specified in CDS' Planning and Operational Directives. The *theory of change* is the commander's big idea of how the operation will change the current operational conditions to the future desired conditions and will be guided by the strategic narrative." *Campaign Planning*, Joint Doctrine Publication (JDP) 5.00 (2008), paragraph 248. It is also a useful way of breaking down a scenario into sequential parts.
5. Ross Babbage, "Learning to Walk amongst Giants: The New Defense White Paper," *Security Challenges*, 4:1 (2008): 13–20; "Questioning Australia's Beowulf Option," *Security Challenges* 4:2 (2008): 147–64.

6. On the "balance of interests" factor in wars between the strong and the weak, and the extent to which it is decisive, see Andrew J. R. Mack, "Why Big Nations Lose Small Wars: The Politics of Asymmetric Conflict," *World Politics* 27:2 (1975): 175–200; Richard Betts, "Interests, Burdens and Persistence: Asymmetries between Washington and Hanoi," *International Studies Quarterly* 24:4 (1980): 520–24; Jeffrey Record, *Beating Goliath: Why Insurgencies Win* (Washington, DC: Potomac Books, 2001), 2–22; Ivan Arreguin-Toft, "How the Weak Win Wars: A Theory of Asymmetric Conflict," *International Security* 26:1 (2001): 93–128.

7. On the dynamics of weaker states resisting distant stronger states, see Andrew Davies, "History Shows Need for Rethink on China Tactics," *The Australian*, October 23, 2010; on the difficulties of the Falklands War and how close Britain came to defeat, see Jeevan Vasagar and Alex Bellos, "Falklands Victory a 'Close Run Thing,'" *Guardian*, April 3, 2002.

8. As Hugh White argues, *The China Choice: Why America Should Share Power* (Melbourne, Canada: Black Ink, 2012), 70–71.

9. See the important revision of "imbalance of interest" theory by Michael J. Englehart, "America Can Win, Sometimes: US Success and Failure in Small Wars," *Journal of Conflict Studies* 9:1 (1989): 20–35.

10. See the alternative argument of Theodore L. Gatchel, *At the Water's Edge: Defending against the Modern Amphibious Assault* (Annapolis, MD: Naval Institute Press, 1996). Gatchel claims that it is defenders who historically have the harder job and that the history of amphibious assault is mostly one of success. Gatchel, however, acknowledges only a few cases of amphibious assaults turned away by defenders, namely the assault on Gallipoli, Turkey, in April 1915, and Japanese landings at Wake Island and Milne Bay in December 1941 and September 1942, respectively. He does not mention several cases of failure: the failed allied assault at Anzio in Italy in January 1944, the failed British assault on Norway in 1940, and the failed Cuban rebels' assault at the Bay of Pigs in April 1961.

11. Basil Liddell Hart, *The Defense of Britain* (London: Faber & Faber, 1939), 130.

12. Zachary Keck, "Why D-Day Would Fail Today: Modern Defense Technology Has Made Seaborne Invasions All the More Difficult," *The Diplomat*, June 7, 2014; Brett Friedman, "No, the Amphibious Assault Isn't Dead," *War on the Rocks*, June 12, 2014.

13. Office of the Secretary of Defense, *Annual Report to Congress; Military and Security Developments Involving the People's Republic of China*, 2013, 54–59.

14. China's People's Liberation Army has recently sponsored a video game, *Glorious Mission Online*, where players fight to retake the East China Sea Islands from Japan: "Game Lets Players Retake Disputed Islands," News 24, August 1, 2013. I am grateful to Jane Rogers for bringing this to my attention.

15. Michael Evans, "Power and Paradox: Asian Geopolitics and Sino-American Relations in the 21st Century," *Orbis* 55:1 (2011): 85–113, 98–102; Robert Kaplan *Monsoon: The Indian Ocean and the Future of American Power* (New York: Random House, 2010), 276–93; James R. Holmes and Toshi Yoshihara, "An Ocean Too Far: Offshore Balancing in the Indian Ocean," *Asian Security* 8:1 (2012): 1–26, 2.

16. As Stephen Biddle suggests, "Rebuilding the Foundations of Offense-Defense Theory," *Journal of Politics* 63:3 (2001): 741–74, 744.

17. For this argument, see Richard N. Rosencranze, *The Rise of the Trading State: Commerce and Conquest in the Modern World* (New York: Basic Books, 1986); Carl Kaysen, "Is War Obsolete?," *International Security* 14 (1990): 42–64.

18. Stephen G. Brooks, "The Globalization of Production and the Changing Benefits of Conquest," *Journal of Conflict Resolution* 43 (1999): 646–70.

19. Mark Zacher, "The Territorial Integrity Norm: International Boundaries and the Use of Force," *International Organization* 55 (2001): 215–50; Anna Simons, "The Death of Conquest," *The National Interest* 71 (2003): 41–49, 41–42; Tanisha M. Fazal, *State Death: The Politics and Geography of Conquest, Occupation, and Annexation* (Princeton, NJ: Princeton University Press, 2007).

20. On the "offense-defense" debate, see Keir A. Lieber, "Grasping the Technological Peace: The Offense-Defense Balance and International Security," *International Security* 25:1 (2000): 71–104; Charles Glaser and Chaim Kauffmann, "What Is the Offense-Defense Balance and How Can We Measure It?," *International Security* 22:4 (1998): 44–82; Stephen Van Evera, "Offense,

Defense and the Causes of War," *International Security* 22:4 (1998): 5–43; *The Causes of War: Power and the Roots of Conflict* (Ithaca, NY: Cornell University Press, 1999). For the earlier foundational works on the issue, see George H. Quester, *Offense and Defense in the International System* (New York: John Wiley and Sons, 1977); Robert Jervis, "Cooperation under the Security Dilemma," *World Politics* 30:2 (1978): 167–214. Important critiques of narrower versions of the theory are Stephen Biddle, "Rebuilding the Foundations of Offense-Defense Theory," *Journal of Politics* 63:3 (2001): 741–74; Tang Shiping, "Offense-Defense Theory: Towards a Definitive Understanding," *Chinese Journal of International Politics* 3 (2010): 213–60.

21. As Colin Gray phrased it, *Weapons Do Not Make War: Policy, Strategy and Military Technology* (Lawrence, KS: University Press of Kansas, 1993), and for his critique of "offensive and defensive weapons," see 29–46.

22. "Great powers are those states with enough resources to overcome the disadvantages of distance. Indeed, a major component of US military superiority today is its capacity, far exceeding that of other states, to transport large numbers of military forces over long distances in relatively short amounts of time." Bruce Russett, Harvey Starr, and David Kinsella, *World Politics: The Menu for Choice*, 9th ed. (Boston, MA: Wadsworth, Cengage Learning, 2010), 77.

23. Jeremy Black, "Geographies of War: The Recent Historical Background," in *The Geography of War and Peace: From Death Camps to Diplomats*, ed. Colin Flint (New York: Oxford University Press, 2005), 2–25, 2–3.

24. Christopher J. Fettweis, "Sir Halford Mackinder, Geopolitics, and Policymaking in the 21st Century," *Parameters* 30:2 (2000): 58–71.

25. Daryl Press, "Geography and War in East Asia," unpublished paper ISA 2014; Avery Goldstein, "First Things First: The Pressing Danger of Crisis Instability in US-China Relations," *International Security* 37:4 (2013): 49–89, 66–67.

26. This is the judgment of senior military commanders, some of whom are veterans of the Anglo-Argentine war of 1982: for the "lunchtime" warning, see Sandy Woodward, "The Truth Is We Couldn't Defend Anything Further than the Other Side of the Channel," *Daily Mail*, June 15, 2011; Christopher Parry, "Can Britain Defend the Falklands?," *Prospect*, February 22, 2012; Thomas Harding, "Argentina to Invade Falklands after 30th Anniversary Furor Dies Down, Commander Warns," *Daily Telegraph*, April 12, 2012; United Kingdom National Defense Association, *Inconvenient Truths: Threats Justify Prioritising Defense*, 2011, 24: "Our assessment is that current force levels are inadequate to hold off even a small-size invasion." For the "practically invited" claim, see Deborah Haynes, "Navy Grandees Take Aim at 'Perverse' Defense Cuts; Falklands Vulnerable to New attack, Ex-Admirals Warn Cameron," *The Times*, November 10, 2010.

27. Paul K. MacDonald, "Is Imperial Rule Obsolete? Assessing the Barriers to Overseas Adventurism," *Security Studies* 18:1 (2009): 79–114, 81, 87–91, 111–12.

28. MacDonald points to plausible scenarios that might generate such pressures, such as a political breakdown and Islamist uprising in Pakistan, a successful terrorist strike on the US homeland from a perceived "haven," or a "reentry" into imploding societies such as Afghanistan or Iraq.

29. F. Kaplan, *The Wizards of Armageddon* (New York: Simon & Schuster, 1983).

30. Bernard Brodie, *Strategy in the Missile Age* (Princeton, NJ: Princeton University Press, 1959), 158, 163, 390.

31. John Herz, *International Politics in the Atomic Age* (New York: Columbia University Press, 1959), 107–08.

32. Thomas Schelling, *Arms and Influence* (New Haven, CT: Yale University Press, 1959), 21–22.

33. "America's Delicate Balance of Terror," *Foreign Affairs* 37:2 (1959): 211–34.

34. Albert Wohlstetter, "The Illusion of Distance," *Foreign Affairs* 46 (1968): 242–55.

35. Kenneth Boulding, *The Meaning of the 20th Century: The Great Transition* (London: George Allen & Unwin, 1965), 87.

36. On the influence of Wohlstetter on defense officials and especially neoconservatives, see Stefan Halper and Jonathan Clarke, *America Alone: The Neo-Conservatives and the Global Order* (Cambridge: Cambridge University Press, 2004), 62–64, 91–92; Fred Kaplan *Daydream Believers: How a Few Grand Ideas Wrecked American Power* (Hoboken, NJ: Wiley & Sons, 2008), 11–16; Neil Swidey, "The Analyst," *Globe Magazine*, May 18, 2003; after the Gulf War, one of Wohlstetter's followers, Richard Perle, claimed, "This is the first war that's been fought in a way

that would recognize Albert's vision for future wars. . . . That it was won so quickly and decisively, with so few casualties and so little damage, was in fact an implementation of his strategy
and his vision." Swidey, "The Analyst."

37. For an account of how the military revolution debate evolved through interpretations of
each war, see Keith L. Shimko, *The Iraq Wars and America's Military Revolution* (Cambridge:
Cambridge University Press, 2010).

38. A representative *Economist* article forecast that the RMA would greatly expand American military power, and few had the resources, skills, or will to compete: "Select Enemy. Delete. Only
America is close to mastering the new technologies that are transforming war. That gives it a
huge advantage over potential foes—and allies." *The Economist*, March 6, 1997.

39. Stephen Biddle, *Military Power: Explaining Victory and Defeat in Modern Battle* (Princeton, NJ:
Princeton University Press, 2004), 72.

40. William Owens, Prepared Statement for the US Senate Budget Committee, February 12, 2001.

41. George W. Bush, "A Period of Consequences," September 23, 1999, at www3.citadel.edu/pao/
addresses/pres_bush.html.

42. Text of Bush's Speech at West Point, *New York Times*, June 1, 2002.

43. Stefan Halper and Jonathan Clarke, *America Alone: The Neo-Conservatives and the Global Order*
(Cambridge: Cambridge University Press, 2004), 26; Brian C. Schmidt and Michael C. Williams,
"The Bush Doctrine and the Iraq War: Neoconservatives Versus Realists," *Security Studies* 17
(2008): 191–220, 199.

44. John Barry, "A New Breed of Soldier," *Newsweek*, December 10, 2001.

45. John Lewis Gaddis, "A Grand Strategy of Transformation," *Foreign Policy*, 133 (2002): 50–57, 54.

46. For the sense that America's opponents could not politically survive their first battlefield defeat,
that overthrown regimes such as the Taliban would not make a comeback, that Afghanistan was
"over" and that there would be a decisive shift with minimal resistance after Saddam's fall, see
Eliot A. Cohen, "Iraq Can't Resist Us," *Wall Street Journal*, December 23, 2001; Max Boot cites
early American euphoria that US forces had brought down the Taliban in forty-nine days, com-
paring their success to the Soviets' failure to defeat their Afghan enemies over a decade at much
higher casualties: Max Boot, *War Made New: Technology, Warfare, and the Course of History*
(London: Penguin, 2006), 382. But this is misleading. Boot compares the lengthy post-invasion
phase of the Soviet campaign with the quick initial phase of the American invasion, overlook-
ing that in both wars, initial regime change did not bring violent political conflict to a close.
Both occupiers quickly overthrew the Kabul regime (the Soviets' initial invasion also quickly
overthrew the regime, the time between the first arrival of Soviet airborne forces and the death
of President Hafizullah Amin being three days), and took control of major cities and military
bases. And both stayed to face a protracted resistance. America's stay has gone longer than the
Soviets' occupying period of nine years and two months.

47. James Webb, "A New Doctrine for New Wars," *Wall Street Journal*, November 30, 2001; Max
Boot, "The New American Way of War," *Foreign Affairs* 82:4 (2003): 41–58; Linda Kozaryn,
"US Special Operations Forces Change 'Face of War,'" *American Forces Press Service*, December
14, 2001; this is discussed further in Stephen Biddle, "Afghanistan and the Future of Warfare,"
Foreign Affairs 82:2 (2003): 31–46.

48. As Bob Woodward relates, among Bush's advisers there was great apprehensiveness about
Afghanistan, its history of "rebuffing outside forces," and the prospect of mountain fighting,
quagmire, and even overspill into Pakistan: *Bush at War* (London: Simon & Schuster, 2003),
82–83; but success created momentum and optimism: *Plan of Attack* (New York: Simon &
Schuster, 2004), 5; on November 21, 2001, the day Bush instructed Rumsfeld to prepare plans for
Iraq, he declared that the Taliban were "on the run," "President Shares Thanksgiving Meal with
Troops," at www.whitehouse.gov/news/releases/2001/11/20011121-3.html. Memoirs by admin-
istration officials and officers also recall the emboldening effect of initial success in Afghanistan:
Richard B. Meyers, *Eyes on the Horizon: Serving on the Front Lines of National Security* (New
York: Simon & Schuster, 2009), 187–96; Hugh Shelton, *Without Hesitation: The Odyssey of an
American Warrior* (New York: St. Martin's Press, 2010), 482, discussed further by Melvyn Leffler,
"The Foreign Policies of the George W. Bush Administration," *Diplomatic History* 37:2 (2013):
190–216.

49. Rachel L. Holloway highlights the tradition of techno-utopianism that was then married with late twentieth-century military innovations, "The Strategic Defense Initiative and the Technological Sublime: Fear, Science and the Cold War," in *Critical Reflections on the Cold War: Linking Rhetoric and History*, ed. Martin J. Medhurst and Henry William Brands (College Station: Texas A & M University Press, 2000), 219.

50. On the issue of swords and shields in military history, see Hew Strachan, "The British Way in Warfare," in *The Oxford History of the British Army*, ed. David G. Chandler (Oxford: Oxford University Press, 1994), 399–416, 406; "Time, Space and Barbarisation: The German Army and the Eastern Front in Two World Wars," in *The Barbarisation of Warfare*, ed. George Kassimeris (London: Hurst, 2006), 58–83, 56.

51. Cited in Williamson Murray, "Thoughts on War and Geography," in *Geopolitics, Geography and Strategy* ed. Colin Gray and Geoffrey Sloan (London: Routledge, 1999), 205.

52. On the comparison of both campaigns, see Harold Winters, Gerald E. Galloway Jr., William J. Reynolds, and David W. Rhyne, *Battling the Elements: Weather and Terrain in the Conduct of War* (Baltimore, MD: Johns Hopkins University Press, 1998), 74–97, 94–95.

53. Christopher Layne, *The Peace of Illusions: American Grand Strategy from 1940 to the Present* (Ithaca, NY: Cornell University Press, 2006), 278.

54. Paul Bracken, *Fire in the East: The Rise of Asian Military Power and the Second Nuclear Age* (New York: HarperCollins, 1999), 48–52.

55. In the words of Ian Easton, a researcher at the Project 2049 Institute, China seeks to "adapt an ancient defense method to a modern battlefield." Wendell Minnick, "China Pursues Systems to Keep US Forces at Bay," *Defense News*, September 17, 2013; James Holmes, "China's Underground Great Wall," *The Diplomat*, August 20, 2011.

56. Russell Hsiao, "China's 'Underground Great Wall' and Nuclear Deterrence," *China Brief* 9:25, 2009, Jamestown Foundation.

57. As Stuart Elden notes, *Terror and Territoriality* (Minneapolis: University of Minnesota Press, 2009), xxvii.

58. Roger Cliff, *Entering the Dragon's Lair: China's Anti-access Strategies and Their Implications for the United States* (Santa Monica, CA: RAND, 2007), 17–44; Andrew Krepinevich, Barry Watts, and Robert Work, *Meeting the Anti-Access and Area-Denial Challenge* (Washington, DC: Center for Strategic and Budgetary Assessments, 2003), ii, 3.

59. Roger Cliff, "Anti-Access Measures in Chinese Defense Strategy" (Santa Monica, CA: RAND, 2011). Testimony Before US China Economic and Security Review Commission, January 2011.

60. US Office of the Secretary of Defense, *Annual Report to Congress: Military and Security Developments Involving the People's Republic of China*, 2010, 32.

61. Charles Glaser, "Will China's Rise Lead to War? Why Realism Does Not Mean Pessimism," *Foreign Affairs* 90:2 (2011): 80–91, 83, 91; Iskander Rehman, "Dragon in a Bathtub: Chinese Nuclear Submarines and the South China Sea," *The Diplomat*, March 2013, http://carnegieendowment .org/2013/03/09/dragon-in-bathtub-chinese-nuclear-submarines-and-south-china-sea/fpjl.

62. Klaus Eugen Knorr and Patrick M. Morgan, eds., *Strategic Military Surprise: Initiatives and Opportunities* (Brunswick, NJ: Transaction Books, 1982), 250; Victor Davis Hanson, "Tomorrow's Wars," *City Journal* (December 2010): 80–86; Robert L. O'Connell, *The Ghosts of Cannae: Hannibal and the Darkest Hour of the Roman Republic* (New York: Random House, 2010), 266.

63. Kieren Webb, "The Continued Importance of Geographic Distance and Boulding's Loss of Strength Gradient," *Comparative Strategy* 26:4 (2007): 295–310, 297.

64. James R. Holmes and Toshi Yoshihara, "An Ocean Too Far: Offshore Balancing in the Indian Ocean," *Asian Security* 8:1 (2012): 1–26, 6.

65. Toshi Yoshihara, "How Vulnerable are U.S. Bases in the Pacific Now?," *Global Public Square*, December 7, 2012.

66. "Big Mistake: How America's Opinion of the Iraq War Has Changed," *The Economist*, August 31, 2010; "On 10th Anniversary, 53% in US See Iraq War as Mistake," at www.gallup.com/ poll/161399/10th- anniversary-iraq-war-mistake.aspx;

67. President George W. Bush, "Remarks in Greeley, Colorado," October 25, 2004, in Public Papers of Presidents of the United States: Administration of George W. Bush, 2698–705, 2701.

68. According to polling by Pew, CBS/*New York Times*, and CNN/Gallup, by the period October– December 2004, more than 50 percent of Americans disagreed with the proposition that the

United States did the right thing in taking military action against Iraq, a majority opinion that mostly endured. For the breakdown of the polling trends, see Ole R. Holsti, *American Public Opinion on the Iraq War* (Ann Arbor: University of Michigan Press, 2011), 39. As resistance and disorder increased in Iraq, members of the public who believed the Iraq War was "worth it" became a quickly shrinking minority already by the second half of 2004. From then on, even with a lowering of the levels of violence and US casualties, no poll reported a majority agreeing that it was worth it. Holsti, *American Public Opinion*, 61. Looking back, according to the Pew Research Center survey of public opinion, only about four in ten Americans who fought there believe the reasons for going to war justified the loss in blood and treasure. Of post-9/11 veterans, 50 percent say the decade-old war in Afghanistan has been worth fighting, while 44 percent view the eight-and-one-half-year-old conflict in Iraq the same way. In comparison, just 41 percent of the public says the conflict in Afghanistan has been worth the costs and just 36 percent hold a similarly approving view of Iraq. Pew Research Center, *The Military-Civilian Gap War and Sacrifice in the Post-9/11 Era* (Washington, DC: October 2011), 12.

69. Benjamin Lambeth, *NATO's Air War for Kosovo: A Strategic and Operational Assessment* (2001), 87–88, note 4.
70. On the difficulties that skillful weaker defenders can present to bombing campaigns, in both the Gulf War and Serbia, see Daryl Press, "The Myth of Air Power in the Persian Gulf War," *International Security* 26:2 (2001): 5–44, 42; Steven Lee Myers, "Damage to Serb Military Less Than Expected," *New York Times,* June 28, 1999; "How the Serb Army Escaped NATO," *Guardian,* March 9, 2000.
71. Barry Posen, "Battling for Baghdad," *New York Times,* October 13, 2002.
72. Peter John Paul Krause, "The Last Good Chance: A Reassessment of US Operations at Tora Bora," *Security Studies* 17 (2008): 644–84, 646, 650, 651; Anthony Cordesman, *The Lessons of Afghanistan: War Fighting, Intelligence, and Force Transformation* (Washington, DC: Center for Strategic and International Studies Press, 2002), 26; Stephen Biddle and Michael Evans both refute theories that precision technology or air power eclipses traditional land dimensions of warfighting: Stephen Biddle, *Afghanistan and the Future of Warfare: Implications for Army and Defense Policy* (Carlisle, PA: US Army War College Strategic Studies Institute, 2002); Stephen Biddle "Allies, Air Power, and Modern Warfare," *International Security* 30:3 (2005–6): 161–76; Michael Evans, *The Continental School of Strategy: The Past, Present and Future of Land Power* (Land Warfare Studies Center, 2004).
73. National Public Radio, "Among the Costs of War: Billions a Year in A.C.?," June 25, 2011.
74. Office of Secretary of Defense, *Annual Report to Congress: Military and Security Developments Involving the People's Republic of China 2013* (2013), 21, 57.
75. Richard C. Bush and Michael E. O'Hanlon, *A War Like No Other: The Truth about China's Challenge to America* (Hoboken, NJ: John Wiley & Sons, 2007), esp. 187–95; David A. Shalpak, David T. Orletsky, Toy I. Reid, Murray Scot Tanner, and Barry Wilson, *A Question of Balance: Political Context and Military Aspects of the China-Taiwan Dispute* (Santa Monica, CA: RAND, 2009); Anthony H. Cordesman and Nicholas S. Yarosh, *Chinese Military Modernization and Force Development: A Western Perspective* (Washington, DC: Center for Stategic and International Studies, 2012), 176–216; US-Taiwan Business Council, *The Balance of Air Power in the Taiwan Strait* (Arlington, VA: May 2010).
76. Toshi Yoshihara and James Holmes, "Command of the Sea with Chinese Characteristics," *Orbis* 49:4 (2005): 677–94.
77. Aaron L. Friedberg, *A Contest for Supremacy: China, America and the Struggle for Mastery in Asia* (New York: W. W. Norton, 2011), 177.
78. On this process, see Bruce Gilley, "Not So Dire Straits. How the Finlandization of Taiwan Benefits US Security," *Foreign Affairs* 89:1 (2010): 44–60.
79. Andrew S. Erikson, "China's Modernization of Its Naval and Air Power Capabilities," in *Strategic Asia 2012–13: China's Military Challenge,* ed. Ashley J. Tellis and Travis Tanner (Washington, DC: National Bureau of Asian Research, 2012), 66.
80. M. Taylor Fravel, "International Relations Theory and China's Rise: Assessing China's Potential for Territorial Expansion," *International Studies Review* 12:4 (2010): 505–32, 509, 523.
81. Field Manual 3-34.2, *Combined Arms-Breaching Operations* (Washington, DC: US Department of the Army, August 31, 2002), paragraph 1.32.

82. On this issue, see Michael Cole, "Would Taiwan Fight?," *The Diplomat*, September 24, 2012.
83. Michael O'Hanlon, "Why China Cannot Conquer Taiwan," *International Security* 25:2 (2000): 82–83.
84. International Institute of Strategic Studies, *The Military Balance* (London: Routledge, 2013), 335.
85. US Department of Defense, *Military and Security Developments Involving the People's Republic of China 2012*, 47.
86. Sheryn Lee and Benjamin Schreer, "The Taiwan Strait: Still Dangerous," *Survival* 55:3 (2013): 55–62, 60.
87. Lyle Goldstein, "China's Falklands Lessons," *Survival* 50:3 (2008): 65–82, 66, 74–75, 79.
88. Jason Miks, "Taiwan War Games," *The Diplomat*, August 10, 2010.
89. I derive these phases and the principles they are based on from Evans, *Amphibious Warfare* 91ff, and Gatchel, *At the Water's Edge*.
90. As summarized in the US Office of the Secretary of Defense, *Annual Report to Congress*, 56.
91. Bush and O'Hanlon, *A War Like No Other*, 189; Martin Edmonds and Michael Tsai, *Taiwan's Security and Airpower* (London: Routledge, 2004).
92. The US-Taiwan Business Council warned in 2010 that the situation then was "both widening the quantitative gap in the cross-strait power balance, and narrowing TAF's [Taiwan Air Force's] qualitative edge in aircraft performance and pilot training/experience." *The Balance of Air Power in the Taiwan Strait* (Arlington, VA: May 2010), iv. It should be borne in mind that the council through this document was agitating for the United States to sell F-16C/Ds to Taiwan, so it should be treated cautiously. Since then the quantitative gap (at least) with regard to fighters has shifted back in Taiwan's favor, as reported by Cordesman, *Lessons of Afghanistan*, 2002, 205.
93. Shalpak et al., *A Question of Balance*, xv, 43, 78; "circular error probable" means the margin of accuracy expressed as the size of the circle outside the intended target that includes the landing points of 50 percent of the rounds.
94. Ibid., 89-90. In the RAND model, for the "blue team" of Taiwan to give its air force greater survivability (such as terminal defenses against missiles) in the air war would take a large and expensive program to construct aircraft shelters.
95. Ed Ross, "Taiwan's Ballistic Missile Deterrence and Defense Capabilities," *China Brief* 11:3 (2011): 9–13. I also assume in the scenario that Taiwan does not yet have the "Cloud Peak" missile capable of reaching into southern and eastern China, due to begin production in 2014: Wendell Minnick, "Taiwan Working on New 'Cloud Peak' Missile," *Defense News*, January 18, 2013. Nor in this scenario has Taiwan yet upgraded and expanded the antiballistic missile systems. It currently plans to upgrade the three batteries of PAC-2 antiballistic missiles, and will acquire seven additional PAC III systems that fire PAC-2 and Patriot Guidance Enhanced Missiles. According to Ross (11), Taiwan at that stage "could have an adequate number of missiles to intercept a large percentage of incoming PRC missiles. Provided its missile early-warning, tracking, target prioritization and C⁴ systems are up to the job, Taiwan's missile-defense capability would be a formidable one."
96. James Hardy, "Taiwan Inducts Upgraded E-2 Hawkeyes," *Jane's*, April 1, 2013.
97. Shalpak et al., *A Question of Balance*, 106.
98. "Tien Kung 1/2/3 (Sky Bow) (Taiwan) Defensive Weapons," *Jane's Strategic Weapons Systems*, October 31, 2012.
99. For the most developed articulation of this option, see William S. Murray, "Revisiting Taiwan's Defense Strategy," *Naval War College Review* 61:3 (2008): 14–31.
100. James R. Holmes, "Partner in the Pivot?," in *Taiwan and the U.S. Pivot to Asia: New Realities in the Region?*, ed. Shihoko Goto (Washington, DC: Woodrow Wilson Center, March 2013), 25–32.
101. J. Michael Cole, "A New Definition of Military Success," *Taipai Times*, February 22, 2013.
102. Republic of China, *National Defense Report* (2011), 131–32: "In the past, 'victory' was perceived as overcoming the enemy on the battlefield. However, considering the military strength of the two sides of the Taiwan Strait, we must use a practical attitude to reconsider the definition of 'victory' if we are to achieve 'resolute defense and credible deterrence.' After studying and analyzing the current situation of the Taiwan Strait, the definition of 'victory' was adjusted from 'defeating the enemy in a full confrontation' to 'striking the enemy half way across the Taiwan

Strait and preventing the enemy from landing and establishing lodgment'; the force structure of the Armed Forces was planned with a focus on gaining a relative advantage in this critical period of war. This will not only allow a 'small but superb, strong and smart' force to achieve 'resolute defense,' but also avoid engaging in an 'armaments race' with the PRC, which might affect the nation's overall competitiveness."

103. Republic of China, *Quadrennial Defense Review* (March 2013), 41 ("sudden and high intensity assaults"), 38–40.

104. See Dan Blumenthal, "Rethinking Taiwan's Defense," *Wall Street Journal*, September 29, 2011; James Holmes, "Partner in the Pivot?," *The Diplomat*, April 23, 2013, at http://thediplomat.com/the-naval-diplomat/2013/04/23/partner-in-the-pivot/.

105. For discussions of Taiwan's various measures to ensure its forces' survivability: Wendell Minnick, "Taiwan's Hidden Base Will Safeguard Aircraft," *Defense News*, May 3, 2010; J. Michael Cole, "Carrier Killer Launcher: A New Road-Mobile Launcher for the HF-3 Supersonic Antiship Cruise Missile Will Increase Its Survivability," *The Diplomat*, August 16, 2013; "Taiwan's New Rocket Launchers? Taiwan's Military Recently Inadvertently Confirmed the Deployment of the Ray Ting-2000 (Thunderbolt-2000)"; "Taiwan Takes Delivery of First Thunderbolt Rocket Launcher," *RP Defense*, September 13, 2012; J. Michael Cole, "ROC Navy and the War of the Flea," *Strategic Vision* 1:5 (2012): 20–24, 22; US-Taiwan Business Council, *The Balance of Air Power in the Taiwan Strait* (Arlington, VA: 2010), 29; "Rapid Runway Repairs for Taiwan," *Defense News*, December 29, 2012.

106. Cordesman, *Chinese Military Modernization*, 198.

107. On "swarming"' in general and with regard to a straits battle and sea denial in particular, see James Holmes and Toshi Yoshihara, *Defending the Strait: Taiwan's Naval Strategy in the 21st Century* (Washington, DC: Jamestown Foundation, 2012).

108. In the words of one Taiwanese analyst, the objective is "to complicate Chinese strategic calculations by raising the strategic uncertainty of military action against the island, to disrupt the tempo of People's Liberation Army operations, thereby mitigating their intended effects and affording Taiwan more time to seek outside assistance/intervention." Wendell Minnick and Paul Kallender-Umezu, "Japan, Taiwan Upgrade Strike Capability," *Defense News*, May 7, 2013.

109. At the time of writing, Taiwan's active-duty army numbers have reduced to approximately 235,000, but the figure of roughly 60,000 comes from RAND's assessment that its approximately one-hundred-ship armada could transport a maximum of 31,000 troops at a time, and that conducted over a matter of days in a time-sensitive campaign, we can reasonably assume two crossings. RAND and I assume that it is still to China's benefit in this scenario that this would be enough to constitute a 1:1 manpower ratio.

110. On this phase, see Shalpak et al., *A Question of Balance*, 114–15.

111. Despite its wider skepticism about Taiwan's defensive chances, the *Military Balance* in its survey of the capabilities of both sides finds that Taiwan "has developed world-class capabilities in detecting, analyzing and countering cyber intrusions from the PR." *The Military Balance*, 273.

112. Though Vietnam could be expected to lose heavily in a capital and technologically intensive war with China, it also bears the capacity to punish Chinese adventurism on the way down, with an access-denial system made up of impressive air defense network, antiship cruise missiles, and *Kilo*-class submarines: Robert Farley, "If Vietnam and China Went to War: Five Weapons Beijing Should Fear," *The National Interest*, July 12, 2014.

113. Mark S. Bell, "Can Britain Defend the Falklands?," *Defense Studies* 12:2 (2012): 283–301, esp. 293–94.

114. Sean Rayment, "Defense Chiefs Prepare New Plans to Defend Falkland Islands," *The Telegraph*, January 12, 2013.

115. Shalpak et al., *A Question of Balance*, 102–3.

116. Sydney J. Freedberg, "Marines Seek New Tech to Get Ashore against Missiles: Reinventing Amphib Assault," *Breaking Defense*, April 16, 2014.

117. Paul K. Davis and Peter A. Wilson, *Looming Discontinuities in U.S. Military Strategy and Defense Planning: Colliding RMA's Necessitate a New Strategy* (Santa Monica, CA: RAND, 2011), 13–14.

118. As James Holmes describes, "Partner in the Pivot?," *The Diplomat*, April 23, 2013.

CHAPTER 5

Wide of the Mark
Drones, Cyber, and the Tyrannies of Distance

Give me $1 million and 20 people and I will shut down America.

—ANONYMOUS FORMER INTELLIGENCE OFFICIAL

Inside those trailers you leave North America, which falls under Northern Command, and enter the Middle East, the domain of Central Command [CENTCOM]. So much for the tyranny of geography.

—ROBERT KAPLAN

It might be the most precise, most sophisticated system for applying lethal force ever developed—the Platonic ideal of how an air war should be run.

—WIRED.COM

For too many people—including defense "experts," members of Congress, executive branch officials and ordinary citizens—war has become a kind of videogame or action movie: bloodless, painless and odorless.

—ROBERT GATES

T his chapter turns to two emerging technologies that some observers regard as "globalizing" in their effects. These are remotely piloted vehicles (RPVs) and "cyberwar." The arrival of new tools and domains of war is one of the most frequent contexts for claims of a globalizing revolution. Our age of unmanned aerial vehicles and cyber conflict, like revolutions in robotics and information technology, it is said, both collapses distance and for at least one side, removes the visible human being from the battlespace.

Visionaries do not exactly claim that these systems annihilate all distance, but that they neutralize the problems of distance for those who wield them. Seemingly, people can assault targets without the political or economic costs or risks that traditionally come with military actions. Both are becoming instruments of the worldwide projection of power. Both attract claims that because of their properties, the weapons are changing the nature of war itself to the point where new strategic theories are needed. And both generate mixtures of fear and confidence typical of globalism. On the one hand, because these weapons are assumed to be "offense dominant" in that they hand great power to attackers and render distance unimportant, they cause anxiety about what could happen in the event that the innovations were turned on the United States or its allies. At the same time, they are seductive. For those drawn to force as an instrument of policy but weary of the grinding wars of the recent past, new tools hold out the promise that a superpower can now strike quickly and precisely with minimal risk. They seem to offer what air power perennially seems to offer, what Eliot Cohen called "gratification without commitment."[1]

But on closer inspection, as I argue, both the worst fears and the greatest hopes are overstated. Both utopian and dystopian visions replicate the flaws of the more dubious speculations about air power in the twentieth century. As it is evolving, cyber "space" is not necessarily a freeway through which aggressors can wander through at will. Cyber attacks may supplement but will probably not supplant the territoriality of warfare. "Drones" are fallible and must navigate through weather, the difficulties of targeting, the psychological problems pilots endure fighting in a state of "virtual" intimacy from afar, and other problems and tradeoffs that come with standoff combat. The current one-sided model of a president vaporizing adversaries with drone strikes may not be the model of the future. As they spread to other countries, drone "space" will probably get more geopolitically contested. In both cases, mutuality and competition blunt the offensive potential of the instrument. Technical breakthroughs remove the human being from the battlespace, at least for one side, but not from the dilemmas of fighting from afar. War remains nonlinear and tragic.

Cybergeddon: Does the Electron Always Get Through?

Cyberwar is a long-anticipated but relatively new form of conflict. I define it as hostile action by networked computers against networked computers for political purposes. Opinion is split on the implications of the emerging "fifth geography" of war. This debate represents the extreme case of a form of war that bypasses physical distance but whose consequences for strategic space are open to debate. There is no question that cyber collapses physical space. Armed with cyber capabilities, actors can potentially wage war remotely, stealthily, and secretly. In contrast to "normal" warfare, victims may be unaware for some time after offensive penetration occurs. Obviously, the ability to attack networked information systems from anywhere in the world collapses physical gaps, to the point where a computer in a room on the other side of the planet works its mischief as quickly and identically as a computer in the room next door. That should not be confused with the more ambitious claim that it is therefore a postgeographic, nonphysical phenomenon.

The real question is to what extent its compression of space and time overturns the force of strategic space. Does it confer decisive offense dominance that destroys distance? Does it enable actors to bypass the battlefield and the terrestrial struggle, and inflict direct hits on an adversary's vitals for major strategic effect? Those vitals are typically seen as the critical industrial control-systems, or ICS, such as air control traffic, electrical grids, and military weapon-control systems. Does the coming of this kind of capability promise to alter the balance profoundly between the strong and weak, the state and the nonstate? Or is it merely a distinctive new instrument that supplements existing warfighting operations, adding tactical utility but not, on its own, amounting to a force of grave strategic danger like nuclear weapons? In short, is cyber really a strategic-level "game-changer"?

Because these are early days in the strategic history of cyberwar, critical observers of the phenomenon can only make provisional arguments. We do know substantially more about cyber than we did even a few years ago. We can draw on a great deal of information about a high-profile recent cyber incident, the "Stuxnet" case, which has been subject to inquests available in open sources. If, as it turns out, there is little direct evidence or inferential logic supporting claims that cyber represents the death of strategic distance in a shrinking world, it would be wise to examine the assumptions globalists make not only about the capabilities, but the fragility of the societies under attack.

Some claim that cyber is geophysically extraordinary. Because it is free of the encumbrances of distance and is hard to shield against directly in advance, it confers the upper hand to the offense over the defense, in the sense that electrons, like the bomber feared by Stanley Baldwin, always get through in strategically lethal quantities to strike critical targets. In turn, this has vast strategic implications, making the connected, network-dependent United States especially vulnerable.[2] We are dealing with a new, man-made geography of war. This domain is born of the spread of the internet, the expansion of computer networks, and the increasing dependency of urban, modern states on them. Cyber aggression can threaten critical financial, military, or utility systems with viruses and bugs. It is prone to hacking, probing, disruption, infiltration, and espionage. Cyber is revolutionary, they argue, because it transcends the laws of geography.[3] By destroying barriers and sidelining concrete or material forms of territorial control, cyber allegedly hands great power to weaker, nonstate actors who can bring havoc to powerful adversaries and by so doing, overturn the power structures of international relations.[4] Thus cyber fears spring from perceptions about the revolutionary and subversive nature of the technology. Its easy access, connectivity to critical infrastructure, and the anonymity it confers on users means that it cheats the traditional geopolitical barriers to aggression, such as distance, visibility, and the high costs of the "ticket to play." Several high-profile breaches of system security suggest that the information domain is a volatile and insecure environment that is hospitable to would-be aggressors. It seems to obliterate distance as an instantaneous and virtual medium of communication, exchange, commerce, and mischief. Some claim that it is even "ageographic" in its transcendence of traditional spatial limits. If conquering territory is now more difficult and less rewarding, cyber infiltration could represent the postindustrial, twenty-first-century version of conquest.

According to dystopian portrayals of this new technology, it could be the vehicle of a new barbarism that could lay waste to societies. Cyber continues to excite nightmare scenarios among government officials and military commanders. "Electronic Pearl Harbor"—even "digital Armageddon"—is the day of reckoning that cyberwar prophets warn of, from Richard A. Clarke, former national coordinator for security, infrastructure protection, and counterterrorism, to former secretary of defense Leon Panetta.[5] "Digital Pearl Harbor" was the title of a US Naval War College Exercise in 2002. After 9/11, fears of cyber terrorism increased. Sen. Charles Schumer warned, "Terrorists . . . could gain access to our power plants, our air-traffic-control systems, our utilities and our banking systems, which translates into rolling blackouts, dead phone lines, and wiped-out bank accounts. Frankly, I fear we're on the verge of a digital Armageddon."[6] It poses an "existential threat," according to the former chairman of the Joint Chiefs of Staff, Mike Mullen, as "a space that has no boundaries. It has no rules."[7] With these fears, in the world of cyber alarm, a kind of "cult of the offensive" has grown. Assuming cyber is "offense dominant," government officials and commentators assume that the best defense, or the only one, is attack. For obvious historical reasons, this is a disturbing development.

Paradoxically, the same phenomenon with its imputed powers also attracts a kind of techno-utopianism, visions of a more antiseptic and "cleaner" form of conflict. Israeli deputy prime minister Dan Meridor characterized information war in the shadows as an alternative to "ugly" war, a "new battleground."[8] More beautiful war, supposedly, can conduct conflict without the violence and emotions of pre-cyber eras. It is not clear whether Israel would respond in non-ugly, nonviolent ways to a digital attack on its own information systems. But it is an open secret that the United States and its allies are covertly preparing to wield cyber as an offensive weapon. Convinced that a deadly new era of information war has arrived, states study how to harness this offensive weapon for themselves, fulfilling their own prophecies. As we will see, like air power, cyber power lends itself to tempting hopes of finding technical solutions to strategic problems. This is not so much the opposite of techno-pessimism, and more the sunnier side of the same coin, where inventions remove the gravitational constraints of space.

Against that argument, skeptics believe that while cyber presents a nontrivial nuisance, the sky is not falling.[9] It is an adjunct and a member of a strategic "team" of capabilities that could marginally enhance military advantages, rather than a substitute for the use of violent force. Doomsday prophecies reflect not just technical awareness of the instrument, but also assumptions about human fragility in the face of chaos. They wrongly conflate the nuisance effect of "hactivism" and internet criminality with major strategic assaults. Cyber is not directly violent or bloody. It has nothing like the direct, devastating impact on human life of nuclear weapons. With regard to typical war aims, such as seizing territory or overthrowing governments, it does not offer an "end run" independent of other uses of military force.

There is no such thing as a purely "virtual" battlespace. Cyber capability is territorial, in that it is embodied in physical, nonvirtual systems. Much of it depends on undersea telecommunication cables. And information systems rely on hard physical infrastructure systems that depend in turn on maintenance and repair.[10] But even if the materiality of new tools and domains is conceded, doesn't cyberspace still have a profound impact on distance?

The policy implications of this alarmism are serious. It has led to the establishment of a dedicated military command (USCYBERCOM). It generates increasing levels of state spending. It could be creating a cyber-industrial complex of groups with a material interest in hyping threats and leading to the wasteful misallocation of resources. It could lead to the further extension of state power and, in America, the imperial presidency that is at the heart of the "national security state," reflected specifically in recent debate over empowering the executive branch with a "kill switch" that would shut down large swathes of the internet. Such an initiative would have major implications for the Constitution and could jeopardize further its checks and balances. It would also potentially create the kind of concentration of threat in one pair of hands that a terrorist network could only dream of. For a country whose constitution is designed to prevent the creation of unchecked power, that would be a serious blow. More generally, theories of cyber power as a revolutionary game-changer feed an overall view of a lethal world where states are so vulnerable to proximate enemies that their security interests are universal and that they must project power globally. It creates an offensive mindset, where countries like the United States develop cyber-strike capabilities in ways that could increase escalation and lead to unintended spirals of hostility. In other words, overblown notions of a post-geographic cyber era could indirectly further erode the coherence of Western statecraft, making it harder generally to define and rank interests, measure threats, and manage risk prudently.

The Problem with Cyber Alarmism

I now make two counterarguments against the proposal that cyber represents a radical kind of offense-dominant weapon that kills strategic distance.

First, it is empirically flawed. In framing cyber as an offensive silver bullet, it underestimates the capacity for cyber defense. The internet is already quite resilient. Several measures can be taken to blunt the offensive power of cyber. Defenders may have the disadvantage of not knowing an attack is "on," of not knowing the assailant, and because aggressors attack "zero day" vulnerabilities that have not yet been shielded, defenders constantly must play "catch up" with aggressors. But they enjoy an advantage that they do not have with regard to other geographies: because it is a man-made system, they get to redesign and fortify it with greater latitude than they can with the sea, the air, or the land. On the evidence we have, cyberwar waged for strategic effect is difficult, resource intensive, and needs to orchestrate highly tailored intelligence penetration with a critical mass of expertise. The major, coordinated attempt by a superpower and a determined ally to disrupt a nuclear program via cyber means, the Stuxnet project, took a vast, complex effort and yielded only modest results.

Second, it is conceptually flawed. Cyber alarmism falsely conflates nuisance potential of "hactivism" and criminal activity with strategic-level danger. To appreciate the nature of this capability and its limits, we need to discriminate more carefully between general nuisances and strategic threats. Cyber alarmism is not just about the attacker and the system target. It also makes sociological assumptions about the people on the receiving end. It recycles the myths of air power from the twentieth century, and its flawed conception of societal frailty in the face of offensive weapons. Alarmism about cyber reflects a flawed, one-way conception of technology and of space without attrition, cost, or defensive reaction. Cyber-technology does reconfigure the relationship between strategic behavior and space. But seen as a medium like the ocean, it is still a battlespace that is anchored in the physical and material world, that if defended imposes costs, presents obstacles, and if sufficiently large-scale, is open to lethal countermeasures. Like the strategic bomber, seen as a tool it expands and possibly intensifies war but is not a wonder-weapon that alters its nature. Ultimately, the more extravagant cyber fears reflect not only assumptions about the potency of new technology, but about the vulnerability of human defenses and the fragility of humans themselves. Such fears restage the illusion of technology destroying space.

What does a sober analysis tell us about these nascent cyber capabilities, from what we already know? We do have evidence from prominent serious episodes: DDOS (distributed denial of service) attacks and the Stuxnet attack on Iran. First, the question of what counts as "war" is an important one and goes beyond semantics, because there are a range of behaviors that those on the receiving end would not necessarily classify as "war" in other contexts. The treatment of a hostile act as "war" obviously can escalate responses more than other classifications. Much cyber activity is "probing," the equivalent of testing systems or "trying doorknobs." It is not clear why we should assign the status of "war" to what amounts to "spying," mapping, or "testing" another nation's vulnerabilities. That is a de facto accepted form of competition between states, within bounds, and its discovery in contexts other than cyber is treated seriously but not normally as grounds in itself for a declaration of war. Russia reportedly in 2010 flew right to the edge of British airspace with its Blackjack bombers to be warded off by the RAF on at least twenty occasions.[11] For Britain, these are grounds for concern. But if muscle flexing, response-testing, and "signaling" are not treated as war in the nonvirtual world, if targeted states still allow themselves a ladder of probing and controlled escalation rather than an absolute condition of "peace" or "war," it is not clear why this should be different in the virtual world.

Thinking of direct attacks, what can cyber attacks really "do"? Thus far, more ambitious cyber operations can inflict disruption and damage. But the scope and timeframe of the damages inflicted are often limited. Consider one of the most prominent and successful direct cyber strikes on an adversary's strategic power, the Stuxnet computer worm launched against Iran's uranium-enrichment facility at Natanz that was discovered in June 2010. We now know, to a high degree of probability, that it was carried out collaboratively by Tehran's major adversaries, Israel and the United States, to disrupt its nuclear program. It took great effort and coordination, requiring expertise in nuclear engineering, intelligence operations, and the mechanics of Iran's ICS, as well as a series of expensive tests and trial runs. It also took time, with preparations beginning years in advance (the journalist David Sanger dates its origins to 2006), and with reconnaissance building on ramped-up intelligence penetration of the country. Far from easy, cheap, anonymous, and instant, Stuxnet was complex, costly, gradual, and eventually attributed.

Stuxnet was created and launched as a substitute for military airstrikes precisely because long-range military offensive power had not killed off the problems of distance. A conventional bombing would probably have met difficulties in damaging a remote facility that was placed underground and would have required an intensive bombardment and skillful weaponeering, an action that was possible but that would have brought diplomatic costs that the United States was not willing to bear. A cyber strike might do the job more covertly and in a less inflammatory way internationally, while persuading Israel not to inflict its own unilateral air attack. As a blow to the attackers' hope for anonymity, the program of cyber operations against Iran, Operation Olympic Games, was later pieced together and described in the New York Times.[12]

According to the Institute for Science and International Security (ISIS), the damage inflicted amounted to roughly 10 percent of Iran's centrifuges (disabling one thousand out of nine thousand), which was barely above the normal error rate, and did not reduce (though may have limited) Iran's production of low-enriched uranium in that year, and mostly struck empty centrifuges.[13] Iran promptly took action to prevent further damage by shutting down centrifuge cascades, eliminating the malware and replacing disabled machines. As the International Atomic Energy Agency chief Yukiya Amano affirmed, Stuxnet had merely a temporary impact on Iran's uranium-enrichment process.[14] A later study of 2012 found that the attack delayed the centrifuge program by about a year. In itself this is not negligible and arguably succeeded in purchasing Iran's adversaries an extra year for other coercive measures and diplomacy to work. But it was hardly a fundamental blow relative to the elaborate investment the operation required and was modest compared to the dramatic announcements of a new transformed era of war that observers announced when it was revealed.[15] Stuxnet's chief effect was delay, distress, embarrassment, and inconvenience, but ultimately not destruction. Other constraints also hindered the operation: The target was complicated, so that every part of its architecture had to be mapped out and understood in advance. High-value ICS targets are likely to be complex assemblages of systems, not a single vulnerable device that can be switched on or off. And contrary to the view of cyber offense as instantaneous, to allow the worm to work its damage on centrifuge cascades gradually and below the radar, time was needed before the Iranians realized they were under attack rather than suffering malfunctions for other reasons, in turn limiting the damage that could be inflicted.

This would seem to be a particularly instructive "crucial case" if the assailants included the "cyber superpower," the United States, with its unmatched capabilities, and Israel, a state that declares an existential interest in terminating or at least seriously delaying Iran's nuclear program. One or both of these parties would have had a strong motive in making a more damaging attack. Either they attempted and failed a more damaging attack or deliberately limited the attack to prevent early discovery or unintended consequences. If it is because, as ISIS hypothesizes, that "it may be harder to destroy centrifuges by use of cyber attacks than often believed," exactly how dangerous would cyber aggressors be with less capability or will? And if it was to limit the damage and the fallout, this suggests that cyber is not immune, after all, to the logic of retaliation and escalation. As for the argument that Stuxnet itself lowered the barrier to cyber operations by creating a code that others could copy, it also provided a detailed tutorial for defenders and intensified technical study by "computer security communities."[16]

The Stuxnet case is significant not only because it suggests the possible limitations attached to the "cyber bomb" that futurologists warn against. It is also a caution against cyber utopianism and the resort to narrow technical solutions to dilemmas such as the confrontation in the Gulf that involve more intractably difficult diplomacy. As Ilan Berman argues, "for all of its tangible benefits, Stuxnet may also turn out to have played a distinctly unhelpful role: feeding the hopes of policymakers desperately seeking to avoid a confrontation with Tehran over its nuclear ambitions that such a conflict has, in fact, been deferred. The stubborn reality, however, is that Iran's nuclear program is moving ahead anew—and that Stuxnet's impact, while significant, was just temporary."[17] Since then, the United States and its allies have brought other pressures to bear, such as economic sanctions, on Iran's nuclear program. The ultimate fate of this process of coercion and negotiation is unknown. But as a way of shutting down Iran's nuclear program, the cyber bomb was not a substitute for the more prosaic attempt to combine activities to get a result. It hit with a whimper, not a bang.

Evidence drawn from other cases fits a similar pattern. A serious, first-order assault on an information system is more costly, complex, and demanding than often presumed. DDOS attacks typically disrupt a website for a few hours and can normally be mitigated with practical steps such as more resilient servers or with technical means such as "edge caching."[18] To date, attacks have sometimes disabled systems temporarily, but only for limited stretches of time. Not only can effective guardians—systems administrators—often restore their systems within forty-eight hours, but they can then "close the breach" to curtail repeated attempts of the same method. As Martin Libicki reports, every large server that was derailed in the February 2000 DDOS attack was back in service within three hours.[19] Even the infamous attacks on Estonia had only "minimal" impact, only disrupted public-facing government websites for a few days, and permanently degraded almost no critical services.[20] Defenders can also insulate vital systems such as stock exchange computer systems and military networks from the Web, dismantling any electronic connection between the system and the rest of the world, a practice known as "air gapping." Nuclear weapons are not physically connected to the internet and cannot be operated remotely by outsiders, just as airplanes cannot be hijacked remotely.[21]

As with the evolution of air power in the twentieth century, there is visible a spiral of offense and defense in the cyber realm. Put simply, the same technology can be deployed by a determined defender to resist attack as well as perpetrate it. As with air power in the last century, defenders can harness this man-made battlespace to identify, resist, and possibly attribute their adversaries. In terms of the shifting balance, there is nothing predetermined within the intrinsic qualities of cyber weapons about the relative strength of offense and defense. Defenses can be shored up with sound doctrine, talented network engineers, and "Plan B" procedures for disruption or suspension of systems. A cyber attack may look instant, but it must successfully survive through multiple steps of a "kill chain": According to a former head of the Defense Information Systems Agency, an attack must carry out reconnaissance, build a weapon, deliver that weapon, and pull information out of the network. Each step creates a vulnerability, and all have to be completed.[22] Even if an attack does penetrate without being parried by the defender, there is increasing attention to cyber resilience and to developing the ability to recover quickly and ride out the assault. Increasingly alert to the problem, security communities can take active steps to place a virtual distance between their critical systems and cyber access. "Really critical information should never see a computer; if it sees a computer, it should not be one that is networked; and if the computer is networked, it should be air-gapped."[23] Defenders can buy redundant capabilities for command-and-control systems. While the offense has multiple advantages that should be taken seriously, the defense has a notable advantage here more than in any other geography, in that it has the discretion to redesign, "complexify," and "layer" its network in advance.

The cyber case reflects the overdetermined quality of "offense-dominant" theories. What Britain's official historian Noble Frankland wrote of the bomber could also apply to this new weapon: "The whole belief that the bomber was revolutionary in the sense that it was not subject to the classical doctrines of war was misguided."[24] Defenders have agency, and the "structure" is not one where all vital systems must be dangerously wired. Part of the problem is that analysts are still searching for an appropriate metaphorical language through which to characterize virtual war. There are two dominant languages employed: First, the rogue nuclear attack, which turns out to be flawed as a description of the scope of damage and the capacity for defense; and second, the strategic bomber, along with the extravagant prophecies made about offensive air power in the interwar period. But unlike nuclear weapons, cyber is mostly confined to an immaterial electronic environment and cannot directly wreak material havoc except through extraordinary difficulty, luck, and investment. It cannot seize territory or overthrow governments. Contrary to conventional military power, it would be very difficult using cyber means to inflict the equivalent damage of a Pearl Harbor attack, a complex operation well beyond the capabilities even of the most well-funded and cohesive terrorist group.

The Stuxnet case suggests an alternative language that better captures the ambiguities and limitations of the domain: the ocean as an alternating buffer and highway. Or as Jon Lindsay and Lukas Milevski argue, cyberwar is better reimagined as "a commando raid into enemy territory defended by superior forces. For special operations, detailed prior intelligence and mission planning and rehearsal are required to insert a team into the target area, to enable it to infiltrate through enemy security and counterintelligence obstacles, and to ultimately perform some sort of actions on the objective, in this case, sabotage."[25] If we conceive distance as the spatial aspects of power rather than physical territory, cyber should be understood as a thickly defended, cluttered, and heterogeneous structure where breaches are possible, but deep and lasting offensives are far more difficult to execute. Familiar patterns from strategic history are reconfigured in a new context, from cores and peripheries to the offense-defense cycle.

It is also possible that we may be seeing an "attribution revolution," an increase in the ability to identify the "signature" of cyber attackers. Attackers "are only human. They make mistakes when they're in a hurry or overconfident. They leave bits of code behind on abandoned command and control computers. They reuse passwords, email addresses, and physical computers. Their remote access tools are full of vulnerabilities. These are openings that we can exploit to trace cyber attacks first to the command and control computers used to carry them out, then to the homes and offices of the hackers that perpetrate them and then, hopefully someday soon, to the customers that sponsor them."[26] This is supported by the extensive evidence of the cyber hacking by the People's Liberation Army, exposed by the American cyber-security firm Mandiant.[27] Not only is there motive for attribution in the event of a serious breach, there is also a set of emerging forensic techniques. So the fear that future major cyber offensives will be invisible, and because invisible undeterrable, and therefore empowering the weak as a "game-changer," may also be overstated.

All of this suggests that cyber may not be a "game-changer" for world politics. To be sure, the skeptical assessment here draws on the limited evidence that currently exists in the public domain. But it is less speculative and more evidence-based than portrayals of electronic Pearl Harbor and Digital Armageddon, scenarios that proponents typically conjure on the basis of graphic description and strategic and sociological assumption, rather than inference from specific evidence. It is more likely that "online" cyber capabilities will reinforce rather than alter offline power structures—if cyber offense on a strategic scale of disruption is more difficult, involved, and complicated than often imagined, if the most concentrated attack so far by a superpower and its ally had at best limited impact, and if defenders have the ability to create resiliency and create virtual distances between vital systems and networks. If the United States and Israel, with plentiful resources, expertise, and preexisting intelligence networks, could not convert technical wizardry into a decisive strategic dividend, it is not clear what poorer, weaker, and less advantaged actors could achieve. That is not to deny that cyber attackers, like bank robbers, can wreak mischief at lower levels and deserve the attention of government. But superpowers can live with criminal nuisances. It would be prudent to discriminate between the lower levels of cyber activity and what really counts as a "strategic-level" capability. Based on the evidence we do have, the days are still far off when networked guerrillas can break into and disrupt military command-and-control systems, bring down electrical grids, or somehow endanger our very existence.

The drumbeat of fear about cyber tells us more about the anxieties of Western states about their own population's resilience, inflated by the melodramas of science fiction, than about the material capabilities of digital weaponry. This fear is embedded in Richard Clarke's warning, offered without direct evidence, that within fifteen minutes, Chinese hackers could disable the Pentagon's networks, take down air traffic control, delete all data held by the Federal Reserve, and cause a nationwide blackout, causing looting and rioting. It reflects a deeper techno-pessimism common to globalism and echoed in the interwar fears of strategic bombing, that "access" with direct assaults will rapidly bring civilian populations to their knees. But people under attack by a common adversary do not necessarily behave this way. If the experience of strategic bombing by far more directly damaging instruments tells us anything, societies on the receiving end will usually adapt more robustly. The most intensive campaigns of terror bombing in the last century reveal populations not reacting as helpless, passive, and fragile modern victims, who cannot cope without their functioning infrastructure. Instead, they have proven to be pragmatic, adaptable, and often cooperative and showing social solidarity under fire.[28] The shrinking-world ideology supposes people to be more vulnerable because they are more "wired," but the will of nations under the coercive bombing of distant enemies can endure even beyond the life of their hi-tech networks.

To return to the analogy of an "electronic Pearl Harbor," even in that unlikely event, American society would probably be more resilient than its rulers seem to fear. Pearl Harbor was horrific for those at ground zero, but it was not apocalyptic nor did it paralyze US society. It destroyed only two aging battleships, while the United States repaired or resurfaced other damaged ships, and only temporarily neutralized the US Pacific Fleet that returned to action much faster than Imperial Japan desired. It precipitated the mobilization of American society to unprecedented levels.[29] And what subsequently happened to the country that carried out the Pearl Harbor attack is not exactly an encouraging precedent for future aggressors.

Drones: The Clinical Kill?

"Drones," or remotely piloted weapons, are becoming ever more central to the waging of modern war. President Obama in particular has increased and institutionalized their use. On his watch, the United States has developed a "disposition matrix" database that lists the details and whereabouts of people selected for assassination in places where the host state either won't or can't do the job.[30] They are becoming standard in the repertoires of the US Air Force and the Central Intelligence Agency. Many other countries also adopt them, either off the shelf or as indigenous systems. Depending on one's politics, this system marks the sinister rise of a "Predator empire" that normalizes extrajudicial homicide at the flick of a joystick and facilitates casual "video game" murderousness, or it means the evolution of a more discriminate way of war that will create fewer body bags and kill fewer bystanders.[31]

Critics and advocates of drone use may differ over whether drones are effective and legitimate. But they often share an assumption that drones represent a radical transformation in warfare because they distance the killer from the target. What critics lament as a loss of military virtue and a loosening of restraint, supporters welcome as a way of reducing human and political costs and an affordable alternative to the other options on the table.[32] Both stake their arguments in part on geopolitical claims about drones as a technology that is special because it alters the normal rules of space and time. Both assume that drones, like long-range artillery fire but at a greater remove, sanitize, "numb," and make easier the act of killing by offering distance that is physical, moral, emotional, social, and mechanical.[33] Both take at face value the ideal-typical image of the drone as a weapon that transcends the constraints of distance, for better or worse.

Drones are seductive as they seem to offer a clinical, detached, and relatively cost-free way of projecting power. Evidence suggests that the availability of drones lowers inhibitions against using lethal force. Policymakers resort to drone killings in situations where they might not otherwise apply force. Claims made about the revolutionary significance of "drones" are more sober than prophecies about "cyberwar." Nevertheless, at first glance drones seem to be a "game-changing" instrument. Because they are "unmanned," they offer their wielders the chance to conduct surveillance and strike at minimal direct risk or cost, or even "costless" war in the excited terms of some media coverage.[34] They hold out the almost perfect possibility of killing without being killed, a formula warmakers have pursued ever since ranged combat first appeared on the battlefield. Drones smite adversaries from afar without the visible difficulties that attend putting planes in the air or boots on the ground, and without the trouble of prolonged nation-building projects or high-stakes raids. For those concerned about humanitarian questions, drones with their precision and smaller payload are relatively discriminate. They offer a more clinical kill than the F-16 fighter aircraft or the Tomahawk missile fired from offshore. And they do the job more humanely than proxies such as the Yemeni military with its torturing, indiscriminate bombing, and scorched-earth habits. Drones' munitions strike fast. A Hellfire missile, for example, travels quicker than the speed of sound, hitting its target before the targeted can hear it. They are a model for the compression of time and space in the kill chain between live video surveillance and death. And they are farsighted, seemingly giving the superpower a panoptic "eye." As the Pentagon oracle Thomas Barnett declares, drones mean "the end of off-grid locations, no where to hide, etc. You will be held responsible for what you do. There will be no frontiers in which you can disappear."[35] Such exhilaration in the reach of one's power may be hard to avoid. Barack Obama's own joking threat to would-be suitors of his daughters that he had Predators at his disposal points to a less humorous possibility, that the ramped-up use of drones, in the words of the former US NATO ambassador, readily "allows our opponents to cast our country as a distant, high-tech, amoral purveyor of death."[36]

Drones also pose grave questions about constitutional authority. They appeal to the commander in chief as a way of short-circuiting or sidestepping the decision-making process, such as the War Powers Resolution that requires congressional authorization of military operations after sixty days. During Operation Unified Protector in Libya, which went well beyond that period, the Obama administration argued that it did not require congressional approval for continuing its drone bombings of that country because the operation did not "involve the presence of US ground troops, US casualties or a serious threat thereof."[37] As well as bearing a sinister Orwellian claim that hostilities are not hostilities if they are conducted by remote vehicles, this use of drones to bypass congressional deliberation invests the president with enormous discretionary power, literally, over life and death. To put it bluntly, drones attract policymakers because they seem to make war easier. In the words of Leon Panetta, the former head of the CIA, drones are "the only game in town."

Yet again, the same confidence can be turned on its head. In the hands of adversaries, drones could be turned on the American homeland. To paraphrase the fearful governments of the interwar period, distance will offer little security if we are entering an era where the drone-warrior always gets through.

There is already much debate about the ethics, laws, and prudence of their use. But here I focus on one question: Do drones enjoy the benefits of distance while overcoming its burdens, and do they decisively shift the balance toward "offense" at low cost? Both the reported experience and the geopolitical complexities of the use of drones suggests not. Of course, drones like cyber have a physically compressing effect. Nevertheless, I argue that they do not strategically shrink the world to the extent that they offer the gains without the costs of distance, for three reasons. First, the force of distance is evident in the fog of misinformation and ambivalence that surrounds drone targeting, a problem that complicates marginal decisions to kill or not to kill. Second, drones are proliferating, and current trends suggest that the recent history of the United States striking targets at will from an uncontested sky will not be the dominant pattern. Third, it turns out that drone pilots themselves are not operating as "disembodied warriors" waging virtual war with ease from afar.

An important misconception about drones is that they form part of an automated and near-perfect information system and kill chain. Stereotypically, drones loiter in a clear sky and are directed by immaculate sensors. In real life, they can be impeded by clouds, rain, or fog. In terms of intelligence, they must also navigate a fog of war that is hard to penetrate. Like any human-made instrument, drones are fallible and can fall short of the high expectations that they generate. They sometimes break down. More importantly, they sometimes strike the wrong target or inflict unintended collateral devastation. They kill civilian innocents. Supporting teams with high volumes of data and real-time images may not have perfect information about whom, precisely, they are striking. This is compounded by the politics of war on the ground. It is difficult to determine the failure rate of drones because of the very circumstances in which the United States deploys them. Precisely because the United States is reluctant to risk a military presence there, most strikes are carried out in remote locations such as the "tribal" territories of Pakistan beyond the writ of the state. These places are hostile to journalists, officials, and nongovernmental organizations seeking to identify and count the corpses and to gather on-the-ground information. Therefore, the estimate of how far a strike killed only genuine sworn adversaries or whether it also killed blameless bystanders is a difficult judgment call from afar. This is one reason why estimates for the success rate of drones vary greatly.[38] Transparent visuality is not the same thing as rock-solid intelligence, especially in human terrain where civilians and nonuniformed adversaries dress the same.

If policymakers regard drones as inherently more surgical and discriminate, and if this makes them more prone to use force, the net effect could be to make bombings more indiscriminate. In a recent classified study of drone strikes in Afghanistan and Pakistan by the Center for Naval Analyses funded by the Pentagon, it turned out that unmanned bombings had "close to the same number of civilian casualties per incident as manned aircraft, and were an order of magnitude more likely to result in civilian casualties per engagement."[39] The actual content of the study and its attribution of causes is not yet in the public domain. But it must be significant that the Department of Defense has produced findings that argue against its own interest, its claim that drone strikes are surgical and minimize civilian casualties, in a report whose summary stresses the problems of sifting the dead.

This problem of knowledge is compounded by the propaganda opportunities that bombing of such uncontrolled terrain offers. Actors on the ground can falsify the numbers or disarm the dead to increase the impression of a civilian slaughter, while executioners from afar can work hard to minimize their estimates.

Cause-and-effect has always been a difficult question with regard to bombing targets that contain civilian people and buildings, and drones do not eliminate this problem. Against the accusation that drones kill too many civilians, proponents of the method argue that the Taliban fabricate figures, or that the lack of ground presence and the politicization of the casualty question means that the extent of misfires cannot be more than roughly "known."[40] But this observation limits the argument that drones offer a clinical kill. Even if they are mostly precise and more effectively humane than other weapons, the force of distance interferes with the narrative of a clean kill. Physical speed and exact targeting do guarantee a desired reception. Reliance on drones, especially on "signature strikes" aimed at whole groups of people in one spot, easily feed the impression of civilian slaughter. Within the rapid cycle of drone strikes, distance still takes effect including in ways that are not desired by their architects. Drones may provide televisual detail but that is no substitute for the painstaking local data needed for more rigorous verification. In this respect, even attacks via "remote control" must still be made through a glass darkly.

These insights in themselves are not necessarily a decisive judgment against their use. After all, this book has pointed out the shortcomings of armed occupations, so unless a purely "law enforcement" approach were taken with its own limitations, it would be frivolous not to consider drone strikes as alternative measures for containing those who mean harm to the United States. But it is a reminder of what it costs and the importance of debating the threshold and protocols of use. Decisions about individual drone strikes must balance the very mixed effects of their use: They unquestionably thin the ranks of AQ's talent, as we have heard bin Laden himself acknowledge. At the same time, they do not curtail the output of propaganda, and because they kill civilian bystanders and are seen to do so, may energize it.[41] Contrary to the *Wall Street Journal*, the case is not "easy."

Today's debate about drone strikes reflects a "presentist" view of the United States with its near monopoly of the market using drones at will, with the United Kingdom and Israel a distant second and third, respectively. But drones are now proliferating.[42] By 2011, according to the US Government Accountability Office, seventy-six countries had acquired drones of some kind. Current trends suggest that the recent history of the United States with its Predators and Reapers roaming in an empty sky seeking earthly targets will not be the dominant pattern in future. Iran also fields armed drones, claiming that one of its vehicles has the range of two thousand kilometers. We are already seeing the introduction of indigenously made drones into Asia's troubled security environment, for purposes ranging from maritime surveillance to combat. China, Japan, Vietnam, and Taiwan are running and stepping up their unmanned arial vehicle (UAV) programs. The rise of remote systems means that we are likely to see "more crowded skies and seas in the years ahead." This is sparking fears that the proliferation of the technology will bring new hazards: encouraging greater risk-taking where the pilot's life is not on the line, or through software or communications failures or inexperienced operators leading to accidents. Drones falling out of the sky or drifting off course could trigger inadvertent escalation.

And most relevant for the argument here, countries involved are also researching counterdrone capabilities. Drones are slow and vulnerable, and relatively easy to shoot down compared to manned jet fighters. They cannot compete in air-to-air combat against the greater speed, mobility, and sensors of modern fighter planes.[43] Their current design reflects the assumption of American dominance, which it enjoyed as a pioneer of the robotics revolution. But this may well change. Ground-based air defenses or aerial fighters could knock them out of the sky. Concerned about China's turn to remote vehicles, Japan's defense ministry is looking at options to shoot down unmanned drones that enter its airspace. The future may well see drones going up against other drones. In full-scale warfare, the ability of these vehicles to survive would be in doubt. The shift from undefended to defended airspace would again widen that space. While it is too soon to know, the proliferation of drone technology could also offer states struggling to match US capabilities an alternative way to compete. For example, while attempting the hard task of building the capability of manned naval aviation, Beijing might equip its *Liaoning* carrier with UAVs because of the difficulty of training pilots to land on carriers. But for China's rivals, like Japan, the resort to drones could help Tokyo compensate for its disadvantage in manpower and balance against China's military buildup.[44] If states in crisis or conflict situations are likely to see their own drones shot at, and if they can field drones as a way of adding to the firepower they can deploy, this should make it even harder to capture and hold territory against resistance. We should expect the net pattern to reinforce rather than reduce the barriers to expansion.

There is another respect in which drone warfare is less than clinical. "Unmanned" aircraft in reality are manpower-intensive. They require a ground-based platoon of a pilot, maintenance crew, sensor operators, and surveillance analysts to operate, and at present, a Predator drone requires 168 people to stay aloft, which is more than an F-16 fighter jet.[45] Recent reports suggest that the experience of drone operators is not that of disembodied warriors or mere "video game players" unencumbered by the strains of the battlespace. Fighting at long range via a cubicle induces combat stress in drone pilots. Fatigue and unnatural hours diminish performance. Though "unmanned" systems take the pilot out of the combat zone, they do not relieve pilots of combat stress. A recent survey of 426 operators of MQ-1 Predator and MQ-9 Reaper drones found that just over a quarter (26.35 percent) of active-duty operators and 13.85 percent of National

Guard / Reserve operators exhibited symptoms of occupational burnout, namely emotional exhaustion and cynicism.[46] Other surveys indicate evidence of combat stress manifested in depression, cardiovascular and respiratory problems, sleep disturbances, erratic behavior, or apathy.[47] The job, as pilots report, is not like playing a video game.[48]

There are several likely, interrelated causes of these stresses. First, there is the high tempo and long shift hours of the job, over fifty hours per week, involving the relentless working of data overloads while sitting in cubicles. Second, drone pilots witness their kills in high definition via their video feeds. This distinguishes them from other distanced killers in Dave Grossman's study, such as artillery combatants, who do not "witness" the point of destruction so closely. As the commander of the 163rd Reconniassance Wing observed in 2008, in a fighter jet, "when you come in at 500–600 mph, drop a 500-pound bomb and then fly away, you don't see what happens." But when a Predator fires a missile, "you watch it all the way to impact, and I mean it's very vivid, it's right there and personal. So it does stay in people's minds for a long time."[49] And after the strike, typically the drone coverage will linger in order to attempt a damage assessment. As Derek Gregory argues, the video interface lends a certain kind of distressing intimacy to the process. Testimonies of operators themselves suggest that even killing from a world away creates an intensity that is not easily brushed off. "You see a lot of detail. . . . When you let a missile go, you know that's real life. There's no reset button."[50] This must be balanced against opposite findings, such as a recent air force study of almost fifteen hundred operators of Reaper, Predator, or Global Hawk drones, that in one-on-one interviews there was a sense of real accomplishment in adding supporting fires to the troops on the ground.[51] But the point is that they are involved in the action in ways that create a sense of complicity and identification, whether they are distressed by the broadcast of killing or proud of their part in supporting combatants at the front and saving lives.

Aside from combat-related stress, there is the difficulty of moving between worlds. As they command their vehicles typically from tens to thousands of miles away, they commute to and from work, switching between military and domestic civilian roles. Thus they enter the archetypal moment of distress and dislocation in war films and literature, the moment of encounter and reintegration of the combatant in the home front. Unlike in other parts of the armed forces, it is harder for people so close to the civilian world splitting their time between family and other combat personnel to forge "primary group" loyalties and unit cohesion that traditionally help ease the strain. To reflect these realities of the human element, the US Air Force changed its terminology, from UAVs to RPVs (remotely piloted vehicles).[52]

Conclusion

The new, man-made geography of war, the electronic and cyber domain, as well as the expanding innovation of "remote" war, attract ambitious claims. Cyberspace, some argue, is a new, "ageographic" form of battlespace and at the same time, a revolutionary weapon of the weak that radically empowers the adversaries of the state. The age of remotely piloted vehicles and cyber conflict, revolutions in robotics and information technology, it is said, both collapses distance and for at least one side, removes the human being from the battlespace. The easy access offered by cyber, its connectivity to critical infrastructure, and the anonymity it confers on users mean that it cheats the traditional geopolitical barriers to aggression, such as distance, visibility, and the high costs of the "ticket to play." If conquering territory is now more difficult and less rewarding, cyber infiltration could represent the postindustrial, twenty-first-century version of conquest.

But as this chapter has demonstrated, these dramatic speculations run ahead of the evidence. Drones in important ways do not offer a clinical kill, as they risk misidentification and blowback, generating propaganda opportunities to adversaries. Fired from a distance, they do not sidestep the political problems of fighting from distance. Problems of distance already impose themselves and are likely to increase as the technology proliferates. And while their use extricates the killer from the battlespace physically, it does not antiseptically remove them from the distress and emotion of killing. In the case of cyber, while the argument must be provisional, the cyber domain offers the "offense" some advantages, but contrary to apocalyptic visions of cyber capabilities, the cyber domain is difficult to launch crippling attacks within. That it is the first entirely human-created geography poses a problem to the offense, because it can be redesigned and refortified, to the point where launching major offensives is a demanding and costly exercise. We know that the most intensive and sophisticated attack by two leading cyber states inflicted only modest disruption, and that forensic attribution techniques are improving.

Notes

1. Eliot A. Cohen, "The Mystique of Air Power," *Foreign Affairs* 73:1 (1994): 109–24, 109.
2. Joel Brenner, *America the Vulnerable: Inside the New Threat Matrix of Digital Espionage, Crime, and Warfare* (New York: Penguin Press, 2011); Richard A. Clarke and R. Knake, *Cyber War: The Next Threat to National Security and What to Do about It* (New York: HarperCollins, 2010); Lukas Kello, "The Meaning of the Cyber Revolution: Perils to Theory and Statecraft," *International Security* 38:2 (2013): 7–40; William Lynn III, "Defending a New Domain: The Pentagon's Cyberstrategy," *Foreign Affairs* 89:5 (2010): 97–108; Mark Clayton, "The New Cyber Arms Race," *Christian Science Monitor*, March 7, 2011.
3. For example, Lukas Kello argues, "A unique feature of a cyberattack is its virtual method. To reach its target, a weapon traditionally had to traverse a geographic medium—land, sea, air, or outer space. Upon arrival, it inflicted direct material harm. The cyber revolution has dramatically altered this situation. Malware can travel the information surface and obeys the protocols of TCP/IP, not the laws of geography. It is little constrained by space and obliterates traditional distinctions between local and distant conflict." "The Meaning of the Cyber Revolution," 22–23.

4. Joseph Nye Jr., "Nuclear Lessons for Cyber Security?," *Strategic Studies Quarterly* 5:1 (2011): 18–38, 20.

5. Elizabeth Bumiller and Thom Shanker, "Panetta Warns of Dire Threat of Cyberattack on US," *New York Times*, October 11, 2012; Alex Spilius, "Cyber Attack Could Fell US within Fifteen Minutes," *Telegraph*, May 7, 2010.

6. Neil Graves, "Schumer: Holes in 'Net' Give Terrorists 'Modem' Operandi," *New York Post*, February 18, 2002.

7. Adm. Michael Mullen, *Defense News*, July 10, 2011, at www.defensenews.com/article/20110710/ DEFFEAT03/107100301/Adm-Michael-Mullen.

8. Dan Williams, "Israeli Official Sees Cyber Alternative to 'Ugly' War," Reuters, February 3, 2011, at http://uk.reuters.com/article/2011/02/03us-iran-nuclear-israel-cyber-idUSTRE71259U2011 0203.

9. Skeptics include Thomas Rid, *Cyber War Will Not Take Place* (New York: Oxford University Press, 2013); Erich Gartzke, "The Myth of Cyberwar: Bringing War in Cyberspace Back Down to Earth," *International Security* 38:2 (2013): 41–73; Colin Gray, *Making Sense of Cyber Power: Why the Sky Is Not Falling* (Carlisle, PA: Strategic Studies Institute, 2013); John R. Lindsay, "Stuxnet and the Limits of Cyberwarfare," *Security Studies* 22:3 (2013): 365–404; also, Michael C. Horowitz, "Coming Next in Military Tech," *Bulletin of the Atomic Scientists* 70:1 (2014): 54–62, 59. This chapter will examine catastrophist visions as it proceeds.

10. S. Graham and N. Thrift, "Out of Order: Understanding Repair and Maintenance," *Theory, Culture and Society* 24:3 (2007): 1–25.

11. Sam Greenhill, "Pictured: The moment RAF jets intercepted Russian bombers flying in British airspace," *Mail Online*, March 25, 2010.

12. David E. Sanger, "Obama Order Sped Up Wave of Cyberattacks against Iran," *New York Times*, June 1, 2012.

13. Institute for Science and International Security, Report, "Did Stuxnet Take Out 1,000 Centrifuges at the Natanz Enrichment Plant?," Preliminary Assessment, December 22, 2010, cited at http://isis-online.org/uploads/isis-reports/documents/stuxnet_FEP_22Dec2010.pdf; "Stuxnet Malware and Natanz: Update of ISIS December 22, 2010, Report," 10.

14. Lally Weymouth, "We Don't Have a Smoking Gun; We Have Concerns," interview of IAEA Chief Yukiya Amono on nuclear programs in Iran, North Korea, and Syria, *Slate*, February 13, 2011.

15. David Albright, Paul Brannan, Andrea Stricker, Christina Walrond, and Houston Wood, "Preventing Iran from Getting Nuclear Weapons: Constraining Its Future Nuclear Options," Institute for Science and International Security, March 5, 2012.

16. As Lindsay observes, "Stuxnet and the Limits of Cyberwarfare," 388.

17. Ilan Berman, "No Magic Bullet for Iran's Nuclear Efforts," *Defense News*, February 28, 2011, cited at www.ilanberman.com/8837/no-magic-bullet-for-iran-nuclear-efforts.

18. Jerry Brito and Tate Watkins, "Loving the Cyber Bomb? The Dangers of Threat Inflation in Cybersecurity Policy," *Harvard National Security Journal* 3:1 (2011): 39–84.

19. Martin Libicki, *Conquest in Cyberspace: National Security and Information Warfare* (New York: Cambridge University Press, 2007), 37.

20. R. Ottis, "The Vulnerability of the Information Society," *futureGOV Asia Pacific* (August/ September 2010), 70; Peter W. Singer, "The Cyber Terror Bogeyman," Brookings Institution, November 12, 2012.

21. Joshua Green, "The Myth of Cyberterrorism," *Washington Monthly* (November 2002), 8–13.

22. Cited in Peter Singer and Allan Friedman, "Cult of the Cyber Offensive: Why Belief in the First-Strike Advantage Is as Misguided Today as It Was in 1914," *Foreign Policy*, January 15, 2014.

23. Libicki, *National Security and Information Warfare*, 105–6; Libicki, *Cyberdeterrence and Cyberwar*, 19, endnote 24.

24. Noble Frankland, *The Bombing Offensive against Germany* (London: Faber and Faber, 1965), 105–6.

25. Lukas Milevski, "Stuxnet and Strategy: A Space Operation in Cyberspace," *Joint Forces Quarterly* 63:4 (2011): 64–69; see also Jon R. Lindsay, "Cyber Attack in Iran: A New Kind of Warfare?," International Studies Association, San Diego, CA, April 1–4, 2012, 9–10.

26. Stewart Baker, "The Attribution Revolution," *Foreign Policy*, June 17, 2013.

27. Lee Ferran, "Report Fingers Chinese Military Unit in US Hack Attacks," ABC News, February 19, 2013.

28. As Sean Lawson argues, "Beyond Cyber-Doom: Cyber-attack Scenarios and the Evidence of History," Mercatus Center, George Mason University, working paper 11-01, January 2011.

29. John Mueller, "Pearl Harbor: Military Inconvenience, Political Disaster," *International Security* 16:3 (1991): 172–203.

30. G. Miller, "Plan for Hunting Terrorists Signals US Intends to Keep Adding Names to Kill Lists," *Washington Post*, October 23, 2012.

31. Ian G. W. Shaw, "Predator Empire: The Geopolitics of US Drone Warfare," *Geopolitics* 18:3 (2013): 536–59.

32. For opposing critiques of the use of drones, see Medea Benjamin, *Drone Warfare: Killing by Remote Control* (New York: Verso, 2013); Mary Ellen O'Connell, "Seductive Drones: Learning from a Decade of Lethal Operations," Notre Dame Law School Legal Studies Research Paper No. 11-35; Laurie Calhoun, "The End of Military Virtue," *Peace Review* 23:3 (2011): 377–86. For more sympathetic treatments, see P. W. Singer, *Wired for War: The Robotics Revolution and Conflict in the 21st Century* (New York: Penguin, 2009); Brian G. Williams, *Predators: The CIA's Drone War on Al Qaeda* (Washington, DC: Potomac, 2013).

33. Lt. Col. Dave Grossman, *On Killing, The Psychological Cost of Learning to Kill in War and Society* (New York: Back Bay Books, 1996), 187; Johansson, "Is It Morally Right to Use Unmanned Aerial Vehicles (UAVs) in War?," 283; Christian Enemark, "Drones and the Disembodied Warrior," unpublished paper, International Studies Association 2013; Christian Enemark, Armed Drones and the Ethics of War: Military Virtue in a Post-Heroic Age (London: Routledge, 2013).

34. P. W. Singer, "Do Drones Undermine Democracy?," *New York Times*, January 22, 2012.

35. Thomas P. M. Barnett, "Drones + Biometrics: Weapons That Conquer Globalization's Frontiers," *Time*, July 14, 2011.

36. Kurt Volker, "What the US Risks by Relying on Drones," *Washington Post*, October 27, 2012.

37. White House, *United States Activities in Libya*, report to Congress, June 2011, 25.

38. Contrast the estimates of the New America Foundation, *The Long War Journal*, and The Bureau of Investigative Journalism, and the far lower estimates by US government officials: cited in Micah Zenko, *Reforming US Drone Strike Policies* (Council on Foreign Relations Special Report No. 65), January 2013, 13.

39. Joint and Coalition Operational Analysis (JCOA), *Drone Strikes: Civilian Casualty Considerations*, June 18, 2013. Executive summary available at http://cna.org/research/2013/drone-strikes-civilian-casualty-considerations.

40. "The Drone Wars: Weapons Like the Predator Kill Far Fewer Civilians," *Wall Street Journal*, January 9, 2010; Daniel Byman, "Why Drones Work: The Case for Washington's Weapon of Choice," *Foreign Affairs* 92:4 (2013): 32–44, 36–37.

41. D. Kilcullen and A. Exum, "Death from Above, Outrage Down Below," *New York Times*, May 16, 2009. As Megan Smith and James Igoe Walsh argue, "Do Drone Strikes Degrade Al Qaeda? Evidence from Propaganda Output," *Terrorism and Political Violence* 25 (2013): 311–27. Smith and Walsh astutely argue that propaganda output is part of AQ's war and find that drone strikes do little to affect the "rate" of propaganda output. But this doesn't tell us much about the "purchase," reception, or credibility of that propaganda. A terrorist network must rely on conducting impressive operations to sustain its fame and following, otherwise it risks becoming a mere producer of words that can sound hollow without a track record of success. To turn the analysis on its head, continued violent resistance in Iraq did little to prevent the Bush administration from issuing its own propaganda output. But it would be an incomplete analysis to conclude that the Iraqi insurgencies had little impact on the ability of President Bush to "operate."

42. On the proliferation of drones and the rise of countermeasures against US dominance of the field, see Sarah Kreps and Micah Zenko, "The Next Drone Wars: Preparing for Proliferation," *Foreign Affairs* 93:2 (2014): 68–79; Shaun Brimley, Ben Fitzgerald, and Ely Ratner, "The Drone War Comes to Asia: How China Sparked a Dangerous Unmanned Arms Race," *Foreign Policy*, September 17, 2013; David Axe, "Will US Lose Its Drone Edge?," *The Diplomat*, November 21, 2011; Walter Russell Mead, "Game of Drones? Asian Militaries Shift toward Cutting Edge,"

American Interest, November 5, 2012.

43. Robert Farley, "America's Troubled F-35: Five Ways to Replace It," *The National Interest* July 20, 2014.

44. Wilson T. VornDick, "Exploring Unmanned Drones as an Option for China's First Carrier," *China Brief* 12:7 (2012): 11–14.

45. Micah Zenko, "10 Things You Didn't Know about Drones," *Foreign Policy* (February 27, 2012).

46. Joseph A. Ouma, Wayne L. Chappelle, and Amber Salinas, *Facets of Occupational Burnout among US Air Force Active Duty and National Guard / Reserve MQ-1 Predator and MQ-9 Reaper Operators* (Wright-Patterson AFB, OH: Air Force Research Laboratory, School of Aerospace Medicine, June 2011), 11.

47. As discussed by Scott Fitzsimmons and Karina Sanga, "Killing in High Definition: Combat Stress among Operators of Remotely Piloted Vehicles," unpublished paper, International Studies Association Conference, San Francisco, CA, 2013, 6; on the risks of long-term PTSD, see Committee on the Assessment of Ongoing Efforts in the Treatment of Posttraumatic Stress Disorder, *Treatment for Posttraumatic Stress Disorder in the Military and Veteran Populations: Initial Assessment* (Washington, DC: National Academies Press, 2012), 39–41.

48. Rob Blackhurst, "Drone Pilots Say Their Job Is Not Like a Video Game," *Business Insider*, September 24, 2012.

49. Scott Lindlaw, "UAV Operators Suffer War Stress," Associated Press, August 7, 2008.

50. Derek Gregory, "From a View to a Kill: Drones and Late Modern Warfare," *Theory, Culture and Society* 28:7-8 (2011): 188–215, 198.

51. Elizabeth Bumiller, "Air Force Drone Operators Report High Levels of Stress," *New York Times*, December 18, 2011

52. David Zucchino, "Stress of Combat Reaches Drone C rews," *Los Angeles Times*, March 18, 2012.

CONCLUSION

The Geopolitics of Hubris

In recent months, nobody's been asking me about why we didn't go to Baghdad.

—COLIN POWELL, 2007

In this concluding chapter, I do three things. First, I summarize my argument. I then anticipate some possible objections. Finally, I consider the "so what" question, the policy implications of the argument, and where it leads.

The global village myth is a claim about the impact of technology on space, an account of security for the United States and its allies. Globalists perceive a transformed, dangerous environment, a shrinking world where technology trumps terrain, where the offense has advantage, where America's security interests are virtually limitless and on which American power can be imposed, if only its leaders had the will. An imperial and restless ideology, globalism is a potent force for belligerence as well as cosmopolitanism, for messianic expansion as well as open coexistence.

But as I have argued, it is more than this. It is tied to the question of identity, reflecting and reinforcing the notion of the American-led West as a bringer of order into chaos. The received "knowledge" that the world is threateningly small is the expression of a dubious ideology that masquerades as a disinterested, objective map. It has attracted American policymakers ever since World War II, when the United States married its rapidly growing power with an expansive, liberal conception of its security interests. Even though one of the most influential globalists, Franklin Roosevelt, was drawn to maps and spoke as America's geography teacher, he articulated an ideology that was antigeographic. Roosevelt, like Halford Mackinder with his focus on railways, was not primarily a geographer, but a machinist, impressed by the ability of instruments to transcend space. If the ideology of the American Century "portends a quintessentially liberal victory over geography," it also carries the anxiety that illiberal forces could do the same thing.[1]

After "12/7" (1941) and 9/11 (2001), Americans and their allies took away a grand lesson: Their enemies were unconstrained by geography. Because the security of Americans rested on the security of others, no longer could they tolerate even remote dangers. Like a contagion, insecurity could spread. Or, like dominoes, eruptions even on the outer periphery could trigger a chain reaction of threat. Hence, policymakers reasoned, Americans were obliged to embrace "national security," the projection of power far beyond its hemisphere with no obvious limit, and tame the world back into order. The myth's ultimate logic is to keep going, heedless of limitation.

In this study, I have asked whether globalism does a good job when applied to three areas where it should perform well, cases that are an "easy test" for the concept and a "tough test" for theories that bring distance back in. These three cases are terrorist "netwar," amphibious offensives, and emerging technologies of "cyber" and drones. As these cases suggest, technology does not kill distance. It may accelerate movement and compress physical space. But it does not necessarily shrink strategic space, the ability to project power affordably and effectively across the earth. In important ways, tools also have the reverse effect, and the state with its power has an important vote in widening the space around it.

The global village myth is a pernicious mentality because it can tempt even secure states into self-defeating behavior. Time and again, the American experience of war challenges the assumptions of liberal crusading, demonstrating that it endangers the very values it claims to uphold, and loses sight of the limits even on the power—and knowledge—of the American hegemon. And it forgets that states that suppose themselves the guardians can also be agents of chaos. By deterritorializing the concept of America's security domain, the replacement of large mental maps by small ones has led to the neglect of limits, an insensitivity to strategic cost, a boundless conception of interests, and the pursuit of absolute security at almost any price. By dismissing distance as a shaping force in world politics, the capacity of America and its allies to think strategically has suffered.

Despite its claims to singularity, America like great powers before it has fallen prey to overextension. To be sure, many of its overseas ventures were not hubristic failures. America carried out impressive postwar reconstructions of Japan and Europe, and helped build the prosperity of the Pacific Rim countries. But against Asian communists in Korea from 1950, Vietnamese revolutionaries from 1964, and the multifactional Iraqi resistance from 2003, Americans tasted the shock and disappointment that struck great powers before them. None of these were decisively fatal to American power. After all, Washington bolstered its position in Asia after withdrawing from Vietnam, a clear demonstration that retrenchment can strengthen rather than weaken a great power. But each step inflicted costs that were not anticipated. The Iraq War contributed to a broader long-term fiscal overstretch that the United States has yet to recover from and that threatens its unipolar position.

In Korea, the United States expanded what could have been a successful limited territorial war to preserve the status quo into a conflict against communist China, a clash that escalated America's Cold War and poisoned its domestic politics. The escalation of the Vietnam War by the insertion of ground troops in 1964 led to the most polarizing and costly conflict of the Cold War. It had perverse results, jeopardizing rather than bolstering America's containment of communism. Instead of fortifying American democracy in the world, it polarized and poisoned it at home. And expanding the war into Cambodia helped to produce a genocidal totalitarian regime in the form of the Khmer Rouge. In America's wider competition with the Soviet Union, the "sideshow war" drained resources and political will from the main struggle. The invasion of Iraq, driven by inflated threats of globalized insecurity and inflated confidence in America's capacity to project power at will, resulted in a tragic Pyrrhic victory. In all three conflicts, the embrace of territorially unlimited war aims contributed to the problem. Policymakers moved from territorially conceived and bounded security interests to psychological and universal ones. Korea and Vietnam were part of a global effort to counter communism, conflated into a single adversary that had to be checked everywhere. Iraq was part of a war on terror with no boundaries.

Objections Anticipated

Lastly, let us now consider three possible counterarguments to the case I have made here. First, some might object that technology may not kill distance now, but it could create offense dominance and shrinkage in the future. Second, it might be argued that the global village myth is mere rhetoric. And third, that this is yesterday's problem, as Americans have already become disenthralled with global wars.

One possible objection to my argument is that in the ceaselessly competitive dynamic of swords and shields, offense and defense, there are no "last moves." Offense-defense strivings are permanent. Even if the global village is down for now, we can't count on it staying down.[2] If this criticism holds, theories based on the global village are not so much wrong as early. It may be that the medium-term future could introduce technologies that tilt the advantage to the offense, to the extent that expansionists exploiting new weapon systems with sound doctrine could project power at lower cost and with greater ease.

This is in principle possible. Indeed, as I have argued, the relationship between humans, their tools, and space is constantly in flux. But a dramatic shift in the offense-defense balance is at least some way off and will require considerable breakthroughs. It may be that the technological future introduces offense-empowering innovations. These might include exoskeletons and biological enhancement that enable soldiers to run faster, carry more, endure longer, and avoid harm. It could involve new stealth technologies that make possible a surprise mass assault by conventional forces. And it could feature the elusive nuclear missile shield that by deflecting every warhead of a saturation attack, an aggressor could strike without nuclear retaliation.

Each of these innovations would have to overcome substantial obstacles. For example, though stealth technology to protect aircraft carriers is likely to improve, as James Holmes argues, "there's only so much you can do to disguise a 100,000-ton behemoth."[3] A strategic missile defense system would have to perform to perfection to prevent even a few warheads getting through to devastate cities, and the coming of lower-altitude, hypersonic missiles would make the job even harder.[4] As for empowered, super-armored soldiers, it would still be hard to get them successfully from sea to shore without suffering a prohibitive level of attrition.

Beyond technical difficulties, expectations of a global village still suffer three drawbacks. First, most innovations have a double-edged effect and can be turned into defensive as well as offensive capabilities. A technological and doctrinal shift in favor of offense would need to be so great as to tilt the balance decisively toward power projection at affordable cost. It is doubtful whether a surge in offensive capabilities could neutralize the defensive potential of precision munitions, tactical nuclear weapons, or access-denial technologies. Second, the strategic history considered here shows that the agency of determined defenders with a greater stake in the struggle can challenge even stronger, hi-tech opponents, and states combating shadowy guerrillas close to home can do much to thwart their capabilities and disrupt their designs.

Finally, while innovations may reduce the costs of physical distance, strategic distance and its dilemmas are likely to reintroduce themselves in each era. Indicative of the problem is the fate of America's Conventional Prompt Global Strike (CPGS) initiative, the attempt to develop nonnuclear weapons that can strike distant targets rapidly. Here is a textbook case of the gap between physical and strategic space. While very fast and accurate, such a system with its intercontinental range and its launch platforms such as sea-based ballistic missiles or land-based rocket launchers would risk being mistaken for a nuclear missile attack. An attempt to compress time and space to this global scale would risk miscalculation and inadvertent escalation. It would suffer warhead ambiguity (misidentification of the incoming bomb as nuclear), destination ambiguity (an observing state being uncertain about whether it is being targeted), and target ambiguity (uncertainty about whether the target is conventional or nuclear).[5] An observing state could misinterpret a CPGS launch on a third party as a strike on itself or misinterpret a CPGS strike on itself as nuclear. Even if the probability of such a misperception leading to nuclear retaliation were low, even a low probability would be dangerous given its high costs. In deteriorating political circumstances where hostilities and apprehensions were raised, the likelihood of a worst-case interpretation would presumably increase. Distance in this instance would make signaling difficult, and at short notice and with imperfect information, this would pose serious risks of escalation. In gaining speed, the superpower would be incurring the penalty of risk at the highest level.

Turning to the second objection, it might be argued that the globalism scrutinized here does not really matter, as it is largely a body of rhetoric that is marginal to US strategic practice. My argument, some might suggest, pays too much attention to what policymakers say in their speeches and formal documents, instead of the more detailed calculus that informs their substantive debate about policy choices behind closed doors.

This objection fails to recognize the complex dynamics between words and deeds, especially in a society where politicians compete to offer the public security as the leaders of a superpower. As I have argued, it is not necessarily the case that presidents, government officials, congressional representatives, or military leaders personally believe in the claims of globalism, though there is plenty of evidence to suggest that strategic shocks like North Korea's invasion of South Korea and the 9/11 attacks really did take a grip on the minds of decision-makers and shape their assumptions.

More importantly, the global village myth with its fears and ambitions defines a politics of "liberal terror," a politics that exerts such power that leaders evidently feel compelled to live up to it. Politicians who disown the notion of a fragile country needing to tame a dangerous globalized world are open to attack. The myth exerts its power in several ways, whether as genuine belief, as a form of rhetoric that can entrap governments that articulate it, or as a justification or rationale for expansion. Recent pressures on Washington to be seen actively "doing something," even intervening directly, in conflicts from Syria to the Ukraine suggest the ongoing, discursive power of the myth.

Some may argue that the argument here addresses yesterday's problem. The liberal crusading impulse is unpopular in the second decade of the twenty-first century. American society is tired, struggling under the weight of wars and debt. Large-scale military interventions, especially ones that commit ground troops, have gone out of fashion as once-vocal supporters of American hegemony now concede.[6] Former secretary of defense Robert Gates judges that any defense secretary who advises the president to send a big American land army into Asia or into the Middle East or Africa should "have his head examined."[7] US forces are no longer scaled to conduct large-scale, prolonged "stability operations."[8] America's security interests as an increasingly energy-independent power are less tied to the oil-rich Gulf, and a takeover of the Gulf by one hostile state doesn't seem like it could happen any time soon. Standoff, hi-tech weaponry bombing from afar seems to serve as a better, cheaper defense than troops inserted into dangerous places. The Obama administration has been increasingly careful to limit its liability. Having fought wars in Libya and Afghanistan and been blocked by Congress from bombing Syria, it is now determined to exhaust diplomatic options, avoid entanglement, and begin limited retrenchment of US commitments.

Despite these trends, there are three reasons why an interrogation of globalism and its liberal wars is needed. First, we are still living with its legacies. We are entitled to ask how we got to this point, to audit how well the globalist agenda fared, and the assumptions that drove it. Citizens spent tax dollars, lost limbs, or died in the name of this set of ideas, so it is reasonable for those who paid and those who mourn to take stock.

Second, globalism is being recast and lives on. President Barack Obama may warn against the danger of putting America on a footing of "perpetual war" and the need to limit the scope of its hostilities.[9] Yet he also articulates an ideology of a dangerous borderless world in need of American guardianship, an outlook that excites the movement to perpetual war in the first place. In deeds, his bombing of Libya, his escalation in Afghanistan, his expansion of the drone assassination program, and his slouching toward an escalating rivalry with Beijing does little to tilt Washington away from the state of endless war.

A persistent lobby still carries the torch for liberal wars in a dangerous world. In August 2013, a group of senators, state governors, and public intellectuals cosigned a letter calling on the president to bomb Syria and become the armorer and backer of rebels in its civil war.[10] Hawkish idealists at the Project for a New American Century who helped craft the Bush Doctrine have created a successor institution, the Foreign Policy Initiative. There is also an overlapping counterinsurgency lobby. Liberal internationalists, and a wider faction of defense intellectuals, argue that the United States should accept the likelihood of future small wars as a fact of life and not let its new counterinsurgency expertise go to waste.[11] In Washington, strategic debate is still defined and dominated by an ascendancy of liberal internationalists and neoconservatives. The central debate in post–Cold War United States is whether grand strategy remains mostly about what form of hegemony to seek, not whether to pursue it.[12]

Third, globalism is larger and more resilient than just an ideology of nation building and goes beyond the "War on Terror" that officials are now uncomfortable with. The temptation to put boots on the ground may have weakened after years of depletion. Yet there is still the pressure to use military force from afar in other ways to tame the dark side of globalization. There is the liberal humanitarian impulse to act with force against atrocities and exercise the "responsibility to protect." Converging with this, there is the nationalist impulse to back up idealistic words by reaching for the gun, for fear of losing credibility. Debate about the use of force abroad still widely assumes that the world has become America's military protectorate, battlespace, and theater for the testing of its resolve. There persists an assumption that security problems stem from state failure, with the debate narrowed to one about tactics and antidotes.

America and its allies have been here before, after Korea and after Vietnam. And despite these disappointments, globalism still proved resilient. After hard wars, US diplomatic history shows cycles of overexpansion followed by recoil, followed by renewed confidence. In the future, if America enjoys a return of peace and prosperity, this could raise the temptation once again to seek security through expansion. Given its survival as an entrenched assumption and its strong institutional platform, it would be premature to assume that the global village myth is just a curiosity of recent history. It needs not an epitaph, but a warning.

So What? Policy Implications

If my arguments against globalism hold up, there are important policy implications to be drawn. There are fears that stalk each of case studies, whether borderless terrorists, an expansionist China, or cyber predators. As I demonstrate, these are overblown.

Today's "global guerrillas" and practitioners of "netwar" are less mobile and deadly than often presumed. 9/11 was an aberration, not a forerunner for an era of catastrophic mass-casualty attacks. By arousing state hostility, the space enlarged and grew more deadly around them. AQ then fragmented into a network. Network theorists hailed this as an inspired move. But increased flexibility cost AQ the ability to direct its jihad. It lost its coherence, attracted indiscriminately brutal figures, and provoked the angry blowback of Muslims from northern Iraq to Algeria. The guerrillas of the information age can still inflict atrocity, but our resilient nation-states have reduced their ability to inflict mass-casualty terrorism on Western soil. The creation of terrorist capability relies on experiential knowledge and in-person training, and the space for doing this safely has been strangled. No longer do they pose a first-order threat. To keep them off balance, disrupt their capability, and ensure they remain a low-level nuisance, they can be contained through the interdiction of unspectacular police work, interstate intelligence sharing, the scrutiny of financial transactions, clandestine operations, selective raids with commandos, or, in restricted circumstances, drones. Given that they have become far less capable of the thing most feared, of serial, major assaults on the heartlands of major states, they pose a serious threat mainly to the extent that they can bait the West into self-defeating responses, either expensive liberal crusades or the excessive dismantling of civil liberties. This is not an easy balance to strike, but a sober appreciation of the limits of netwar can steer the debate toward proportionality.

What about security in East Asia? Those who fear a rising China, and its bid for hegemony, base their fears partly on China's presumed offensive ability to expand and tilt the regional balance in its favor. Now that Beijing and its neighbors are engaging in saber-rattling, territorial disputes, and standoffs, these fears are growing. A revisionist China, allegedly, looks eerily like Wilhelmine Germany, "a second great military-authoritarian-capitalist rogue regime, with an army partially independent of civilian authority, a navy aimed at knocking the United States off its perch, the world's second-largest economy, a racist-nationalist mythology that legitimates world domination."[13] But even if Beijing does entertain such imperial ambitions, it is unlikely to develop the capability and find an opportunity to realize them. As I have shown, it is likely that in the event of an invasion, even an isolated Taiwan could give China a world of trouble. While China would probably prevail, Taiwan could raise costs to make it a Pyrrhic victory. This fits a wider pattern, that while China's booming economy and large population have propelled it to the rank of a great power rivaling the United States in the region, China's ability to expand affordably and to convert its strength into a land-sea empire is modest.

This should put alarmist fears in perspective. East Asia is not a power vacuum open to the predations of a single aggressor like Nazi Germany or Imperial Japan, but a region crowded with states developing their own formidable defensive maritime-air capabilities to deter and respond to one power's adventurism. The likes of South Korea, Japan, India, and Vietnam are wealthy enough to defend themselves and would have the means to check and punish Chinese expansionism. That is not to argue that America's grand strategy should be to come home. But it can afford to abandon the costly and difficult effort of attempting to hold on to primacy and prevent the emergence of new great powers. Chinese expansion faces many obstacles, so the task of US diplomacy should be to coexist and share power, while retaining the ability to act as balancer of last resort. It could still have alliances, but no longer must act as adult supervisor and guarantor of first resort, an arrangement that creates moral hazards by encouraging risk-taking by allies. If East Asia is essentially a defense-dominant region, that strengthens the argument that America can oversee a transition to multipolarity, instead of its current collision course. An awareness of the power of distance can assist the world's most consequential, bilateral relationship.

With regard to the emerging technologies of drones and cyber power, the greatest hopes and worst fears are not supported by what we currently know. Drones do not defeat distance as strategic space, do not eliminate the tradeoffs between fighting "up close" on the ground and striking from distance. And we are entering an era of proliferation that may make it harder even for America to wield them freely as offensive weapons. Awareness of the difficult tradeoffs of use and nonuse should inform the debate. Prophecies of offensive cyber doom are also overstated. The most ambitious cyber attack yet conducted, probably by two allied states, took a vast, coordinated effort that yielded only modest gains.

Cyber attackers are not the equivalent of nuclear bombers bringing on electronic doomsday, but are more like special forces infiltrating increasingly complicated ground, and systems that are increasingly layered to make them more resilient against hostilities. Great skills and resources are needed to pull off an attack of the first order. At best, cyber is an adjunct to terrestrial military forces fighting over the control of ground. With both drones and cyber, as with air power, we should beware of notions of revolutionary weapons that transcend limitations.

The overall pattern is that defenders with geography on their side and instruments to exploit it can ward off, punish, or wear down attackers in many domains, thereby raising costs on aggression and containing threats. But when they switch from defense to offense, they struggle to eradicate threats. And if technology and human agency empowers defenders in today's strategic space, this means that estimates of the West's great global power are also exaggerated. That the United States can endanger itself more readily than external enemies was Abraham Lincoln's argument: "Shall we expect some transatlantic military giant, to step the ocean, and crush us at a blow? Never! . . . At what point then is the approach of danger to be expected? I answer. If it ever reach us it must spring up amongst us; it cannot come from abroad. If destruction be our lot we must ourselves be its author and finisher. As a nation of freemen we must live through all time or die by suicide."[14] Today's technologies make Lincoln's message more applicable. In other words, we are less powerful, but more secure, than we think. The prophecy of Nicholas Spykman during World War II, and Henry Kissinger today, is all the more sound. If the global strategic order of the twenty-first century has one defining characteristic, it is that the world is increasingly unconquerable. No single power will be able to dominate it.

Against the logic of eradicating insecurity at unaffordable cost, Washington should tilt toward the logic of containing threats and living with insecurity. Because America is more secure and less powerful than often imagined, it should proceed on the basis that it can place limits on threats, curtail adversaries' ability to operate, and wait patiently for them to wither into an irrelevance or nuisance, without exhausting or overextending itself. This logic applies well to a self-defeating enemy, whether the Soviet Union with its doomed Marxist-Leninist system, or Al Qaeda, a movement that habitually alienates the very Muslims it claims to represent. Containment is not only about outlasting the enemy, but also about keeping costs down and avoiding self-defeating behavior. This stands in contrast to the alternative, of "rollback," an endless project of going on the offensive to defeat threats. Those who believe Washington should pursue security this way do not intend endless war. But that is where their logic leads. A more restrained approach would focus military power most on what it does most effectively: secure the territory and sea lanes, deter would-be expansionists, and exist as an insurance policy for emergencies. By shifting from eradication to restraint, the United States could begin to reverse its state of insolvency and accumulate a surplus of power with which to respond to the unknown and the unexpected.

Beyond these specific questions of national security, a turning away from the global village myth is an important step in rethinking the terms of national security debate. Being more aware of the geography of hubris will not lay out where the United States should go or avoid. But it can assist the cultivation of prudence, the most important quality of statecraft. Prudence is the practical wisdom that weighs the consequences of competing political choices and recognizes the conflicted nature of any political situation.[15] To be prudential is to deliberate carefully between means and ends in a dynamic field, balance competing interests weigh costs against benefits, and act effectively within the limits of power and in the face of unexpected contingencies, with an eye to the dangers of self-defeating behavior. Finding the right balance between resources and goals, power, and commitments is never a certain equation. The search for guiding "lines" is provisional and never-ending. But maps are one way of fixing a point of limitation, even if it is never final or definitive, around which to define and rank interests and to separate the vital from the desirable and the core from the periphery. Rather than falling back on Vietnam-haunted countermyths of inevitable quagmire abroad, decision-making will benefit from rediscovering the principle that rulers should be wary of the strains of distance as they roll the iron dice. Attention to the most compelling insights of geopolitical thought, whether classical or modern, can put states on guard against hubris, not only the hubris of overstretch but also the intellectual hubris of believing that doctrinaire creeds of "global leadership" can replace strategic judgment. In striving for prudence, attention to the assumptions within our mental maps is a good start.

By breaking free of the global village myth, we could break free of the dichotomous habit of mind that it encourages. There can be good reasons for exercising power beyond the water's edge. The United States has security interests at stake in the balance of power abroad, in the security of the sea lanes and choke points of the global "commons," and in complex problems that it can help address, from the supply of renewable energy to disaster relief to nuclear proliferation. But the debate about America's commitments abroad, the dialectical relationship between means and ends, is corrupted by the reductionist mentality of "globalism versus isolation." As Hans Morgenthau observed during the Vietnam War, the ideologies of globalism and isolation share a common failing. Isolation, like globalism, is an absolute stance that denies "that middle ground of subtle distinctions, complex choices, and precarious manipulations, which is the proper sphere of foreign policy."[16] By stepping back from globalism, the makers of American strategy could clear space for considering measured choices, neither running the world nor hiding from it.

As the Soviet Union crumbled, one of Mikhail Gorbachev's aides warned Americans that "we will do a terrible thing to you; we will deprive you of an enemy." That sardonic remark rightly touched the pathology that afflicts most great powers, the need for a defined conflict and a sworn enemy to affirm one's own role and importance. And since World War II, American policymakers did not measure threat only in terms of particular opponents. Threats, they believed, were inevitable because they were more systemic than discrete and were created by the shrinking of the world. If the temptation to inflate threats and fall prey to overstretch poses a danger to modern great powers, the problem lies not only in misperceptions of specific adversaries.[17] It lies also in the view of a radically altered security environment. To see the world as a constant, existentially threatening village is to look for the next opponent after the defeat of the last.

The fall of a totalitarian empire in 1989–91, without a major war, was an extraordinary emancipation, achieved jointly by civil society behind the Iron Curtain and adroit American diplomacy. It should have reduced insecurity. It was an opportunity to revise grand strategy in changing conditions. On the contrary, given the ascendant politics of endless emergency, the foreign policy "class" refused to demobilize its mind even in the resumption of peace. The Soviet Union's demise prompted an effort by security elites to find new threats and new adversaries, chiding their compatriots for lapsing into civilian normality. Hence the perverse relief among some commentators, from David Brooks to George Packer, that at least the 9/11 slaughter clarified things, creating a "fear" that was a "cleanser" of "self-indulgence," summoning Americans back to seriousness.[18] This reflected an atavistic ideology of "redemption by war," where violent clash is intrinsically desirable. The embrace of war, not as a regrettable, illiberal "lesser evil" but as a positive and invigorating good, showed the fatal contradiction that globalism creates. To secure liberty by permanent mobilization in its name, to exist "in continual war" abroad, as James Madison warned, was to endanger it at home.

Many in the foreign policy commentariat claim that America's only choice is "global leadership" to superintend a shrinking world, and chide others for their lack of appetite for fresh wars.[19] But today, Americans in opinion polls and even some in Congress say differently.[20] If the people who pay taxes, fight, or lose loved ones in American wars are increasingly skeptical about the pursuit of global hegemony and its fruits, if they sense that there are more prudent ways to pursue security, they are right. Globalization has not, after all, turned the world into a single, closed battlespace that threatens the republic. America can afford to do less, not to isolate itself but exercise more restraint. It can rebalance its depleted power with its overextended commitments, unshoulder some burdens to others, husband its resources, accommodate the rise of other states, reverse the damage that expansion abroad has inflicted on institutions and liberal values at home, and ensure its future as a heavyweight in a multipolar world. It can contain its most potent adversary, itself.

Notes

1. Neil Smith, *American Empire: Roosevelt's Geographer and the Prelude to Globalization* (Berkeley: University of California Press, 2003), viii.
2. I am grateful to Colin Gray for suggesting this problem in our correspondence.
3. James Holmes, "Twilight of the Aircraft Carrier?," *The Diplomat*, December 13, 2013.
4. Zachary Zeck, "Will Hypersonic Capabilities Render Missile Defense Obsolete?," *The Diplomat*, February 7, 2014.
5. James M. Acton, *Silver Bullet? Asking the Right Questions about Conventional Prompt Global Strike* (Washington, DC: Carnegie Endowment for International Peace, 2013), 111.
6. Victor Davis Hanson, "America Is Intervened Out," *National Review Online*, October 15, 2013; Francis Fukuyama, "Why Shouldn't I Change My Mind?," *Los Angeles Times*, April 9, 2006; *America at the Crossroads: Democracy, Power, and the Neoconservative Legacy* (New Haven, CT: Yale University Press, 2006).
7. Thom Shanker, "Warning against Wars like Iraq and Afghanistan," *New York Times*, February 25, 2011.
8. Department of Defense, *Sustaining US Global Leadership: Priorities for 21st Century Defense* (January 2012), 6; Sydney J. Freedberg Jr, "VCJCS Winnefeld Tells Army: Forget Long Land Wars," *Breaking Defense*, September 13, 2013.
9. "President Obama's Speech at National Defense University: The Future of Our Fight against Terrorism, May 2013," Council on Foreign Relations, May 23, 2013.
10. "Experts to Obama: Here Is What to Do in Syria," *The Weekly Standard*, August 27, 2013; one of these signatories, Max Boot, also calls for putting boots on the ground to deny terrorists a safe haven. Oren Dorell, "Syria Conflict Could Last Years, Killing Continues," *USA Today*, February 13, 2014.
11. David H. Petraeus, "Reflections on the Counter-insurgency Era," *RUSI Journal* 158:4 (2013): 82–87.
12. Michael J. Mazarr, "The Risks of Ignoring Strategic Insolvency," *Washington Quarterly* 35:4 (2012): 7–23, 9.
13. MacGregor Knox, "Thinking War—History Lite?," *Journal of Strategic Studies* 34:4 (2011): 489–500, 498.
14. Cited in Eric Foner, *The Fiery Trial: Abraham Lincoln and American Slavery* (New York: W. W. Norton, 2010), 26.
15. Robert Harriman, *Prudence: Classical Virtue, Postmodern Practice* (University Park, PA: Penn State University Press, 2003); Hans J. Morgenthau, *Politics among Nations: The Struggle for Power and Peace* (New York: Alfred A. Knopf, 1978), 12.
16. Hans Morgenthau, "Globalism: The Moral Crusade," reprinted in *Vietnam and the United States* (Washington, DC: PublicAffairs Press, 1965), 81–92, 81.
17. As Stephen Van Evera argues, "Foreword," in *American Foreign Policy and the Politics of Fear: Threat Inflation Since 9/11*, ed. A. Trevor Thrall and Jane E. Kramer (Abingdon, UK: Routledge, 2009).
18. David Brooks, "Facing Up to Our Fears," *Newsweek*, October 22, 2001; George Packer, "Recapturing the Flag," *New York Times Magazine*, September 30, 2001; see also C. Robin, "Liberalism at Bay, Conservatism at Play: Fear in the Contemporary Imagination," *Social Research* 71:4 (2004): 927–57.
19. Richard Cohen, "Obama Is Bush 2.0, but It's No Upgrade," *Washington Post*, September 16, 2013; Bret Stephens, "The Robert Taft Republicans Return," *Wall Street Journal*, September 3, 2013.
20. On popular support for more restraint, see Benjamin H. Friedman and Christopher A. Preble, "Americans Favor Not Isolationism but Restraint," *Los Angeles Times*, December 27, 2013.

INDEX

234 INDEX